HIGHER EDUCATION
IN
THE SOUTH

HIGHER EDUCATION
IN
THE SOUTH

SAM P. WIGGINS, Director

Southern Study in Higher Education

Supported by a grant from the General Education Board
to George Peabody College for Teachers

McCutchan Publishing Corporation
2526 Grove Street
Berkeley, California 94704

Copyright © 1966 by

SAM P. WIGGINS

TO THE READER

"Some men have been virtuous blindly, others have speculated fantastically, and others have been shrewd to bad purposes; but you, sir, I am sure will give under your hand, nothing but what is at the same moment, wise, practical, and good."

Letter to Mr. Benjamin Franklin from Mr. Benjamin Vaughan, dated January 1, 1783, and quoted in the commemorative edition of *The Autobiography of Benjamin Franklin* (Boston: Houghton Mifflin and Company, 1906), p. 77. —From this assumption, the author proceeds.

Preface

Higher education is passing through a crucible of heightened responsibility in America, and the colleges and universities in the Southern region appear to be facing the most severe test of all. In addition to the problems the South shares in abundance with every region of America, there are three kinds of endemic problems confronting Southern higher education that press their claims for special attention. These are the problems associated with race, with poverty, and with substandard precollegiate education.

None of these problems is restricted to the Southern region, but they are all most prevalent there. The South cannot be held solely responsible for this cluster of problems, nor will it be able to cope successfully with them alone. They are American problems that especially challenge educators in the American South, but that have immediate and direct meaning for all of America.

The Southern Higher Education Study Grant

The General Education Board, in 1963, made a grant to George Peabody College for Teachers to study biracial higher education in the Southern region. The grant was made in the belief that the accumulated experience of many Southern colleges and universities during the past decade, and before, was of sufficient duration to provide a fruitful area of research that could have an important influence on policy and on the execution of policy in higher education. No restrictions were imposed by the grant upon the scope of the study, its methodology, or upon the interpretation of its findings. The study was officially initiated late in 1963, and the staffing for it was completed in the spring of 1964.

The Staff

The grant made staff provisions for a director, an assistant director, graduate student assistants, and a staff secretary. Late in the summer of 1963, President Felix C. Robb of Peabody College, now Director of the Southern Association of Colleges and Schools, invited this author to direct the study and to seek out an assistant director to collaborate in its development. Dr. Harold Stinson (now President of Stillman College) was granted an eighteen months' leave of absence from the superintendency of the Boggs Academy, in Georgia, to join the staff in the spring of 1964. From the beginning, his counsel and assistance proved most valuable in countless ways.

The graduate students, as they do, came and went. But in passing each made a creditable, indelible mark on the study. Dr. Garland Millett is now at Fisk University. Dr. Robert Koepper is at Southern Illinois University. Mr. Forrest Rollins is at North Texas State University. Mrs. Shirley Williams is now at Wisconsin State University-Oshkosh. Mr. Archie Jordan has joined the faculty at Western Kentucky State University. Their assistance to this study has ranged from the tedious verification of data to the challenge of joining in the unending search for answers to unfathomable questions.

Mrs. Faye Reedy completed the staff complement in the capacity of secretary, and served skillfully and devotedly in the total enterprise. When she left the study because of her approaching maternity, Miss Carolyn Smith joined the staff as her able replacement. The diverse outlook of members of the staff, a desegregated team of men and women, argumentative and agreeable, strengthened our tolerance of diversity while unifying our purpose and commitment to it.

THE ADVISORY BOARD

From the outset, a need was envisaged for an eminent advisory board, of educators and other insightful Southern leaders, to consult together and give the staff the benefit of their experience and varied judgments. We sought not only some of the most able presidents of Southern institutions of higher learning, but regional educational directors and outstanding citizens from the business world as well, including private industry and the daily press. However diverse, the views of members of the board were consistently thoughtful and straightforward. To its full credit, it did not become a governing board, but carefully retained its significant advisory role. The membership of that board is listed in Appendix A, both as a matter of record and as a public acknowledgment of deep gratitude for their helpful guidance.

Miss Flora Rhind, who in 1963 was the Vice President of the General Education Board and subsequently became the Special Assistant to the President of the Rockefeller Foundation, consented to serve as an unofficial member of the Advisory Board. Her counsel and encouragement throughout the study was greater than any conventional acknowledgment could convey. The General Education Board has shown a long, sympathetic interest in the many human problems within the South, and Miss Rhind's active participation in the development of the study was a fitting personification of that interest and commitment.

THE STUDY'S UNFOLDING DESIGN

The initial focus of the study was to have been upon the plight of the Negro with special reference to desegregation. An early examination of these problems revealed the need to deal with the cluster of problems mentioned earlier, since the problems of poverty and educational disadvantage confronted both Negro and white youth. A more discrete study of any one of these topics would have been far more manageable, and more "sanitary" by the conventional measures of scholarly productivity. But this was to be an action-oriented study, and emphasis needed to be on the relationship of these inseparable aspects of disadvantage, however valuable such discrete studies might be for other purposes. Indeed, the topic of desegregation eventually seemed to warrant special treatment, and an ancillary monograph was developed and recently published under the title, *The Desegregation Era in Higher Education.*[1]

The problem of central concern, however, was that of dealing with these related barriers to higher education in a functional perspective. As Robert Hutchins once observed, "If we split the world up in order to gain some detailed knowledge of it, at some point we have to put it together again to understand it."[2] After two half-day sessions with the Advisory Board this problem-cluster approach shaped up as the task. The mission was to ferret out the detailed knowledge already available (or in the process of being discovered), to search for some of the remaining missing parts, and to put the parts together into a coherent pattern. This pattern must convey an accurate picture of the problems, of what was being done about them, and what courses of future action would most likely yield beneficial results. To accomplish these aims, the problem-cluster itself had to be viewed in the moving stream of higher education, not as a static isolated phenomenon. As the reader is well aware, the years of this study, 1964-1966, have been rapidly changing, almost frenetic years in American higher education. Major action has been taken in each of the areas of our concern, and the job of merely keeping abreast of national events has been a time-consuming one. Action in many areas has, indeed, far outstripped the planning for it.

Early efforts were made to locate and survey the published and unpublished studies, completed or in process, directly germane to this study. A good deal of literary sleuthing proved rewarding as we picked up leads to sources through personal contacts. Yet, there was a paucity of success stories or even of sustained institutional effort.[3]

We went into the field, then, to interview officials and students of dozens of Southern colleges and universities. The more significant the data,

---

[1] McCutchan Publishing Corporation, 1966.

[2] Hutchins, *The University of Utopia* (Chicago: The University of Chicago Press, 1953), p. 24. The author prefers the Spanish version: "La cuestión no es cómo fragmentar el mundo, sino de qué manera animar esos fragmentos."—It is not a question of how to fragment the world, but how to activate those fragments.

[3] As an example, the report of Earl J. McGrath, *Negro Colleges and Universities in Transition* (New York: Teachers College Press, Columbia University, 1965), saved us untold weeks of original work. The data-gathering of the Southern Education Reporting Service also made possible the use of some data that we could not otherwise have obtained.

in general, the more "off the record" it had to be. Our interest, though, was in getting at the heart of the problem without undue concern about being able to footnote our data in due primary-source form.

A list of the institutions visited by one or more of the staff is provided in Appendix B. Officials of these institutions were uniformly kind and helpful. To minimize embarrassment to institutions due to race, and to gain fuller information, our decisions concerning separate and joint visits varied. The point seems worth noting, however, that Dr. Stinson and I traveled and conducted joint interviews in the states of Arkansas and Mississippi, and were cordially received wherever we went, separately or together.

The scores of interviews with individuals and groups were helpful, but they were not sufficient for our total purpose. As a means of supplementing interview data, we queried the presidents of forty diverse, additional Southern institutions to delve pointedly into matters of institutional action and presidential judgments. This inquiry emphasized that the presidents would help the study more by *declining to respond* than by *delegating the assignment* to subordinates or by giving only hurried attention to the five questions put to them. Some presidents accordingly obliged by declining to respond, but twenty-two provided thoughtfully worded responses that proved to be exceptionally useful. The institutions thus represented are identified in Appendix C.

Despite the combination of related current literature, the pattern of observations and interviews throughout the South, the insightful opinion-naire returns, and our continuing reference to various members of the Advisory Board, we anticipated significant gaps of ignorance that the staff would not be able to fill. We needed to identify these areas of strategic importance, and then call on experts to help us. We set about to identify scholars who could develop such research memoranda and working papers for our use.

An official of the United States Office of Education prepared a valuable document expressly for this study, entitled "The Federal Government's Emerging Role in Southern Higher Education." His name is withheld at his request in accordance with government policy. Other informative documents prepared for our use are listed here with appreciation to the several contributors. None of these contributors, of course, is accountable for any portion of this study, since different interpretations may have been placed upon their data by this author. Besides, even a rearrangement of data may do violence to the purpose achieved by the original papers although they are highly useful in a new context for different purposes. Aside from the unidentified contributor from Washington, special working papers were prepared by these scholars within their respective fields of specialty:

Dr. Robert Bjork Visiting Professor of Economics Syracuse University	"An Economic Glimpse of Today's South, Yesterday and Today"
Dr. Robert Cleary Associate Professor of Government The American University	"Gubernatorial Politics and Southern Higher Education"
Dr. James W. Reynolds Professor and Consultant in Junior College Education The University of Texas	"The Southern Community College"
Dr. Gordon Sweet Executive Secretary, Commission on Colleges Southern Association of Colleges and Schools	"The Role of Accreditation in Southern Higher Education"
Dr. Myron Wicke General Secretary Division of Higher Education The Methodist Church	"Church Related Colleges in the South"

Numerous other individuals have been of special help through interviews and by providing unpublished materials from their personal files. Notable among these are Dr. Guy B. Johnson, Kenan Professor of Sociology at the University of North Carolina; Dr. J. Curtis Dixon, National Representative for the Woodrow Wilson Foundation; and Dr. Frank Dickey, Executive Director of the National Commission on Accrediting. (The latter two persons were also members of the Advisory Board.) To assist the reader in finding the "South of the moment," Miss Martha Palmer and her assistants, at Peabody College, prepared the helpful maps contained in Appendix D.

The unfolding design of the study has been one of clarifying issues with the assistance of our Advisory Board, and of going to sources most likely to yield the needed information, no matter how esoteric, as in psychological research, or how commonplace, as in conversations with student civil rights demonstrators. The concern has been less for scholarly respectability than for an accurate perception of conditions that will not sit still long enough to get a time-exposure view of them.

We have been beset a bit by this phenomenon of documentation, that the closer one approaches a significant datum, the more difficult it is to get it on the record. Yet the veteran social science researchers will have empathic respect for this difficulty. We have found no way around the problem except, as an esteemed colleague expressed it, to lie a little in order to tell the truth.

The help and encouragement received from many people in the development of this study have been substantial. The freedom to report and to interpret findings as one individual is a humbling freedom. With no restrictions imposed by terms of the grant, by the Advisory Board, or by the contributors of research memoranda, the author alone is to blame for its shortcomings. In the final analysis, this is only one man's view of the current salients and challenges in Southern higher education as he has been helped to see them by his fellow Americans. Higher education must soon become a force leading to a more humane as well as a more prosperous society, or the word *higher* will eventually become only a figure of speech. Among the author's several biases, this is his prevailing one, as this study clearly reflects.

List of Graphs

List of Tables

Contents

PART I.

THE AMERICAN SOUTH

THE AMERICAN SOUTH

There are numerous souths, and most of them have been written about at length in recent years. A generation or so ago, a collective attempt was made by many authors to describe Southern culture, and that effort divided the culture into thirty-one chapter-length treatises.[1] Our purpose here is far simpler, maybe even naive. This profile simply aims to provide a limited social context in which the distinctive problems of Southern higher education may be more easily comprehended by those readers not fully "at home" either in the Southern culture or in Southern higher education. The introductory focus will be mainly on politics and religion; on conditions of race, and of family life; and on conspicuous poverty. This choice of focus requires brief explanation.

The word politics somehow implies sinister connotations while its American companion, democracy, conveys a heartwarming faith, a patriotic appeal. Yet politics, pure and simple, forms the structural means by which our ideals of self-government are put to work. One cannot understand the South, or its efforts to provide higher education for its citizens, without some insight into the rapidly changing circumstances of Southern politics.

In a different manner, the South puts its faith in religion. As the South has been a one-party political system, containing divisions within it, so has it been largely a one-party religion, the party of Protestantism.[2] Church and state in America, we say, are kept apart by historic American doctrine. Walter Lippmann explained the relationship between church and state advisedly: "Church and state need to be separate, autonomous, and secure. But they must also meet on all the issues of good and evil."[3] The South prides itself in being regarded as the Bible Belt of America.

---

[1] W. T. Couch (ed.), *Culture in the South* (Chapel Hill: University of North Carolina Press, 1935). More copious yet, of course, was Howard Odum's *Southern Regions of the United States* (Chapel Hill: University of North Carolina Press, 1936).

[2] For theological reasons, the Southern Baptist Convention does not officially regard itself as a "protesting" but as an "affirming" denomination, although many Baptists and other Protestants overlook these distinctions.

[3] Lippmann, *Essays in the Public Philosophy* (New York: Mentor Books, 1956), p. 119. [Originally published by Little, Brown and Co. in association with the Atlantic Monthly Press.]

Yet in that South, church-related colleges are entering the public sector, largely by dint of public monies. Southern religion, like politics, is a basic part of the ABC's of Southern higher education.

Ethnic divisions within the South have placed it in the national and international limelight for more than a decade. There have been more authorities on the subject than students of the problem. Even Gunnar Myrdal cautioned the readers of *An American Dilemma* against stretching the findings and conclusions of his study beyond their proper sphere. [4] Southern higher education now has the challenge of assuming a leadership role in facing a new ethnic dilemma, one of an emerging postdesegregation era in the public domain and a continuing predesegregation era in the private sphere of Southern life and thought.

The Southern family is in a state of increasing social disorganization. The Negro family, from the standpoint of social crisis, creates problems and issues that are tragically reflected in higher education.[5] The white family, in different form, presents its share of problems as well. Higher education can ill afford to proceed unmindful of the family problems it inherits and to some degree compounds. It must seek a more intelligent role in either stabilizing family life or in finding some acceptable equivalents for its social functions. The uprooting effects of urbanization, of technology, of manpower and womanpower needs, combine to place new demands upon what college should offer toward strengthening our primary social institution.

There is always the matter of money. Politics and religion, ethnic divisions and family life are all influenced by—some would say governed by—economic interests. The South is far more prosperous than it was a generation ago when Franklin Delano Roosevelt named it the nation's number one economic problem. Yet both chronic and acute poverty remains in the Southern regions, and the current "war on poverty" is falling short of its worthy goals. Higher education must be a business as well as an educational enterprise. A study of the economics of the South will provide a clearer view of the magnitude of the poverty barrier in higher education—with which this study is deeply concerned—a poverty both of persons and of institutions.

In this uprooted cultural milieu, a major purpose of this study is to discover the tasks that Southern colleges and universities are setting for themselves, and are having set for them. First of all, is Southern higher education genuinely relevant as viewed against society's need for it?

---

[4] Myrdal, *An American Dilemma, The Negro Problem and Modern Democracy*, Twentieth Anniversary Edition (New York: Harper and Row, 1962), p. *lxxxiii*.

[5] See: Office of Policy Planning and Research, *The Negro Family: The Case for National Action* (Washington, D.C.: U.S. Department of Labor, March 1965).

Secondly, does it concern itself sufficiently with "the needs of the Negro, the poor, the deprived, and the socially depressed?"[6]

The well-informed student of the South and of Southern higher education may gain little by reading Part I of this report unless it be to sense the bias of the author. Less profound scholars of these subjects, it is hoped, will find these opening chapters helpful before proceeding to the main body of the study.

---

[6] Harold Taylor believes that American higher education has concerned itself too little with these needs. See: "American Idealism, 1965," *Saturday Review* (June 16, 1965), p. 16. Our scope of inquiry will be limited to the Southeastern quadrant of that proposition.

1. POLITICS AND RELIGION

To define the South in terms of geographical boundaries is a difficult task, as we have observed. Yet many have tried. Some refer to the South as contiguous regions; others, as sections. A fundamental difference between regionalism and sectionalism was pointed up by Howard Odum, who explained that regionalism puts the nation first, with the national culture the superior judge of this priority, while sectionalism emphasizes "states rights," local loyalties, and a loose confederation of the nation's many political parties.[1] The South, wherever it is, combines the views of sectionalism and regionalism, but this admixture of views is not coterminous with the Mason-Dixon line.

Curiously enough, the South probably could be identified on an annual rainfall map as that portion of America enjoying the optimum rainfall of 40-60 inches per year; or, with a few notable exceptions, as the temperate region boasting a growing season of 200-300 frost-free days per year. But rainfall and growing seasons are not the South.

If the South consists of any agreed upon group of states, it is impossible to determine which they are. The eleven states of the Old Confederacy extend from Virginia along the Atlantic seaboard through the Carolinas, Georgia, and Florida, turning westward into Alabama, Mississippi, Louisiana, and Texas, and then edge northward to include Arkansas and Tennessee. These states also may be alluded to as the "deep South." The South, however, cannot be thus definitively identified. This grouping does not correspond with that of the Southern Governor's Conference, which includes Maryland, nor with that of the Southern Association of Colleges and Schools, which excludes Arkansas. None of those souths agrees with the seventeen-state area covered by the Southern Education Reporting Service, which represents the area most closely touched by the Supreme Court rulings on desegregation in public education, including the "border South." *The World Book* identifies fourteen Southern states without explaining the basis for its selection. The United States Bureau of the Census identifies the South Atlantic, the East South Central, and

---

[1] See: William H. Nicholls, *Southern Tradition and Regional Progress* (Chapel Hill: University of North Carolina Press, 1960), p. 75.

the West South Central sections. extending far beyond any South of liter-
ature and legend. The "Southern Baptists" hold state conventions from
Florida to Alaska. Certainly religion and politics know no homogeneous
South.

Rupert Vance observed that the "solid South" was made more by history
than by geography, and Wilma Dykema added that if this were true, then
geography had given the South its infinite variety.[2] Its rivers and moun-
tains reach in from adjoining sections of America. The Appalachian
Mountain range, nearly three hundred miles wide, stretches from Maine
to Alabama. Miss Dykema identified thirteen specific geographical entities that make up the regions we commonly call the South.[3]

In these pages dealing with politics, and those beyond it, the "map
South" cannot always be the same. The obligation remains, as we "change
souths" with the reader, to keep before him the South to which we refer
at a given moment. Appendix D contains six maps of different souths to
assist the reader in geographical identification. To bind ourselves to any
fixed South that does not exist in fact is to perpetuate another legend.
Of that we do enough already.

To know the South's inner self, to probe the covert aspects of its overt
behavior—its compassion and its aggression, its genteel and its cavalier
character—one must cultivate an empathy with those dimensions of life
and thought so close to the heart of the Southerner. The house of Southern
politics and of the Southern religious establishment, in a loosely defined
region, with their varied expressions of thought and feeling, give a glimpse
of that South. Politics and religion, certainly within the South, find much
of each in the other, and together they provide a primer to an understanding
of the most written about region of America.

THE HOUSE OF SOUTHERN POLITICS

Southern politics has been historically dedicated to the idea that only a
house divided against itself can stand. That house has been divided, in
part, by the white voting constituency and the largely disfranchised Negro
Southerner. It has consisted, too, of the powerful rural voter, and of
the less influential city dweller whose vote has often counted much less
than half that of his country cousin. Even among the voting "equals" and
their political leadership, the South, though appearing to be "solid," has
not consistently been so. Dewey Grantham amply documented the position that "the monolithic South was and is a myth."[4] Within the one party,
factions have arisen to air economic grievances and to mirror other real
divisions in Southern life and thought. The new divisions in Southern

[2]Wilma Dykema, "The Face of the Solid South," *Current History,* 35 (November 1958),
259-260.
[3]*Ibid.*
[4]Grantham, "Politics Below the Potomac," *Current History,* 35 (November 1958), 265.
See also: Grantham, *The Democratic South* (New York: W. W. Norton and Company, 1963).

politics, however, will increasingly be divisions among peers rather than amid the rural white ruling class, the voiceless Negro, and the under-represented citizen of the city, whatever his color.

To consider Southern politics requires one neither to condone nor to condemn it. The task is to describe its changing character. Those evident changes appear to reside mainly in the variables of race, of legislative reapportionment, of federal spending in its relation to Southern political strategy and tactics, and finally, of a redefinition of gubernatorial role.

The Historic Theme—Race

The penetrating study of V. O. Key, Jr., in 1949, revealed that the character of politics of individual Southern states varied roughly with the Negro proportion of the population, from Virginia to Georgia to Arkansas. Key observed that the whites of the Black Belt[5] gave the South its dominant political tone, and that "in the last analysis, the major peculiarities of Southern politics go back to the Negro."[6]

The "last analysis" still holds true in a general sense, but the historic theme, while still focusing on the race-centered character of Southern politics, has been dramatically changed. Today the whites of the Black Belt have diminished power over national and state elections, and this lessening of power extends increasingly to the local levels.

The enfranchisement of the Negro Southerner is becoming a major new equalizer in politics. It was introduced in significant form in 1944, when the Smith v. Allwright decision knocked out the legal underpinnings of the "white primary." In that decision, the United States Supreme Court held that the right to vote in political party primaries is a right secured by the Constitution.[7] Thus ended a twenty-year legal battle to invalidate the expedient by which the Democratic party had so systematically excluded Negroes from political influence. The Republican party, except for patronage purposes, did not count in Southern politics.

During the ensuing decade, the registration of Negroes assumed considerable proportions. In Florida, for example, Negro registration increased from about 20,000 in 1944 to 137,535 in 1956; from 5.5 to 37.5 percent of the 1950 adult Negro population.[8] According to Hugh Price, a study of that period in Florida's history ". . . demonstrates the growing ability of the Negro to use the ballot with traditional aims

[5] The Black Belt refers, authentically, to that strip of fertile black soil, extending mainly through central Alabama and into west central Mississippi, ideally suited for plantations where cotton was king. Politically, the Belt refers to a heavy ratio of Negro population (40 percent or more) from Virginia to Georgia to Arkansas.

[6] V. O. Key, Jr., assisted by Alexander Heard, *Southern Politics in State and Nation* (New York: Alfred A. Knopf, 1949), p. 5.

[7] Smith v. Allwright, 321, U.S. 649 (1944).

[8] Hugh D. Price, *The Negro and Southern Politics* (New York: New York University Press, 1957), p. 3.

and values in mind. "[9] The Negro votes were evidently not susceptible to "delivery" in bloc vote form. A half century earlier, W. E. B. DuBois had remarked that "The Negro voter . . . has in his hand the tremendous power of emancipating the Democratic party from its enslavement to the reactionary South. "[10] In that same hand is now also the ominous power to crush the tender prospect of ethnic community.

This acceleration in the registration of Negroes was not limited to Florida, but has been a major movement for more than a decade throughout the South. In Georgia, more than 163,000 Negroes were registered in 1956, compared with only 10,000 or so in 1944. In the eleven states of the Old Confederacy, Negro registration rose to about 1,238,000 by the end of 1956, or about 26 percent of the five million Negro residents of voting age in those states.[11] Yet, in the Black Belt of the South, characterized by a high ratio of Negro population, the legal destruction of the white primary made little perceptible difference. In Mississippi only 6 percent of Negroes of voting age were registered in 1954.[12] A decade later, in 1964, that percentage was raised only to 8 percent.

The Civil Rights Acts of 1957, 1960, and 1964 failed to break the hold on the disfranchised Negro in the Black Belt. Yet, in this time he was becoming an increasing political power that could not be ignored with impunity. According to the best available estimates, the number of Negro registrants in the eleven former Confederate states climbed in 1964 to 2,174,000, or 43.3 percent of the Negroes of voting age.[13] C. Vann Woodward pointed out that the five Southern states in which Senator Goldwater was victorious in the 1964 presidential campaign were those with the lowest Negro registration, and that the Negro vote clearly represented the balance of power in four or five other Southern states.[14] Corroborating this view, Lloyd Elliott observed that Negro Southerners gave President Johnson 1.4 million votes, which consisted of forty-three to fifty-six electoral votes in the Electoral College, depending on one's analysis of North Carolina's thirteen electoral votes.[15]

The most recent page in the ethnic chapter of Southern politics was the Voting Rights Act of 1965. Ten weeks after its passage on August 6, 1965, 110,000 Negroes registered in the states of Alabama, Georgia, Mississippi, South Carolina, and Louisiana. Of these voters 29,213 were in Mississippi,

[9]*Ibid.*, p. 111. A value judgment, to be sure, not a demonstrable fact, and contraindicated in the Georgia and Alabama gubernatorial elections of 1966. In Virginia, in 1964 and 1965, however, the Negro vote, *en bloc*, was decisive.

[10]As quoted by Dewey Grantham, *The Democratic South*, p. 86.

[11]Estimates of the Southern Regional Council, as reported by Grantham, p. 83.   [12]*Ibid.*

[13]Voter Education Project news release by the Southern Regional Council, November 15, 1964. Mississippi had risen only from the 6 to the 8 percent level in that ten-year period, while Alabama had climbed to 23 percent.

[14]Woodward, "From the First Reconstruction to the Second," *Harper's*, 230:1379, p. 132.

[15]Elliott, "The Negro Voter and National Politics," *New South*, 20 (September 1965), 9.

and 36, 219 were in Louisiana,[16] areas where civil rights legislation had
been so largely impotent. The Negroes' vote in 1966, while in no true
sense a balance of power, has changed ingredients in the recipe for success in Southern politics. Louis Lomax expressed the significance of this
change with his poignant but compassionate wit, "they ain't Niggers,
they are colored citizens."[17] They are now more than two million strong.
The whites of the Black Belt, in state and national terms, no longer rule
supreme. They share their power, man for man, with colored voting
citizens. They know there is no turning back. Yet in Alabama and Mississippi, the small Negro bloc vote is overwhelmingly counteracted in state
elections by white segregationists. The Meredith march in 1966, dividing
Negro leadership, has not altered that fact. The subsequent voter education projects in Mississippi conducted by the Southern Regional Council,
however, may make a difference two years hence.

The Equalizer of Apportionment

Second in import only to the changing political power of the Negro, if
not transcending it, is the impact of legislative reapportionment. The
apportionment issue, of course, is of massive national significance, but
the scope of immediate concern is with the increasingly urban South,
which has been trying, since 1936 and the days of Governor Hugh White's
BAWI program of Mississippi, to Balance Agriculture With Industry.

The South is becoming urbanized less rapidly than other American
regions, but it is moving in the same direction. During the 1950-1960
decade, the Census showed that 604 Southern counties gained in population;
in 743 others, it decreased. Yet seventy-four metropolitan centers
with populations exceeding 100,000 showed a population increase, while
only one did not. In the category of cities of 10,000 to 100,000 population,
363 showed a population increase and only 37 showed a loss. The urbanization of the South points to an urgent need for legislative reapportionment,
and the Supreme Court has made clear that this principle will hold fast.
The Southern politician, of course, wonders how—and how soon.

As many readers will recall it all began in Tennessee. In 1959, Charles
Baker, of Memphis, a "citizen and voter" of the state, challenged the
existing legislative apportionment as unconstitutional, under provisions
of the due process and equal protection provisions of the 14th Amendment
to the United States Constitution. It would have been difficult, in Tennessee
or elsewhere, to find an informed citizen who privately would disclaim the
challenge. Tennessee's constitution had for a half century "required"
reapportionment by the General Assembly each ten years. The assembly,

---

[16] William J. Taylor (staff director), *The Voting Rights Act . . . The First Months* (Washington, D. C.: U.S. Commission on Civil Rights, 1965). The act is applicable to the states
of Alabama, Georgia, Mississippi, South Carolina, Alaska, twenty counties in North Carolina, and one in Arizona.

[17] Lomax, *The Negro Revolt* (New York: Harper and Row, 1962), introductory comment
relating an imaginary conversation between two Southern senators.

decade after decade, simply paid no official attention to the requirement. How could a rural ruling legislature be expected to "comply itself" out of its unquestioned position of authority and loyalty to its rural constituency?

The familiar Baker v. Carr case was decided in 1962; it asserted the jurisdiction of both state and federal courts on matters of legislative apportionment, based on the "equal protection" clause of the 14th Amendment of the United States Constitution. Subsequently, in 1964, in the Reynolds v. Sims decision, the Court enunciated the "one man one vote" doctrine, to the effect that both houses of bicameral legislatures must be apportioned "substantially" on the basis of population distribution.[18]

Congress responded against the second Supreme Court decision in various but, thus far, ineffectual ways. Efforts to amend the Constitution, to permit states to apportion one legislative house on a nonpopulation basis, could not muster the necessary two-thirds majority of the 89th Congress so as to get the amendment wheels turning.[19]

Most Southern states are moving and counter-moving in final efforts to preserve as much rural power as possible by legislative negotiation and compromise. The unhappy option, of course, is that the courts will apportion the legislatures if they do not apportion themselves promptly and in a manner satisfactory to the courts.

The apportionment controversy may be revived, but its substantial outcome is clear. The half-disfranchised city dweller will be strengthened by the one man one vote doctrine, thus introducing another ingredient in the recipe for success in Southern politics. This will have—it is having—an unhappy effect upon the dispossessed ruling class of the rural minority, and will leave its scars, but the diversified South, in developing its economic growth potential, is more self-determining as it moves into a future that will be less limited by a nineteenth-century balance of political power.

The Friendly Federal Government

Since the ante-bellum period, the South has been looked upon as the "states rights" region of America. The label has not been misplaced. The desire for self-determination is exceeded only by the use of the phrase as a defensive pattern against the claimed rights of others within the South. Efforts to establish states rights, sometimes through independent political parties, have a sporadic history. The Dixiecrats movement of 1948 and the free election movement of 1960 were examples of these efforts. The most recent and most devastating instance was in the party bolt to Goldwater Republicanism in 1964. The South now knows that its real choices will

---

[18] "Legislative Apportionment," *Congressional Digest*, 44:1 (January 1965), 1.

[19] On August 4, 1965, such an effort failed in the Senate by an insufficient majority vote of 57 to 39. On September 8, 1965, the Senate Judiciary Committee ordered a similar bill, sponsored by Senator Dirksen of Illinois, to be reported without recommendation, in view of the August 4 vote. Again, in April 1966, the Dirksen proposal was voted down.

be made within the two existing major parties, and that the predominant national platform-makers leave little room for the traditional states rights plank. Yet many believe the prospect for a revived third party in 1968 to be a credible one.

Far more important to the South today, is the massive fund dispensing facility of the federal government, since 1964, toward what has been called, among various names, the Great Society. There is an unprecedented disposition on local and state levels within the South (not unlike the non-South) to "cooperate" with the federal government. For the South, the facility to cooperate has not come easily. Few believe that the South has been deeply converted from its views of sectionalism to those of regionalism— of suddenly subordinating state to national interests. The Metropolitan Action Commission, various education acts, and other channels of federal disbursements combine to place the South in an unseemly "beholden" position. But, since 1964, the practice has become respectable within the South to commend programs of the federal government, or to criticize them in subdued terms that do not threaten the prospects for financial recipiency. The continuation of that practice depends, of course, upon continued massive benefits in the shifting sands of politics.

The Southern Governor's Changing Role

The titular head of the state is, of course, the governor. Some view him as a political weathervane; others as a shaper of public opinion and policy. The observation of Theodore White states the general problem of political leaders succinctly: "They must devote as much of their time looking backward to make sure the people continue to follow as looking forward to find where they should go." [20]

We select here for illustrative purposes, the governors, in 1965, of the states of Alabama, Mississippi, and Georgia, because in combination they represent the spectrum of gubernatorial positions on major issues in Southern politics. The illustrations, however, are selected from the recurring racial theme.

Governor George Wallace, formerly a moderate Southerner on the racial issue, first campaigned for that high office in 1958, against John Patterson. In that campaign, according to R. G. Sherrill, "he was so moderate on the race question that one saw only Wallace bumper stickers in many Negro districts." [21] The Ku Klux Klan openly supported Patterson. Wallace was defeated. On election night, as he viewed his certain defeat from the election returns, George Wallace is reported to have remarked, "They outniggered me that time, but they'll never do it again." [22] Wallace looked back to see where the people were going, and soon thereafter got

[20] White, *The Making of the President 1964* (New York: Atheneum Publishers, 1965), p. *x*.
[21] Robert G. Sherrill, "Wallace and the Future of Dixie," *Nation*, 199 (October 26, 1964), 268.
[22] *Ibid.*

out in front of them. Attorney General Richmond Flowers, of Alabama, was looking ahead in 1966 to where Alabamans might be influenced to go, but was told by his friends and advisers that he was ahead of his time in Alabama, and risked political oblivion. They may have been correct. Mrs. Lurleen (George D.) Wallace won by a majority in the Democratic primary without a run-off. Flowers took the Negro vote and little else. John Patterson polled a negligible 3 percent.

Governor Paul Johnson of Mississippi appeared, in a different manner, to be politically adroit. There is little doubt that his earlier political position was that of a Southern moderate, here used to mean a gradualist, a slowly changing segregationist who honors the law. Mississippians, including members of the then powerful White Citizens Council, recalled his strong support in 1963 of Governor Barnett in the Ole Miss last ditch stand against desegregation; and the campaign slogan, "Stand Tall with Paul, " echoed the segregationist battle cry of defiance. But Governor Johnson's inaugural address of January 21, 1964, gave the Council and other segregationists pause for concern; and gave desegregationists and those who could "take desegregation or leave it" a new basis for hope of economic prosperity and social stability within the law: "I will say to you that you and I are part of this world, whether we like it or not; what happens in it, through no fault of ours, affects us. Too, we are Americans as well as Mississippians. As a practical matter, we are at this moment in the mainstream of American life. National policies have direct bearing on our economy, on our political freedom, on our daily living, whether we like it or not. "[23]

In August 1965, Governor Johnson moved a step further with Mississippians in seeking their support of a constitutional amendment that was opposed by the Ku Klux Klan and by the White Citizens Council. He declared, in substance, that defiance and loud talking would not protect the people of that state, that theirs must not be a rear guard defense, but that they must claim for themselves and the welfare of the rising generations their "share of tomorrow. "[24]

Governor Carl Sanders, of Georgia, was one of the most ardent supporters of Lyndon B. Johnson in the presidential election of 1964, but Georgia switched its loyalty temporarily to the Republican party despite his efforts. Thanks to the "mandate" of the nation, however, Governor Sanders proved to be a "winning loser. " Since 1964, he has worked toward mending some political fissures. As a young governor looking at the new realities of Southern politics, he knows that he is a bit out of step; Black power and Lester Maddox have turned Georgia back.

---

[23] Inaugural address of Governor Paul B. Johnson, January 21, 1964, p. 7 of text.
[24] Televised address, August 16, 1965. The referendum passed by a three-to-one majority. Although its purpose was to offset the Negro bloc voting with a new bloc of 400,000 unregistered and functionally illiterate whites, his position was honest and lawful.

These cases have been drawn neither to vilify nor to eulogize any individuals, but to illustrate the new ambiguities in Southern politics on the gubernatorial level. These and other governors ostensibly wish to serve their people well—and long. Doing both sometimes seems to create contradictions. We must understand the basis for adamant positions on the racial issue, and we need to recognize as well that in other areas of public responsibility, all of these governors have shown constructive leadership.[25] The governors of Alabama, Georgia, and Mississippi, for example, have done well and are doing as much as any other three governors to meet the new challenges of public higher education in their respective states.

Higher education in the political sphere, however, presents two nettling, challenging questions:

1. In the South of changing political realities, how can colleges and universities, accustomed to patterns of using education for politics, learn effectively to use politics for education?

2. In the educational programs of both public and private Southern colleges and universities, how can future civic leaders, today's college students, be prepared to use the changing political power in the public interest rather than, wittingly or unwittingly, against it?

Both questions require studied plans and prudent action.

THERE STANDS THE CHURCH

The South, the Bible Belt of America, is building its share of churches. The new ones, whether colonial, Gothic, or modern, will depart considerably from the traditional church steeple design. Changing the tenets of the old time religion, however, is a different matter. Wilhelm Worringer's *Form in Gothic* symbolizes the interest of some Southern Protestants far more than does Robert Raines' *Reshaping the Christian Life.* One spokesman lamented that: "Churchmen hear the drums of their culture beating above the small voice of their Master." However apt the view, Americans in general and Southerners in particular like to be affiliated with a church whether they choose to attend it or not, and Southerners, white and Negro, show a marked preference for Protestantism.

Man, in an anthropological sense, appears to have made God in his own image, obtaining godly sanction for his biases, rather than the other way around. Then he is shocked to be told that God is dead, believing it to be the god he made. This predicament is explained by Arnold Toynbee, who commented that if the religions of the world are to save our time, each must realize that it has only a partial hold on the truth. His stated prerequisites to the victory of religion are: (1) to seek a common moral

---

[25]Dewey Grantham, *The Democratic South,* p. 49, gives several illustrations of Southern governors who have made inflammatory use of the race question, such as Vardaman and Bilbo, but who, in other respects, have been good governors.

code—not a creed, (2) to be concerned with issues relevant to the times, and (3) to strip itself of the unnecessary accretion of doctrines of particular epochs in history. He was speaking in the South, and pointedly to it as well.[26]

A prevalent, inaccurate notion persists that the American church stands as a headquarters for bigotry, and research of a demographic nature has supported the view that Americans with church affiliation are, on the average, considerably more prejudiced than are the unchurched. More intensive psychological research, however, reveals that "frequent attenders and total nonattenders are most tolerant," and that "it is irregular church attendance (not membership) that correlates most highly with bigotry."[27]

TABLE 1

AMERICAN TRENDS OF RELIGION'S INFLUENCE

General Public Opinion	1957	1965
Increasing	69%	33%
Losing	14	45
No difference	10	13
No opinion	7	9

College Viewpoints		
Increasing		24%
Losing		62
No difference		11
No opinion		3

If the American church is declining in its religious or social influence— if we are living in an increasingly post-Christian era—is it explained by a lack of personal commitment to the moral code inherent in all great religions? Do Americans believe that organized religion is obsolete? A Gallup poll on the status of religion in the United States, which asked: "Is religion increasing or losing its influence?," strongly reflected a

[26]*Nashville Tennesseean* (February 14, 1965), p. 8-C. The remarks are from an address given at the University of the South, February 13, 1965.

[27]Gordon W. Allport, "Prejudice: Is It Societal or Personal?," *Journal of Social Issues,* XVIII:2 (1962), 131.

national sentiment in which religion, of whatever denominations, is losing its grip. [28]

Does this mean that organized religion is becoming less sacred—and more secular? Is the American church becoming more prosperous and less influential? Or is it, on the other hand, assuring its economic life so that spiritual life may grow and prosper in a secure context? These are not questions for the South alone. The South, however, is the scope of our present interest, and its answers, past and present, are unique and highly relevant for higher education.

Southern White Protestantism

In the South, Protestantism "reigns supreme." As Kenneth Bailey expressed it, "Nowhere else, almost surely, is there a Protestant population of equal size so renowned for its piety or . . . its commitment to old fashioned Scriptural literalism." [29] An eminent anthropologist, who is a Southerner, recently observed that because of this scriptural dimension of the culture, Southerners have a more deeply ingrained conscience; they want to do what is "right," and they feel deep guilt when they fail to do so. Whether or not this perception is accurate, the South is known for its "fixed commitments" in religion, in politics, and in general.

Within Southern Protestantism, the Baptists continue to be religious leaders with respect to total membership and to the size of their budgets. They were not always "Southern" Baptists, however. It was in 1845 that the Southern Baptists seceded from the General Missionary Convention, basically over the question of slavery. Except for limited activities in the North and on the West Coast, they remain more than a century later a separate Southern group. The aggregate membership grew from 2,700,155 in 1936 to more than 10,190,000 in 1962. Bailey ascribed this surge of growth to a heavy reliance on "studied promotional techniques," and to the local church control that frees each church for self-determination on crucial matters of controversy: Each congregation is virtually a law unto itself. In Texas, for example, more than 230 congregations have adopted a policy of desegregation, but each acted on its own authority, [30] unlike the connectional Methodists.

The Methodists, like the Baptists, seceded from their national religious body principally because of the slavery issue. After many subsequent efforts at compromise, the Methodist church reunited in 1939 with regionally and racially segregated "jurisdictions." This was a step forward, but far from achieving church unity. National membership of the Methodist church in 1962 exceeded 10,150,000, only 38,300 short of that of the

---

[28] George Gallup Survey, reported in the *Nashville Tennesseean* (April 18, 1965), p. 5-B.
[29] Bailey, *Southern White Protestantism in the Twentieth Century* (New York: Harper and Row, 1964), p. *ix*. Southern Louisiana, predominantly Catholic, is the notable exception.
[30] *Ibid.*, pp. 152-153.

Southern Baptist Convention. Within the Southern (white) jurisdiction, Methodist membership climbed from 2.8 million in 1940 to more than 4 million in 1962. If the Methodists were to add the membership of the counterpart African Methodist Episcopal (and Zion) church, this would swell the membership figure by two million more.

The Southern Presbyterians ("U.S." as distinguished from the Northern "U.S.A."), like the Baptists and Methodists, seceded from the parent organization over the issue of slavery, and are also doing well as a separate entity, judging from the business indicators of membership and budget. From 1936 to 1962, the Southern Presbyterian membership more than doubled—from 449,045 to 928,055.[31]

Southern Protestantism is big business. In 1962, the Southern Baptist Convention received contributions in excess of half a billion dollars ($50.24 per member). The Methodist church (nationally) also received "tithes and offerings" in the amount of more than half a billion dollars ($57.37 per member). The Southern Presbyterians contributed nearly a hundred million dollars to their church ($105.33 per member).[32] In social and economic terms, then, the Southern white Protestant church has established itself as a highly stable social institution. Yet it exerts social control over its members only through suasion. Since the individual member is under no enforceable obligation, the double standards of church position (on abstinence from alcoholic beverages, for example) and normative behavior are often taken for granted.

This individual freedom grows upon a sound theological base. Protestantism, of course, was historically a protest movement against the dogma of authoritarianism. Built into the mechanism of its governing controls was a guarantee of representative government on various levels. Thus, the religious or ethical plateau is not determined by ministerial edict, but by the highest ethical level at which church leaders can achieve reasonable consensus. The grass roots approach is at once a strength and a weakness of Protestantism. If each man is his own priest, especially in a South conditioned by a relatively unchanging culture until of late, then the sporadic starts and stops of Protestantism are understandable. The individual tends to resist any infringement on his private life. The Anglo-Saxon white Protestant presumably wants to do "right"—but he sees through the eyes of his culture.

The quandary of the Southern white clergy remains. The clergy's dramatic examples of "taking a stand" have not been accorded the public recognition they deserve. Kenneth Bailey cites case after case of clergymen, both Northern and Southern, risking their lives as well as their

[31]*Ibid.*, p. 152.

[32]Benson Y. Landis (ed.), *Yearbook of American Churches* (New York: National Council of Churches, 1964), pp. 277ff.

tenure in support of civil rights, for example. True, there were some—now a dwindling number—who championed the cause of segregation. Both the Honorable Baptist Brooks Hays and the Baptist Governor Orville Faubus, differing widely on that issue, had a good measure of support from the Arkansas Baptists.

The Southern evangelist may make a temporary emotional impact among the less "sophisticated," but sustained value is realized only through the patient forbearance of the minister who stays with his flock—he understands them, marries their young, buries their dead, rejoices with them in time of gladness, and mourns with them in time of grief. But he, like the politician, is not a leader unless he is being followed. On the civil rights issue, non-Southern ministers have come South and some have done a beneficial "evangelistic" job of creating a moral ferment within which Southern ministers can work constructively within what they call a "doctrine of limited goals." Some have left behind untended problems of equal magnitude. It takes time, but many ministers are now using that time to strengthen bonds of brotherhood and to heal the raw, salted wounds. Southern religion and human rights have, in the main, been helped by non-Southerners serving a function that only they could serve. The predominantly white church, in broader perspective, is not just standing there. Its leadership is working with measured success to get it on the move, but inertia is a powerful deterrent.

The Negro Church

The Negro church in the South, evolving as a kind of "invisible institution," became a focal point of social organization and cohesion many years ago. Professor E. Franklin Frazier termed it "a nation within a nation."[33] In that context Negro leadership could emerge, and there the emasculated Negro man could establish his manhood. In the Methodist church, members enjoyed a limited opportunity to experiment with the concept of democracy by voting and participating in the election of church officials. Many Negro churches were "family churches," and strengthened attenuated family ties. The Negro church was described by Frazier as the most important agency of social control among Negroes, transcending even the law and family mores, until a generation ago.

As Negroes moved into urban areas, the church decreased in its social control over and demand of high loyalty from them. Urbanized Negroes are being drawn into a newly emerging class structure that finds expression in a different kind of church affiliation. With secular desegregation has come the tendency of the middle-class Negroes to remove from the names of their organizations anything that identifies them by race. Another tendency, in this striving for status, is leaving the "low brow" Baptist and Methodist churches to join the more elite Presbyterian, Episcopalian,

[33]See: E. Franklin Frazier, *The Negro Church in America* (New York: Schocken Books, 1963), p. 33.

and Congregational churches.[34] The shopping around for status and *bona fide* integration has included the Catholic and Christian Science churches. But if Negroes sometimes achieve such status, they rarely gain true integration. The Negro church has, by its nature, impeded the integration of Negroes into American society. For the masses of Negroes, in contrast to the mobile middle and upper classes, the Negro church continues to be a refuge. Despite liberalized church polity, it appears apt to remain so.[35]

The pattern of control of the Negro church continues to be highly authoritarian. The church's recent doctrinal emphasis has shifted from that of salvation after death (an excellent form of social control used in India with the Hindu untouchable and in America with the Negro slave), to matters of an economic, social, and political salvation here and now.

All One Body, We? [36]

Southern Baptists have insisted on local and state control of their affairs. The Methodists, though organized in a connectional or episcopal sense, insist upon church control through the democratic processes of the clergy and laity. In contrast to the Negro church, the white Protestant church remains a weak instrument of social control. On moral issues, where the church has taken an official stand, the members of the church act as "free moral agents" unbound in any sense by church sanction. Following the 1954 Supreme Court decision on public school segregation, nearly every denominational organization acclaimed it. In 1956, the Methodist church urged that segregation in the Methodist church be abolished "with reasonable speed." In local congregations, however, church attendance proceeded about as usual. The Southern Presbyterians, in 1954, asked local churches and church colleges to open their doors to all races. In that same year, the Southern Baptist Convention acknowledged the decision to be in harmony with Christian principles.

Each denomination had left the national organization when the Confederacy seceded from the Union. The Confederacy failed, but the secession of Protestantism was successful. Now these same Southern denominations, once pro-slavery, are opposed to segregation, while local congregations stand fast. The tokenism of Race Relations Sunday each year continues,

---

[34]*Ibid.*, p. 79.

[35]*Ibid.* The major causes seem to be these: Negro leadership does not wish to lose its own following or get into ethnic competition; and Negroes are "comfortable by habit" in their own churches. Segregated housing militates against a natural desegregation of churches on a natural basis of having a community in common.

[36]Like a mighty army   We are not divided; all
  Moves the Church of God   one body we,
  Brothers, we are treading where   One in hope and doctrine,
    the saints have trod.   one in charity.
                                                    Onward, Christian soldiers.

while segregation continues, to a great degree by mutual consent.[37] Thus, by an ironic twist of history, desegregation was stalled in Southern white Protestantism by the exercise of the democratic process itself in the church establishment. (As an example of deliberate speed, in the year 1957, 35 of 45 Catholic schools in the South were desegregated, while only 55 of 188 Protestant institutions of higher learning were so classified).[38]

Southern Christian soldiers are surely not all one body. Even within Protestantism, the churches, their ministers, and their related colleges are divided by race, by denomination, and by social class. Add to this diversity the changing Catholic church, found mainly in southern Louisiana and increasingly in the urban South; add Judaism, the Church of Christ, and the Unitarian church—which like Confucianism is regarded by some as more of a philosophy than a religion—and, in a different vein, add the unnumbered sects that employ religious garb for political diatribes. Obviously, then, there is much more good and ill associated with Southern religion than is contained within Protestantism. Yet, within the South, there is an increasing tolerance of diversity along with the increase in urbanization, population mobility, and economic prosperity.

SOUTHERN RELIGION AND HIGHER EDUCATION

The churches, Southern and non-Southern, list an impressive array of Southern colleges and universities that receive some measure of support from them. The Methodist church, which leads that list, contributes to four Southern universities, more than a score of predominantly white senior colleges, and eight or more predominantly Negro senior colleges. Yet the Southern churches provide relatively meager support to many of their church-related institutions. The church has not caught a vision of its responsibility for a distinctive role in higher education, but has become mainly a creature of uncoordinated habit in providing modest support of higher education, spreading its contributions incredibly thin and without systematic purpose.

Somehow, organized religion and church-connected colleges, if they are to help society advance instead of simply joining its slow moral evolution, must concern themselves with their joint *raison d'être*, and combine a new rationality with an old fashioned "human heartedness." The clergy of the South, the educational leadership of church-related colleges, and the church-connected citizens of the South together face a challenge of a high order in reassessing and reshaping church-sponsored higher education.

In this setting, they are confronted by a peculiar decision. One of the church's concerns in higher education is traditionally for the socially

[37]See: Bailey, *Southern White Protestantism in the Twentieth Century*, chaps. 7 and 8.
[38]*Ibid.*

ostracized, the poor, and the educationally disadvantaged. But the culture of secular higher education prizes its high selectivity, based on an aristocracy of the intellectually and socially elite, of those most likely to distinguish the institution. The church may still discover a form of service through higher education more consonant with its range of avowed commitments.

SELECTED REFERENCES

A. Politics

Grantham, Dewey W., Jr. *The Democratic South*. New York: W. W. Norton, Inc., 1963.

Key, V. O., Jr. *Southern Politics in State and Nation*. New York: Alfred A. Knopf, Inc., 1949. (Also published in paperback by Vintage Books.)

Nicholls, William H. *Southern Tradition and Regional Progress*. Chapel Hill: University of North Carolina Press, 1960. (See especially chapter 4, "The Undemocratic Political Structure.")

Price, Hugh D. *The Negro and Southern Politics*. New York: New York University Press, 1957.

B. Religion

Bailey, Kenneth K. *Southern White Protestantism in the Twentieth Century*. New York: Harper and Row, 1964.

Frazier, E. Franklin. *The Negro Church in America*. New York: Schocken Books, 1963.

Harmon, George. "How to Tell a Baptist from a Methodist," *Harper's*, 226:1353 (February 1963), 58-63.

Landis, Benson Y. (ed.). *Yearbook of American Churches*. New York: National Council of the Churches of Christ in the U.S.A., 1964.

Sellers, James Earl. *The South and Christian Ethics*. New York: Association Press, 1962.

2. ETHNIC DIVISIONS, MONEY, AND THE FAMILY

The South faces major problems that have concerned higher education only peripherally in its traditional upper- and middle-class orientation. These problems relate to the undefined status of the Negro citizen, to the increasingly disorganized social institution of the family, and to the effects of conspicuous poverty. These problems, unchecked, are breaking the South apart, and one cannot understand the region's internally changing character without a sense of the chaotic stress so prevalent in these areas. The foci of the present chapter are upon the current racial tenor of the South, upon the Southern family and "nonfamily" units in Negro and non-Negro households, and upon the parasitic effects of poverty.

ETHNIC DIVISIONS AND EDUCATION CORRELATES

The director and assistant director of this study have viewed and experienced racial aspects of Southern life from many vantage points. We have traveled as desegregated companions throughout the South. A companion, in terms of etymology, is one who "shares bread" with another. We have shared bread in Kentucky, Arkansas, and Mississippi; but, more significantly, we have shared our perceptions and insights as we have traveled in the South, separately and together. More than that, we are "socially indigenous" to a South that is changing its mind, if not its heart, about race relations. For more than forty years, since early childhood, each of us has studied "race relations" in the South. Neither of us yet claims to understand its mystic character, but only to recognize a part of its mystery that has been rolled away.

Gunnar Mydral described, in *An American Dilemma*, the racial paradox of creed and practice as being something unique. Not only is it now *not* unique, but there is not even a distinctly American variety of it, as has recently been made patently clear around the world. The wave of "freedom" came to Africa with a headlong rush as colonial possessions became independent nations. With this gush of freedom, a trend developed to forbid opposition to the ruling groups. Some African countries have become models of police states. In this brief interval, however, a strong need for the skills of white men from Europe has been sensed. As Tanzania's President Julius Nyerere expressed it: "What our nation must

23

quite deliberately avoid is the attempt to Africanize management with untrained people. This would be as disastrous to the economy as the Africanization of hospitals with witch doctors would be to the health of the people."[1]

The most explosive situation in Africa rises out of the white minority domination of a few African nations. From Basutoland, with a white population of only 0.5 percent to South Africa with a white population of 24.1 percent, the African variation of the "reapportionment" question has been volatile indeed. The Chinese and Soviet agitation for immediate "one-man, one-vote" rule, in contrast with American hopes for a peaceful, evolutionary transition, suggests a risk in moving too slowly or too rapidly. The problem of racial tension is among the major conflict situations in Africa, as leadership reverses color, missing meanwhile much of the point of democratic freedom.

In England, the issue of whites v. nonwhites has created an increasing disturbance. The Labor party has discovered the politically explosive character of the issue, and Britain's variation of the recent Klan movement, combined with other race-linked issues, show that racial tensions have been rising steadily.[2] Indeed, the greatest international ethnic threat may be, as many have cautioned, the coalition of nations along color lines.

But America is not without its problems, and can take little comfort from the misery of others. Their misery is our misery, too. This entire nation, as well as the South, has come to grasp the widespread character of the problem, with its many variations, and most civil rights barriers in the public sphere have been removed. Civil rights in the South, while still a harsh reality for many, are being accepted as a new way of life. Agonized or gratified, the American South is facing facts. It is *cooperating* with, or *accommodating* itself to the inevitable.

Good Business

The Negroes' quest for freedom began, of course, as soon as they were made captive, to become the lucrative "black ivory" from Africa. A voyage of nine months or more across stormy seas, crowded between decks for fifteen hours or more a day, naked and chained together in pairs, was not calculated to cultivate a liking for slavery. Yet, for the Portuguese, the British, and for many Americans, it was good business.[3]

That was, of course, a different time, and largely a different world. In 1954, the quest for freedom pointed toward equal educational opportunity, with its spearheading legal effort aimed at the desegregation of America's public schools. The quest had to start somewhere, and the strategy of

[1]"For Black Africa: Five Years of Freedom, and Now," *U. S. News and World Report,* LIX:7 (July 5, 1965), 56.

[2]"Klan Comes to Britain: What It's All About," *U. S. News and World Report,* LIX:1 (July 5, 1965), 30-31.

[3]See: Frank Tannenbaum, *Slave and Citizen, the Negro in the Americas* (New York: Alfred A. Knopf, 1946).

the National Association for the Advancement of Colored People was based on selecting a field of contest where the odds were good and where the stakes were high. That was democratic public education, and the world knows the story. The United States Supreme Court ruled in 1954 that equal education could not be forcibly separate, and instructed the schools of the nation to proceed "with all deliberate speed" to be guided accordingly. The North, not fully conscious of its own vulnerable position of *de facto* segregation, applauded the decision. The South, reeling under the impact of the blow, said to the court, you can't be serious!

A decade later, the Civil Rights Act of 1964 opened public life to Negroes in many of its major dimensions outside of education. In public accommodations, commerce, entertainment, housing, and, last of all, equal job opportunity (July 1965), the Negro was to enjoy the rights of full-fledged citizenship.

In public education, the "good business" factor of Title VI, economic interests, accomplished far more in one year than the ruling of the Supreme Court had done in ten.[4] Federal money was to be withheld from state and local school systems that did not comply with the provisions of the act. Schools were also pressed by the Office of Education to demonstrate their compliance by deeds as well as by words. A Mississippi school superintendent confided that there were two federal governments in Washington—the courts and the Office of Education—and that his school system chose to be governed by the courts because they were more understanding and sympathetic.

The avalanche of compliance, whether "voluntary," by court orders, or by negotiation with the Department of Health, Education, and Welfare, was unparalleled in the annals of Southern history. Money was speaking with a loud voice. The unanswered question was whether "feeling" in support of the changed behavior, i. e. of *de facto* desegregation, would follow in the wake of the overt behavior. A limited amount of research evidence, in the realm of social psychology, said that it would.[5] The South's schools and colleges, in any case, were "complying."

Because of the massive volume of agreements to comply, the Office of Education was hard-pressed to catch up with its backlog, and to assure careful examination of compliance forms to estimate the real extent of compliance. Thus, while 84 percent of the school systems had agreed to comply, only 32 percent had, in June 1965, been accepted as having in fact complied. Nearly all were subsequently accepted, however. Higher

---

[4] In a sense, this is a specious comparison since that Act could not have been effectively passed without the earlier sanction of the U.S. Supreme Court. The reference here is to expression of compliance and measurable desegregation.

[5] See: Gordon W. Allport, "Prejudice: Is It Societal or Personal?," *Journal of Social Issues,* XVII (April 1962), 120-134 (see especially, page 134); and Leon Festinger, *A Theory of Cognitive Dissonance* (New York: Row, Peterson Co. , 1957).

education was virtually exempt from being questioned, not because colleges were trusted, but due to the magnitude of the school systems' reports
of challenged or doubted veracity.

TABLE 2

TITLE VI COMPLIANCE OF PUBLIC SCHOOL DISTRICTS

State	Total Districts	Agreed to Comply		Accepted	
		Number	Percentage	Number	Percentage
Alabama	118	112	95	15	13
Arkansas	411	325	79	204	50
Florida	67	67	100	17	25
Georgia	195	195	99	11	6
Louisiana	67	5	7	1	1
Mississippi	163	66	40	0	0
North Carolina	170	159	94	9	5
South Carolina	111	96	86	7	6
Tennessee	152	152	100	20	13
Texas	1,420	1,220	86	661	47
Virginia	137	133	99	12	9
Total	3,011	2,530	84	957	32

Source: U.S. Office of Education, June 2, 1965, as reported in *Southern School News*,
11:12 (June 1965), final issue.

With these gains in agreements to comply came reports of Negro teachers losing their jobs in several states. Some believed that a wholesale
discriminative movement was under way. Others stoutly averred that
Negro teachers were being eliminated in fair, open competition. Teaching
was no longer a "protected profession" for Negroes, and the mixed results
of that fact were far from clear. The National Teachers Examination was
increasingly employed as an objective measure of equality or as a weapon
to discharge Negro teachers, according to the bias of the individual. North
Carolina, Florida, Texas, and Virginia were identified by the NAACP as
being the major offenders. The issue of faculty desegregation promised
to become a new center of controversy. It had no demonstrably valid
resolution.

In higher education, only a dozen of the 221 public Southern colleges and
universities remained segregated. In nonpublic colleges, 201 of the 298
Southern institutions had formally filed their compliance agreements by
May 1965. Across the nation, 2,197 colleges and universities had done so

by June 29, 1965. Yet, many of these were complying only insofar as they felt compelled to do so, for "good business" reasons.

Nonpublic colleges were financially influenced to file compliance agreements because they were relying increasingly on public funds for their expansion and prosperity if not for their survival. The Higher Education Act of 1965 strengthened the bond of dependence of private colleges on public funds. Meanwhile, of course, public institutions were receiving increased support from various private philanthropies, which also insisted upon *bona fide* desegregation.

But, widespread as desegregation was in higher education, its application to faculty recruitment was negligible. There was a gentle tug of war for some of the best Negro professors, except in the "sensitive" areas of education, psychology, and the "social sciences." There was a number of white professors in historically Negro colleges, but there were fewer than a dozen or so Negro professors in predominantly white institutions. Why should they go there? They risked the social threat of overacceptance or of isolation. They risked the threat of failure. There would still be residential isolation from their colleagues. Why should they leave a place where they were secure, respected, and found professional challenge at a comparable salary? Desegregation for what?[6]

TABLE 3

HIGHER EDUCATION — TITLE VI COMPLIANCE

State	Public		Private	
	Number of Institutions	Agreed to Comply	Number of Institutions	Agreed to Comply
Alabama	12	12	18	13
Arkansas	8	8	13	12
Florida	34	34	18	13
Georgia	21	21	27	18
Louisiana	13	12	13	6
Mississippi	25	19	20	10
North Carolina	17	17	43	33
South Carolina	7	7	25	12
Tennessee	7	7	41	31
Texas	54	54	45	34
Virginia	23	18	35	19
Total	221	209	298	201

Source: *Southern School News*, 11:11 (May 1965), 1. In May 1966, only one public college had not signed the Assurance of Compliance. All but forty nonpublic institutions of higher learning had done so.

[6]A curious legal circumstance precludes faculty desegregation. Colleges are not required to desegregate faculties, but if they do, they must not dismiss faculty on account of race.

Ethnic Freedom and Responsibility

There has been a justifiable, necessary, and moderately successful push for desegregation in Southern society. The considerable exodus of Negroes has eased the pressure of some economic and racial problems, and has served the useful purpose of educating the nation to the complex nature of ethnic divisions in varying social contexts.

Within the South in 1966, except in rural pockets of isolation, Negroes are generally able to exercise legalized civil rights, with the recognition that there may be other civil rights that are not yet legal. In the nonpublic South, however, there have been only a few superficial changes. As a recent example, the Nashville (Tennessee) Bar Association, in December 1965, narrowly voted to admit Negro lawyers to its organization. This was done with less than a three-to-two majority, and then only after public pressure from students of the Vanderbilt University Law School and an articulate community "conscience." The strange nature of that conscience, in Tennessee and elsewhere, has been that it appears to be a conscience for private desegregation by "others," somewhere else. It is commonly a "third person" conscience.

The desegregation era is near its completion in a *de jure* sense in the South. In its *de facto* public context, it is moving along with increased tempo. In the private sphere beyond the reach of law or of major economic threat, it has hardly begun. It is not likely to do so unless higher education takes a responsible hand in that effort. The pitting of thousands of illiterate Negro voters against other thousands of newly enfranchised illiterate white voters may do something for liberty and equality, but it is unlikely to further the interest of ethnic fraternity. The challenge of achieving ethnic fraternity is not a legal one. It is a problem that can be met only by the instrument and spirit of education. Subsequent portions of this study will suggest ways in which higher education may help to achieve this goal.

CONSPICUOUS POVERTY

There is no doubt that the free enterprise system of capitalism has accounted for much of America's great economic and social progress. Yet Franklin D. Roosevelt was deeply troubled, a generation ago, about the tragic paradox of poverty amidst abundance. He expressed his concern in these words:

> It is my conviction that the South presents right now the nation's number one economic problem—the nation's problem, not merely the South's. For we have an economic unbalance in the nation as a whole, due to this very condition of the South. It is an unbalance that can and must be righted, for the sake of the South and of the nation. Without going into the long history of how this situation came to be—the long and ironic history of the despoiling of this truly American section of the country's population—

suffice it for the immediate purpose to get a clear perspective of the task that is presented to us.[7]

And, in 1965, nearly three decades later, President Lyndon Johnson was facing the same basic problem of spreading economic opportunity throughout the nation which left poverty pockets of major economic distress in Appalachia and other regions.[8] Senator Fulbright of Arkansas was saying that the South was no longer the nation's number one economic problem, but the nation's new economic frontier. Others were saying that the last half of the twentieth century belongs to the South. If so, the South would have to take up its option. And, as W. H. Nichols pointedly observed, this means a deliberate choice of economic progress over those traditions that are inconsistent with achieving it. But the problems of wealth, as Adam Smith noted long ago, involve its distribution as well as its production.

In 1966, the war continued against poverty, but not with the gung ho spirit with which it was first declared. First of all, there was a disenchantment about both the strategy and tactics of that war. Part of the debate hinged on whether the participant leaders among the poor would be the generals or the privates in that army. There were criticisms on other fronts as well. The major abatement of commitment, however, was caused by events outside the South—half way around the world in Vietnam. The tempo of that war, and its financial cost, had to be stepped up—not so much to assure an early victory as to stave off the prospect of a defeat by stalemate. And, there was the cost of the race to the moon. America was leading in that fantastic adventure in outer space. It was America's great commitment to conspicuous consumption. It would be difficult to explain that priority of commitment to the white and Negro poor, but there was no need to explain. The poor had never been an organized political power group.

Po' Mouthin'?

There is a colloquial expression in the South called "po' mouthin.'" Other regions have their variation of the term. It means complaining about hard times or hard knocks far out of proportion to the genuine poverty or hard times experienced. In 1965, for Southerners to complain about poverty was a clear case of po' mouthin' by comparison with the recent past. In the main, Southerners had "never had it so good."

The per-capita real income in the South in 1929, converted to 1963 dollars, was $734. In 1963, the average per-capita real income had climbed to $1,820. (The eleven states of the Confederacy plus Kentucky

[7]Lowell Mellett, *Report to the President on the Economic Condition of the South* (Washington, D. C.: National Emergency Council, 1938), p. 1.

[8]On March 27, 1965, the White House Press Release announced a new "lease on hope" for the 2.5 million Americans living in America's 182 poorest counties, as classified by the U. S. Department of Commerce, Bureau of the Census.

and Oklahoma.)[9] The South was poor no more. Not only that, but it had come closer to the national average with respect to wealth and income. From 1929, with a per-capita income of only slightly more than half that of the national average (55 percent: $372 cf. $680), it had approached in 1945 nearly three-fourths of the national figure (71 percent: $1,005 cf. $1,410). While both regional and national incomes have increased appreciably during the two decades since 1945, the relative position of the South has increased only slightly.[10] In the South Atlantic states in 1961, it was 84 percent; in Kentucky, Alabama, Mississippi, Tennessee (the East-South-Central states) it was 67 percent; in the West-South-Central states of Arkansas, Louisiana, Oklahoma, and Texas it was 82 percent.[11]

But comparisions of incomes are commonly made on the same time line, and the per-capita income for the United States in 1963 was $2,449. The South was better clothed, better fed, better housed, and better schooled in 1965 than it had ever been. Like the rest of the nation, it chased a fleeting illusion of prosperity as being the salvation to its many problems. It was caught up in a culture-bound system of material values, unmindful of the limitations of happiness that can be achieved through material possessions alone.

Poverty is a relative matter in other respects as well. There are other salient bases for comparison. Most of the nations in the world, for example, have no compassion in economic terms for the American South because it, by world standards, fares so well. Furthermore, as Barbara Ward points out convincingly, the wealth and income gap between the rich nations already "in orbit" (that is, having accumulated enough wealth to develop an income momentum) and the poor ones not yet "off the ground," is widening, not narrowing.[12]

In explicit terms, compare the per-capita income of the South in 1963 (Confederacy plus Oklahoma and Kentucky) of $2,449, with the U.S.S.R. ($900), Italy ($800), Poland and Japan ($450), Mexico ($300), or China and India ($75).[13] For the South as a region to complain of poverty is for it to po' mouth. But the poorest of the poor in Mississippi or Kentucky can still feel the pangs of poverty as strongly as those in Italy and Poland do.

[9]Robert M. Bjork, "Income, Employment, and Population Aspects of the Contemporary South," unpublished working paper for this study (Archives of the Peabody Southern Higher Education Study, 1965), p. 6, table 4.

[10]*Ibid.*, pp. 2-3, table 1.

[11]*Ibid.*, p. 5, table 3.

[12]Ward, *The Rich Nations and the Poor Nations* (New York: W. W. Norton and Company, 1962), p. 35.

[13]Bjork, *op. cit.,* pp. 6 and 7, tables 4 and 5.

But Underneath, Dire Poverty

The problem of poverty within the South is so acute because of the striking contrast between conspicuous abundance and relative poverty. Average incomes are misleading because so many individuals are far below the median or mean income, and so many are well above it. Where all people are chronically poor together, poverty is not conspicuous. It does not stand out in bold relief against its opposite. Thus, in the American nation, J. K. Galbraith paints a picture of *The Affluent Society*, giving the illusion, the half-truth, that we like to see. We are properly disturbed, then, by Michael Harrington's realistic description of *The Other America*, and Edgar May's more recent, discomforting portrayal of *The Wasted Americans*, describing the public welfare dilemma and America's "permanent poor."

One of the most striking income disparities in the South has long followed the color line. In the South, the individual income of Negroes is only two-fifths that of whites. Outside the South, the figure is approximately three-fourths. A close look at this contrast of the rich and the poor, in close physical proximity, reveals a built-in cause and effect of ethnic tension and conflict. It is easy for the white man to blame the unschooled, unskilled Negro, so typically lacking in industry and foresighted planning. It is equally easy for the Negro to complain of dead-end training with no hope for utilizing skills once developed. Both statements may be scapegoating or true, depending on who makes them. Both can be copiously documented. But, beginning in July 1965, as a result of the Civil Rights Act of 1964, the Negro was generally assured of employment on the basis of merit, neither handicapped nor privileged by race. It would take time, but at last there was a substance for hope—and the word of that hope was spread across the nation.

Economist Robert Bjork gives this explanation of the urban-rural Negro income. Negro income in Southern urban areas, while greater than rural Negro income, would be considerably greater except for the large pools of poor rural Negroes whose continuous flow into the Southern city creates a substantial number of partially employed workers, and depresses the wage rates of those Negroes of longer urban residence who are fully employed. If the rural Negro moved out from the South instead of into the urban South, the Southern urban Negro would be far better off. Similarly better off, it would appear, would be the rural white. And likewise, the non-South would be handicapped by the exodus.

There is a white poor, too, whose misery matches that of the Negro poor. The rural poverty pockets of eastern Kentucky and the nearby areas of highland Tennessee consist almost exclusively of white citizens. And, according to the 1960 census, of the 54 poorest counties in the South, ten were in Kentucky and six in Tennessee (nearly all white), while sixteen were in Mississippi and seven in Alabama (nearly all Negro). Wherever the poorest counties were, white or Negro, each of them was overwhelmingly rural. Increasingly, the "haves" are in the city; the "have nots" are in the rural areas. With hopes, they move to the city. Disillusioned, they remain there.

TABLE 4

MEDIAN INCOME OF PERSONS 14 YEARS AND OVER BY REGION AND COLOR 1950-1960

Region	White		Nonwhite		Differences In Dollars for Nonwhites		Income Percentage of Nonwhites	
	1950	1960	1950	1960	1950	1960	1950	1960
Northeast	$2,246	$3,304	$1,622	$2,441	-584	-863	72.2	73.9
North Central	2,143	3,090	1,652	2,263	-491	-827	77.1	73.2
South*	1,647	2,473	739	995	-908	-1,478	44.9	40.2
West	2,114	3,298	1,455	2,474	-669	-824	68.9	75.0

*Includes Maryland, Delaware, Texas, Oklahoma, West Virginia, Virginia, Alabama, Arkansas, Florida, Georgia, Kentucky, Louisiana, Mississippi, the Carolinas, Tennessee, and the District of Columbia.

Source: Vivian W. Henderson, *The Economic Status of Negroes* (Atlanta: Southern Regional Council, n.d.), p. 13.

Although there was a dramatic political pull in 1965 to attend to the poverty needs of Appalachia, this was not the area many economists would have identified as the most economically distressed in America. There would be debates, as well, regarding how to help it. A major proportion of the federal legislation to help Appalachia was to be for highway construction through that isolated segment of America. The direct and indirect advantage to the poor was questionable; to many of the nonpoor—particularly road construction contractors—the advantage was clear. But there was already greater poverty where good roads and highways had long since been constructed. The state of Mississippi, has one of the better highway systems in the South, and 51.6 percent of its population live in families with less than a $3,000 annual income. Arkansas is not much better off with 47.7 percent of its population in the present poverty category of $3,000 or less per annum.

Conspicuous poverty within the South, especially in the atrophied portions of the rural South, is cause for deep concern. And because of local control and support (or nonsupport) of the schools, the areas of the poor are also the areas of the most limited educational opportunity. The children of both the Negro and white poor have an ironic equality of non-opportunity.

Is Education the Enemy of Poverty?

Conspicuous poverty is an enigma to the affluent, who are insulated against it and isolated from it, but it is a source of consternation to the puzzled poor. Gerard Piel, writing in international terms, virtually bypassed the role of education in dealing with the inequities associated with abundance.[14] In a similar vein, the Committee for Economic Development appears more interested in a manipulated economy, of guiding Adam Smith's "invisible hand" of *laissez-faire* doctrine, than in recognizing the role of education as a necessary ingredient of individual and collective economic health.

Nevertheless, there is a general correspondence of level of education to level of income. Many figures, in an effort to provide an incentive for more support for schooling, have been compiled and widely publicized. For example, the average lifetime earnings of a college graduate are more than $400,000; of a high school graduate, about $225,000; and of a person with eight years of schooling, in the neighborhood of $125,000.[15] But when you read between the lines, you learn that the earning power of a Negro college graduate in America is only equal to that of a white man who did not go beyond the eighth grade.[16]

When the total picture of education and income is broken into its component parts, we get dramatic examples of dislocation; of schooling that is not educational in terms of economic investment, due either to a callous indifference to or an ignorance about supply and demand in the vocations and professions. To advise any youth that schooling *per se,* on the secondary or collegiate level, is a sound economic investment, is to mislead him, as thousands of disillusioned youth and adults, white and Negro, can attest. Similarly, and with considerable supporting evidence, schooling may be a questionable investment from the standpoint of its liberalizing effect, its general education.

To equate schooling with education universally, as an economic or a cultural investment, is to be naively superstitious. The challenge of Southern higher education, both in its guidance and instructional functions, is to play it straight with students by helping them to see the opportunities, and by helping them to be prepared to avail themselves of them. Higher

[14]Piel, "Abundance and the Future of Man," *The Atlantic,* 213:4 (April 1964), 84-90. See also: CED's "Challenge of Prosperity," *Saturday Review* (January 9, 1965), pp. 23-38.

[15]See: *Education — An Investment in the Future* (Raleigh: North Carolina State College, 1962), p. 10; and *Education: Texas' Resource for Tomorrow* (Austin: Governor's Committee on Education Beyond High School, 1964), p. 16, fig. 6.

[16]See: Herman Miller, *Rich Man, Poor Man* (New York: Thomas Y. Crowell Co., 1964), p. 149.

education can be, as it is now customarily classified by economists, a consumer's item; or, hopefully, it can increasingly become a part of the Gross National Product, both in increasing earnings and in the deployment of the manpower of America in society's best interest as a community utility. The GNP of 1965 was $670 billion. At present, we cannot know how much of that product was attributable to higher education, and how much higher education "siphoned off" as a consumer.

THE FAMILY: SOCIAL INSTITUTION NUMBER ONE

Throughout man's recorded history, the family has been regarded as society's primary unit, and every known society has counted on it as a kind of cultural glue to hold the society together in some meaningful value system. The family is the socializing agency that makes people human. The individual conscience is largely developed there, and the true family provides a security, an intimacy of response, and an individual sense of significance apart from personally earned achievement. There are other necessary views of the family, of course, legal and biological components that do not always fit into the context of familial social function. We are here concerned with both the legal and social views in the American South. The social disorganization attended by decreasing family stability and cohesion is one of crucial magnitude. The problem of the family is intensified by those historic antecedents that almost eliminated the Negro family as either a legal or social unit. Today, however, there are increasing problems confronting families, white and Negro, of low and high estate. If higher education helps to comprise the cultural superstructure of the South, then the family is the foundation on which it must build.

The statistics of family disorganization do not adequately convey the impact of the problem of family instability. To report that each year more than 100,000 couples in the South sever their marital bonds through the divorce courts only begins to tell that story. To report that another 100,000 couples separate each year, choosing "poor man's divorce" as they call it, does not complete the picture. To know that one of every four marriages terminates with divorce does not disturb the mythical picture of tranquil family unity. Many other socially fragile homes are not officially broken by divorce or separation, but those broken homes are quite as real. The divorce rate is lowest in South Carolina, where no legal ground for it was available until 1948; and in Southern Louisiana where Catholic restrictions do not yet sanction it. The statistics do not identify the shattered homes, where so-called family units are held together by laws or by religious tenets. Uncounted thousands of "nonfamilies" in the South result from desertion, and from physical or psychological separation when the prospect of divorce is too overwhelming to contemplate. Within the more stable "adjusted" families, there is an increased depersonalization, food and lodgings are provided without a genuine family of interests.

Although increasing juvenile delinquency does not have a single cause, its incidence is commonly associated with youth growing up in nonfamilies, households where there is no adult who deeply cares or knows how to show that he does. Delinquency statistics are misleading in social class terms, because delinquents from "good" (i.e. middle class) families are not regularly "booked" for their law violations, but are protected by their respectable parents who are frequently community leaders. Legally, these juveniles are not "delinquents." They are only unbooked violators of the law.

Families, across the nation, are coming apart increasingly, and with this disintegration, both as cause and effect, crime and delinquency are increasing. Another indicator of family disorganization is the extent of childbirth, or of conception, out of wedlock. But before examining recent statistics, we should give some thought to their interpretation. The normative sequel to pregnancy out of wedlock among lower-class Negro families is to bear the child, raising him in a father-absent home, admitting his illegitimacy, and claiming financial assistance for his care under Aid for Dependent Children (ADC) provisions. A second option, more available to white mothers who have "made a mistake," is to travel incognito to another state, and, after the birth, to release the child for adoption to couples who pay for the services of private physicians and for the expectant mother's expenses during this period. Virtually all adopted children are white. In a study of adoptions in Cook County, Illinois, the chance for adoption of an illegitimate white child was found to be 166 times as great as for a Negro child.[17] Farther South the odds would surely be no better. The third course of action, reserved in the main for the affluent upper-class, is illegal abortion. Ranging from a few hundred to several thousand dollars, depending upon presumed professional competence and risk, this is the "ultimate solution" for those who can afford it. The cheaper abortion, accomplished by drinking a quart or so of whisky straight, may abort the embryo and risk the life of the mother. Yet the strong moral stand of the Bible Belt maintains its taboo against illegitimacy, and more than 20,000 children in Louisiana were denied aid in a recent year because of the circumstances of their birth.[18]

The taboo against illegitimacy, so long held rigidly in the middle-class white society, is shared by its brown middle-class counterpart. Skin color among Negro families has long been a class symbol, upward mobility being a climb toward whiteness. The conditioned self-rejection revealed in a number of studies such as those by the Clarks[19] may explain this phenomenon. There are signs in 1966 that blackness, however, in the family

---

[17]See: Edgar May, *The Wasted Americans, Cost of Welfare Dilemma* (New York: Harper and Row, 1964), p. 44.

[18]*Ibid.*, p. 47.

[19]K. D. Clark and Mamie Clark, "Emotional Factors in Facial Identification and Preference in Negro Children," *Journal of Negro Education,* 19 (1950), 341-350.

or outside it, is coming into its deserved equal class status, as "Negro-ness" itself loses stigma. (Textbook publishers, in their new emphasis on biracial illustration, cannot be sure just how colored Negroes should be.) As long as illegitimacy is statistically race-linked, however, the taboo against it will militate against any Negro's acceptance in middle- or upper-class America. This personal observation illustrates the case:

> Lower-class Negro males are much less sure of jobs than are their wives whose services are always in demand as domestics. The job picture of unskilled labor is bleak for all men regardless of color, and even more so for those of darker visage who are the last hired, often at lower wages, and the first fired. The lower-class Negro male often feels that he is extra-neous, an extra mouth to feed; less than a man. To his noneducated mind, it seems that conditions will be better all around if he leaves, especially since he knows that his wife and children will then at least have the added income of public assistance. Many unemployed Negro fathers who do not desert their families are forced to lead "double lives," technically living somewhere else, while their wives and children are impelled to lie to authorities, and say they do not know where he is, in order to receive public aid. If the mother has another child (by her legal husband, whom she technically has not seen in months), she is forced to say she does not know who the father is. This, in turn, further distorts society's view of the Negro family.
>
> Negroes must first seek to strengthen the family by helping each male to stay with his family and have some means of support. Archaic welfare laws that say children must go hungry if they live with both parents must be changed. That poor Negroes *do* often have more children than they can possibly support is a fact. Poor families do not necessarily want all these children, but they have been unable to receive birth control information from public health agencies, which they frequent, which middle-class persons receive from their private physicians.
>
> No documentation has been found that the poor are more immoral than the "haves"; only that they have more children born out of wedlock. Be-cause of strong traditional feelings about abortion and placing "ones own flesh and blood" for adoption, Negro mothers much more frequently than white mothers keep such children even in the face of public scorn. Once they are able to control unwanted births, morality will be a personal and private matter as it is with other social classes. [20]

The recent national study of the Negro family reports some facts to American society which we would do well to note. [21] To what extent the South is typical cannot be determined with certainty, although the available indicators suggest that it is. That report contains such facts as these:

---

[20] From an unpublished working paper prepared for this study by Mrs. Shirley Williams, of Chicago, Illinois, and formerly of Jackson, Mississippi. Mrs. Williams is well-acquainted with conditions of Negro families living in both cities.

[21] Office of Policy Planning and Research, *The Negro Family: The Case for National Action* (Washington, D.C.: U.S. Department of Labor, 1965), *passim*.

1. The nonwhite illegitimacy ratio is eight times that of the white ratio. Nearly one-fourth of Negro births are now illegitimate. The white rate, in 1963, was 3. 07 percent.

2. Illegitimacy varies inversely with incomes. The rate among nonwhites with above average ($6, 500) income was less than half that of those below the poverty level ($4, 000).

3. The breakdown of the Negro family has led to 14 percent of Negro children now receiving Aid for Dependent Children assistance, compared with 2 percent of white children. The situation is getting worse, not better.

4. One-third of nonwhite children live in broken homes; the highest rate is in cities, the lowest is in rural farm areas.

5. The unemployment rate of nonwhite men virtually parallels the percentage of nonwhite women separated from their husbands. The prospect increases in bleakness. In January 1965, the unemployment rate of Negro teen-agers was 29 percent.

America in general and the South in particular recognize that whatever other realities are to be faced, the disintegrated family is not "good business. "

The Family and Social Class

E. Franklin Frazier, who made a ten-year study of the Negro-American family, revealed that the value and behavioral pattern of middle-class Negro families corresponds with that of white middle-class families. Family size is small, the wife is unlikely to be employed in menial or subprofessional work, and relations between man and wife, especially where both are employed, tend to be equalitarian.[22] In the middle-class Negro South, Frazier found the husband to be a relatively authoritarian "Southern gentleman, " especially if his wife was unemployed. In both white and Negro middle-class families, wives availed themselves of respectable employment opportunities in order to maintain middle-class standards of consumption.

Lower class families with poorly schooled parents, regardless of race, have a suspicion of the "mental odor" of academic learning, especially beyond high school. And well they might, because higher education in the main has not turned its attention to their needs nor has it recognized their potential for social progress and economic productivity. On the contrary, a student may be denied admission because of conditions about his family, or, if admitted, he may be embarrassed about his family while in

[22]Frazier, *The Negro Family in the United States* (New York: The Dryden Press, 1951), p. 329. Light skin is a normative but not an essential characteristic of the Negro middle-class.

attendance.[23] Upper class families have increasing difficulties in retaining clear status symbols. They relate, however, to "exclusiveness" of
social clubs, church affiliations, college loyalities, ánd residential address. Thus, the upper-class Negro may press for admission by race and
for exclusion by social class.

The Family and Urbanization

Just as yesterday's South is not today's South, neither is yesterday's
rural family the urban family of today. As farm families find agriculture
unprofitable, and eventually economically unbearable, they move to the
city—and discover that there is no demand for farm hands on city streets.
The family loses much of its anchor of values and its way of life. It is
often uprooted by occupational insecurity. Some lean quickly upon public
welfare. Others, in a perceived sense of pride, disdain charity. As the
social reformer Saul Alinsky once expressed it, "I would steal before I
would accept charity." Many do. There is a confusion of ideals, and
patterns of conformity-behavior change atténding the culture shock of
urbanization.

It is as if the social multiplication tables had been done over, and there
is no systematic way to learn that $2 \times 2 = 7$ and $3 \times 4 = 9$. Painfully, each
new combination has to be tried anew to find the new right answer. The
mother often obtains employment when the father cannot, suddenly replacing
a patriarchal pattern by a shaky equalitarian one or by a pretense of retaining the earlier relationship.

In the Southern city, the rate of illegitimacy is higher than in the
country, and the same is true of its upper class equivalent—abortion.
In America as a whole, there are an estimated four abortions for each
child born out of wedlock. Here the racial percentages shift markedly,
with a large majority of abortions, estimates range as high as 97 percent,
among white women. However reliable the statistics, the problems of
family life in Southern cities are deplorable for a large segment of the
population. We do not require a verified accuracy to feel the massive and
growing impact of the problem upon family unity.

As we have considered the race-linked and the social class-linked
conditions and problems associated with family life, both likenesses and
differences have been noted. Although there are some evident cultural
differences independent of income level, this factor accounts for most
differences between the races. The overpowering fact is that such a large
proportion of Negroes are at or only slightly above subsistence income
level while this is true of only a relatively small proportion of white
families.

---

[23] Years ago, a Negro doctoral student, now a distinguished bishop, was asked on his
final oral examination by a member of his doctoral committee if his parents were married.
His eyes blinked in disbelief, and the question was repeated. He quickly managed to regain
his composure and replied, "Yes, how about yours?"

The following table shows these economic contrasts in detail:

TABLE 5

MEDIAN INCOME OF WHITE AND NONWHITE FAMILIES IN SOUTHERN STATES

State	Total	White	Nonwhite	Percentage of Nonwhite to Population
Virginia	$4,964	$5,522	$2,780	50.4
Florida	4,722	5,147	2,798	54.4
Texas	4,884	5,239	2,591	49.4
Oklahoma	4,620	4,824	2,765	57.3
Louisiana	4,272	5,288	2,238	42.2
Georgia	4,208	5,027	2,188	43.5
Kentucky	4,051	4,193	2,570	61.3
North Carolina	3,956	4,588	1,992	43.4
Tennessee	3,949	4,333	2,292	52.9
Alabama	3,937	4,764	2,009	42.2
South Carolina	3,821	4,893	2,189	44.3
Arkansas	3,184	3,678	1,636	44.5
Mississippi	2,884	4,207	1,444	34.3

Source: Computed from U.S. Bureau of the Census, U.S. Census of Population, 1960, State Reports.

The problems of family life, however compounded by economic stress, revolve around the vagueness of role expectation. Whatever the roles, if they are consistently understood and accepted, the stability of family life is virtually assured. This point is briefly illustrated by the following contrast between family life in Ghana (Africa) and in the American South.

The Kongo Family (Africa)

A wife was expected to be obedient to her husband and to be a good worker. A husband was expected to provide housing and clothing for his wife, or wives, and children. Beyond this there might be a great deal of affection and mutual respect in the elementary family. A wife showed her fondness for her husband by preparing for him the tastiest foods possible, and he in turn gave her such gifts as cloth and beads. The children were devoted to their mother because of the care which she gave them from birth. They were expected to obey both parents, but the father was respected and to a certain extent feared. Even when children grew up and married they were expected to make certain gifts to their father, thus assuring his blessing on them. The deepest bonds of affection were generally among brothers and sisters, and this was carried over into adult life where a man became the protector of his sister and her children who would be his heirs.

In spite of the respect due the father throughout his life and beyond, his actual authority over his children extended only for a limited number of years. This might be until puberty, or even until marriage.[24]

The Southern Family (America)

A wife was unsure of whether she was to be obedient to her husband (patriarchal) or he to her (matriarchal) or if each would demand equal rights (equalitarian) from the other. A husband might provide housing and clothing for his wife, or might desert her if he could not, or they might both be gainfully employed. The urban wife could often find employment as a domestic worker when her husband, if unskilled, could not. The white wife, in the South but not in the North, could not "stoop" to that race-linked occupation without loss of face.

This ambiguity of parental authority and responsibility created uncertainty of expectation among the children, and it interfered with both mutual respect and affection as the family became less cooperative and more competitive. The phenomenon called "keeping up with the Joneses" pressed wives into gainful employment to raise the level of consuming the unnecessaries, what Thorstein Veblen called "conspicuous consumption." Wives entered the labor market for other reasons, too; some for professional self-fulfillment, others to escape in a societally approved manner from the children they loved but couldn't bear to be around for extended intervals.

The children looked upon their parents as thing-givers, not self-givers, not sharing of themselves but of their possessions. The upper and middle class, the relatively affluent, had fewer children and less time for them because they were attempting to elevate their social class and to enroll their children, whom they rarely came to know well as children, in the college appropriate to their social class choices. Views of discipline had changed. The sanction of corporal punishment declined with urbanization. Without equivalent substitutes of social control, parents felt unable to cope with their now vaguely defined responsibilities.

Children learned to be more competitive than cooperative through grades at school, athletic contests, and other competitive activities. Bonds of affection were not strong because of competitive parental expectations and frequent desires to fulfill their own latent aspirations through their children. Unlike the extended family system of the Kongo, kinship obligations did not run deep or often extend beyond the immediate family except for the exchange of Christmas "gifts." The government assumed economic responsibility for the elderly, and social progress was moving at too fast a tempo for the young to have much time for their elders. Rights and privileges were commonly demanded, but unenforceable obligations and moral responsibility were, if not taboo, at least not uniformly stressed. The government had assumed the responsibilities for social security but not for psychic or emotional security. There was no bureau for that.

[24]Karl Laman, *The Kongo,* Vol. II (Stockholm: Studia Ethnographica Upsaliensia, 1953), pp. 36-37, as reported by Charles Weaver, *A Comparative Study of Selected Congo Clusters as a Basis for Building National Unity through Education* (Nashville: George Peabody College for Teachers, 1966), p. 132.

The Negro and white families in the South of the same social class levels observed similar value patterns generally, but generally, more of the Negroes were lower class, less schooled and less skilled. Within this so-called lower class, the recorded rate of illegitimacy was high, and relatively little social stigma was attached either to the mother or the child. Artificial birth control devices were more commonly used among the better informed upper social classes, both white and Negro. With the recent advance of medical science and the dissemination of birth control knowledge, problems of abortion and illegitimacy would virtually disappear. Medical science could not solve the social problems of family life, but it could help to erase some of the visible effects of moral decay.

CONCLUSION

We can never see all of the South. The best we can hope to do is to glimpse portions of it. This view of three segments of the American South has been depicted with the hope of achieving that limited goal. We know that ethnic division within the South has been lessened in the realm of legal rights, but we have little evidence of progress beyond that point. A full generation will be required before Negro Southerners will be able to take full advantage of these rights even within the public sphere. Will the South then continue to be separate and equal in the personal, private sector?

We know that poverty amidst abundance plagues hundreds of thousands of white as well as Negro Southerners whose lives and hopes are being hardly touched by the transitory war on poverty. The poor will have to wait again while the war is stepped up against the Viet Cong. We know, meanwhile, that the war against poverty will never be won while adults are unskilled, and unschooled—or ironically—irrelevantly schooled.

Down through the few centuries of Southern history, the family has provided a bond of unity. To our shame, however, the Negro family was all but destroyed, because of the business interests of plantation owners and sometimes for far less worthy motives. The Negro family is still affected by the impact of that willful historic effort to sever family ties. Now white and Negro families find social controls from church, from neighborhood gossip, and from other agencies lessening in city life, where there is more anonymity. The traditional socialization of the individual does not take place in the Southern slums as well as it did in a well-ordered "backward" rural farm. Family life in the South is thus progressing backward with the many new problems attending urbanization.

But within this South there are sources of substantial hope. One of these sources is that of higher education. With more than four hundred colleges dotted about the South, surely these and other problems will soon receive the educational attention and action they require.

SELECTED REFERENCES

Bjork, Robert N. "Income, Employment and Population Aspects of the
    Contemporary South." An unpublished research paper for this study.
    Nashville: Peabody College Southern Higher Education Archives, 1965.
Blair, Lewis H. *A Southern Prophecy* (1889). (Edited with an introduction
    by C. Vann Woodward.) Boston: Little, Brown, and Company, 1964.
Cash, W. T. *The Mind of the South.* Garden City, New York: Doubleday
    Anchor Books, 1956. (Copyright 1941 by Alfred A. Knopf, Inc.)
Cavan, Ruth S. *The American Family.* New York: Thomas Y. Crowell
    Co., 1963.
Frazier, E. Franklin. *The Negro Family in the United States.* New York:
    The Dryden Press, 1951.
Gallagher, Jr., Art. *The Negro and Employment Opportunities in the
    South.* Atlanta: Southern Regional Council, 1961.
Henderson, Vivian W. *The Economic Status of Negroes: In the Nation and
    in the South.* (Toward Regional Realism Series No. 3.) Atlanta:
    Southern Regional Council, undated.
Odum, Howard. *Southern Regions of the United States.* Chapel Hill:
    University of North Carolina Press, 1939.

3. HIGHER EDUCATION IN AN UPROOTED CULTURE

The South is feeling its way to an uncertain future, aided hopefully by higher education. Whether or not this proves to be a vain hope depends on the insight and resolute action of leadership, within and beyond the South. The task of increasing the relevance of higher education for a changing culture, however, is an exceedingly difficult one. Southern higher education is caught in a web of pressures and irrational priorities, both within the colleges and within the society at large. A number of cultural contradictions are immediately apparent as we look at higher education in a rapidly changing, an uprooted South.

Jacques Barzun has likened culture to an enormous pumpkin, "hard to penetrate, full of uncharted hollows and recesses for cultural critics to get lost in, and stuffed with seeds of uncertain contents and destiny."[1] A vignette of Southern culture has a mystic as well as a scientific quality about it. If we are to understand the mission and present activities of Southern higher education, we cannot ignore those uncharted hollows of Southern culture and of the variant subcultures of higher education—the subcultures of the "haves," and of the "have-nots."

STATED GOALS AND EVIDENT GOALS

Very likely, the most serious problem facing Southern higher education is that its stated goals do not agree with the goals evident from its action. This is not to say that the actual goals and observable activities of higher education are unworthy ones. It is only to note a discrepancy between the unfocused activities of colleges and the lofty goals they publicly espouse.

The Commission on Goals for Higher Education in the South developed a statement of goals based on an inquiry into educational conditions and societal needs within the Southern regions. The commission expressed the view that "the continued progress of our civilization and the vigor of our free society depend primarily upon our colleges and universities. Present world conditions give a big urgency to their development."[2] The

---

[1] Barzun, *Science: The Glorious Entertainment* (New York: Harper and Row, 1964), p. 9.
[2] Colgate W. Darden, Jr., *Within Our Reach* (Atlanta: Southern Regional Education Board, 1961).

43

commission then identified five broad goals of central importance for higher education in the South. They are:

1. To provide every individual with opportunity for maximum development of his abilities.
2. To produce citizens responsible to the social, economic, and political needs of their time.
3. To achieve excellence in teaching, scholarship, and research.
4. To accelerate the economic progress of the Southern region through education and research.
5. To guide the region in solving social problems created by population changes, racial differences, urbanization, and technological growth. [3]

To the credit of the Southern Regional Education Board, which sponsored the work of this commission in conjunction with the Southern Governor's Conference, these goals have served as its *bona fide* guide for regional leadership. This commitment, however, has not been uniformly characteristic of colleges and universities throughout the South, either individually or collectively. The culture gets in the way, and higher education has difficulty swimming upstream against it.

Professor C. B. Hoover called attention to the danger of an academic degree breeding "conceit and arrogance" if it is regarded as simply entitling the holder to prestigious leadership. In exhorting a graduating class at Duke University to regard themselves not as future leaders, but as future contributors to society, he called upon university graduates to recognize that the superior advantages they had received obligated them to service on behalf of their fellow men.[4] We give verbal support to this idea as being one of the hallowed virtues of the college-educated man or woman. A proper concern, however, is the limited correlation of graduation addresses and statements of goals by commissions with the everyday practices observable on the campuses. In the main, Southern culture measures the value of higher education in terms of increased earning power and elevated social position.

There is little verbal disagreement about the importance and validity of the goals and viewpoints of the Commission on Goals, or the lack of reconciliation between stated and real goals. Problems of giving unswerving commitment to these objectives appear to arise principally out of two conditions. In the first place, higher education in the South, as is true all over America, is in a scramble. It faces the problem of all the *nouveau riche,* it has more customers and more money more suddenly

³*Ibid.*
⁴Hoover, "The Privilege of a College Degree: Then and Now," *Duke Alumni Register* (June 1964), pp. 8-9.

than it has ever known before.   Frequently uncertain about where it is
going, higher education is anxious to get there.   Many matters are so urgent, such as instant housing and instant staffing, that anything that is
merely important is crowded out of the rapidly paced activity.   The second
condition is that of the status system of the subcultures within higher education.   The professor, the college president, and the student find built-
in conflicts between working toward the avowed goals of higher education
and achieving their own upward mobility according to the social system of
which they are a part.   These two conditions operate as strong deterrents
to the achievement of the verbally assumed goals of Southern higher education.

Pressures and Priorities

The fever of haste is felt within the South, but the urgency is of national,
epidemic proportions.   Many urgencies have originated from pressures
outside the South.   The college-age population boom has been felt less in
the South than on the West Coast and in the East.   Although there are unprecedented enrollment increases in the South, which we shall soon note
in detail, they do not compare with those of some of the more densely
populated areas elsewhere in America.   Yet, zealous activities are accompanied by much lost motion, a plausible disconnection between purported purposes and manifest activities.   As attention is diverted to the
problems of sheer physical institutional growth, the dynamics of educational growth are perforce neglected.   When a college or university becomes edifice-oriented, it is often pressed into declaring a moratorium
on educational progress.

The evidence of the crisis is easy to find—and impossible to escape.
The fitting theme of the 1965 conference of America's Association for
Higher Education was "Pressures and Priorities in Higher Education."
More than two dozen separate bundles of collegiate urgencies, ranging
from the pressures from the federal government to those of college students, demonstrating against they weren't quite sure what, were mulled
over and debated.   Among the pressures discussed were: Pressures
from the federal government; from state and local governments; from the
changing economy; from international responsibilities; from students;
from exponential increases in knowledge; and pressures for educating
the disadvantaged; for quality of undergraduate teaching; for the arts and
humanities; for "educational productivity"; and there were pressures on
students, faculty, and administrators of increasing operating costs.[5]

In this welter of uncoordinated growth, a few institutions, including
some Southern ones, are making good headway in educational progress.

[5] See: Proceedings of the Twentieth Annual National Conference in Higher Education,
Current Issues in Higher Education (Washington, D.C.: National Education Association,
1965), pp. *ix-xi*.

A recent publication described many new procedures in some of the 146 colleges established in the triennium 1962-1964, as well as among a few of the longer-established ones.[6] This description of occasional, modest improvements, however, underscored the relative educational inertia of the more than two thousand other colleges, all over America, which have not forged ahead in pointing society toward its options for the future. The educational innovations described in that study include the use of the community as a resource for learning, "new" learning media, provision for independent study; and a reorganization of the curriculum, its content and methodology, congruent with a rapidly changing scientific and social order. Yet tokenism seems still characteristic of curriculum change. Few colleges can escape being inundated by the urgencies and exigencies that press in on them daily.

And even these innovations, if true to form, will be sporadic, fading out instead of growing, as incentive grants terminate. Southern higher education is caught up in an artificial value system of transitory commitments. Our inquiry into the practices of Southern higher education has provided occasional glimmers of hope that institutions are making new and sustained commitments in dealing with the major social problems within the Southern regions. We occasionally uncovered evidence of deep concern in dealing with problems associated with race, with poverty, and with the educational unreadiness of otherwise college-capable youth. Almost uniformly, however, efforts to give priority attention to these problems were either prompted by outside financial incentives or by the grantsmanship hopes of attracting substantive financial support. Within the South, attention to these problems has been more a result of opportunism and expediency than of humane concern. This is not a criticism of Southern higher education, but a description of distressing conditions within it. Its subculture places a premium on money and position. The genuine concern was most deeply felt where the resources were in shortest supply to deal with the problems.

The Collegiate Status System

A system of higher education cultivates that which it values most highly. Herein lies the ironic paradox of the status system of higher education. Students, professors, and college presidents are exhorted to engage themselves in activities that are the least remunerative and the lowest in social rank order. In a sense, college faculties and administrations are working within a value system of status seekers, and being urged to evolve another from it—a system where social responsibility is of signal significance.

---

[6]See: Samuel Baskin (ed.), *Higher Education: Some Newer Developments* (New York: McGraw-Hill Book Company, 1965).

There is a well-known prestigious order in the higher education class system. The upward mobile drive characterizes each stratum of the college campus. A university professor is "higher" than a college professor who, in turn, is "higher" than a junior college professor. The junior college president aspires to become the president of a "real college." Most capable presidents of "almost colleges" will have their chance, either as their own junior college achieves seniority, or through being invited to take their choice in filling a number of senior college vacancies. In state colleges, the fact of relative status is uniformly reflected in the budgetary provisions for faculty salaries on the various collegiate levels. Freshmen do not "deserve" as many qualified professors as seniors do.

Many students have grasped the idea. Many have gotten the feeling that the junior colleges are the "almost colleges" of last resort. They do not know that when they arrive as freshmen at a university, they may not be regularly taught by professors, but by graduate students who spend part time doing research and the remaining time teaching undergraduate courses. To this general rule there are occasional, heartening exceptions.

The status system of higher education provides the social context in which the "academic market place" takes root. "Getting ahead" is the American way, and the way in which one gets ahead in higher education is not determined by service to students or to concern about the social relevancy of higher education in an upended society. The conventional wisdom of higher education honors conformity to the status system and stresses, with equal vigor, a verbal acceptance of altruistic ideals.

Oddly enough, the "poor colleges," small in enrollment and resources, help students to achieve identity in a personally intimate environment that state universities cannot emulate and are not always seriously interested in attempting. At the small schools, professors work with students outside of the publish-or-perish dogma. Thus, disadvantage has its advantage.

THE HIGHER EDUCATION ESTABLISHMENT: PEOPLE AND MONEY

The recent history of Southern higher education (until two decades ago) showed a paucity of students and an impoverishment of funds, both among the students and among the institutions. While the Southern picture continues to compare unfavorably with that of the remainder of American higher education, its position is improving steadily. But major problems cannot properly be laid to the door of financial limitations alone. While many nonpublic colleges continue to be in financial distress, the prestigious private institutions and the public institutions of the South, in comparison with their own past, are in a favorable position. Among the poor institutions, the financial crisis of endowment and current fund-income and expenditures is dire and real. One of the best over-all pictures of the college boom in the Southern states can be reflected through increases in college enrollment. The table below cites the actual statistics of 1961

and the estimates for 1970. In 1966 nearly all revised estimates for the
1970 enrollments were upward rather than downward. In view of the
multi-billion dollar Higher Education Act of 1965, one may anticipate a
further accelerated increase in enrollment above these predictions.

TABLE 6

COLLEGE ENROLLMENTS IN SOUTHERN STATES IN 1961
AND 1970, IN THOUSANDS

States	1961			1970		
	Public	Private	Total	Public	Private	Total
United States	2,374	1,517	3,891	5,171	2,216	7,387
Southern Regional Education Board	688	307	955	1,326	496	1,822
Other States	1,725	1,210	2,946	3,845	1,720	5,565
Alabama	36	12	48	73	22	95
Arkansas	20	7	27	39	10	49
Delaware	7	1	8	16	3	19
Florida	53	27	80	130	30	160
Georgia	35	17	52	75	23	98
Kentucky	34	18	52	65	35	100
Louisiana	47	16	63	119	13	132
Maryland	37	23	60	64	33	97
Mississippi	31	7	38	62	15	77
North Carolina	44	34	78	80	58	138
South Carolina	18	15	33	37	25	62
Tennessee	37	27	64	84	43	127
Texas	136	63	199	249	114	363

Source: *Statistics for the Sixties, Higher Education in the South* (Atlanta: Southern
Regional Education Board, 1963), adapted from Table 3, p. 25. See also: E.F. Schietinger,
Fact Book on Higher Education in the South 1965 (Atlanta: Southern Regional Education
Board, 1965).

For many reasons, going to college in the South is increasingly the
"thing to do." From the noble to the ignoble, these reasons range from
the altruistic hope of becoming better qualified to serve mankind to the
happy arrangement by which draft deferment is made possible for students who achieve a modicum of academic success. College is known to
be a respectable haven for draft dodgers. Some raise the question of
whether the colleges are becoming cluttered up with the wrong enrollees,
thereby shutting out many others who would be better societal investments.
The fact is clear that the intellectually below average student from a family of moderate means or better is more likely to attend college than is

the above average student living in conditions of economic privation. The problem is a vexing one for the colleges, however; how can it afford to discriminate in admissions policy in the interests of society? To turn away paying students in order to make room for students who require financial help does not, on the surface, appear to be plausible. If collegiate education is a cultural rite of passage into upper-class society, then that function is negated by selecting students on the basis of intellectual motivation and promise rather than social position. This is a major part of the quandary the college faces. Intellect and training can make a tool to serve society or serve as an instrument to exploit it. Colleges cannot be sure which purposes they are serving.

Just as the South believes in college attendance, it is willing increasingly to pay for it through substantial increases in state appropriations. In the South, the increased state support for public higher education has been phenomenal. In the two-year period 1963-1965, for example, the over-all increase of state appropriations amounted to 40 percent above the 1963 figures. The range of increased commitment varied from that of 14 percent in Virginia to 63 percent in North Carolina. Building programs in Georgia in two years exceeded those of the three previous *decades*.[7] Part of these state-by-state differences is explained by the contrast in the pattern of public and private higher institutions. For example, in 1964, only about one-sixth of the students in Mississippi attended private institutions while 44 percent of South Carolina's students enrolled in nonpublic colleges.[8]

The increased state appropriations for public colleges are shown in the following table. These growing commitments alleviate the logistic problems of Southern higher education to a considerable degree. Students will be housed and fed. Libraries will be enlarged and filled with books, and faculty, the best available for the price, will be employed and paid.

But, this uneven progress explains why instructors, in short supply, are employed at inflated salaries and are tempted to get an inflated sense of self-importance. Meanwhile, many nonpublic colleges suffer from a new conspicuous poverty, as their own faculty are raided and their student prospects, athletic and academic, are picked over.

Beyond the state funds for public institutions, a new rush has begun and has picked up momentum for new sources of money for public, church-connected, and private institutions of higher education. Colleges face new temptations to temporize with their basic stated goals both in relationship to the federal government and to private foundations. The president of one university was asked to comment privately on the proper long-range

[7]See: Harry Murphy, "College Construction Spans 32 Years in 2," *The Atlanta Journal* (April 16, 1965), pp. 1, 6.
[8]See: "Southern Colleges Do Better," *Southern Council on Teacher Education Bulletin III*, No. 2 (November 1965), p. 6. (Based on legislative reports of the Southern Regional Education Board.)

goals and commitments of philanthropic foundations to higher education. In his many years of administrative experience, he confided, he had never given the matter serious thought. He had spent his time concentrating on the soft spots of various foundations and capitalizing upon the wisdom of expedience. His institution has done well.

TABLE 7

INVESTMENT GROWTH IN SOUTHERN PUBLIC HIGHER EDUCATION, 1959-1960

States	1959-60	1965-66	Percentage Two-Year Gain (1963-65)	Percentage Five-Year Gain (1959-64)
United States	$1,399,044	(incomplete)	--	75
Southern States	393,478	$836,020	40	59
Alabama	21,823	46,667*	60	39
Arkansas	13,551	28,722	41	50
Florida	40,392	95,476	40	87
Georgia	24,058	50,859	44	74
Kentucky	14,954	49,507	54	186
Louisiana	40,062	72,318	30	62
Maryland	23,818	48,217	39	64
Mississippi	15,118	25,931	48	72
North Carolina	28,419	76,323	63	81
Oklahoma	27,014	41,555*	24	24
South Carolina	12,113	21,403	23	59
Tennessee	17,022	41,106	45	87
Texas	71,021	165,301	44	61
Virginia	25,544	40,830	14	55
West Virginia	18,569	31,805	43	50

*Based on Southern Regional Education Board legislative reports. Alabama and North Carolina gains reflect new networks of junior colleges and trade schools. Virginia, lagging conspicuously until 1966, has begun to catch up.

There is something in the excitement of higher education within the South reminiscent of the gold rush of the forty-niners. There is the problem of the *nouveau riche* alongside that of the conspicuous poor. It is an illustration of David Reisman's law, "The more the more" and of Christopher Jencks' corollary, "The less the less."[9]

[9]See: Jencks, "Diversity in Higher Education," *Consultants Papers, The White House Conference on Education,* VI (July 20-21, 1965), 61.

The Higher Education Facilities Act of 1963 provided new access to funds for both public and private colleges and universities. Millions of dollars were going to colleges throughout America in 1964-1965. Some institutions sought to utilize and circumvent the intent of the federal government by using federal funds for what they regarded to be in their own best educational interest. The federal government decided on priorities of needs in national perspective, and the individual institution attempted to bend legislative appropriations around to educational needs as perceived in its system of local priorities.

The Higher Education Act of 1965 brought new funds for a wide variety of purposes. The President of the United States returned to his alma mater, Southwest Texas State College in San Marcos, to sign the $2.6 billion act, and reminded the several thousand students and others in attendance that they were witnessing a moment in history that they could tell their children and grandchildren about. That act, President Johnson said, which would cost nearly one billion dollars ($845.3 million) during the first year, would be the key to opportunity for many thousands of young people who could otherwise never reasonably aspire to a higher education.[10] The detailed provisions of the Higher Education Act are familiar to most students of higher education, and virtually every institution has already completed a careful study of it with two questions in mind, giving them varying degrees of emphasis: (1) How does this appear to assist institutions of higher education to extend the quantity and to improve the quality and the relevance of their service to American society? and (2) What's in it for us? Uncle Sam, for Southern higher education, risked becoming a "thing giver" not an authentic partner in the educational enterprise, and it was "nobody's fault." The Higher Education Act's title headings are listed below to remind the reader of the various categories of assistance to institutions of higher education.

Higher Education Act of 1965

Title I	Community Service and Continuing Education Programs
Title II	College Library Assistance and Library Training and Research
Title III	Strengthening Developing Institutions
Title IV	Student Assistance
Title V	Teacher Programs
Title VI	Financial Assistance for the Improvement of Under-graduate Instruction
Title VII	Amendments to Higher Education Facilities Act of 1963

Federal aid to higher education has become an important social phenomenon within the Southern culture. The educator, like the politician, finds

[10]See: William H. Gordon, "LBJ Signs the $2 Billion School Bill," *The Houston Post* (November 9, 1965), p. 1.

himself saying less about states rights and more about eligibility for federal assistance. Some educators are privately sheepish about the shift of their positions from openly objecting to federal aid with its threat of federal control to actively soliciting for support under provision of the Higher Education Facilities Act of 1963; its mammoth successor, the Higher Education Act of 1965; and the further provisions of 1966. Underneath this aura of sweetness and light, however, many students of higher education are concerned about the "lure effect" of federal aid unwittingly militating against the educational mission it purports to fulfill. Southern higher education is sorely tempted to place immediate business interests ahead of studied educational priorities. Worse yet, it is caught up in the urgencies of quick proposals based on the premise that action with crash planning is far better than ideas without money. Statesmanship in ordering the business of colleges, which have only an educational reason for existence, taxes both prudence and courage.

With its lofty goals, its immediate pressures, its overriding priorities of urgency, its temptations to get in on a good thing, its being diverted by status-system values of institutional name and size and eminence through esteemed research and publication programs, *Southern higher education is finding the task of being conscious of any centrality of purpose extremely difficult. In the tumult of the total society, which instituted both public and private higher education to further the advancement of all mankind through responsible leadership, Southern higher education itself is upended. How can it be a stabilizer and innovator for social progress?*

HIGHER EDUCATION AND SOUTHERN REALITIES

Higher education is serving a trailing function, mirroring the problems of the region as much as it is coming to grips with them. It was established by society, or by component parts of it, to provide a vision, to show models of ethical and moral commitment as well as to further the economic interests of a technological society. Now it is faltering. Its load is heavy.

Unreadiness for Higher Education

Within the South, a major part of the colleges' problem is the unreadiness of high-school graduates for what is conventionally regarded as higher education. Some graduates are already beyond the level of the average college senior when they first enter college. Others have as low as seventh-to-tenth-grade achievement levels. Some have benefited from excellent schooling and cultural enrichment from their family and community. Others, white and Negro, have been deprived of adequate schooling, of a social unit remotely resembling a family, and even of life within a community, except in that fleshless definition of "an aggregation of people occupying contiguous territory"—which is not a community.

Unreadiness due to poor secondary-level schooling has been dramatically revealed, in words and statistics, in a current survey of objective characteristics of Southern high schools.[11] That carefully documented report provides convincing data that millions of youths do not have a fair chance of achieving collegiate success because of the impoverished academic fare they have experienced through the secondary schools. The small rural schools and the inferior schooling provided in the slums of Southern cities unwittingly conspire against the poor and the lower social classes, regardless of race. The segregation of schools in the rural South, as pointed out in the survey, militates against white youth as well as Negroes because it limits the breadth and quality of programs available.

Unreadiness due to poor schooling is compounded by unreadiness growing out of a depressed social environment: an environment of broken homes and of broken communities, where hope and independence of thought and action have long been largely abandoned because of obstacles perceived as insurmountable. Lewis Jones refers to this as "social unreadiness," i. e. academic unreadiness primarily due to social factors within the environment.[12] The Negro poor and the white poor have suffered together from this obstacle. But the unreadiness of the Negro has been greater for a variety of reasons, the major one being the culturally conditioned knowledge that education did not open doors of opportunity because of prevailing discriminatory practices of housing and of job opportunity. The Negro who "knew his place" was well advised not to get much "book learning." Aspirations are largely governed by role models. Children and youth have developed a sense of the futility of effort. It has not been a "short span" view. It is a historic acceptance of unyielding realities. Negroes have been protected against the disillusionment attending almost certain failure. Now many of them are not ready to earn success.

Some steps have been taken to identify some of the best prospects for higher education among Negro youth. One of the most promising recent efforts at good risk identification has been that of the National Achievement Scholarship Program, a parallel of the Merit Scholarship Program but restricted to Negroes. This leaves the basic sources of academic and social problems, of course, largely untouched.

Because of the combination of academic and social unreadiness, then, many high school graduates are actually on the eighth, or ninth, or tenth grade levels. Colleges that cater to such students have a historic tradition of pretending to be higher education institutions—for the humane purpose of protecting technically eligible students and for the economic purpose of sheer educational survival. As the president of one predominantly Negro university confided, "If our admission standards and academic

---

[11]See: W. D. McClurkin, Rupert B. Vance, *et al., High Schools in the South: A Fact Book* (Nashville: Center for Southern Education Studies, George Peabody College for Teachers, 1966).

[12]See: Lewis Wade Jones, "The Social Unreadiness of Negro Youth," *Saturday Review*, 45 (October 20, 1962), pp. 81-83, 91.

grading standards were comparable to those of white institutions, we would have to close our doors within a year."

Predominantly white universities generally admit such students and then proceed to eliminate them. They "get in the way" of the university's purpose, and harsh attrition of unready college students is culturally condoned in the name of academic standards. A few institutions do make systematic efforts to help students overcome their deficiencies, so they can become *bona fide* college students. But many students balk at this extra time; in their haste to get the bachelor's degree, they are less concerned about its educational value than its monetary and social class significance.

Higher Education and Race

Until the present generation, the segregation of Southern colleges and universities insulated college students against a true awareness of the ethnic issues of the American South. Provisions were made within the protected professions, mainly teaching, for Negro students to grow up and find their places in the Negro world of the South. At a respectable social distance, the white world continued its own apartheid educational system. The meeting of these two worlds was on a casual and super-ficial basis. Not until the decision of the National Association for the Advancement of Colored People to make its first strong stand for deseg-regation in higher education did these worlds begin to meet. In 1966 desegregation is an accomplished fact in the academic sphere of Southern higher education. And, in a few institutions, interpersonal relations have proceeded to a depth level of acquaintance. But in most institutions of higher learning, desegregation has been markedly limited. The impact of the present problems and the challenge of the opportunities associated with race have not found their way into the thinking and action of college administration, faculty, and students in Southern colleges and universi-ties. Very little interinstitutional cooperation has developed in urban areas. Only sporadic attempts have been made to recruit students without reference to race or to recruit faculty members on the same basis. High-er education, again, in the public and private institutions, has followed the mandates of society and, as external pressures have subsided, the internal efforts to enrich educational opportunities have been sharply de-limited. As in the other areas of social import, the colleges have been too occupied with other pressures to give continued study and attention to the racial concomitants of higher education.

In the ante-bellum days of slavocracy, higher education did little to question the institution of slavery. In the past generation, it has done little to promote desegregation. Now it has a "safe" educational challenge of educating for a desegregated society that is already here.

Higher Education and Money

Whether a culture begins with it or works around to it, the topic of money, or what it stands for, is sooner or later recognized as being the measure of things. The question of what higher education is worth prompts an answer in monetary terms. On the one hand, the liberal arts tradition is eulogized; but on the other, the years in college are measured against the potential earning power resulting from those years. The colleges and universities have made efforts to keep apace of the changing professional and vocational demands of a technological era. Yet there are thousands of students miscast, ill-advised or unadvised, with reference to the present and prospective supply-demand situation in the professions and trades.

Higher education can be looked upon as a means of immunizing students from social responsibility or of helping them develop a commitment to the use of money in the public interest as well as in the personal interest. If higher education is viewed exclusively, or even primarily, as a means to affluence and social position, society may increasingly ask the germane question of why this kind of education should be subsidized through taxation or philanthropy. Higher education becomes and remains a social institution only in the measure that it is concerned about and works at the problems of most significance and relevance to the society it has been established to serve. Higher education is thus in the uncomfortable position of a conflict of interests.

The professor's increasing mobility in search of the highest dollar, and the abandonment of the conventional ethics of faculty recruitment illustrate the Sunday ethics and the daily practice of the business world. Until the leadership of administration and faculty can extricate itself from dollar primacy in both personal and institutional life, higher culture will not take root in higher education.

Higher Education and Politics

Southern colleges and universities are beholden to the hands that feed them. Thus politics, in church and state, involves hard decisions involving laudable statesmanlike compromise on the one hand, and a press for position and power at the price of integrity on the other. The highest qualification a state college president can have is often regarded to be his influence with the legislature in relation to funds. In Texas, Representative Jim Cotton explained it this way: "Many legislators think the University of Texas is getting too damned big. So they give the bigger increases to the smaller schools to catch up—the college presidents sometimes become the most active lobbyists, each one looking out for himself and his own school."[13] Texas was not, and is not, unique. In Louisiana, where the Kingfish, Huey P. Long, once stoutly championed free higher education and a chance for everybody to get into college, the low tuition tradition still curtails the growth needs of institutions, and the low admission requirements muddies the issues of when a college is a college.

---

[13]Saul Friedman, "A Series on Higher Education," reprinted from *The Houston Chronicle* (1963), p. 6.

The colleges and universities of the South are not organized into any system or systems, but higher education is, in political terms, in a status of institutional anarchy. An interstate body, like the Southern Association of Colleges and Schools, occasionally checkmates political control of some aspect of higher education. Higher education in the South, however, is deeply imbedded in the political power structure and is largely subservient to it rather than a participant in it. In the current realignment of political power, higher education is keeping its ear to the ground, but it is not making its voice heard in an articulate manner for politics in the public interest. Neither the academic life nor the political life of the college campus is attuned to the task of education for political leadership and responsibility. Higher education, aside from pecuniary interests, is standing by. And the goals of the Commission on Goals for Higher Education in the South, such as: *To produce citizens responsive to the social, economic, and political needs of their time,* and *to guide the region in solving social problems created by population changes, racial differences, urbanization, and technological growth,* are often submerged by political expediency.

Higher Education and Religion

We have viewed the religious dimension of the South in pointing to the predominance of Protestantism by reference to the region as the Bible Belt of America. For better or for worse, however, the South is coming to be more and more like the non-South. A recent audit of church attendance in America, for example, shows that the percentage of attendance in the South is precisely the same as that in America as a whole. According to a recent Gallup poll, 44 percent of Americans and 44 percent of Southern Americans went to church in a typical week during 1965.[14] Yet higher education in the South is more "church-connected" with reference to the percentage of church-related institutions than is the case generally in America. The financial commitment is spread quite thin, but the 15 to 25 percent church support of a number of colleges makes the important difference between marginal survival and the achievement of moderately creditable educational programs.

Questions are being asked about religion in the changing South, both in the secular institutions and in the nonsecular ones. The church-connected colleges have become increasingly liberal in their orientation and have sought to avoid sectarianism and, to a large degree, fundamentalism in their religious tenets. Courses in the Bible are no longer required in a number of church-related institutions. On the other hand, state institutions, despite their secular commitment, are frequently ringed by a coterie of denominational religious centers for students of the Methodist,

---

[14] George Gallup, "Church Attendance Lowest in 10 Years," *Nashville Tennesseean* (December 26, 1965), p. 5-B.

Baptist, Presbyterian, and other faiths. There are religious homes away from home in the state institutions while the church-connected institutions seek to avoid any charges of being narrow or fundamentalist in their recruitment of students and in their educational programs. Church and state institutions are becoming more alike in the religious sphere.

In the South, organized religion is not doing a great deal for or about higher education. Southern colleges and universities by the same token are doing very little except in a perfunctory way about those matters conventionally regarded as being of a religious nature. Thus there remains the unanswered query of the place of the church-connected college in trying to make a reasonably unique contribution in Southern higher education.

Higher Education and the Family

The problem of deteriorating family life has not reached into the priority concerns of Southern higher education. Children who live in broken homes rarely get to college anyway. The appalling statistics of the Negro American family are not directly relevant for historically Negro colleges because the typical Negro is not college bound. The incidence of illegitimacy, of desertion, and of father-absent families is not nearly so acute among Negro college students as among the general Negro population. Colleges have neither found it necessary to educate for effective cohesive family life, nor to inculcate a sense of responsibility to deal with family problems in societal terms. Some courses on the family are available as electives, and some are required as a part of departmental majors, such as in sociology or elementary education. How helpful they are we do not know, but they do not begin to touch the massive societal problem. College authorities are naturally more concerned about immediate issues of morality, of illicit sexual behavior, of alcoholic intemperance, and of avoiding any incidents that would bring embarrassment to the institution or to its students, than they are about family stability outside their province of immediate responsibility.

In conversations with students in Southern colleges, the feeling was repeatedly expressed that "we can look after our own romance, our marriage, and our family. Besides, who would teach us?" Regarding this general cultural problem, there was the feeling that "specialists and social workers should take care of that. It's out of our line." Here again the college seems to have served the purpose of helping students to rationalize their escape from social problems rather than to cope with them in a responsible and committed manner. There is little of the Peace Corps or Vista concept apparent in Southern higher education. College students have had no contact with their less advantaged fellow citizens; but their apathy has developed a sophistication.

CONCLUSION

Southern colleges and universities are churning about in a rapidly changing culture. Their temptations and their opportunities are unprecedented. As social institutions they are afforded three options. The first is that of attempting to hold back social change by reflecting upon the virtues of the present and the recent past in the context of loyalty to social traditions.

The second is for the institution to drift with change in an opportunistic fashion, becoming beholden to monied interests and reflecting the values of a society with a premium upon expedience. This trailing or drifting function is understandable and can be easily rationalized by those committed to it. The third and most difficult option is that of studying the problems of society that may be solved or ameliorated through education and achieving an ethical plane of responsibility in which Southern higher education will become a participant in social affairs and social change, concurrent with its role of educating citizen leaders for the years ahead.

In this maelstrom of higher education in Southern culture, this welter of educational and cultural confusion, these questions are whispered earnestly:

> 1. What will higher education do to minimize racial barriers to opportunity and to achieve an ethnically congenial South?
> 2. What will it do to help college-capable youth to hurdle the barriers of poverty, to provide continuing encouragement and assistance, in a context that will dignify the person rather than his possessions or his social position?
> 3. What will it do to recognize and deal with the problems of academic and social unreadiness of otherwise college-capable youth, both white and Negro, from the slums and from the rural areas of marginal educational opportunity?

The answer comes back too often with superficial abruptness: "We can handle it." Yet, we in the South are not "handling it." We are not dealing with these problems with any depth of sustained commitment. We are not doing so for good reasons, but not for sufficient reasons. Of course, not all institutions should attempt to do so, but some certainly must. These matters, like most others in Southern higher education, claim our attention only when forced upon us as a crisis, or when financial incentives lure institutions into a sudden expression of compassion. It is popular and profitable now to help the poor, the disadvantaged and, of course, the Negro. Will this commitment abide if it ceases to be either popular or remunerative?

Above all others, however, this question presses for attention: What will higher education do to make itself increasingly relevant for all college-capable students in our democracy, aside from the consideration of the Gross National Product, increased individual earning power, and social class? If higher education is the keystone, in the long view, to the society we are making, will higher education provide a leadership through education, and provide the basis for a moral and intellectual commitment? Or will it, on the other hand, serve only to provide a traditional bill of fare in this period of rapid growth—providing more of the same crystallized educational program, remaining insensitive to the pressing demands of society and callous to the failure rates and explicable boredom of students, responding only to the greatest immediate pressures—rolling with today's punches from the society it is presumed to lead and serve? The shape of the future hangs on the answer—not what we say, but what we do.

SELECTED REFERENCES

Baskin, Samuel (ed.). *Higher Education: Some Newer Developments.* New York: McGraw-Hill Book Company, 1965.

Darden, Colgate W., Jr. *Within Our Reach.* Commission on Goals for Higher Education. Atlanta: Southern Regional Education Board, 1961.

Jencks, Christopher. "Diversity in Higher Education," *Consultants Papers, The White House Conference on Education,* July 20-21, 1965, pp. 57-62.

McClurkin, W. D., Rupert B. Vance, *et al. High Schools in the South: A Fact Book.* Nashville: Center for Southern Education Studies, George Peabody College for Teachers, 1966.

Schietinger, E. F. *Fact Book on Higher Education in the South 1965.* Atlanta: Southern Regional Education Board, 1965.

Statistics for the Sixties, Higher Education in the South. Atlanta: Southern Regional Education Board, 1963.

PART II.

THE COLLEGIATE SCENE

THE COLLEGIATE SCENE

The Southern collegiate scene is a combination of mobility, of academic pressures and personal stress, of sanctity of spirit and of moral turpitude; of goal fulfillment, of sanctions and taboos, of pride and prejudice, and of social class strivings. Underneath, despite the millions of players on the stage of Southern higher education, each member of that cast is a real individual, whatever mask or make-up he may be required to wear, whatever behavioral part he may feel called upon to play.

The centrality of concern in this scene is one of guiding the individual student—the person—as he seeks equality of opportunity and excellence of achievement with reference to his capacity. But professors and administrators are, behind their degrees and desks, persons, too. If the stresses, the strains, and the challenges emanating from this simple fact can be learned in operational terms, the collegiate scene will become not only an academic community, but a model of democratic living.

4. ACCESS TO HIGHER EDUCATION

Admissions practices in higher education form a tangled web within the South and around the world. A recent international study of university admissions, directed by Frank Bowles for UNESCO and the International Association of Universities, attests to the significance of this area of growing concern.[1] This nation, affluent and increasingly college-bound, has its unique variations of admissions problems, but we Americans are also tied to our traditions and vested interests. We, like other nations, grapple ineffectually with the task of discovering and cultivating the talents of many of our most capable human resources, despite our sophistication in test construction.

In a number of countries, questions of admission and retention policies are pressing for high national priority. In Yugoslavia, in 1963-1964, 9,657 new students enrolled at the University of Belgrade, but only 3,190 of these could pass their tests at the end of the first year.[2] For Yugoslavia, this posed an item of urgent business. In the Orient, in the Republic of Korea, for example, the loss of "face" resulting from denial of admissions and from academic failure creates vital crises. The occasional suicides and suicide pacts attributable to these failures dramatize the seriousness of the issues of access and attrition for higher education and for the society it purports to serve. In Colombia, South America, with less than 3 percent of college-age youth enrolled in institutions of higher learning, admissions practices are exceedingly complex.[3] In the United States, present college admissions practices have been described as "increasingly chaotic, wasteful, and unfair."[4] Here, with a third of the world's enrollment in higher education, and with the most favorable economic conditions,

[1] Bowles, *Access to Higher Education* (New York: International Documents Service, Columbia University Press, 1963).

[2] *The Nashville Tennesseean* (July 16, 1965), p. 11.

[3] This author was privileged to work with the Association of Colombian Universities in the summer of 1966. Previously, he became acquainted with the trauma associated with admissions in Korea, when he assisted the Ministry of Education through an A.I.D. project. In the American South, similar problems are dressed differently, but have much of the same baffling character.

[4] Fred E. Crossland, "Policies and Practices in College Admissions," *Phi Delta Kappan*, XLIV:7 (March 1965), 299-302.

the lack of coherent effort among institutions is increasingly critical. With more than a million freshmen now entering American colleges and universities annually—a number that will increase to three million by 1980—there is a growing national urgency about changing our ways of getting the job done.[5] The alternatives to responsible action are grim to contemplate. And many colleges still show more inclination to achieve a competitive position than to cooperate in the public interest.

These fundamental problems appear around the world, a world in which higher education enrollments will easily double within a decade. If somehow the American South can find a way to break through its own basic admissions problems, it will not only help itself, but may also perform a service to higher education in many kindred spots where the search goes on in vain for national or regional models of success. The American South may be the best present hope, as a manageable geographical unit, to provide a model of measured success. If it does not, it will have bypassed or stumbled over one of its own chief problems, and other nations may despair increasingly of their comparable dilemmas. The admissions problem, unhappily, is not simply a question of whom to admit and whom to deny admittance. The whole fabric of higher education, soon or late, is touched by the trigger of admissions that energizes it. The South, in recent years, has become peculiarly aware of that fact.

THE SOUTHERN CIRCUMSTANCE

In 1962, a survey of admissions practices of member colleges and universities of the Southern Association of Colleges and (Secondary) Schools was conducted by the Association's Commission on Research and Service. The commission reported that decisions affecting admissions were often being made in the absence of comprehensive institutional planning, following a trend to "accommodate policies to pressures as far as possible, and then draw the line."[6] The commission urged that the admissions policy makers not be "swayed willy-nilly by academic or economic forces which may or may not have logical meaning for the situation."[7] The report exhorted colleges, before enrollment increases became fully realized, to explore policy alternatives and to assess their likely consequences to individual students, to the institution(s) of higher education, and to society. Despite some valiant efforts of admissions officers, of

---

[5] *Ibid.* Crossland recommends a plan akin to that of the British Central Council on Admissions. Whatever the plan, he argues, American higher education must find ways of developing a cooperative enterprise to coordinate the mounting task—both in the interest of students and of institutions.

[6] Southern Association of Colleges and Schools, *Changes in Admissions Policies of Colleges and Universities in the South* (Atlanta: Commission on Research and Service, the Association; quoted by Kenneth M. Wilson, in the Southern Regional Education Board's *Research Related to College Admissions* [Atlanta, Georgia, 1963]), p. *iii.*

[7] *Ibid.* (The word Secondary has since been dropped from the Association's name.)

relatively low station in the hierarchy of the higher education establishment, that timely counsel has gone largely unheeded since 1962, and its consideration is now more urgent and more difficult than ever.

Visits to Southern colleges and universities and interviews with individuals from many others during the period of 1964 to 1966 revealed four modal patterns of policy and practice. The first is that of open admissions accompanied by burgeoning enrollments. In the state universities and quasi-universities (expanding state colleges, by whatever name), there is evident a pattern of high attrition (except among out-of-state students where selective admissions practices frequently obtain). With more students enrolled than the institutions are educationally equipped to serve, a mounting indifference to student failure is apparent. Where enrollment limits are established only by considerations of logistic limitations—housing, food services, classroom seating, and library accommodations—student attrition is viewed less as a problem than as the solution to a problem.

In one state university, a dean of one of the colleges reported how anxious the professors were to "cull out" the poor students so that they could concentrate on students with suitable background and demonstrable ability, who did not require special help. In another university, students reported being in a section of a class in which a majority of the students were failed. In still another, a successful college senior confided that "the university shows no interest in you as a person until the junior year. If you survive with credit, you become a name and have an identity. Until then, you aren't much of anything except among your fellow classmates." In a rapidly growing state college, professors reported that legislators, for political reasons, insist upon giving every student "a chance" in the public institution of his choice. The professors reluctantly submit to the practice, but show apathy toward students thus admitted. In one state university, a selective admissions policy applies during the fall quarter, but an open admissions policy becomes effective with the subsequent quarter. Based on experience tables, admissions reservations are made with the certain knowledge that professors will "make room" for new applicants to take their temporary turn. Some professors clearly equate professorial and institutional prestige with a "high flunk rate" in open admissions universities and colleges.

In very few cases are there provisions for special courses or for systematic instructional assistance. There is an intracollege struggle, also. In more than one state college, professors reported their president to be anxious to have the institution expand as rapidly as possible, stepping up recruitment, and dormitory and classroom construction. In one state, something akin to a building campaign contest was reported among state college presidents. The typical president's explanation, however, was that every student in his state should be encouraged to get a college education, and that his college had to tackle that job no matter how rapidly it forced the college to grow.

Admissions practices of state universities do not square with their graduate and research oriented functions. The axiom is well established that an institution takes greatest pride in the program leading to its highest earned degree. When freshman applicants appear in the thousands, the large universities see nothing inhumane about high attrition rates. "It is a functional process of screening," some say, "and the university is not a missionary society. The high dropout level is no secret, and weak students get what they have coming to them." As state colleges aspire to the research status image, they surrender the historic concept of the land-grant colleges, that the open door to learning implies a responsibility on the part of the college to those who enter it with reasonable capacity and the will to learn. As graduate programs are introduced, freshmen tend to be overlooked unless they show graduate potential.

Many students who enter the universities and state colleges do so without the motivation to avail themselves of its educational opportunities. The motivations for such college attendance are so blurred by social expectations that many dropouts clearly represent action in the best interest of students and institutions. If, however, the large universities were free to select capable, academically oriented students most likely to succeed in the context of the university's graduate and research orientation, accepted students would have less fear of failure; professors, less sense of guilt or impatience.

The second pattern is that of the institution that has come to grips with the question of its own special reasons for existence. It has secured resources to perform its mission creditably, and makes a systematic effort to limit its enrollment to students for whom the educational programs are relevant and for whom success with high effort is possible. Rice University, in Texas, with dozens of National Merit Scholars in each beginning class, is a twentieth-century version of the Jeffersonian concept of an aristocracy of the intellectually elite. Highly selective in academic and other terms, financial limitations have never been, *per se,* a barrier. Students are admitted regardless of their financial means, and provisions are made to assure each admitted student that he or she will not be denied access or continuance at Rice due to limited financial resources. As it turns out, of course, most students who are financially poor are so educationally disadvantaged that they cannot meet the academic requirements.

Berea College, in Kentucky, has developed a varied program for academically talented students of financially limited means. Preference is given to students from the mountain territories of eight Southern states having limited financial resources, but excellent high school records and satisfactory test scores (Scholastic Aptitude and the "College Boards"). The college provides remedial courses in basic general education areas for students who are intellectually capable but whose schooling has limited their opportunity and motivation for academic learning. In keeping with their tradition, no tuition is charged. All students work, for economic and educational reasons.

Similarly, Morehouse College and others in the Atlanta University complex, the largest predominantly Negro higher education center in the world, have provided precollege instruction for their freshmen. Knowing of the accumulated educational disadvantages of the students admitted, systematic efforts have been made to articulate admission expectations and educational program offerings.

Fisk University, far more selective than most predominantly Negro institutions, applies rigorous academic standards, and its graduates move into graduate schools all over America, consistently establishing good records wherever they go. [8]

Within the highly selective institutions other problems, of course, arise. First of all, is there too large a homogeneity of social class background? Are many good prospects excluded because their rough edges show? Where are the brilliant, but nonbookish? What level of confidence do the selective institutions have that they have not become creatures of habit, relying excessively upon test scores, academic grades or class standing, and elected offices in school? How do they create a community of cooperative scholars when their students are pricked by the drive of successful competition? How do they find the Lyndon Johnsons and the Harry Trumans? Like the West Point Academy, which sees some of its earlier rejects become distinguished admirals while many of its carefully chosen cadets live out their army careers in mediocrity, even the selective institutions in the South are searching for innovative admissions practices that will improve their choice among the scholars and the nonscholars.

The third pattern is that of the small college or junior college, public, church-connected, or private, which admits and recruits virtually all high school graduates and tends to struggle along with limited resources to provide some form of collegiate environment. [9] In this situation of disadvantaged and weaker institutions, there is still a frequent stirring of intellectual curiosity, a sense of learning together and a personal identity that is sometimes overlooked, or minimized in institutional assessment.

They face, however, an unending struggle for students, for competent faculty, and for adequate financial resources to attain or maintain the respectability of accreditation. Frequently located in isolated areas of the South, these institutions, both predominantly Negro and predominantly

---

[8] At a luncheon of student leaders of the Fisk senior class, each student reported his plans for the following year. Nearly all were entering graduate schools, in the East, the West, the Midwest, and the South, with assured or anticipated fellowships awaiting them.

[9] A number of state colleges tend to be more concerned about good instruction, and less about research activities.

white, are struggling against heavy odds to perform a crucial task in higher education. In one such college, many freshmen measured from the eighth to the eleventh grade achievement levels in reading, mathematics, English, and science. Because they were in college, however, they were turning the pages of college textbooks—college teaching "had to be" from college books. They were learning, but not with efficiency, since neither instructors nor students were functionally able to accept their level of learning needs.

The other side of the picture is represented by the president of a junior college enrolling fewer than 150 students, who explained in detail the reasons for their two unavoidable dropouts. This presidential concern about two students, and the family-like learning atmosphere, with a faculty whose real qualifications seemed to exceed their transcript paper qualifications, and who would "stoop to teach," combined to reveal this to be an institution of promise.

Title III of the Higher Education Act of 1965 refers to these colleges euphemistically as "developing institutions," after the pattern of the chronically underdeveloped nations around the world. The fact is that they are disadvantaged colleges attempting to educate disadvantaged youth who hold high school diplomas. Until of late, they have been more criticized for their limited success in their low prestige enterprise than they have been helped to succeed in it.

There are also colleges in which professors have found a sinecure, a freedom from responsibility, a license to stagnate. The "developing institutions" are not all developing, and financial resources are not their only limitations. Indiscriminate, unguided support of all such institutions would be against educational interests. These colleges admit students who will conform. They do not have to worry excessively about dropping out. The colleges' compassion, apathy, and the student shortages in such colleges, in the face of this period of crowded colleges, will keep them there. In many instances, the student's college experience will consist of a lower education, unsuited to his ability and needs. Yet, there are no "admission" problems from the standpoint of access. Access may be the point at which the problems are generated, and often ignored. *Entry to college does not assure access to higher education.*

The fourth pattern is a heartening one that defies classification by type of college. The admissions policy may be open or moderately selective, but the college is characterized by the combination of generally adequate, but not elaborate resources, and a sense of commitment to help each student find himself, personally and vocationally, to achieve a good measure of success. This commitment is found, for example, in some junior colleges in Florida, where guidance and comprehensive program offerings make it possible for nearly every student to choose a worthy achievable goal. At Virginia State College, programs are planned to provide regular and individualized learning opportunities.

Similar programs are in operation in Texas, at Southwest Texas State College and, in a different context a few miles further south, at Trinity University in San Antonio. This commitment is also found within the individual departments of colleges, universities, and institutes. The School of Agriculture and Forestry of Louisiana Polytechnic Institute, for example, assumes a personal interest in each student, viewing failure as more of a relationship than a condition. This fourth pattern is one of moderately strong institutions in which every student admitted is regarded as someone special, with whatever talents and limitations he brings with him, and the faculty works in a spirit of partnership with him to achieve success.

The Southern Circumstance in Summary

With an abundance of student applicants in Southern colleges and universities, it is little wonder that those requiring special assistance, who do not "fit into" existing programs, are denied access, discarded by attrition, or forced into the mediocrity of a "pot luck curriculum" in frequently unstimulating academic climates. Given our present cultural folkways, it is no surprise. Given our verbalized objectives of higher education, it is little short of shameful.

Some obligations are implicit in the admissions policies of institutions, separately and collectively. Not all institutions need concern themselves greatly with the problems of educational disadvantage. But more of them, public and nonpublic, should. Not all institutions need feel obliged to *guarantee* all necessary financial aid to every in-state student who can prove financial need. Yet, the financial anxiety of students must be recognized as a matter of institutional concern and shared responsibility. Not all institutions need give major attention to problems connected with desegregation in higher education. For many colleges, however, such problems are a matter fairly claiming focal attention.

Within the South, the admissions barriers of race, of poverty, and of marginal precollegiate schooling comprise a formidable cluster of issues facing higher education. These issues involve each institution's unique contribution to higher education. They relate to recruitment practices prior to admission, to the institution's obligations implied by admission, to the relevance and degree of difficulty of the curriculum, and to the college's responsibility for the job placements of its graduates. If there is to be a commitment in higher education to the identification and cultivation of human talent—wherever it is—some institutions must step out in front and respond to that largely unmet challenge.

THE CHRONIC BARRIERS TO ADMISSION

Entry to college cannot be separated from its roots of recruitment or from the educational harvest presumed to succeed it. If we are to avoid a waste of human effort in learning and teaching, and a misuse of capacity, then admissions practices have to be in harmony with the backgrounds,

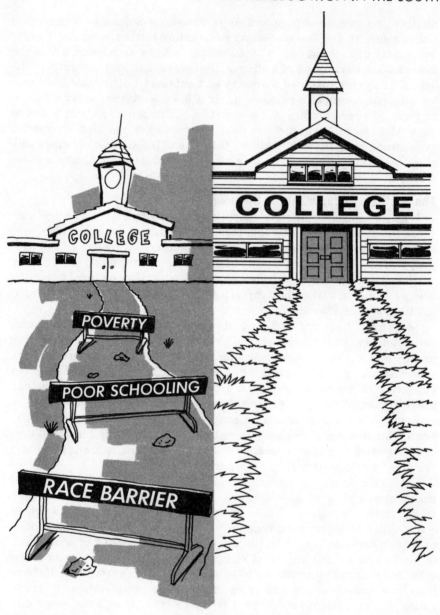

"THE ROAD NOT TAKEN"
"with memories of Robert Frost"

abilities, and industry of students so that a relationship can be established with what higher education in a specific institution has to offer. Within the South, three major barriers to admissions and to successful college continuance persist, thereby impeding the total effort of Southern higher education. The endemic barriers stand firm against those students whose intellectual potential shows clear promise of collegiate success.

The Ethnic Barrier

The barrier to the admission of Negroes in Southern white colleges was erected out of an allegiance to social customs. Prior to the desegregation era in higher education, Negro students in white Southern colleges were an anomaly, which was clearly out of keeping with the times. In 1948, not more than a dozen Southern colleges were desegregated. In 1966, however, the segregated institution has become the anomaly. No more than sixty nonpublic colleges (about 20 percent of the total), four of them Negro, had not yet signed and filed the "Assurance." The total enrollment of these small colleges amounted to fewer than 30,000 students, not more than 3 percent of the million students enrolled in Southern institutions of higher learning.[10] In strict legal terms, students are rarely barred from admission on the basis of race.

Underneath, the facts are different. In many institutions assuring compliance, *de facto* segregation continues. At times this is because of hostile community attitudes. In other cases, the white institution's unwritten policy is to "discourage" Negro applicants, or to limit their number. In some desegregated institutions, the policy is one of reluctant, even grudging admissions.

The reverse situation, of white students enrolling in historically Negro institutions, is of a different character. The college doors are open, but the taboo of the mores is overpowering. The white community says "do not enter." In terms of social banishment, for a white student to do so voluntarily would be almost as "bad" as for a Hindu to become a Christian. It would result in loss of caste, and it just isn't done, with the exception of a few nonconformists and others with a deep altruistic desire to perform a societal service; most of these white students who do enter historically Negro institutions are from non-Southern states.

The ethnic barrier will continue to exist so long as colleges promise to admit students without reference to race but recruit students on the basis of race. It will be removed only after college faculties are desegregated to some degree, establishing a "beachhead" of desegregation; beyond this nucleus minority group, students should be recruited, admitted,

---

[10]Based upon Cumulative Lists Nos. C-26 and C-26-D (up to January 7, 1966) of colleges and universities that have signed an Assurance of Compliance issued by the United States Office of Education (Director, Equal Educational Opportunities Program), and compared with institutions listed in the U.S. Office of Education, Directory of Higher Education, 1964-1965 (OE-50000-65), 1966.

counseled, instructed, passed and failed without regard to race. The barrier is not removed by the formality of an Assurance of Compliance. Indeed, one of the most fundamental ethical issues in Southern higher education is that of the moral and educational implications growing out of such assurance. The honest segregationists have maintained their institutional integrity of public purpose. Their barriers are posted in open view. The desegregated institutions, however influenced, which have decided to comply in full measure are also at peace with themselves. The dilemma deepens for those institutions that attempt to live in the past and in a present that cannot be reconciled with it, for they remove visible barriers only to replace them with subtle obstacles behind masks of compliance.[11]

Removing ethnic barriers will not result in rapidly accelerated desegregation; nor should it. The push should not be to accomplish desegregation, but to permit its natural development. As it is removed, the public schools and other social institutions may gain an intercultural enrichment beyond desegregation; the folkways and mores will accommodate themselves to change as higher education sets a pattern of a social order based on the dignity and potential worth of each student.

The Economic Barrier

After the admissions barrier of race has been removed, the obstacle of poverty continues to block educational opportunity for many capable white and nonwhite students. From the standpoint of available funds, the problem has eased considerably since 1964, but there remain related problems of communicating relevant information to capable deserving students, of effecting equitable distribution of funds, and of helping students to make wise choices among possible college applications, which give the economic problem new dimensions. The problem becomes distorted when students get the impression that they can both avoid the draft and go to college on "nothing a year."[12] Frustration arises as they hear vague reports about millions of dollars being available for needy students, and have no idea how to begin the search for aid. Southern high schools are not prepared, in thousands of cases, to be of much assistance. A previously cited survey of secondary education in the South underscored the marginal educational opportunities afforded youth in the Southern regions, revealing that 34.7 percent of Southern high schools enroll fewer than 250 pupils, and that another 32.1 percent enroll fewer than 500.[13] In virtually all of these schools, and in many others, the guidance and

---

[11]Yet, even this point is arguable. If an institution accepts a legal bribe to desegregate, its moral obligation may extend only as far as legal compliance can require.

[12]See: Lester Velie, "How To Go to College on Nothing a Year," *Reader's D i g e s t,* 88:526 (February 1966), 132–136.

[13]W. D. McClurkin, Rupert Vance, *et al., High Schools in the South, A Fact Book* (Nashville: Center for Southern Education Studies, George Peabody College for Teachers, 1966), p. 85.

counseling programs are virtually nonexistent, and pupils have no place to turn. Somehow, a combination of funds and a personal, encouraging contact with deserving students must be established to bring together the most promising human resources and the financial support they may require.

One highly effective effort in this direction began at Florida State University in Tallahassee ten years ago. It grew out of a professor's concern about a deserving and needy applicant. The plan took substance and grew in the form of identifying private donors, of seeking academically gifted youth not planning to attend college, and of reducing the costs of university attendance through a cooperative housing plan in which students equally shared all household duties including grocery purchasing, menu planning, meal preparation, and other attendant chores of household maintenance and operation. Now incorporated as the Southern Scholarship and Research Foundation, Inc., it continues to reach scores of outstanding young men and women in Florida, of limited financial means, who are distinguishing themselves academically and in the extracurricular activities of the institution. [14]

Students in many institutions, once they become established there, have little difficulty in gaining part-time employment, judging from inspections of bulletin boards on college campuses around the South and from conversations with students. At Southwest Texas State College, where President Johnson worked his way many years ago, there are still more jobs available than there are students to fill them—jobs not connected with government support. In numerous other institutions, especially in urban areas, conditions are the same. In smaller communities, a different condition prevails. At Wood Junior College, in Mathiston, Mississippi, or Fort Valley State College, in Fort Valley, Georgia, community-afforded employment is practically nonexistent.

The point has been made, and perhaps overstressed, that poverty is color blind. Yet, in pendulum-like fashion, we have variously ignored or indulged one poor group or another. The Florida State program was initiated in 1956 for the white poor alone. Private foundations sometimes single out the Negro poor, thereby seeming in the public mind oblivious to white impoverishment. The chief problem, of course, is that the private foundations cannot be omnipresent in dealing with the ignorance-poverty cycle. The National Merit Scholarship Program unavoidably "favors" white students, [15] and the compensating National Achievement

---

[14] Dr. Mode L. Stone, Dean of the School of Education, was the founder of this program, which was established in 1956; he continues to give direction to it—not as a dean, but as a professor deeply interested in students.

[15] Only seven of 1,100 recent NMSP awards were granted to Negroes. The tests cannot be made fully culture-free, and the Negroes bring their complex disadvantages to the examinations. The tests really mirror the Negro's typical, accumulated handicaps. The culturally disadvantaged white youth continues to be overlooked in this arrangement.

Scholarship Program (for Negroes) seeks to balance the scales of opportunity. The National Methodist Scholarship program is reserved for Methodists. In helping the financially deserving, the lines have to be drawn somewhere—to exclude and to include categories of deserving college-capable students. Federal aid, of the most massive nature, attempts to encompass, without prejudice, all of the deserving poor.

The student's admission is not complete until his registration materials have in some way been rung up on the bursar's cash register and been marked "paid" or "charged." The cost of college, a considerable item, varies widely. In the Southern education network, more attention has often been given to the ability to pay than to the combined ability and desire to learn. For the South's problem is compounded by the fact that only about half as much aid per tuition dollar is available at public institutions there as in America as a whole. Outside and within the South, there has been a wide disparity in scholarship aid among the institutions:

> . . . in 1955-56 the 50 top institutions, in terms of scholarship money, held 34 per cent of the funds, although their share of the total enrollment was only 13 per cent. Ten of these top 50 institutions were Southern. Five years later the scholarship resources of the "top 50" had grown 42 per cent but those of the 10 Southern institutions increased only 5 per cent. Meanwhile, average tuition of the 40 increased 38 per cent, and tuition of the 10 Southern institutions increased 49 per cent. In per-student terms, this disparity of Southern resources is perhaps even more glaring—dollars of student aid per student increased 57 per cent for the "top 50" but only 9 per cent for the Southern institutions.[16]

As most readers of these pages know, the Higher Education Act of 1965 made unprecedented provisions for financial aid to students, stretching the concept of need far beyond the unrealistic earlier restrictions to families with incomes below $3,000 to $4,000 per year. Grants are now available on a more elastic basis to families of average incomes ($6,500) or below. Loan arrangements are available to students in families whose net annual incomes do not exceed $15,000, through Title IV of that act. The Higher Education Act was not calculated to supplant, but only to supplement other provisions for financial assistance. The crucial economic admissions barrier now is that of authenticating the talented and the needy students, and encouraging them to go to college. The College Scholarship Service, in Princeton, New Jersey, and in Berkeley, California, gives major assistance in ascertaining the financial need of student applicants, but difficult issues persist:

---

[16]"Undergraduate Student Aid," *Financing Higher Education,* No. 17 (Atlanta: Southern Regional Education Board, 1965), pp. 2-3.

1. Not all confidential statements of parents are accurate and many items of "information" cannot be verified.

2. Not all colleges avail themselves of this service. Some do their own investigation, often haphazard. In some cases, students are encouraged to stretch the truth a bit to receive federal assistance.

3. Many bright students do not know about or avail themselves of the financial benefits available.

A new problem has arisen as the economic barrier has been lifted in the South and around the nation. The enrollment predictions are proving to be low estimates, and the South now appears to be the second most crowded area in America.[17] Thus the caution about a "willy nilly" admissions practice applies to increasingly acute circumstances. The resolution of the economic problem directly gives rise to others.

In a nation rich enough to spend billions of dollars to put men on the moon, in a nation that genuflects to the value of education in giving direction to a prosperous future, we cannot hesitate to afford, through public and private means, the education we espouse. Family income still plays too large a part in determining which of our college-capable youth shall be encouraged and permitted to rise to leadership through educational assistance, and which shall not. Nowhere in America is that problem so chronic, so acute, and so conspicuous as in the American South.

The Academic Barrier

With the racial barrier to admission removed, a major obstacle is overcome. With the poverty barrier lowered a bit, the admission door is pushed ajar. The problem of admissions is still not solved for youth whose schooling, year after year, has been a poor substitute for education. Thousands of youth, of above average intelligence, are far below average achievement levels due to inadequate schooling and to their low aspirations, which have been conditioned by school, by family, and by the neighborhood.

Now it is possible, on the basis of obtainable data about high school seniors, to predict the success of individuals in various collegiate institutions. The cumulative work of John R. Hills and others, for the University System of Georgia, shows what can be done with test scores and academic grades for aiding students to figure their realistic chances for success at various institutions.[18] Unfortunately, their tables of experience do not yet make provision for the prospects of Negro students crossing over into historically white institutions or of white students enrolling

[17]As reported by James K. Hitt, 1965 President of the American Association of Collegiate Registrars and Admissions Officers, in the Association for Higher Education's *College and University Bulletin*, 17:15 (May 1965), 1-5.

[18]John R. Hills, Joseph A. Klock, and Marilyn L. Bush, *Freshman Norms for the University System of Georgia, 1962-63* (Atlanta: Regents of the University System of Georgia, 1964).

in historically Negro colleges and universities; nor does that information carry any interstate information of emigrating students.

A crucial question in Georgia and throughout the South is this: What can and should colleges and universities do to assure a fair chance of collegiate success for talented but academically disadvantaged youth? If a student is academically talented and only a year or so "behind," he can, by dint of his own effort, frequently overcome this educational lag. On the other hand, it is unrealistic to expect that a student who is three years behind his age-grade level, and only moderately college-capable in potential, will be able to make up for this marked deficiency even with considerable assistance. Nonselective colleges face a major dilemma therefore, even after deciding to make a genuine effort to help the educationally disadvantaged student attain academic success. Some students drop out of college because they fail the courses. When standards are lowered to provide for weaker students, the college itself flunks as abler students drop out because they find no academic challenge there.

Other Barriers

There are numerous other barriers associated with college admissions in the public and private spheres. A review of admission requirements in fifty-two Southern higher education institutions reveals that most colleges require standardized tests for admission. All are locked into the nineteenth-century Carnegie unit-credit of measurement.[19] Between twelve and fifteen high school units are required and more than half of the colleges request the recommendation of the high school principal or teacher. Health and character information is required as a part of the application procedure. A few institutions have an age limit, require a "C" average, and use rank in class in the admissions process. Practically all of these institutions prefer graduates from accredited high schools, but provisions are included in the admissions policy for graduates of nonaccredited schools as well. From an examination of the following table the difference between requirements of publicly and privately controlled institutions may be noted.

We must recognize, of course, that college education is not the sole nor even the best avenue toward self-fulfillment and social usefulness for all college-capable youth. To argue otherwise is to take an illiberal, smug view that runs counter to the fundamental goals of higher education. Years ago, John Gardner emphasized the fact that a college education

---

[19] In a recent study of success in trade schools, between high school graduates and roughly equivalent dropouts, no significant difference was noted. Would an academic comparison yield the same results? What college would dare try? See: Garland Millet, *Achievement of Male High School Dropouts and Graduates in Alabama Vocational Schools* (Nashville: George Peabody College for Teachers, 1965).

should surely not be the sole means of establishing one's worth. In some cases, it presents indeed a counterfeit claim. One of the most vexing problems in admissions practices is that of separating the valid premise that all youth should be permitted to develop their intellectual and vocational talents up to the point of marginal return (beyond high school) from the false premise that everybody should go to "college," whatever it offers. As the base of admissions expands, so must the base of educational offerings expand, and institutions are obligated to provide increasingly specialized functions of an academic and nonacademic nature.

TABLE 8

ADMISSIONS REQUIREMENTS IN A SAMPLE OF FIFTY-TWO COLLEGES AND UNIVERSITIES IN ELEVEN SOUTHERN STATES

Requirements	Public	Private	Total
Accredited high school	17	25	42
Health, character, etc.	15	23	38
CEEB or other tests*	15	21	36
Recommendation of principal or teacher	12	17	29
Transcript of high school grades			
16 units	9	9	18
15 units	10	13	23
14 units	1	1	2
12-plus units	0	1	1
Credit by examination or performance	9	11	20
Rank in class	7	8	15
"C" or higher average	4	6	10
16 years of age or older	4	3	7
No test required for admission	3	4	7
Available space	2	1	3

*Across the nation, more than six hundred colleges require College Entrance Examination Board-Scholastic Aptitude Test (CEEB-SAT) scores in the admission process (College Board, SAT Bulletin, 1964).

RECOMMENDATIONS

While there are no easy solutions to mounting admissions problems, there are some guiding principles that make the issues intelligible. The subsequent recommendations are based upon four such principles.

1. Recruitment and admissions policies should be consonant with the educational goals of the institution, and prospective students should be apprised of these major goals.

2. Students should not be admitted who do not have a fair (fifty-fifty) prospect of success with reasonable effort.

3. If educators believe open admissions and high attrition do a disservice to higher education, there is an implicit moral obligation for them to articulate these views to politicians and their publics.

4. Success and failure whether it be academic, financial, or personal, should be regarded as a relationship between each student and the institution.

The Ethnic Barrier

1. Every institution that has filed an Assurance of Compliance has an obligation to examine its meaning in relationship to institutional objectives. It is a document that has vast unused potential as an educational instrument among student groups, the faculty, the administration, and governing boards. The personal view of this author is that, where possible, small groups of ethnic minorities, including some foreign students, should be deliberately recruited as a desirable factor in intercultural, liberalizing education, as truly as out-of-state students are systematically sought and recruited. Beyond that point, students should be recruited and admitted on the basis of their presumed likelihood of success, without regard to national or ethnic origin. Massive desegregation as a quantifiable end, of course, defeats its larger purpose.

2. Some institutions face special problems in the delicate area of race relations. To state the matter plainly, if a predominantly white "compliance" institution will admit, but cannot genuinely welcome Negro students, it should politely and honestly say so and explain why. The following statement illustrates that position:

> South College has filed an Assurance of Compliance with the Office of Education affirming this institution's stance of operating in compliance with the Civil Rights Act of 1964. This administration is committed to honor that pledge in good faith. Students are reminded, however, of the limits of the administration in the enforcement of this act. We can exercise control of demonstrably discriminatory behavior on campus, but cannot make desegregationists of all our students, nor will we presume to trespass upon the convictions of segregationists within the law. South College is located in a community that continues to oppose desegregation. You are entitled to know these facts. The college administration, however, will make every reasonable effort to assure your full acceptance as a student desiring to earn a college education—nothing less, nothing more.

The Economic Barrier

3. Colleges and universities have a new opportunity and face a new responsibility for helping students and their families to plan the financial aspects of higher education. Under present arrangements, the financial aid officer of an institution should become sufficiently informed about the financial circumstances of all student applicants. This officer should, in effect, co-sign the statement of admission for each student applicant along with the director of admissions. Admissions procedures should assure that the student has made adequate arrangements to complete his first year of college, or that through the financial aid officer adequate financial provisions are secured. *Admissions practices should eliminate the financial dropout threat during the freshman year.*

If part-time work is necessary, through provisions of the Higher Education Act's Work Study Program or through other kinds of employment, the academic course load should be appropriately adjusted to minimize the academic hazard growing out of financial hardship. If the college does not follow a policy of a shared responsibility for financial responsibility, it should not indulge in misleading assurance, but should enter an honest disclaimer of responsibility to student applicants to that effect. Students continue to become disillusioned in colleges after they have been assured by recruiters that they will be "taken care of" once they enroll, only to learn that it was only the recruiter talking—not the institution or its financial aid official. The institution needs to speak to students with one voice, making the nature of its responsibility explicit.

4. Without assistance, small Southern high schools can do very little to help college-capable students obtain current, pertinent information about financial aid, and to put it to good use. This places a heavy responsibility upon school systems and upon state departments of education to inform high school principals and guidance counselors about the means of enabling deserving students to obtain aid for their education and training after high school.

5. To facilitate interstate access to higher education, a clearinghouse information service should be provided to serve statewide efforts, and those of schools and of individual pupils who are unable to obtain satisfactory information elsewhere. The person-to-person effect of such a service, with connected field travels to identify economically deprived but academically talented students would increase the efficiency of bringing together deserving students and available funding.

The Academic Barrier

6. The university that is oriented toward its research and graduate school programs should abandon its open admissions policies, and redefine its admissions practices with reference to potential graduate students, who are generally among the first quartile of high school graduates. In many cases, baccalaureate programs should either be discontinued or

built into five-year programs as a respectable dropout point. In-transfer students should be admitted only during the junior year, and only those students wishing to pursue graduate degrees should be considered. Florida Atlantic University has set an example of this nature meriting widespread emulation. A second Florida university will follow suit.

Until such time as such arrangements could become effective, poor-risk students should be politely but honestly apprised of their doubtful chances for success and of the university's limited arrangements for improving these chances. The public policy of "Student, Beware," may seem cruel to some, since the abnegation of responsibility is a weak substitute for positive guidance and educational assistance, but it can serve a useful purpose as a stop-gap measure.

7. The senior college with quasi-open admissions requirements should adjust its freshman curricular offerings to include some half-credit remedial courses in English, mathematics, science, and the social sciences. Just as some students are admitted to advance standing, so disadvantaged students should be admitted on a delayed placement basis. A college education should be established, correspondingly, as a three-and-a-half to a four-and-a-half year program, rather than as a fixed four-year program regardless of the entry achievement level or learning capacity level of its students.

8. A number of public and nonpublic junior colleges should become three-year junior colleges, with one full year of post-high school education consisting of highly individualized instruction for all students measuring below the eleventh-grade achievement level, despite their obviously questionable high school diplomas. High schools and colleges are disconnected, and college education is diluted by having to pretend to be what it is not in scores of Southern institutions.

The North Carolina Advancement School has demonstrated that a great deal can be done to help students of good potential but of poor achievement. The federally supported Upward Bound Project has demonstrated that, within fixed limits, a great deal can be done to help such students in even a short summer program near the completion of high school. In no state, however, have such concepts been built soundly into the educational system. In one southwestern state, and reportedly more, remedial courses are prohibited by law from receiving state aid. Over the years, the purpose for the addition of the twelfth grade has become blurred; it has often become an extension of mediocrity in weak high schools that are already overextended.

With determined effort, flexible three-year junior colleges (i. e. two and a half to three and a half years) can help students to assess their talents and their limitations, and can strengthen their resolve to tackle educational tasks with commitment and purpose. Some would find personal and vocational fulfillment in technical institutes, others in senior colleges. An indeterminant number would transfer to the universities in their junior year and there distinguish themselves. Many of the students now "culled" from the freshmen classes of state universities would attain eminence with this help.

Two Governing Considerations

The validity of these recommendations is a function of two cardinal considerations. First of all, the randomized pattern of college admissions in Southern higher education has to give way to coordinated effort. The Southern Association of Colleges and Schools is a logical place to lodge such a crucial higher education function, but a separated private agency could accomplish the same purpose. The purpose in the American South is not to copy a California plan but to profit from it, not to imitate the British Central Council on Admissions, but to incorporate whatever merit it has for improving Southern higher education. In doing so, a coordinating agency is essential.

The second consideration is in the nature of a joint responsibility of high schools and colleges. It is the task of functionally redefining the basis for what the Latin Americans call *dignidad,* an honor and dignity detached from achievement or prestige. That redefinition is difficult because it runs against the grain of American cultural conditioning, where college choices are based on social status or on economic exclusiveness. Yet, personal dignity according to the American creed resides in what a person is rather than who he is or where you find him. Dignity and indignity can be found at Rust College in Louisiana, or at Harvard College in Massachusetts. They can be found at East Mississippi Junior College in Scooba, and at the University of California in Berkeley. If this principle can be taught by precept and "caught" by example, students can be guided to choose the colleges that can do the most for them. That is the point of admissions policies, guidance, and recruitment. Fewer than half of college freshmen complete the college program on which they embark. Colleges should strive for a holding power of not less than 80 percent.

A successful admissions policy is one which is, in effect, a contract— a meeting of the minds about the mutual expectations of the prospective student and of the college faculty and staff of the institution that will assist him to "heighten" his education. The college should be aware of whatever academic hiatus, or financial difficulty, or ethnic problems a prospective student may encounter, and it should be prepared to assist him in surmounting these problems. In this context, this chapter concludes with a proposed "Contract of Student Admissions," intended only to convey the spirit that admissions is a relationship of commitment.

A Proposed Contract of Student Admissions

South College accepts its share of responsibility with each student for his or her success. This college is "with" each student, not "against" him. Yet, it can only offer educational services to industrious students.

It cannot forcibly educate them, and it does not presume to do so. If each student and South College measure up to the expectation of this admissions contract, we believe that dropouts and disappointed students will be a rarity and that the college experience will be a personally satisfying and intellectually exciting chapter in each student's life. South College recruiters and admissions officials confidently expect each student to respond maturely to these mutually binding obligations. South College is committed to assume its responsibilities, as herein expressed, in full measure.

The Student's Commitment

1. I agree to apply myself with diligence to the academic requirements of the college curriculum, reserving a minimum of fifty hours weekly, as a full-time student, for class attendance and in fulfillment of academic requirements.

2. I have made firm provisions for financing my first academic year of college, either independently or through the Financial Aid Director of South College, based on savings, loans, part-time employment, or other means.

3. Beyond the customary observance of duly constituted regulations of the college, I will not treat with disrespect any person on account of his economic situation, his social position, his race, his religion, or his academic circumstance.

4. As a citizen of the college community, I will seek to improve it. In doing so, I will act through the student council or other duly elected or appointed student officers empowered to represent the interests of all students, or through the groups of which I am a part.

South College's Commitment

1. In assuring the earning of maximum academic success, South College pledges itself to make these special provisions for students:

   a. Freshman booster courses will be offered to students whose limited academic advantages or achievement appear to warrant such preparatory work or improved study skills.

   b. A reduced program of courses will be arranged for intensive student effort during the freshman year or some portion of it, for students who may encounter more than average academic difficulties, or who need considerable part-time employment.

   c. Tutorial instruction, for individuals or small student groups, will be provided by upper division students or by other qualified persons under auspices of the student council and under further direction of the faculty.

   d. Each student will have ready access to an assigned faculty adviser who will counsel him on academic matters, and who will refer him to other qualified college officials for advice on personal and financial difficulties beyond the adviser's competency.

2. South College will expend every reasonable effort to secure needed financial assistance for each student beyond his freshman year, in the form of loans, scholarships, work-study, and other part-time employment aid, and by other means. While South College cannot guarantee all needed assistance, and while such arrangements may extend the normal period

required for completion of the student's program, the student has assurance of the college's strong efforts to assure that he may continue in it until his graduation. Marriage and added dependents are not a part of this agreement, but in no way lessen the college's other educational commitments to the student.

3. South College aspires to become a model of social and political democracy. In this sustained effort, its regulations and services are periodically reviewed and revised by the representative deliberation and decision making of students, faculty, administrators, and the Board of Trustees. Each student will have a genuine chance, as a citizen, to improve the college—on matters that "count." In that same democratic spirit, the college further seeks to assure the condition in which each student shall be accorded the rights and respect due him as a full-fledged citizen. The personal dignity of each student here will be honored and protected as a high-priority commitment of South College.

4. The responsibility of the college continues beyond the student's college education. Through its placement service, South College seeks to help each student attain employment suitable to his qualifications and interest. The placement service will operate in each student's behalf throughout his entire career, whether he becomes a graduate or not.

Under the above terms, _____ is hereby admitted to South College.

_____, Dean of Admissions. _____ (Financial Aid) Officer.

Under these terms, I confirm my acceptance by South College, to begin enrollment in September, 196_.

_____, Student. _____, Parent or Guardian.

SELECTED REFERENCES

Allen, Herman R. *Open Door to Learning: The Land Grant System Enters Its Second Century.* Urbana: University of Illinois Press, 1963.

Bowles, Frank. *Access to Higher Education.* Vol. 1. New York: Columbia University Press, 1963.

Hamilton, Horace C. *Community Colleges for North Carolina.* Raleigh: For the North Carolina Board of Higher Education and the Governor's Commission on Education Beyond the High School, 1964.

Hills, John R., Joseph A. Klock, and Marilyn L. Bush. *Freshman Norms for the University System of Georgia, 1962-63.* Atlanta: Regents of the University System of Georgia, 1964.

Jones, William C. (ed.). *Higher Education for All?* Proceedings of the Twenty-seventh Annual Pacific Northwest Conference on Higher Education, April 1-3, 1965. Corvallis, Oregon: Oregon State University Press, 1965.

Montgomery, James R. *Proceedings of the Research Conference on College Dropouts*. Cooperative Research Project No. F-065. Knoxville: University of Tennessee, 1964.

Wilson, Kenneth M. (ed.). *Research Related to College Admissions*. Atlanta: Southern Regional Education Board, 1963.

5. CONDITIONS OF ACADEMIC LEARNING

Statistics can reveal a good deal about academic learning but students can tell more. One white university coed described a math class in these words: "All through the class the professor didn't talk. He just stays at the blackboard and draws circles and lines and mumbles occasionally. I s'pose he thinks he's teachin'." In a private college, a young man in the cafeteria line pumped the recall capacity of a fellow student about the exam questions given in his morning section of English 101. This was not cheating—it was only "academic guidance." His section would get a modified version of the same test the next hour. A Negro coed, in a hostile white college climate, found her nerves wearing thin. Academic learning was impeded by the feeling that no one in the college wanted her to succeed. With this hurt came a renewed drive to succeed, an alternating futility about its possibility, and an occasional cynicism about its value. A fourth student, a Negro man in another predominantly white college, discovered a stimulating world of thought that he never knew before—among friends.

While able young instructors would "vote" for first rate academic learning, they hardly have the time or inclination to work at achieving it. In one Southern institution, a brand new Ph.D. spent half of an "education" class period reading some esoteric published material to his listless students; he had no prepared comments on the material. Immediately after class, he resumed revising a paper soon to be read in a professional meeting of his learned peers. It dealt with research in teacher education. It would increase his visibility in the academic market place.

In another class in that institution, an undergraduate seminar of future teachers came to grips with some theoretical and practical aspects of teaching. The instructor, deeply interested in the personal and professional lives of the students in this enthusiastic group, was reconstructing the students' processes of arriving at value judgments of the ends and means in teaching. But he will never "amount to anything." He does not now hold an earned doctorate, and he never will.

The president of a public college, a self-appointed champion of good teaching, feels "in all fairness" forced to rely on objective measures, the earned doctorate and published writings, to determine promotion in rank and advancement in salary. His institution needs to be in a competitive position in research and graduate education. It will soon begin offering doctoral programs, and thus become a university.

A consideration of academic learning extends far beyond the statistics of over-all curricular patterns, of the forensics of curriculum balance, of the machinery for credit computation, into a basic reappraisal of educational function. As Manning Pattillo and Donald Mackenzie emphasized in their recent analysis of church-connected colleges, "A college ought to know what it stands for, and these values should be perceivable in the daily lives of faculty and students."[1] The purposes of higher education are a function of who the learners are and what they bring to college with them: their aspirations, their academic backgrounds, their affluent or modest means, and their attitudes about themselves and others.

WHO ARE THE LEARNERS?

Since learning is a personal affair, the students establish or largely modify the climate in which it takes place. Admissions practices can almost assure a docile or an impatient campus climate. The more attention we pay to the learner as a person, and to learning as an interactive process, the less attention we shall need to pay to the techniques of pedagogy. The true objectives of a college prove to be a combination of the expectations students bring with them and those they "encounter" when they enroll. This joining of objectives may help to explain the disenchantment related by students in prestigious colleges and universities, whose hopes were high, and the placid behavior of students in unknown institutions who were not expecting any distinctive opportunities anyway.[2]

Within the South, both public and private colleges consist of white and nonwhite men and women in upper, middle, and lower classes; of domestic and foreign students; of those well and poorly qualified, intent or indifferent about a college education. For some, college life will be a fulfillment of a long-time dream; others will simply be status-seeking flotsam on a college-bound tide of students, conforming to the prescribed behavior of their social set. Beneath these almost meaningless generalizations are some noteworthy statistical facts.

Negro students drop out of the elementary and secondary schools on the road to college far more frequently than white students do. While nearly a third of white students begin college, only a tenth of Negro students do. Even after high school graduation, the contrast is appalling. In South Carolina, for example, 38.3 percent of white high school graduates entered college in 1963-1964, compared with only 17.7 percent of Negro

[1]Manning M. Pattillo, Jr., and Donald M. Mackenzie, *Eight Hundred Colleges Face the Future* (St. Louis: The Danforth Foundation, 1965), p. 23.

[2]See complaints about Oberlin College in John Keats' *Sheepskin Psychosis* (Philadelphia: J.B. Lippincott, 1964), *passim.* The outstanding student may find more "wrong" with a good institution than a poor student would with a weak one.

high school graduates.[3] The percentage of admissions for white students in South Carolina was no higher than in surrounding states.

Sex ratios of college students reveal another significant imbalance. Among white students, men outnumber women by the rate of 100 to 60, while in predominantly Negro institutions a reverse ratio is the case, women outnumber the men at the rate of 122-100.[4] The reasons for this difference go deep into the history of the South. Two explanations go back to the emasculation of the Negro male: historically and currently he has been cut adrift from an adult familial role; and occupational opportunities in skilled and professional fields have been denied him until recently. He has been bright enough not to prepare himself for positions that, for him, did not exist. Now that the doors are opening, he is not in college to prepare himself to enter them.

Each Southern state has a number of foreign students within its colleges and universities; these students present both a challenge to academic learning and an excellent resource for international education among American students. The South, however, does not have its proportionate share. Of a total of 82,045 foreign students enrolled in American colleges in 1964-1965, ten of the Southern states had a combined enrollment of only 4,432. Adding Florida, North Carolina, and Texas to the list more than doubles the Southern enrollment of foreign students. Yet, in that thirteen-state area, slightly more than 10,000 students were enrolled in 1965—fewer than in either New York State or California.[5]

In the South, which is in such obvious need for developing this international "consciousness of kind," colleges are providing the most limited opportunity for doing it. A year abroad is an unthinkable dream for the average Southern college student. Yet in virtually every college it is possible to attract some foreign students, to help them learn and through their presence to enrich the general education for all students.

The South retains a major share of its superior high school graduates, but "loses" many of them. In 1964, among the 1,849 National Merit Scholars, 494 were Southerners, and a third of these (161) planned to obtain their higher education in their home state.[6] Probably an equal number would enroll as out-of-state residents in other Southern states. Among the first group of 224 finalists, mostly Southerners, in the National Achievement Scholarship Program (restricted to Negroes), 52 enrolled in Southern institutions; most of these institutions were predominantly white

[3]See: Jesse T. Anderson, *Report on Scholastic Record of College Freshmen, 1963-64* (Columbia, South Carolina: State Superintendent of Education, 1964), pp. 2-3.

[4]See: Earl J. McGrath, *The Predominantly Negro Colleges and Universities in Transition* (New York: Institute of Higher Education, Teachers College Press, Columbia University, 1965), p. 85.

[5]See: *Open Doors, A Report on International Exchange* (Washington, D.C.: Institute of International Education, 1965), pp. 40ff.

[6]E. F. Schietinger, *Fact Book on Higher Education in the South, 1965* (Atlanta: Southern Regional Education Board, 1965), p. 31.

universities and colleges.   The more than 1,000 finalists and 2,000 additional commended candidates of the 1965-1966 list are likely to remain
increasingly in the South.[7] The interstate flow of white and Negro students
is moderate, averaging about 15 percent.[8] A sampling of college-bound
students in Nashville, Tennessee, revealed a third would remain in
Nashville, a third would leave Nashville but remain in Tennessee, and
a third would enter colleges in other states. They do not go far from
home.

TABLE 9

FOREIGN STUDENTS ENROLLED IN SOUTHERN COLLEGES AND UNIVERSITIES, 1964-1965

Alabama	404
Arkansas	166
Florida	1,616
Georgia	623
Kentucky	603
Louisiana	924
Mississippi	279
North Carolina	1,017
South Carolina	221
Tennessee	883
Texas	2,704
Virginia	476
West Virginia	308
Total	10,224

GENERAL AND LIBERAL EDUCATION

In a political sense, the purpose of education, as Thomas Braden of the
California Board of Education expressed it, "is to make self-government
work."[9] A more sophisticated view is that of Horace T. Morse, who
distinguished between liberal and general education by saying that liberal

[7] Information furnished by the courtesy of the National Achievement Scholarship Program
of the National Merit Scholarship Corporation, Princeton, New Jersey.
[8] Schietinger, p. 21.
[9] Quoted by Ronald A. Wolk in an address at the Twentieth National Conference of the Association for Higher Education, "Pressures and Priorities in Higher Education," *Current
Issues of Higher Education* (Washington, D. C.: National Education Association, 1965). p. 2.

education, in the liberal arts tradition, is concerned first with a body of subject matter, "relatively fixed," which is designed to impart the cultural heritage; that general education is more concerned with the learner than with the content, "which may be organized or reshuffled with less regard to traditional fields."[10] Thus the "great books" approach at St. John's College in Annapolis would be an example of the former; the "student-personnel oriented" approach at the General College of the University of Minnesota, the latter.

More than a decade ago, the Harvard College faculty attempted in vain to resolve the semantic differences of general and liberal education. Reasonable consensus was reached that four "traits of mind," whatever called and however cultivated, were worthy of faculty attention. Effective thinking and communication of that thinking, making relevant judgments, and discriminating among values were the objectives of general and/or of liberal education. The paradoxical statements of *General Education in a Free Society* accurately reflected a diversity of outlook among independent scholars and teachers.[11]

Students, to be sure, cannot be educated in a vacuum. To rule out the heritage of the past, some argue, is to start the slow climb to civilization all over again. To neglect the personal centrality of the present, which is rushing into the future, others rejoin, is to fail to profit from our past— to worship it instead of gaining perspective from it to govern society's present direction. Whatever we call it, the persisting question is what are we doing about it? In medieval times, the curriculum consisted of a study of the *trivium* and the *quadrivium* . In many Southern colleges today, students believe it to be a study of the trivial for a quadrennium.

From the standpoint of objectives, virtually any subject matter or any nonbookish experience could contribute to one's general education, to personal development in some sphere of activity. In the formal curriculum, it can consist of Bible study where the view of beating swords into plowshares and spears into pruning hooks is exalted; or of military science where the strategy and tactics of waging war are learned; or in social science where one learns of the Peloponnesian War or of the anguish of trying to wage peace and war together in Vietnam. In conventional terms general education refers to the "natural" sciences, the "social" sciences, to the arts, and to the humanities. In its most venerated sense, the broad area of the humanities constitutes the subject matter most abounding in its potential for general education.

[10]Horace T. Morse, "Liberal and General Education: A Problem of Differentiation," *Association for Higher Education, College and University Bulletin,* 14:13 (April 15, 1962).
[11]The Harvard Committee, *General Education in a Free Society* (Boston: Harvard University Press, 1950).

The Humanities in Southern Higher Education

One of the most thorough and significant studies of general education in Southern higher education was a regional survey of the humanities in public and nonpublic institutions, *The Humanities in the Colleges and Universities of the South*.[12] The study began with an examination of institutional bulletins, appropriately supplemented through correspondence. Responsible officials from each institution were asked to provide a structural description of the activity or program in the humanities area. Two hundred and ninety-one institutions were included in this phase of the study, from which fifty-eight were selected for more intensive study, based upon their representative or distinguished character. The director of that study visited fifty-six of these institutions, conducting formal interviews with fifty deans and more than two hundred humanities professors, most of whom were departmental or divisional chairmen. (Regrettably, provision could not be financially afforded for interviews with students. This, of course, was before the "Year of the Student.") The study represents the best available data, and their analyses, from official publications and from the responsible leaders of these programs, interpreted by a highly regarded scholar in the field of the humanities.

The disciplines of art, history, language and literature, music, philosophy and religion, were incorporated into the category of humanities for the purposes of the study. The institutions are located in the sixteen states that were signatories of the Southern Regional Education Compact (Delaware has since withdrawn). The variety in the degree of attention given to the humanities among the institutions is illustrated by the liberal arts colleges, some of which required courses in the humanities to represent *more than half* of the total courses necessary for graduation, down to the technical colleges in which the requirements in the humanities were *less than 10 percent* of the total graduation requirements. The notable lack of correspondence between college catalog descriptions of course offerings and data gained through questionnaires and interviews suggests that the business world is not unique in providing misleading advertising. Many colleges simply do not deliver what their catalogs promise, even in the simple matter of course offerings. The excerpt below presents the essence of the pathetic humanities problems in general education in the South:

> When 54 per cent of the humanities people and 80 per cent of the deans avow that departmental programs and offerings are not being reappraised and revised as they might be; when 47 per cent of the humanities professors and 40 per cent of the deans suggest that the humanities teachers are not adequately relating their specialties to the needs and interests of students; when 35 per cent of the humanities professors and over 57 per cent of the

---

[12]A. Edwin Anderson, *The Humanities in the Colleges and Universities of the South* (Atlanta: Southern Regional Education Board, 1961).

deans concur in the thought that departmental offerings are more often the result of the instructor's specialized interest than his interest in students; when 45 per cent of the humanities people and one-third of the deans agree that departmental programs are lacking in breadth and unity; when more than half of the humanities folk tend to believe that humanities professors do not sufficiently cultivate the essentially humanistic values and some 40 per cent of the deans go along—it is evident that some serious reappraisal of the humanities as such, and of our services as individual proponents of the values which they represent and have represented perennially, is in order. (Pp. 48-49.)

If the conditions were unsatisfactory in 1960-1961, the prognosis was more disquieting. On all sides, Edwin Anderson found "so many expressions of concern from so many different persons on so many campuses" that the prospect for the future was depressing. As enrollments continued to swell and course sections increased in number, humanities professors were feeling the increased pressures and attendant problems. Freshman English sections continued to increase alarmingly with each new academic year, and appeared to be increasingly staffed with "anyone live enough to make it to the classroom with some regularity."[13]

Coupled with this problem was the "prevailing and sustained dissatisfaction" among responsible educators with the recipient of the doctoral degree. As a teacher, he was found to be uninitiated into the art and science of the process of instruction. With pressures increasing in nearly every area of the humanities, department chairmen were becoming more concerned about the quality of classroom instruction and conduct. The conventional expedience of "simply letting the young Ph.D.'s loose on the unsuspecting undergraduates" was untrue to the concept of higher education. But colleges were still looking for degree holders first; good instructors, second.

Anderson sought a mechanism for correcting the inadequacies of graduate instruction through an in-service training program, but reported that such programs in the Southern region were almost nonexistent. His analysis concluded with the legitimate solution of "reviewing, reassessing and reforming" the graduate instruction in the several areas of the humanities. He urged a provision for more breadth and synthesis of subject matter, for more expeditious adaptation of the content of the field, and of the instructor himself, to the interests and needs of students.[14]

No studies of so comprehensive a scope have been conducted in other areas of general education, but some uncomfortable inferences are evident from this one. There is no reasonable basis for the assumption that

---

[13]Anderson, p. 31.

[14]Anderson, pp. 83-84. William James, a half-century ago, decried the "Ph.D. Octopus" to no avail. Instead of reshaping doctoral programs for collegiate instruction, we continue to produce more of the same, according to Everett Walters, "The Immutable Ph.D.," *Saturday Review*, XLIX:3 (January 15, 1966), 62-63.

conditions are appreciably better in other areas of general education. With the added expenses required for equipment and materials in the sciences, and competent instructors at a premium, there is reason to believe that conditions are not above the standards achieved within the humanities area. Nor is there a supportable basis for believing that conditions are appreciably better in 1966 than in 1960 when the Anderson study was conducted. The enrollment swell had hardly begun at that time. It is now at an unprecedented peak, and competent instructors cannot be produced as rapidly as dormitories can be constructed.

If general education in the South as a whole is characterized by a prevailing mediocrity, then what is an honest assessment of the predominantly Negro colleges of the Southern region? A recent study by Earl McGrath points out that in the great majority of these colleges, faculty members rely heavily on the textbook-lecture system as a "low-cost low-energy means of instruction."[15] Edwin Anderson concluded that the Negro colleges were in the main handicapped by the same problems confronting the predominantly white institutions, the difference was in the acute degree of the problem. He emphasized, however, as did McGrath, that distinctive programs of high quality were found in leading Negro colleges as well as in those that are predominantly white.[16]

Students in Southern colleges are not complaining much, publicly or off the record. They may protest being unable to sun-bathe on the roof, or being denied admittance to a risqué dramatic performance, but they do not protest mediocrity in the general education curriculum. Some are inured to boredom from their high school years. As one student commented, "you have to learn to endure some courses to get a degree. That is part of the price you expect to pay." Where instruction is good, students are often highly appreciative.

The "Values" Aspect of General Education

The area of science has become a focal point of controversy in the general education sphere. It is indeed unfortunate if, in our higher education culture, two cultures are arising, splitting the men of science and the men of nonscience, the Science Foundation as opposed to the Arts and Humanities Foundation. Yet, this schism runs deep in society and within the general education curriculum in higher education in particular.[17] An English professor at a famous Southern technological institute commented, tongue in cheek, that English was regarded as a foreign language there. The queen of the sciences was the native tongue.

[15] McGrath, *The Predominantly Negro Colleges and Universities in Transition*, p. 97.
[16] Personal interview, July 1965.
[17] See: Jacques Barzun, *Science: The Glorious Entertainment* (New York: Harper and Row, 1964).

There is little doubt that the liberal arts emphasis in general, and the attention to the area of the humanities and social sciences, is under unprecedented pressure in the surge toward scientism in our increasingly technological society.[18] The national concern over the problem resulted in the creation of the National Commission on the Humanities in 1963, which forthwith recommended that a National Arts and Humanities Foundation be established. The foundation has since been established, but that does not solve the problem of values in the curriculum, to which the humanities largely address themselves.

During the past decade a substantial body of literature has shown that academic learning makes little difference in the values of students, in degree or in kind. They tend, in the main, to move toward the norm of the value system of which they become a part.[19] Despite some of the initial findings of Philip Jacob, some student groups were found to be particularly potent in providing a moral, cultural, or intellectual climate that created a "high level of expectancy of their students." This community of values can be achieved for a student, according to Jacob, only "when it penetrates the core of his life and confronts him with fresh and often disturbing implications which are different from those which he and his society have taken for granted."[20]

A cogent analysis of factors associated with value change in the academic world has been contributed to the literature by Paul Dressel. He reckons with the prospect that for any change of direction, there is always the possibility of the opposite. Thus, when we are "tinkering with" value change, we should not delude ourselves into the wishful thinking that we can encourage others to pursue independent analyses and invariably arrive at our own conclusions from them. He further examines the process of value change "when a different normative base is accepted."[21] The changing collegiate subculture in the Southern region with reference to desegregation serves as a prime example of this situation. The position of the "moderate" has reversed its acceptance level. Once untenable, it is now modal in this respect. Dressel's conclusions regarding approaches

---

[18]See: "The Plight of the Humanities: A Special Report," *Duke Alumni Register,* 51:5 (May 1965), 13-28.

[19]See: Philip E. Jacob, *Changing Values in College: An Exploratory Study of the Impact of College Teaching* (New York: Harper & Bros. , 1957); Gordon Allport, "Prejudice: Is It Societal or Personal?," *Journal of Social Issues,* XVIII:2 (1962), 120-134; and Paul L. Dressel, "Factors Involved in Changing the Values of College Students," *The Educational Record,* 46:2 (Spring 1965), 104-113.

[20]Jacob, "Does Higher Education Influence Student Values?," *NEA Journal,* 47 (January 1958), 38. A study in a Jesuit University, financed by federal funds, showed greater changes, and some lesser ones, in values held by students than in secular institutions. See: Julian F. S. Foster, "The Impact of a Value-Oriented University" (Santa Clara: Santa Clara University, 1961 [Cooperative Research Program OE-50043]).

[21]Dressel, *op. cit.*

to value change are especially noteworthy in the context of Southern colleges and universities:

1. Students should be helped to become increasingly conscious of value problems.

2. A values approach should emphasize a comparative rather than a normative use of reference or groups of authority. If we start with the "right" value and compare the weaknesses of the "wrong" values, colleges abort their function by being miseducational institutions.

3. The emphasis should be on encouraging internal rather that external initiation of value change (this viewpoint, however, may be questioned in view of Gordon Allport's studies regarding the societal and personal dimensions of prejudice). [22]

4. The emphasis on values should be more upon the process of examining them rather than upon the ultimate values derived from humanistic history.

5. Students should be encouraged to act on a value-oriented basis rather than on living lives of fortuitous inconsistency where values are dropped at the point of decision. [23]

Interviews with students in Southern colleges revealed a fairly consistent outlook. Most overwhelmingly, students were suspicious of any overt or covert effort on the part of instructors to "change students' values." They felt entitled to the privacy of their views about controversial issues. Yet they endorsed highly those instructors who made them think without trying to "bend them around to instructor's dogmas." They were convinced that their values were largely set, and that the college was limited in what it should or could do to modify values through academic activities. In the main, students felt that values can really be modified in only two ways: (1) By the example of instructors as authentic models whom they get to know in informal situations, in class or elsewhere. (2) By experiences with people, which cause them to see things differently. They were confirming, in a variety of ways, what Dressel's analyses led him to conclude.

The question of values in general education is under current reappraisal in many quarters. One of the students of the problem expressed it this way: "The question is whether the college will prove adaptable and imaginative enough to continue to be collectively one of the most significant institutions in the country. And the answer to that question at the moment is far from certain." [24] Within the South, the question is surely in doubt. Some instructors develop effective thinking, while others focus on effective rote learning. Some, in and out of English departments, improve effective communication; others dwell on its writing and listening aspects. Some

---

[22] Allport, *op. cit.*, pp. 120ff. This author's observation.

[23] Dressel, *op. cit.*, pp. 112-113.

[24] Conrad Hilberry (Associate Director, Study of the Future of Liberal Arts Colleges), "Hardy Perennials," *Antioch Notes*, 43:4 (January 1966).

help students to make relevant judgments in the academic domain; others make judgments on what students view as irrelevant for our time. Some attempt to aid students to discriminate among values; others save the students the effort, by discriminating for them.

The problem arises in part from a tradition of respectability; that "dirty politics of today" is unworthy of study along with Plato's *Republic* or More's *Utopia*. Part of it comes from our fragmentary knowledge of the present, and our inability to teach it as a closed system of knowledge. Issues involved in burning draft cards, for instance, would presumably contaminate the curriculum. Yet, with the national draft law coming up for renewal in 1967, it is surely relevant subject matter for young adults. The problem comes also from the academic taboo associated with administrative inquiry into the quality of teaching. *Academic freedom for professors often transcends academic opportunity for s t u d e n t s.* There is finally the mixed blessing of the instructors who are enthusiastic about their own special interests. Interest begets interest, regardless of subject matter, but are students' interests stirred over the subject matter most educationally significant for them? They think not.

In large measure, the general education curriculum in Southern colleges suffers from the same additive process, and subject proliferation that seems to characterize the nation.[25] Professors commonly teach what they have already been taught, and new forms of old problems cannot work their way into the curriculum. Thus, a current analysis of Southern and national politics is "too hot to handle," and students are diverted from considering the live issues confronting our citizenry. A study of the humanities deals with the Protestant reformation, but gives little attention to the current Catholic reformation, which Martin Luther could not accomplish but which Pope John, Pope Paul, and the Vatican Council recently could. It may deal with the nineteenth-century philosophy of Friedrich Nietzsche, but it stops short of a consideration in depth of the "God is dead" philosophy, which can be traced back to it. State institutions separate their secular gods from the Sacred God, in deference to the United States Constitution.

The curriculum may deal with a broad consideration of ethnic and cultural principles, and students may be required to define "ethnocentrism," but they are seldom afforded direct experiences that lessen their culture-bound feelings. A consideration of our affluent society and of the paradox of poverty amidst wealth may form the basis for intellectual calisthenics, but the curriculum provides no opportunity to get to know and help the "other America" in a significant, internalizing fashion. A study of social institutions may be encountered, along with an intellectual acquaintance with problems of family disorganization, but the problems of social disorganization remain unreal to students in large part despite

---

[25] See: Paul L. Dressel, *The Undergraduate Curriculum in Higher Education* (Washington, D. C.: The Center for Applied Research in Education, 1963).

their increased erudition because they do not know any juvenile delinquents personally *and* the empty-shell families out of which these delinquents typically come.

The study of the sciences, the social sciences, the arts, and the humanities does not achieve a wholeness in the making of free, responsible human beings and citizens. Only in the mathematical sense of adding enough credit-hours to achieve the specified total do they amount to general education. Yet the professor is not the responsible culprit for an admittedly unsatisfactory state of affairs. He is a part of a system from which he finds it difficult to extricate himself.[26] He has little opportunity or encouragement to be the kind of instructor he would like to be. From "above," the administration likes to play it safe, and current significant issues are not safe. From "below," students have established a sense of security in the system, like the monk copying page after page of someone's manuscript, and a sense of futility in attempting to improve it. One may ask therefore, if all participants are reasonably satisfied with the system, why be concerned with improving its character? The faculty, administration, and students are all "getting ahead" in the increasingly lucrative business of higher education and upward mobility. The professor is not the hero in academic learning, but neither can he be made the villain by others who share the responsibility for general education, including the students themselves. If professors could be stimulated and helped to give instruction their most creative efforts, and if students were to become genuinely involved as participants in curriculum change, then liberal education might come increasingly to liberalize the student, and to liberate the professor from being the creature of habit that he has often become— with little incentive to be otherwise.

SPECIALIZED EDUCATION

Problems of specialized education are commonly associated with an economic base and with social status. Senior colleges that have traditionally "turned out" teachers have done so in the main because programs can be provided as inexpensive adjuncts to a traditional liberal arts program. An extension into master's degree programs as the highest degree offered has also proved highly economical, particularly in the field of professional education. In the South, where the master's degree is thus offered, current expenditures per student are lower than in those institutions offering only the baccalaureate degree.[27]

---

[26]Aware of the severity of this problem, the Southern Region Education Conference recently recommended establishing a regional experimental center to improve instructional competence in higher education. See: *Proceedings of the Seventieth Annual Meeting of the Southern Association of Colleges and Schools: Education: The Southern Hope* (Atlanta: Southern Association of Colleges and Schools, 1966), p. 49.

[27]See: Gustave E. Metz, *Current Fund Expenditures* (Atlanta: Commission on Colleges of the Southern Association of Colleges and Schools, 1964), p. 15. Reference is to accredited institutions of the Southern Association of Colleges and Schools.

The social status factor is convincingly reported by Norman Harris:

> Semiprofessional and technical personnel are needed in greater numbers than ever before. The fact is, however, that most semiprofessional workers and technicians today were, when they were high school students, planning on professional careers. The recognized professions (though they comprise only 11 per cent of the labor force) are the rather ill-defined goal of over 50 per cent of high school students. Pressures from parents, fellow students, and from high school teachers and counselors motivate thousands of high school youngsters to elect the academic program when their interests and abilities actually lie in more practical fields. [28]

Junior colleges face the same status problem. Nationwide, the average junior college freshman class, *even with and after testing and counseling procedures,* shows a predilection for the "transfer" programs. Leland Medsker reports that two thirds of junior college freshmen choose the academic or transfer program rather than terminal programs. The lack of realism in many of these choices is evident by the fact that only about a third of junior college freshmen ever matriculate in a senior college. [29]

Within teacher education, areas of specialized education in Southern colleges bear little relationship either to supply-demand situations or to projected needs. For college freshmen to be informed about supply-demand, by subject areas or school levels, creates a threat to established collegiate departments. In the interest of amicable faculty relations, students continue to major in oversupplied fields and to teach outside their areas of special competence. Nearly a tenth of all Southern secondary school classes in science and mathematics are held by teachers not even presumed to be competent by meager certification standards. [30] The percentage of elementary school teachers who never "dreamed" they would be there is far greater. Many thought they would be teaching Home Economics.

A recent estimate for national labor needs in 1970 predicted that of the total labor force, 6 percent of workers would need only a grade school education (unskilled workers); 26 percent would require a high school or vocational school education (semiskilled, skilled, and service workers); 50 percent would require posthigh-school training in technical institutes, community junior colleges, and business colleges; and 18 percent would require baccalaureate and graduate study programs. [31] Southern institutions of higher education, with the exception of some leadership from the

[28] Harris, *Technical Education in the Junior College / New Programs for New Jobs* (Washington, D. C.: American Association of Junior Colleges, 1964), p. 81.

[29] See: Leland L. Medsker, *The Junior College: Progress and Prospect* (New York: McGraw-Hill Book Co. , 1960), p. 97.

[30] See: W. D. McClurkin, *et al., High Schools in the South, A Fact Book* (Nashville: Center for Southern Education Studies, Peabody College, 1966), p. 87.

[31] Harris, p. 27. (Based on data from the United States Office of Education and the Bureau of Labor Statistics.)

Southern Regional Education Board and from some state systems of higher education, are making no systematic effort to balance supply and demand.

The specialized curriculum continues to be largely restricted to what the incumbent, tenured faculty can already "deliver." Career programs are largely oriented to the needs of yesterday, a problem particularly acute in the predominantly Negro colleges. Career opportunities for Negroes have historically been open only in the "protected" areas of teaching and agriculture. With these limited opportunities for advancement, it was natural that the college curriculum should concentrate on these areas. Otherwise, a proficient person would find his diploma to be a dead-end certificate. Thus the recent report of Earl McGrath is not surprising, that out of 163 professional schools or divisions in predominantly Negro colleges and universities, sixty-five are in education and seventeen are in agriculture. By contrast, there are only six in law, one in medical technology, one in architecture, four in technical education, and four in pharmacy. As McGrath emphasized, "the curricular options in the predominantly Negro colleges must be expanded if Negroes are not to be kept in low economic and social status by narrow curricular options."[32] Visits of this staff into predominantly Negro institutions fully confirm that conclusion.

The situation in the liberal arts colleges, predominantly white in composition, presents a close parallel. Public and private four-year colleges continue to be teachers' colleges under various cloaks. The percentage of students preparing for or entering teaching is commonly the largest group of a graduating class.[33] The situation would not be so great a problem if the teacher preparation were uniformly creditable, let alone distinctive. The pathos appears in the South, however, when teachers can be certified in the guise of a liberal arts program that is doing only a marginal job, both in liberalized education and in professional preparation of teachers. The South, of course, is not unique in this respect. Across the nation, prestigious private colleges and universities are among the worst offenders.[34]

In other areas of serious shortage and of impending shortage, a highly anomalous situation is apparent. In the field of medicine, it has been estimated that the South will require 86,000 additional physicians in 1975. According to the present rate of supply, we are apt to have only 72,000, falling short of our need by 16,000 doctors. With the advent of Medicare,

---

[32] McGrath, p. 75. Of the 123 predominantly Negro colleges and universities, 119 are in the South. The picture described, therefore, is essentially a Southern picture.

[33] Radford College, in Virginia, guides more than 80 percent of its students through its creditable teacher education curriculum. It is a teachers college for women, but for good reasons would not dare assume such a title.

[34] The Middle States Association's Commission on Higher Education commended teacher education to liberal arts colleges that were willing to undertake it seriously and to make it a central interest: "If not, they had better leave it alone." (Document 4.65, June 1963.) But they do not.

the estimate of the required supply will be increased and the imbalance will be greater. Opportunities for premedical education as well as medical education are extremely limited. In Tennessee, in 1965, a thousand additional registered nurses were needed to meet the present demand. The semiskilled area of dental hygienists is understaffed. We are not yet prepared for yesterday, but we brace ourselves for tomorrow. Needs in agricultural education, not in farming but in such areas as chemical agriculture, are mounting. Although the Southern Regional Education Board and other agencies are keeping abreast of the professional and semiprofessional demands, the colleges are not organized or coordinated to meet them. They offer what their endowment and current funds will most comfortably permit. In some fields, shortages increase, while only half of the students who prepare for teaching enter the profession.

Innovations in Academic Learning

In the bewilderment of general and specialized education, academic learning has been bombarded by a variety of promising and threatening innovations, but they have met a wall of resistance. As Lewis Mayhew observed, "almost everything about colleges has changed . . . except college teaching. Research, scholarship, publication, academic content . . . but not teaching."[35] John Gustad strikes an equally grim note growing out of his study on faculty evaluation for the American Council on Education. He points out that while college presidents uniformly list teaching effectiveness as the most important trait considered, "not a single one had an approximately effective system of finding out whether faculty members were or were not good teachers."[36] The problem as he described it was one of national proportions.

There are numerous innovations, of course, and some of them are appropriately described in glowing terms, such as independent study, programmed learning, educational television, and fuller use of the community as a laboratory for learning.[37] The South appears to be doing its share of innovating, both for better and for worse. But wherever innovations appear in the South, they tend to emerge from hasty grantmanship considerations rather than from a long look at the educational process.

THE TALENTED DISADVANTAGED

In the midst of academic concerns, what is the prospect in Southern higher education for the young man or woman with a capacity for excellence, but whose prior schooling and cultural circumstances have placed him at an initial disadvantage, and whose disadvantage is coupled with the problem that he is not a star athlete?

[35] Mayhew, "The Professional Needs of College Teachers" (address to the conference of the Association for Higher Education, April 9, 1964).

[36] Gustad, "On Improving College Teaching," *NEA Journal* (March 1964), p. 37.

[37] See: Samuel Baskin (ed.), *Higher Education: Some Newer Developments* (New York: McGraw-Hill Book Company, 1965).

The entire area of academic learning raises the question of compensatory preference, a matter that deserves considerable study and more experimental action. At the present time, some educators are concerned about the "inequality" of providing special attention to the educationally disadvantaged Negro or Caucasian who is intellectually capable of "catching up." Side by side with this reluctance to provide "compensatory preference" by race or class, is the prevalent practice of providing tutorial instruction for college athletes who may be required to drop out of varsity athletics unless they can maintain satisfactory academic standing. The going rates for graduate tutors has been found to be upwards of four dollars per hour. Questions such as this are tied in integrally with the climate of academic learning on the Southern campus. For the liberalized learning and specialized training commonly associated with higher education to be possible, the student once admitted must be able to enter into an academic relationship that affords at least a sporting chance of success, whether he be an athlete or not.

Unlike the privileged students who take college for granted, as a fashionable debut into their adult social class, students who face economic, educational, or racial barriers to success in college are more likely to be responsive to an academic helping hand, to a warm acceptance into the academic community, and to a regard for their inherent worth. If upper class higher education can break out of its own culture-bound value system, it will discover that the underprivileged are often more responsive to educational opportunities than are many of their more privileged peers.

RECOMMENDATIONS

Conditions of academic learning in Southern higher education, with heartening exceptions, are not good. They are not getting better. Yet the "establishment" consists of men and women of good will. As colleges increase standards for student selection, they are forced to lower them for faculty recruitment. The South is not alone in that regard. On the day these lines are being written, a recruiter from a midwestern state is on the Peabody campus as a part of his search for 500 faculty members for the system of state colleges there. No wide-scale miracle will upgrade all of higher education in the South or anywhere else. Yet, a massive coordination of effort will be required to raise the qualitative level of academic learning to make it more relevant to social ends and economic goals. Beyond such a large effort to work together in the public interest, a few individual institutions within the South should become openly committed to make academic adequacy their consuming goal. When a few institutions determine to work resolutely at academic learning, and many others give it at least moderate attention, then it will become truly elevated in higher education.

The recommendations contained here have been winnowed from many discussions with students, professors, and presidents. They have been studied in the context of the experience of collegiate efforts outside the South and of applicable professional literature. Some proposals may appear trite; others, unrealistic; some, inappropriate in a given circumstance. Whatever they do, they point to needs in academic learning in Southern colleges. Whether the needs are met in these ways is not the chief concern. The concern is that the needs they reflect be given the kind of deliberation that leads to constructive action.

1. *Academic intimacy.* Faculty advisers should establish a "Unifying Seminar," a meeting weekly for a two-hour period, in which students can develop a peer group intimacy and a depth association with a college official, a personalized *in l o c o parentis*. Each seminar should be limited in size to ten or fifteen advisees. Professional faculty meetings should give attention to problems of unifying the educational program, and should consider the part of seminars in doing so.

2. *Tutorial a n d remedial assistance.* In addition to systematic remedial programs, a tutorial plan should be inaugurated for the abler, or more advanced students to help those in need of academic assistance. (Such as a Frank Laubach "each one, teach one" variation.) Financial payment may or may not be appropriate. It would hardly make sense, for example, for students of modest means to pay the more affluent students. A college fund might remunerate the tutors.

3. *Student committee f o r improving teaching.* Such a student group should work constructively with the faculty and administration in improving the calibre of teaching, of "finding out" those reputed instructors who, allegedly, do not instruct, and exploring with the faculty promising innovations in curriculum teaching. The student chairman might well serve a liaison function on the faculty curriculum committee or its equivalent, so that students are not working against the faculty but with them.

4. *Dignity for t h e deserving.* This principle can be assured by an administrative and faculty respect for students. A special responsibility for minority groups, foreign and native born, that have not been assimilated, and for individual isolates should be assumed. In many instances, faculty deliberations on the departmental level on ways of doing this would be useful. Some colleges have long outgrown their need for this; others should give it high priority.

5. *Library holdings and usage.* The library is generally believed to be a fair indication of academic learning. The number of volumes is far less significant than why students are reading, or why they are not. A recognized student group should have its own budget, however limited, for library book orders independent of course requirements.

6. *T e s t i n g programs.* Such programs should be administered for individually planned student loads. One student might proceed at a regular pace; another at an accelerated pace with an overload; another at a decelerated pace with a reduced load, depending on achievement, scholastic aptitude, and estimated time available for study. The flexible rate

of advance plan should be regulated by background, brightness, and need to work.

7. *A VIEWS program (Volunteers in Educational Work and Service).* Most students entering college should at some time during their college career engage in some volunteer community service or in some form of gainful employment or both. In kinship with the VISTA program, some educational objectives studied in books cannot be learned in depth except in direct experiences. A well-conducted VIEWS program should be an integral extension of the general education program in a number of institutions. Both military and nonmilitary service should be recognized as worthy of educational credit.

8. *Models.* Within each state a limited number of public, private, and church-related institutions should set themselves the task of becoming exemplary models in the academic learning of students representing one or more of the three endemic problems of race, poverty, and inadequate prior schooling. The state, church body, or other supporting agency, should in some cases designate these unique institutions, and should provide additional financial support necessary to increase the chances of demonstrable success worthy of widespread emulation.

9. *Continuing attrition assessment.* Such an assessment should be conducted and should involve more than routine interviews. The "unifying seminar" leaders should be helpful in this respect.

The obvious burden of academic leadership, from the entering freshman to the chairman of the board, is to clarify the academic objectives of the institution and to formulate an over-all curricular design consonant with them. Some colleges can shut out most of the problems associated with economic, ethnic, and educational disadvantage by selective admissions requirements. Some can and should limit their function and their clientele. Somewhere in Southern higher education, however, the responsibility for discovering and educating capable youth beyond high school remains. To pamper the economically privileged while neglecting to cultivate the potential for excellence among the disadvantaged is a parody of higher education.

For college-capable youth the door of relevant academic learning beyond high school must not be closed by artificial barriers. But simply to allow students to get to college and hope they survive to graduate may be doing them a disservice. Academic learning must not be allowed to become a primitive pageantry for any student, but must be an intellectual adventure relevant for today and tomorrow.

SELECTED REFERENCES

Anderson, A. Edwin. *The Humanities in the Colleges and Universities of the South.* Atlanta: Southern Regional Education Board, 1961.

Dressel, Paul L. *T h e Undergraduate Curriculum i n Higher Education.* Washington, D.C.: The Center for Applied Research in Education, 1963.

Educational Policies Commission. *Education and t h e Disadvantaged American.* Washington, D.C.: National Education Association, 1962.

————. *Universal Opportunity for Education beyond the High School.* Washington, D.C.: National Education Association, 1964.

Harris, Norman C. *Technical Education in the Junior College.* Washington, D.C.: American Association of Junior Colleges, 1964.

McClurkin, W. D., Rupert Vance, and others. *High Schools in the South, A Fact Book.* Nashville: Center for Southern Education Studies, George Peabody College for Teachers, 1966.

McGrath, Earl J. *The Predominantly Negro Colleges and Universities i n Transition.* New York: Bureau of Publications, Teachers College, Columbia University, 1965.

6.

THE STUDENT
IN THE COLLEGE COMMUNITY

The college is a miniature society, and the ethos of its culture gives it significant meaning. The college is an artificial community in the sense that it is not self-sufficient but is economically dependent upon the larger society of which it is a part. The "unreal" dimension of the community is "academia," where students and instructors don their academic masks and permit only the intellectual fragments of their personalities to become revealed. The "real" part of the college community takes on substance before and after class, in which students actively participate and feel a primary group relationship with others; where matters of a perceived intrinsic significance for the present and the nearby future are talked about and acted upon. These two institutional subcultures may be separate ghettos of college life and thought, but there are those fortunate institutions where faculty and students sense their common humanity and show it.

The large university, like urban society, is plagued by a high level of depersonalization; the small college, like the small town, is characteristically a neighborhood in which professors and students come to be known for what they are. The freshman moves into his new society, whether large or small, uncertain of the esteem to be accorded him, anxious to conform both to the expectations of his professors and his peers, and remembering his loyalty to his own convictions and to the high hopes of his parents for him. The new society goes to work on him long before he reaches the campus. He has selected his college, insofar as the choice is his, so as to be highly regarded and on the right socio-economic track. He has chosen his fall wardrobe with a careful eye to what will be proper. When he arrives, he may see most of the upper classmen at the student center drinking coffee. He will promptly forego his high school milk. This will not create a moral problem for him, but will only require the cultivation of new tastes. He will puzzle over whether to keep wearing his high school graduation ring or not, and he will be guided by custom. He will establish himself in the new social order by conforming to its expectations, and this conformity will wear into his thoughts and feelings.

At times conformity will be accomplished with ease; at times, with exceeding difficulty. He will hang on to varying degrees of his former

107

self, depending on his inner security. Whatever he has to surrender of himself, he will work at accommodating his behavior to a new set of cultural and educational expectations, of sanctions and taboos. He may experience a genuine culture shock, or he may find college life much akin to what he has known before. This may be for him an experience of self-discovery, or one of self-effacement. He is an almost-man; the coed, an almost-woman. Being almost but not quite is an exciting, exasperating condition of becoming. At one moment, the college is leaned upon as being *in loco parentis;* at another, it is a community of scholars and nonscholars—or a new locus for rebellion against the parental substitutes of college regulations.

THE YEAR OF THE STUDENT: 1965

The "Free Speech Movement" on the Berkeley campus of the University of California, in the fall semester of 1964, received full pictorial coverage in the national press, with both glib and scholarly explanations of this massive student revolt.[1] The consensus of the Byrn Committee, which investigated the stretched-out incident, was that students were not so concerned about free speech as they were about the lack of interest shown in them by the faculty. One astute observer noted that students were protesting the utter loneliness of freedom from responsibility in an apathetic university environment.

From many quarters came the spectacular conclusion that Berkeley is America. But it is not. As a professor from Stanford University wryly observed, it is not even California. With an enrollment of nearly 30,000 students, representing the "elite" among the top 12 percent of California's high school graduates, Berkeley is atypical in size and selectivity. As a multiversity cell of 90,000 students in seven universities in California, it rises in striking contrast against the public and private colleges across the land, but it was and is a leader in American higher education. It would be followed.

Shortly after the Berkeley incidents, some students of its small prestigious neighbor to the South, Stanford University, became exorcised over issues of judicial procedures, women's social regulations, and something called academic freedom.[2] In October 1964, students at Trinity College,

---

[1]See: Michael V. Miller and Susan Gilmore (eds.), *Revolution at Berkeley* (New York: Dell Publishing Company, 1965). A concise account is related by James Cass, "What Happened at Berkeley," *Saturday Review,* XLVIII:3 (January 16, 1965), 47ff. (A year after the Berkeley eruption, the American Council on Education selected as the theme for its annual conference, "The Student." Ironically, the 10-15 percent of Berkeley students creating the incident have been studied far more than the 85 percent not actively associated with it.)

[2]See: Marvin B. Freedman, "Pressures on Students," paper presented to the Twentieth National Conference of the Association for Higher Education, Chicago, March 8, 1965.

in Hartford, Connecticut, marched to the state capitol to protest against prohibiting alcoholic beverages to those undergraduates under twenty-one years of age. Their chant was simply, "We want booze."[3] In violation of state law in Connecticut, their college should be a privileged society, they claimed, not subject to the usual legal statutes, the obligations and restrictions imposed upon their noncollege peers. The college community, of course, has long been a traditional sanctuary for draft deferment. Beyond this, on matters of illegal behavior, what is defined as a crime or misdemeanor among other young adults is often regarded as only a college prank on the "adolescent reservation." The Trinity students thus felt they merited an immunity from the laws that governed adolescents of lower estate.

The student protest movement was showing a new surge of power, and many students wanted to give it full rein. The civil rights techniques were put to use for many purposes, some clearly focused, some highly blurred. Some administrators, shaken out of their authoritarian lethargy, seemed to face the dilemma of distinguishing between those protests directed toward irresponsible anarchy and those that provided promising opportunities to enlarge responsible freedom. The grasp for student power would not assure a campus of tranquillity or a vibrant democratic college community. The students, however much they cherish freedom and symbols of maturity, whether free speech or cheap beer, wish to be cared about and even disciplined— not as children, but as young men and women. That is about the only point of national consensus among educators concerning the year of the student.

That seemed to be the element of universality within the Berkeley incident. Sarah Lawrence College, an experimental college devoted to the concept of student education through responsible freedom, provided a cue to it in a carefully documented case history covering a period of more than thirty years. Student government, initially a vital, exciting experience for students, eventually lost the freshness of its challenge. Many able students declined to accept nomination for leadership positions, preferring to spend more of their time with their studies and their friends.[4] They had, in one sense, achieved a student Utopia, and wanted someone else to keep it going. The faculty, meanwhile, had left the government to the students' devices. Students, with all their freedom, began to speak of the need for the continuing interest and guidance by the faculty. Sarah Lawrence was not a high rise multiversity, but a small woman's college in Bronxville, New York, with an enrollment in 1964-1965 of 599.

---

[3] *New York Times* (October 25, 1964).
[4] See: Harold Taylor, "Freedom and Authority on the Campus," in Nevitt Sanford (ed.), *College and Character* (New York: John Wiley and Sons, 1964), p. 209.

Protests in the Southern Manner [5]

The South is different. There is no Southern counterpart to Berkeley with reference to the combination of size and intellectual selectivity of its student body. Only three Southern universities have an enrollment half the size of Berkeley's university. There are other un-Berkeley factors operating in Southern higher education, too. To understand the "Year of the Student" in the South, two kinds of protests require separate identification. The first consists of protests in the interest of shared institutional goals; the second refers to protests against institutional policy and practice. [6] Both show, within the South, a high level of student-faculty solidarity, a concern for individuals, and a respect for duly constituted institutional authority.

The civil rights movement has had a great deal of appeal to many college students within the South. The chief organization for student action has been the Student Non-Violent Coordinating Committee (SNCC). Yet it has drawn its major support from Southern students at institutions where it has received official or unofficial institutional sanction. Boldness has appeared where courage has been sanctioned by authority. Thus Fisk University in Tennessee, Miles College in Alabama, and Greensboro A and T College in North Carolina have been actively associated with student demonstrations. In a Negro college in Louisiana, however, the president quickly quashed such efforts. In a predominantly white institution in Tennessee, the president called in three freedom riders, and explained how such behavior, with the best of motives, could embarrass their families and their alma mater. They "graciously" refrained from such "unseemly" conduct thereafter. Protests in the civil rights movements have been largely an expression of "conformity to the institutional culture," where the index of student-faculty solidarity has been high. Whether liberal students choose liberally oriented institutions, or whether such institutions "liberate" students may be only a circular question.

Student protests at the University of North Carolina in 1965 focused on an issue unrelated to the racial controversy. This was the so-called Communist speaker ban law growing out of Chapter 1207 of the North Carolina Acts of 1963. That provision prohibited state colleges and universities from permitting any person to use its facilities for speaking purposes who was known to be a member of the Communist party, or had been known to advocate the overthrow of the Constitution, or had pleaded

[5] The data upon which this analysis is based extend beyond the interviews with students and officials of colleges comprising the study. They include reports from a conference of the Southern University Student Government Association at Gatlinburg, in April 1965, and a conference of student leaders from four institutions in Nashville, Tennessee, on March 30, 1965, expressly convened for the purposes of this study.

[6] The civil rights movement, an example of the former, is described in a well-documented report by Pat Watters, *Encounter with the Future.* (Atlanta: Southern Regional Council, May 1965). The latter category is not publicly disclosed except in rare instances. It is generally kept out of the papers, "in the public interest."

the Fifth Amendment to avoid answering questions dealing with communism or Communist party activities. In the relatively liberal academic climate of the University of North Carolina, an organized student protest measured up to expectations of the faculty. More than a hundred faculty members indicated intentions of resigning unless the law was repealed or altered. The Southern Association of Colleges and Schools threatened the entire system of public higher education in the state with loss of regional accreditation unless such political interference in affairs of higher education was withdrawn. The protest of students was tacitly approved, but not officially sanctioned behavior. The legislators compromised.

Protests against institutional policy and practice, however, are apt to meet with a different fate. The "Free Campus Party" at the University of Tennessee, following the Berkeley incident by a few months, died a-borning. The self-appointed minority group, in April 1965, demanded abolition of dormitory closing hours for women, a student referendum on compulsory ROTC and repeal of a rule prohibiting coeds from visiting the apartments of male students. The group made some derogatory remarks, in passing, about the popular university president. After a strong adverse comment from a Knoxville newspaper, and a sharp rebuke from the president of the university, the party made efforts at conciliation, and went into political oblivion at a student election shortly thereafter.[7]

Months later, at Middle Tennessee State University, a student aggregation marched to the home of its president on a weekend, demanding an audience with the president over the right to attend a play declared "censored" by the university. The president sent a message to the demonstrators that he would discuss the issue with a small representative group in his office at 9:00 on Monday morning, but not before. They said, in effect, "O.K.," and promptly disbanded.

For each publicized protest, there are dozens of others in Southern colleges that are talked out or negotiated before they reach a climax. A threatened college demonstration among coeds for the right to sun-bathe on the flat dormitory roof was averted after an alleged architectural verification that the roof was not structurally sound enough to bear the weight of the bodies. Students in a small private university appealed, in vain, to university officials to reschedule the calendar to provide spring holidays. Having been refused the year before, they were making a survey of practices and student opinions to "convince the president and dean" of the validity of their position. If this did not prove successful, they would concede. The students felt the administration would at least listen to their views, and that they were reasonable adults. They would abide by administrative decisions after receiving a sympathetic hearing.

In conferences with student leaders throughout the South, the question has been repeatedly posed concerning their reluctance to protest publicly

[7]See: David Hall, "New Party Fades After Big Splash," *Nashville Tennesseean* (April 11, 1965), p. 10a.

the grievances of the students they represent. A high degree of similarity is evident among the responses. In a complimentary sense, the spirit of those responses has been caught by Nevitt Sanford, who regards the South as a place where "the human community is still very much alive and enormously important; people are accepted and valued unconditionally; the underachiever or ne'er-do-well is not rejected; family solidarity, friendship, fraternity, still matter a great deal—often more than success or status." [8]

Students explain that demonstrations generally short-circuit the established channels for resolving issues, that these private protests are generally placated or that a substantial explanation is furnished for not doing so. Their analyses of other protests, aside from civil rights, lead them to conclude that they either did not arise from worthy purposes or that they did not first explore established channels of communication and negotiation. There are other ways of "getting attention," they feel, which are more socially approved. There is also a respect for tradition and for established authority within the South. Students honor the view that a protest against a man or woman of integrity who has demonstrated interest in their welfare is the height of ingratitude, no matter how "old-fashioned" he may be. They would demonstrate only as a last resort, to which they are rarely pushed. They find ways around their problems without a direct encounter with authority. (If social dancing is not officially permitted by a church-related university, for example, they have unofficial dances in a downtown hotel with required [unofficial] chaperones.) There are, of course, also a number of paternalistic institutions where students would not give serious thought to challenging official authority. Reticence in some cases is due to the feeling of friendship and fraternity, but it is sometimes clearly due to fear.

The deepest concern among elected student leaders in the South is not the fear of excessive discontent about conditions as they are, nor the channels to be used or by-passed in getting problems identified and solved. The engulfing anxiety of student leaders in the South is rather the smothering apathy among students about problems and vital issues in college education and their unwillingness to confront and grapple with them. The view was repeatedly expounded at one interinstitutional conference of student leaders of Fisk, Vanderbilt, Tennessee A & I Universities, and Peabody College. The same sense of futility among student leaders was expressed at the 1965 Conference of Southern University Student Government Association. The elected leaders are worried about their followers and about their own leadership roles.

At a small private college somewhere, the student-body president, with some of his fellow officers and this author, deliberated into the late evening hours over these three questions:

[8] Sanford (ed.), *College a n d Character* (New York: John Wiley and Sons, 1964), p. 295.

1. How can we arouse the students' sustained interest in working at the problems of concern that students, faculty, and the administration have in common?

2. How can a responsible student voice make itself felt, where the president is a benevolent paternalist we do not wish to offend?

3. Shall we focus on a specific grievance and protest with that focus, winning the battle but losing the "war," or shall we instead take the slow and doubtful path of articulating the fundamental issue of establishing student participation in improving the college, so that petty grievances will not become distorted?

A demonstration was considered to dramatize the problem. But it never materialized.

Students do not protest their grievances due to fear, a sense of futility, or apathy. Some do, to good purpose and with good effect. The example set by many student groups, and the attentive reception accorded student views provides an example worthy of emulation. There are signs within the South of a growing awareness of responsible freedom on the part of students, and of an administrative willingness to "risk" student participation in significant college affairs. Public demonstrations against an institution, however, are not yet in the Southern manner, and are not soon likely to become so. They do not befit the folkways of Southern higher education on intrainstitutional differences of opinion.

COHESIVE FORCES IN THE COLLEGE CULTURE

Morale within a college can be measured, in substantial terms, by the forces that tend to hold its culture together in opposition to those that pull it apart. Cohesion need not mean uniformity of activities or outlook, of course, but may mean, instead, a respect for differences. Unity through uniformity creates a static condition, which may prove to be better—or worse—than social disorganization attending change. Unity in diversity reflects a condition of cohesion and can provide a leeway for progress— or for retrogression.

Within Southern higher education, a number of familiar forces affect the cohesion, the morale, and the homogeneity of a given college culture. Interscholastic athletics, with all of its pomp and circumstance, and with its attending social functions, provides a centrality to university and college spirit, or dis-spirit. The collegiate newspaper, as in the larger society, provides an organ of communication about events that matter to students. Fraternity and sorority life, with dances and other social events, provide some cohesion and some fragmentation of collegiate groups. Collegiate conversation, within social organizations and in small informal groups, unites the institution. The matter of "academics" becomes a dependable conversation piece, like the weather, during examination time or at low ebbs of conversation. College regulations, card games, parties, and questions of personal honor emerge for sustained deliberation or for hasty disposition. Politics, within student affairs, may rise or fall as a force for solidarity, depending on gripes and elections, in the student community. Yet each of these forces, along with many others, impinges on the institutional culture and helps to reveal some important aspects of Southern higher education.

Intercollegiate Athletics

The game is the thing among state universities, and it is not to be eclipsed by academic considerations. The senior and junior colleges follow suit. That is where higher education "comes alive." This fact is illustrated by a state board of control in higher education in the deep South, which schedules the dates and places for its fall meetings to coincide with the gridiron contests of greatest interest, assuring adjournment before kick-off time. The *Razorback*, the annual of the University of Arkansas, expressed the central fact dramatically:

> The first warm signs of spring began to appear on the campus: and then "Peace" arrived, a small, gray-haired lady with the words, "Walking 25,000 miles for World Peace" across her blue shirt, explained that she was walking until man learned the way of peace . . . not so unique, but of much more interest to the student body, were the cheerleader tryouts . . . and even less unique was the school by the Democratic Party on how to put on a political campaign. Like the debate between the Demo's and the GOP's, it fizzled.[9]

The able president of a Kentucky state college rushed to Nashville, Tennessee, for a conference on alleged violations of recruitment of college athletes in the Ohio Valley Conference. It was a top priority item for the top administrator . . . A Negro high school senior, a scholar and a basketball star, was being wooed in 1966 with offers by Vanderbilt University, the University of Kentucky, and other Southeastern Conference teams. Three years earlier, his being a Negro would have precluded such recruitment. Now it is a marked asset, and recruitment efforts by predominantly Negro institutions are stymied by this new competitive recruitment from white quarters. Thus, Perry Wallace, a Negro scholar and athlete, enrolled in 1966 at Vanderbilt to break the Southeastern Conference color line, along with another Negro student at the University of Kentucky . . . A Negro coach in Georgia expressed the problem this way: "I have a fair chance to recruit athletes against other Negro colleges, but when a leading coach of a predominantly white university bids against me, I'm sunk. Only if he is anxious about his academic background will a first rate Negro athlete listen to my recruitment sales pitch."

Large universities are often rated by the public as institutions of higher learning on their win-loss records in football. In 1964, an administrator at Florida State University (formerly Florida State College for Women) confided that Floridians would never regard that institution as a

[9]*Razorback*, 65 (Fayetteville: University of Arkansas, 1962).

real university until it defeated the University of Florida in football. The event transpired that fall. F.S.U. thus came of age.

Some smaller, private universities have entered into a pact agreeing not to offer athletic scholarships, thus subordinating athletics to academics. In other quarters the words of Grantland Rice about "how you played the game" fall on deaf ears. The operational slogan is that a good loser is a *loser*.

Athletics comprise an indispensable part of college life. They are the means of gaining or retaining institutional status. Athletics are also essential as an expression of allegiance to conformity. That is how manliness is expressed. Emory University has managed to get by on minor sports, but only because it has been compensated for by other factors, such as an exclusive medical school. But the game also has to be preserved because so much of the institution's life revolves around it. The cheerleaders, the dances and parties, the social calendars of fraternities and sororities, the homecomings, the spirit of convivial togetherness make up a cohesive ceremonial that will not release its hold on higher education. Nor should "the game" be separated from higher education. Collegiate sports have meant a great deal to education in the South. The Olympic sprints of Wilma Rudolph and others in the famed Tennessee A & I University track teams have signified much to the individuals involved, to the sense of significance of the university, and to the image of sportsmanship that transcends race or poverty or other artificial means of measuring a man's or woman's worth.

In state colleges and smaller institutions, sports tend to be viewed in a different perspective. The hand of athletics continues to distort some of their major purposes. "Logically" (i.e. from the academic viewpoint), the athletic and physical education program should be built around the physical and educational needs of college students. The difficulty arises when this "logical" thinking is distorted, making athletics and its attending ceremonies essential to the college culture. The issue becomes a standoff. One reaction leads to a "no scholarship" conclusion, taking the game back from the alumni and returning it to the students. The other view, once espoused by Norman Cousins, is for the universities to buy their own professional teams, and may the best, bought team win. Meanwhile, Southern colleges struggle unsuccessfully with the necessary, noneducative burden. Among 269 institutions of higher learning in the Southern Association of Colleges and Schools, only sixty-five reported that their income from intercollegiate athletics exceeded their expenditures, while 204 reported that such expenditures exceeded income.[10]

The problem of intercollegiate athletics was expressed succinctly and with feeling by a group of students in a small university that had not fared so well in the win-loss column. "Athletic scholarships go to second-rate

[10] See: Gustave E. Metz, *Current Fund Expenditures* (Atlanta: Commission on Colleges of the Southern Association of Colleges and Schools, 1964), p. 21.

athletes who cannot qualify for academic scholarships, draining off resources for serious, capable students. Then we lose most of our games.
We hurt our academic program and our university's reputation through the
competition when we come out the loser. Maybe, as a last resort, we
ought to try cooperating with other institutions on some things—so there
would be no losers." But competition is too deeply ingrained into the college culture for this view to gain widespread acceptance. If cooperation
cannot supplant competition, however, it might very well come to supplement it. Meanwhile, athletics are a cohesive force in the college culture,
especially winning teams and financial profits.

The Collegiate Newspaper

The college newspaper is designed to serve as the center of student
communications, but it may become a standing campus joke. In some
institutions, the student body feels that the editorial staff is either a
stool pigeon of the institution or devoid of original ideas. It is not always
a high-status activity. In other cases, the tendency is clearly to imitate
the sensational journalism of some of the less responsible daily news-
papers within the South. There are also, of course, distinguished examples that the faculty, students, and public relations officials properly
point to as models of responsible freedom in journalism. The Georgia
Institute of Technology and Auburn University provide such models of collegiate journalism, and of responsible freedom of the press.

The educational significance of the press as a barometer of student
interests, opinions, and political activities is often overlooked, both from
the standpoint of future journalists and of the responsibility of students to
make of their news media what they want it to be. Whether the college
press emulates the objectivity of the *New York Times* and its Southern
counterpart, the *Chattanooga Times,* or the vindictive, propaganda pattern of publishers who use the press for economic and political power,
is a decision within the domain of college education. But for the faculty,
the press may be only a thankless sponsorship chore, another extra duty,
perhaps because the paper has little newsworthy or mature editorial content. It is often a vehicle for venting student frustration or for giving
coverage to routine affairs, rather than being a rallying point for unifying
progress in the college community.

Fraternity Row

The same social force that can unify a collegiate society can, if mis-
directed, shatter it. No better case in point could be found than fraternities and sororities in Southern colleges and universities. Here is where
the student finds a primary group sharing interests and aspirations, where
"brothers" or "sisters" regard themselves as a closely knit social unit,
with a mature awareness of near equals in other groups. It is also where
a student can have her self-concept destroyed, if it has been built on a
fragile identification with the"Number One"sorority. In fraternities and

sororities, nobility and cruelty go hand in hand. It is understandable that this should be so. In search for superior recognition, one must be exalted and another debased. In search for belongingness, one must embrace his fellows' similar need. Thus, in competition may be witnessed ruthless strategems, in cooperation a deep compassion.

Fraternal orders serve many functions. They provide some immunity from college regulations. They provide some measure of academic insurance, usually in the form of libraries of former examinations and of other information, but sometimes a step short of blatant cheating. They enter into social service competition as in donating blood to the American Red Cross. Their interfraternity organizations sometimes build patterns of activity that bind the institutions together. With few exceptions, however, they are divorced from the academic community, except insofar as it is necessary to remain in good standing. If every student has his own group of fellow students, thirty or so, with whom he feels akin in spirit and sentiment, he has found "his college." This may be within or outside a fraternity or a sorority. Whether the institution's enrollment is 300 or 10,000 is of no great consequence. The fraternity, in the main, fills that need for community. Unless the student finds "his thirty," the college is simply a population aggregate. Such a condition is characteristic of much of dormitory life, where administrative concern over the enforcement of regulations exceeds the positive concern about developing a sense of community during off-hours.

In scanning the national scene, Nevitt Sanford observed that one useful way to work with fraternities is to focus efforts there to create academic communities. If he were to undertake an experiment, he indicated, to integrate "living and learning," he would as soon start with the fraternity as with any other group. [11] The fact is evident within the South that existing social organizations can be more readily turned in a new direction than they can be abolished or replaced. Where no variations of such organizations are in vogue, the institution can establish houses or societies with most of the advantages and fewer of the limitations of the traditional fraternal societies.

The Collegiate Conversation

A student can feel alone in a small college, or at home within a large university. The correlation of enrollment and anonymity does not show causality. Aloneness depends on whether a student has someone he can talk to, who will listen with feeling, someone he can turn to, in anxiety or exultation; whether the school provides the freedom to hold on to "himself" rather than exerts pressure to surrender himself at the altar of conformity; and whether there is connection with some "power figure" so that major injustices can be corrected.

[11] See: Sanford, *College and Character*, p. 295.

A coed at a state university was asked whether a student could elect *not* to drink alcoholic beverages, and still be acceptable to her peers. Her reply was, "Yes, if she doesn't happen to get in with a drinking crowd as a freshman. We have talked about it, and feel that it's a shame to value freedom and insist on drinking to be a part of the crowd, but that's usually the way it is."

Student conversation also deals with morality and with institutionalized religion. Whether the institution is private or public, its campus is ringed with denominational "houses." The Catholics have their Newman Clubs, the Presbyterians their Westminister Houses, the Methodists their Wesley Houses, and there are many others. There is also a so-called Religious Emphasis Week which stimulates "bull sessions" on matters of moral and religious values. With higher education, and the sophisticated discovery that someone's God is dead, the ideas concerning God and man get a light going over—not one of sustained depth.[12]

After the religious interlude, the talk reverts to dating, love, parties, courtship, and marriage—all combined in the magic word of sex. The publicized studies and pseudostudies on the subject of morality and sex relations are considered, and the discussion continues with conjectures and ambivalent feelings. With a strong sex drive and the awakening search for a life-long mate, calling for delayed gratification or for sublimation, the heart and mind have trouble seeing matters the same way. Talk continues in an unending search for answers to relevant questions of the moment or of eternity.

There is the continuing matter of civil rights. In one college, which has long championed human rights, an "out group" of students wanted to do something dramatic to unseat the elected student leaders. In this case, civil rights almost became a tool for manipulating people. However, the students were talked out of their demonstration. The debate over civil rights continues there and elsewhere, now in a desegregated context, but it is on a polite, shallow level in most institutions. And talk, even over time, will only bring people together to the extent that it is followed by listening.

Thoughtful talk is important. In one university, the Vietnam problem is being considered, along with draft cards, ROTC, preferential treatment, and social ideology. These issues have no assured place in the formal curriculum, and learning is by conversation based on public speeches and magazine articles for classes are over and the professors have gone home. College regulations and their alleged inanities also come in for a share of the conversation, but the discussions rarely move to the point of plans for action.

Whatever the topic, it largely relates to the major question of individual significance and purpose, of how college can be bent toward an expansion

[12] They may reject conventional dogma, but have little help in filling the new vacuum. See: Pierre Burton, *The Comfortable Pew* (Philadelphia: J. B. Lippincott Co. , 1965).

of personal worth and a clarification of human purpose. Near the end of the college career, the focus of discussion shifts to the problems of becoming freshmen again, this time to face life's demands in the larger society, of how to show courage safely,[13] of how to be a "conforming individualist," and of how to climb the economic and social ladder without being smug about those who must be climbed over in the process.

Collegiate conversation is the general education curriculum in action, and it is too bad that professors do not have a more active part in it. In the formal curriculum, there is an evident chance relationship between what students want to learn and what instructors feel constrained to teach. Yet, the formal curriculum and nonbookish learning are directed toward the same end of personal development and of social usefulness. Students do not want professors to intrude on their conversational privacy. They do not want them to be inquisitive, but they do want them to be interested in them and in the world they live in together—but apart.

Campus Politics

Politics may serve as a cohesive force in the college community or as an empty ceremonial gesture. The difference may generally be traced to the significance or insignificance of student leadership in the governance of college affairs. If student leaders enjoy a genuine partnership with the faculty and administration, student elections are of central importance. If students have their own isolated sphere of responsibility and autonomy, the significance of political activity is lessened, but still genuine. When student participation in government is known to be a sham, student elections become a popularity contest and a mockery of democracy.

In very few places is a sustained effort made for political candidates and their supporters to study the premises of politics, of courage and compromise, and of a public philosophy. Campus politics and the behavioral sciences have little in common. Thus it comes as no great surprise that elected leaders have no enthusiastic followers. They are usually not going anywhere anyway. Where are the models of team effort, where professors of social science help student leaders to achieve a collegiate social and political democracy?

DIVISIVE FORCES IN THE CULTURE

The most significant divisive force in Southern higher education is the blocked conversation. It is blocked in both overt and covert ways. In subtle or unintended fashion it is blocked when a student feels that the faculty views him principally as a naive student and only incidentally as a person. It is blocked when a student feels that he is looked upon as a stranger by virtue of the religious or ethnic group of which he is a part.

---

[13]As a theological student viewed it, "The only time you feel safe around here is after you graduate. Then you're gone and it doesn't matter." A short-sighted view, perhaps, but the degree is the pearl of great price, and students do not forget or jeopardize their chances for it.

In overt ways, division becomes apparent when students are relegated to the roles of little children, in a highly distorted patriarchal system of *in loco parentis;* of monologue instead of dialogue.

A college becomes separated from other colleges by its own resources, by its policy of selective admissions, or by its high rate of attrition. As it becomes a like-minded group, it loses the effect of intercultural contacts except as it can arrange for them in extramural activities with students from other colleges with dissimilar backgrounds, abilities, aspirations, and outlook. If the "have" colleges educate for smugness, and the "have not" colleges helplessly inculcate feelings of inferiority, a divisive force of major proportions is at work. "Pure" colleges fear contamination. Liberal ones abhor piety. That is the present case of segregation of values.

Mobility of student population is a further divisive force. Dropouts, dropins, and out-transfers, like water seeking its level, flow against a solidarity of institutional tradition. Nonresident students, whose interests take them away from the college community after classes, do not grow deep roots of college identity. The junior college faces a special problem, with at least a 50 percent turnover each year. Many students do not know who they are or where they are going, and the students who might tell them have just left. Some faculty members may still be on the scene, but many are leaving. Hearing the bell of the faculty market temple, they are off to the senior colleges and universities. The college culture is uprooted by a bewildering continuity—one of coming and going.

Caste and Class in Southern Colleges

The fact is common knowledge that some institutions are predominantly upper class; some are middle class, and others are lower-middle class from the standpoint of students' social class origins. There is a tremendous difference among institutions with reference to the social class systems and the attitudes taken about the customary status symbols of the "outside world." In one private college, a student leader commented: "We don't try to keep up with the Joneses. We are the Joneses." This was not an invidious comparison. In that institution, a student would be ostracized if he were ostentatious about wealth or social position. In a private university, students identified various student organizations with reference to their social rating. The wealthy fraternities and sororities came first, with academic honor groups running a close second. The third group was that of service organizations; the fourth, fraternity and sorority organizations consisting of a miscellaneous pattern of club joiners without active programs. Finally, there were the nonjoiners, who ranged from the top to the bottom of the social ladder, from the competent independents to the isolates. Within this pattern of "consciousness of kind," however, a number of crossovers occur, such as some well-to-do or brilliant students being active in service organizations. An unwritten code of behavior places on eac: group a responsibility to avoid a spirit of condescension. In another institution, where a variation of the Oxford-Cambridge residential college system is employed instead of fraternities, the assignments of students preclude a system of snobbery by group identification. Two incoming students may be assigned to the same house or college, for example, but they cannot specify the house of their preference.

David Riesman and Christopher Jencks view the college as "an initiation rite for separating the upper-middle from the lower-middle class, and for changing the semi-amorphous adolescent into a semi-identified adult."[14] This is true in general, which means that it is sometimes untrue in particular. Some Southern colleges are strictly upper and upper-middle class, to begin with. Other Southern colleges graduate students who, at best, could not lay claim even to middle-class designation. They can all say that they were elevated, however, by this rite of passage.

In personal terms, the Southern college culture does not deliberately ostracize the student who is poor. Generally, he is already in a quasi-ostracized institution. When he is not, wealthy students may not comprehend his poverty or why he cannot take full part in college life. He is not treated with disdain so much as he feels inadequate, that his background is apt to "show" and be noted in nonverbal communication.[15] Academically disadvantaged students who are intellectually capable are subjects of sympathy unless they become sources of academic competition. The Negro in the predominantly white college represents an anomaly both for himself and for his white classmates. It is not the temperament of the Southern culture for him to be a stranger long, despite his race. The gregarious white Southerner cannot ignore students around him, whatever their color. As soon as the definition of the situation is reasonably clarified, the ethnic factor is not apt to constitute a rigid caste relationship, but is likely to be one of a fluid class condition. Negroes will find their places all along the spectrum of social class in the college community in the changing South.

In predominantly Negro institutions the caste and class system seems to prevail, in general, more rigidly. The alienation of upper-class Negroes from those of the lower classes is a commonly observable phenomenon. The non-Southern white student looks for a prestigious Negro institution, if he elects to attend one at all. The white Southerner, except as a non-residential "day" student, is not apt to do so. If he does, his motives may be initially suspect because he is defecting from his own traditions. Why should he, Negroes ask, become one of them? Is it out of compassion, or a misguided missionary spirit, or is it prompted by a desire to be a

---

[14] Riesman and Jencks, "The Viability of the American College," in Sanford (ed.), *College and Character*, p. 39.

[15] With student aid programs, under the 1965 Higher Education Act so varied with respect to eligibility, students may no longer be ashamed to be "poor," but will establish their eligibility for benefits. The nonrecipients and nonapplicants may be the ones who have to explain their nonconformity.

white leader in a Negro context, or is he having trouble with grades? The class consciousness of the upward mobile Negro blurs the cues to the behavior of the white Southerner who has chosen to violate a clear cultural taboo—to an unsure end.

Within the divisive caste and class system of students in higher education, another factor, related to social acceptance, cannot quite be captured in words. The nuances of speech articulation and of mannerisms "mark a man." Dr. Sidney Spivack, of Princeton University, refers to them as the cultural poker chips. They are the tremendous trifles which anyone can learn with a little effort and timely tutoring. And, they are matters that socially mature individuals would tend to overlook. But the matter of diction only illustrates the principle. It is more than that. Poor articulation, with a plantation dialect, identifies a man or woman as different. Precise articulation, on the other hand, pricks sensitive ears as being ostentatious and fastidiously incorrect. Then too, reading habits fail to provide topics in common. *Mademoiselle* is not *Ebony*, and neither is *Look* nor the *Saturday Evening Post*. Bridge is not blackjack, and a fork is not a spoon. The disadvantaged student, in social terms, has to learn how to conform "naturally." Only then can he put some of his distinctive, even colorful rough edges back on again.

The quaintness of accent of a foreign student is regarded as having some special charm. A different quaintness among native whites or Negroes, however, places them in a stereotype against which the upper and middle class have a conditioned bias. An interesting phenomenon may, wishfully, be in prospect. As the socially disadvantaged student, with excellent or equal capacity, learns the cultural ropes of his more advantaged peers, those artificial class symbols may gradually lose their significance.[16] Such interclass experiences in Southern higher education today, unfortunately, are at a minimum. Due to the basic homogeneity of social class within each institution, and to sharply delimited student contacts among institutions, colleges are reinforcing rather than reducing social class distinctions of wealth and of position. Desegregation by race within the South is moving well along, by some standards. Desegregation by social class is only beginning.

RECOMMENDATIONS

There is no certain way to know what recommendations have sound possibilities for making the college culture one which is more concerned with its own political and social democracy, with excellence and equality, and with responsible action for improving the larger society. To that purpose, however, three postulates appear to be evident:

---

[16]As Robert Burns expressed it, "The rank is but the guinea's stamp,/The man's the gowd for a' that."

The Year of the Student

The first postulate stems from the protest movement among students in higher education. That general observation has been descriptively expressed by Vice-President Hubert Humphrey in a relevant societal context: "Self-government is not a luxury on which men may grow fat and indulgent. Rather it is an instrument by which men can, if they have the wisdom, safeguard their individual freedom in the pursuit of happiness . . . We must summon all of our talents for citizenship, for self-government, for public service . . ." This is a challenge for the college student, but not for him alone. It is a mandate for his professors, and for the array of administrators—up to the institution's chief administrator, where the "buck" stops. The year of the student must be regarded as the beginning of shared responsibility among students, faculty, and administrators, not simply as an adolescent interlude.

Cohesive Forces

The Southern college has a great deal "going for it." It is not as susceptible to the vagaries of capricious student action as are so many colleges in the non-South.[17] It is even patient with mediocrity and "unreal" education. Yet there comes a time when patience ceases to be a virtue. The demand is urgent in the South for a merging of the more formal dimensions of academic learning with the college culture where life is real and urgently earnest. There is an increasing necessity for making higher education relevant, in both its general and specialized dimensions. The curricular and extracurricular ghettos, the segregation of faculty from students, the "mental odor" of academia must be dealt with if the college is to become unified in purpose and in spirit.

Forces of Diversity

For a college to achieve a special reason for existence, its student body must be homogeneous with reference to the institution's unique purposes. Yet this quality of sameness can make it colorless by denying it a valuable intercultural diversity of communication and shared experience. The specialized or "single purpose liberal arts" college is much like the obsolescent single purpose teachers college, where students came only to know others of like background and plans. The teachers colleges become, in dozens of instances, sequestered teacherages; the isolated liberal arts colleges, bastions for medieval learning.

To accomplish both the ends of special function and of diversity of outlook, a major new effort toward intercultural, intercollegiate cooperation is required. Competition blocks communication. Cooperation cultivates it. Higher education, with all due deference to alumni, is not for them.

[17] The pressure of fragments of student bodies continues into 1966, with 400 of the University of Chicago's 8,000 students staging a sabotaging sit-in to protest the university's compliance with federal regulations in providing information to the draft boards.

They have had their opportunity for it. The chief concern of colleges should be the education of students. That concern leads us then to consider specific ways in which it can be given focus.

Cues for Action

1. The student council, or its equivalent, should be an increasingly responsible partner in collegiate affairs; it should be helped to "grow up" from representation in planning social functions and traffic court policy to representation on major faculty and administrative committees. *In strengthening the student council's position, the c o l l e g e administration should not give official attention to student grievances not properly channeled through such a body.*

2. Professors in the social science and humanities divisions should be charged with leadership responsibilities in developing with students a democratic academic community.

3. The faculty and administration should work continuously with student officials in cultivating school spirit, initiative, and taking action on matters, on campus and in the community, which are worthy of attention and action. The "unifying seminar" proposed in the preceding chapter should bring faculty members into the "orbit of interest" of students to provide stimulation and appropriate faculty-student action.

4. A "breakfast of the deans" (of academic and student life) should be held regularly as a means of integrating "life and learning." Some form of continuing conversation involving possible channels of action should be held centrally inviolate in this effort, taking precedence over trivial urgencies. Individual students, faculty members, and others should be invited to join the deans, guided by the interests of the moment and by long-range planning for the future.

5. Growing out of such deliberations, numerous extraclass contacts in art, music, drama, and in off-campus study, work, and play, in the local community and afar should be developed.

6. College concern about morality should demonstrate that the college is taking the long-range societal view rather than a short-range, regulatory morality dubbed "morality in our time." In faculty-student affairs, a continuing focus needs to be placed upon the relevance of the collegiate community for the larger American democracy.

7. Efforts at interinstitutional cooperation in metropolitan areas often overlook a crucial student dynamics ingredient. Rather than simply "permitting" student leadership groups to form intercollegiate councils, this should be encouraged as a high order of business. Interinstitutional cooperation properly begins and culminates in student activity, and administrative agreements of reciprocation that by-pass students' ideas, interests, and participation are apt to eventuate into an empty form of cooperation.

8. The fraternal concept needs to be strengthened in the collegiate culture. The dormitory, or a floor or a wing of it, does not provide this

natural sense of community. Many "communities of thirty" should be formed on the basis of factors of compatible diversity developed by students and faculty. Then, in large institutions, computers should make the selection of individuals, including faculty representation. Computers may be irrelevant for matchmaking, but in group formation, they should prove to have unusual merit.

Not until the students' real world combines with the academic imperatives of the classroom will higher education achieve its lofty objectives of general, liberal, and professional education. The issue is not one of the current concepts of the academic community vis-a-vis that of *in loco parentis*. The issue is one of how the institution may help students to achieve social maturity, personal integrity, and economic self-sufficiency; of how social control can be pointed away from symbols of status and conformity to matters of inner dignity and enriching diversity.

SELECTED REFERENCES

Keats, John. *T h e Sheepskin Psychosis*. Philadelphia: J. B. Lippincott Co. , 1964.

Miller, Michael V. , and Susan Gilmore (eds.). *Revolution a t Berkeley*. New York: Dell Publishing Company, 1965.

Morris, Peter. *The Experience of Higher Education*. London: Routledge and Kegan Paul, 1964.

Nicholls, William. *Southern Tradition and Regional Progress*. Chapel Hill: University of North Carolina Press, 1960.

Sanford, Nevitt (ed.). *T h e American College*. New York: John Wiley and Sons, Inc. , 1962.

———. *College a n d Character*. New York: John Wiley and Sons, Inc. , 1964.

Shoben, E. J. , Jr. *Students, Stress and the College Experience*. National Conference on Student Stress, Airlie House, Warrenton, Virginia. Washington, D. C. : United States National Student Association, 1966.

Watters, Pat. *Encounter with the Future*. Atlanta: Southern Regional Council, 1965.

7. THE PROFESSOR'S PREDICAMENTS

If the limelight in higher education is upon restive, protesting students, the searchlight is upon the American professor. National publicity attended the strike of professors at St. John's University in New York as strike-breaking professors were imported to keep that institution's operation moving. In California, three-fourths of all publicly employed professors declined to divulge their nonsalaried extra earnings in a query of the California Coordinating Council for Higher Education. Such sensitive questions might jeopardize prospects for salary hikes. Besides, they violate privacy. Professors in the South bestir themselves about civil rights, about the alleged death of God, and about the speaker ban law of North Carolina. The peculiar recurring themes about professors, however, are that they are overpaid fortune hunters who are insensitive to the instructional and personal needs of students, that they are crassly materialistic, guilty of subordinating professional ethics in their bids for fame and affluence; and in view of increasing college enrollments, America needs many thousands more of them.

Paul Goodman identified the professor as a part of a vicious system from which it is difficult to escape. In sweeping terms, he decried the "cash accounting mentality prevalent in administrators, professors, and the students themselves, the mania for credits and grades, the tight scheduling, the excessive load, the false economy of huge classes, the lack of contact between teacher and teacher, and teacher and student; the lust for rank, buildings and grounds, grants and endowments; the mobility for advancement and salary hikes; and the over-estimation of the 'tangible evidence' of publication. All this adds up to no educational community at all."[1]

This indictment carries a stain that smears the noble with the ignoble, in high and low stations of higher education. Nevertheless, numbers of dedicated individuals. including American professors, are earnestly seeking to identify and assume their responsibility within the total life and purpose of their college or university. They are not organized for

---

[1]"Dialectics in Academia," *Faculty Forum* (October 1965), unnumbered. [Nashville: P.O. Box 871.]

effective action, and they may be in the minority, but this study has uncovered a goodly share of them within the Southern regions. Of course,
the South, like all of America, harbors its malingerers as well.

THE SOUTHERN PROFESSOR

The professor in Southern higher education defies any stereotype. There
are no "typical" professors, but there are clusters of similar professors
engaged in like tasks. One such cluster, with its parallel in virtually
every Southern state, is employed in the four tax-supported, predominantly
Negro senior colleges in North Carolina. A questionnaire was conducted
from the total faculty population of 216 professors engaged in lower-division
instruction; 125 respondents participated in the faculty-data analysis. Of
this group, 22.4 percent held the doctorate. In the departments of mathematics, art, music, and in several others, none did. Their choice was
not to publish or perish, but to persevere or languish. They were assigned
work in the classroom, with the usual advisory and other collateral duties.
Over a five-year interval, three of these 125 faculty members participated
in the writing of a book. Fewer than 15 percent had written an article
for publication in an average year during that interval. Forty-eight percent
were gainfully employed at other occupations, including professional duties,
skilled trades, and sales and clerical positions. [2]

In contrast with this group of instructors of freshmen and sophomores,
350 other professors, at Vanderbilt University, in the fall of 1965, were
engaged in research activities with grants representing more than $8
million. [3] One of these professors privately reported himself to be "an
independent contractor with the university," bringing funds into the institution that added to its economic health as well as to his own. A good deal
of the Vanderbilt research effort is in the medical field, and it is designed
to have considerable impact on the improvement of physical health in this
nation and around the world. Who is to gainsay either research or teaching? The point is to value excellence in whatever worthy activities professors engage in, or in the specialized services they contract to perform.

A third faculty group illustrates yet another dimension of the Southern
professor's character. Deep in the Black Belt of Alabama, Tuskegee
Institute continues to look more to the future than to its estimable past.
Located where academic isolation would be so easy, its faculty are characterized by notable achievements in both research and teaching. Recognizing the handicaps of the mediocre previous schooling of many otherwise capable entering freshmen, the faculty have engaged in developing

---

[2] See: Philip D. Vairo, "Teacher Qualifications in Lower-Division Four-Year Colleges, "
The Negro Educational Review, XIV:3, 4 (July-October 1963), 127-131. These professors
have been kept out of the mainstream of much of academic life, and results of this accumulated isolation have a telling impact on the kind of teaching they are able and motivated to do.
They are victims of circumstances; their students, victims once removed.
[3] See: *Nashville Tennesseean* (February 13, 1966), p. 6-A.

effective prefreshman summer programs. Upper class students offer
tutorial assistance of a further remedial nature; a student-faculty partnership exists in the guiding of learning. An extensive exchange of teachers
and consultants has been arranged with the University of Michigan, and a
visit to the Tuskegee campus discloses a quickening tempo of intellectual
activity. This significant progress has been accomplished with the essential ingredients of financial support and of competent, dedicated faculty
service. [4]

This is a glimpse, in a few paragraphs, of the faculties of a half dozen
Southern institutions. There are more than six-hundred others—each
unique, but forming kindred clusters. The Southern professor, in whatever
institution he finds himself, quickly begins to conform to the expectations
of the faculty or of his own department in it. If research is highly regarded,
he works at it. If the faculty values good teaching, he busies himself with
an application to that. If consultation services or other travel-related
professional activities are highly esteemed, he moves into an airport-to-
airport existence. If he senses a nonprofessional apathy within the faculty,
he will accommodate himself to it or will move on to a less stagnating
intellectual climate. The professor becomes institutionalized, and clothes
himself with the values of his surroundings. Yet, wherever he is, or
wherever he moves, he is aware of a relationship between faculty salaries
and faculty status in the social system of which he is a part, whether it
be a worldly school of economics or an other worldly divinity school where
pastors "await the call. "

Salary Profiles and Social Status in the South

The Southern professor has long pitied himself for the lower salary
he receives in comparison with his colleagues in other regions. Yet the
current state-by-state variations of salary medians within the South (up
to $2, 500) are far greater than those between the Southeast ($8, 340) and
the nation as a whole ($9,081). [5] The Southern professor is no longer at
the sharp disadvantage of former years, and that financial gap is narrowing
further.

The professor in the smallest private Southern colleges, with enrollments of 500 or less, receives an average salary for the academic year
of less than $6,000, while in the largest such colleges, with enrollments
of more than 2, 500, his average salary is $7,438. The formal faculty
qualifications, of course, are commensurately higher in the larger institutions, and they have "first pickings" at the academic market. But there
are exceptions. The University of the South (Sewanee), and the much

[4] See: "Tuskegee Institute Annual Report of the President, 1964-65," *Bulletin of Tuskegee Institute*, LVIII:3 (December 1965), 10-11.

[5] See: William S. Graybeal (ed.), *Salaries in Higher Education, 1965-66* (Washington, D.C.: Research Division, National Education Association, 1966), p. 13.

larger Duke University, pay an average faculty salary exceeding $10,000,[6] having respective enrollments of 821 and 6,360.

TABLE 10

AVERAGE SALARIES OF PROFESSORS IN COLLEGES AND UNIVERSITIES OF NINE SOUTHERN STATES

State	Average Salary
Alabama	$7,324
Florida	7,834
Georgia	5,824
Louisiana	7,452
Mississippi	6,126
North Carolina	8,283
South Carolina	7,647
Tennessee	7,116
Texas	7,200

Source: *American Association of University Professors Bulletin*, 51 (June 1965). Averages are medians.

Professors in the nonpublic junior colleges in the Southeast fare the poorest of all. Four-fifths of them (783) receive salaries of less than $6,000; 150 others are within a salary range of $6,000 to $7,500. Only ten receive more than $7,500; and no professor receives more than $8,500.[7]

The salary profile is a rough indicator of the peaks and valleys of qualifications as well as of prestige. And it lays bare a number of the professor's several predicaments. Where salaries are lowest, the teaching and service loads are typically the heaviest, frequently to the level of oppression. According to a previously cited investigation by Earl McGrath, the salaries of professors in nonpublic Negro colleges in the South are notoriously low and are accompanied by demanding teacher loads. The annual turnover rates amount to only 3 to 7 percent in the stronger institutions, but up to 15 to 25 percent in the weaker colleges.[8]

[6]See: E. F. Schietinger, *Fact Book on Higher Education* (Atlanta: Southern Regional Education Board, 1965), p. 47. (Quoted from *American Association of University Professors Bulletin* [Summer 1964].)

[7]See: Graybeal, p. 47.

[8]McGrath, *Predominantly Negro Colleges and Universities in Transition* (New York: Bureau of Publications, Teachers College, Columbia University, 1965), p. 114.

Unsystematic investigation shows similar conditions among predominantly white institutions as well.

The Southern professor has fewer of the conventional worries than he had before. He has little cause to be concerned about tenure if his formal qualifications are adequate, unless he becomes embroiled in controversial issues that might embarrass the institution. (Even having moderate ability may involve administrators in a tug of war over him.) He knows the rules for advancement within the profession, including Rule One, which is to go along with the institution's system. This is a venerable tradition, a part of the Southern way of life in higher education. The American Association of University Professors and the United Federation of College Teachers do not flourish in the South. The Southern faculty is submissive to the enforceable administrative "don'ts," although it may not be so responsive to the unenforceable administrative "do's."

The Epidemic Predicaments

The Southern professor shares some major frustrations with his colleagues across the nation. These predicaments are so spread across the pages of professional literature that they require no elaborate footnoting here. Suffice it to note that their pronounced presence has been observed throughout the South, and confirmed vicariously beyond it.

The professor's first predicament involves the necessary monetary sacrifice involved in full-time, first-rate undergraduate teaching. A professor whose personal value system would permit him to forego the prestige associated with research or graduate instruction is also required to endure low financial ceilings and heavy teaching loads. If salary alone could be held constant, a number of competent professors might be induced to give more time and effort to college teaching, even in the lower collegiate divisions. This would, of course, cause the status of the activity to rise promptly.

In public institutions, salary schedules throughout the South provide a built-in pattern of low-cost and low-grade instruction on the lower division levels in the form of scaled state budgets for faculty salaries. In many of the top-ranking private universities with top-level faculty salaries, the salary level is achieved in large part by assigning instructional duties to graduate assistants. In some instances, the qualifications of teaching instructors in colleges of doubtful standing is equal to that of actual (graduate student) instructors in leading universities with many prestigious faculty members but few instructing professors except in the graduate schools and upper divisions of the various colleges.

The professor who prefers to teach may agree to take his chances on matters of reputation within the profession. To ask then that he and his family make a financial sacrifice is to stretch the limits of ethical obligation. The administration extols the virtues of good teaching, but gives little sustained financial attention to its improvement. The professor's predicament therefore is that he must endure criticisms for not teaching and advising with students, or of placing students first in his priority system and permitting his success within the profession, by conventional standards, to be placed in a subordinate position, including a salary penalty prospect.

The second predicament confronting the professor is that his doctoral program did not lay any serious claim to preparing him to become a competent teacher. He knows of his initial ignorance about good teaching, but he must presume to be a scholar in pedagogy because his Ph.D. attests to that in higher education. Whatever the reasons for it, two things have customarily happened to the graduate student en route to the doctorate. First of all, he has lived within a value pattern where the instruction of undergraduates is looked upon with condescension, if not with disdain, and where the science and art of teaching on all levels have been given only casual attention. Secondly, whatever direct experience he has had in college teaching has been haphazard, and he has sandwiched it into his more vital tasks: the hurdles of foreign languages, preliminary examinations, and the investigation of esoteric dissertation problems in a zealous effort to make a "contribution to knowledge," one rarely of deep interest even to his own doctoral committee.

He has internalized a number of dogmas about teaching effectiveness, although he may have also learned along the way some useful principles of teaching from both positive and negative examples. He has accepted the dogma that class size is more critical to teaching effectiveness than the quality of the teaching-learning relationship, despite research evidence to the contrary.[9] He gives unquestioning credence to the superiority of one "general method" of teaching over all others, although no one method has been demonstrated to produce more or better learning than another.[10] He rejects, in operational terms, the hypothesis that the important thing in learning is that the student should "inquire into" rather than "be instructed in" a subject matter.[11]

With his research-oriented degree, the new professor, ironically, is not functionally literate in the crucial area of research about the nature and conditions of learning, and the reasoned implications of that body of research for his own teaching responsibilities. He may defensively scoff at the mundane practicalities of such research. He is frequently untaught about the rudiments of teaching, and is "above" making a determined effort to overcome his deficiencies.[12]

[9]See: Winslow Hatch and Ann Bennett, "Effectiveness in Teaching," *New Dimension in Higher Education,* No. 2 (Washington, D.C.: U.S. Office of Education, 1964), pp.3-9.

[10]*Ibid.*, p. 10.

[11]*Ibid.*, p. 15.

[12]These observations refer to the holder of the earned doctorate. The final year of the doctoral program, by common consent, is alien to the tasks of improved college teaching.

The third predicament is the conflict the professor finds between his impatience with the task of achieving the purported goals of higher education in the social order, and the inertia of traditional resistance to educational change. He feels his faculty to be suspicious of innovations unless they are introduced through federal or private foundation grants. His predicament is that of losing his professional vitality in becoming institutionalized. He may add his own favorite course to the program offerings, and the specialty of his predecessor may be discontinued, but he must not question the arrangement of the substantive aspects of the program offerings except on a small-talk level, and then he must not be too persistent.

The predicament is compounded with increased enrollments and the imbalance of faculty supply and demand. The professor becomes frustrated with innovations and proposed innovations, both the panaceas and those proposals with reasonable prospect of success. Even proposals designed to promote the faculty's economic interests as well as educational quality, such as the ill-fated Ruml plan,[13] are frowned upon because they make threatening assumptions about traditional academic dogma. The professor cannot exercise initiative for basic change without being disloyal to his colleagues. Above all, he must not forget that whatever share of the total curriculum is allotted to his department, it is not enough.

The individual professor finds himself within a kind of cult, and cannot unbind himself from its sanctions and taboos. One critical description of the "average professor" claims that he believes education to be for the intellectual aristocracy, "an arcane rite which ought to be conducted by (and largely for the benefit of) its own Sanhedrin, without interference from the peasantry."[14] Mr. John Fischer, editor of *Harper's Magazine,* writes in like vein of the professor's stereotyped attitude: "However liberal a professor may be on the political or social issues, when it comes to his own professorial environment, he is almost invariably as conservative as Charles I—believing, indeed, in the Divine Right of the Professoriat to do as it damn well pleases, with a minimum of accountability to anyone, whether president, parent, taxpayer, or student."[15]

The Southern professor faces these criticisms along with his colleagues all over America. He is confronted with the choice of trying to become a first-rate instructor, or of achieving success within the profession by its conventional standards. He is not prepared for effective teaching, but he must act as if competent instruction is a natural concomitant of graduate degrees. He must champion academic freedom, but he must not question the conservative tradition of content or of methodology in college teaching. If he is to become successful, he must pledge allegiance

[13] See: Beardslee Ruml, *Memo to a College Trustee* (New York: McGraw-Hill Book Company, Inc., 1959).

[14] T. R. McConnell and Paul Heist, "Do Students Make the College?," *College and University,* 35:4 (Summer 1959), 443.

[15] Fischer, "Is there a Teacher on the Faculty?," *Harper's,* 230:1377 (February 1965), 18.

to ritualistic instruction. He must believe that good teaching can take place whether learning does or does not occur in the process. In the name of higher standards, he may reveal a conviction that learning is in inverse relation to teaching—that the best professor holds the highest standards and records the lowest grades. He must champion academic freedom, but must not exercise it in a nonconforming manner. The sooner he accepts these things, the sooner he will achieve a peace of mind in higher education, and be comfortably assimilated into his esteemed culture.

The Endemic Predicaments

In addition to the professor's nationally shared predicaments, the Southern professor faces a few that are largely his own. The professor is culture-bound by his ethnic ancestry. Whatever his behavior, it imputes special meaning as that of a white man or white woman, or a colored man or colored woman. Professors are largely recruited on the basis of race. By weight of habit, and by formalized recruitment procedures, a pool of available candidates for a position is generally segregated. To recruit a Negro professor for a predominantly white institution involves searching for a competent Negro. It does not mean a regularized consideration of Negro candidates along with white candidates, leading to a selection of the best available candidate.

Similarly, a white professor must not be "offended" by being tendered an invitation to teach in a predominantly Negro college. His attitudes about race must first be discretely ascertained. While many institutions have a "policy" of faculty recruitment without reference to race, none has yet fully achieved a desegregated condition without a deliberate will to accomplish that purpose. There is no routinized mechanism for the Southern professor to be considered for positions he is competent to fill without regard to race. He is either sought on the basis of race—for purposes of segregation or of desegregation—or his consideration is rejected on account of race. Nor can he, without misunderstood motives, make known his own availability without regard to race. There is no established provision for him to do so.

The second special predicament of the Southern professor relates to instruction in a recently desegregated institution. How can he, with his own ethnic predilections, be certain that he is working with students with no regard to race? How can he be sure that he should? If his standards are uniform, he is not providing for individual learning needs. If he bends his special efforts to establish security among disadvantaged minority groups, he may be, or may appear to be, prejudiced in a reverse sense. How does he work toward establishing an academic community as a "color blind" professor? The answer is not simple. He wishes to respect the residual prejudices of those colleagues who came by their biases honestly as acculturated Southerners. The glib solutions and cliches do not get at the fundamental dilemma.

The professor, among the most ethnically liberal groups in higher education, has been unable to channel his liberality in constructive, creative fashion. What he has championed, in *d e facto* terms, has become achieved or possible of achievement. The white professor, with folded hands and puzzled mind, communes about the new freedoms with colleagues of a different race at desegregated professional meetings. The Negro professor, with deep ambivalence, says "Yes, isn't it great." But there is no exclamation point at the end of his sentence.

The Southern professor is one step removed from the poverty predicament of the institution and of his own students. Yet he cannot escape the burden that poverty imposes upon the fulfillment of his academic role. If he works in an impoverished institution, he recognizes that economic interests must perforce take precedence over important educational considerations. In the long run, the budget has to balance for the institution to continue to serve the cause of higher education. The professor is handicapped in obtaining materials and facilities to enable him to perform at peak effectiveness. Within the "developing institution," he sees limited opportunities for his own advancement and he begins to look for escapes to institutions less handicapped by economic stress. But he also sees the quality of education declining about him and feels badly about leaving an institution where his services are sorely needed. In another sense, he may be attracted outside the region, where his services will be better rewarded but may also be less crucial in terms of societal needs. As he studies collegiate dropout problems, he comes to understand that many able students, particularly those in predominantly Negro institutions, are leaving college as a result of economic pressures or due to short-sighted economic inducements. If he is employed in one of the weaker colleges, he is a part of the mutual despair of poor institutions attempting to assist poor students.

The Southern professor is pleased to learn of the support to developing institutions and of the various forms of student assistance promised by the Higher Education Act of 1965. These developments are complicated, however, by a chain of events related to proposal writing and of establishing need within an institution. He is not schooled in the art of grantsmanship. The funding provisions are further compounded by the lack of selectivity of poor students without reference to their educational promise. The professor notes, also, that these provisions do not come immediately to his personal aid in increased salary or reduced loads.

The Southern professor in the more affluent institutions experiences the predicaments of poverty in vicarious ways. He knows that many capable students are not admitted to his institution for economic reasons. They do not bother to apply. But even for those there, he senses the economic problems of keeping up with the Joneses, within both the faculty and the student body. The student of moderate means may face embarrassment within an affluent circle of acquaintances. Perhaps the professor faces most acutely a student attitude of sophistication about the reason poor people are poor. The students of inherited economic wealth look about them and conclude that poverty is a direct result of ignorance, or of laziness, or both. Their attitudes about the poor may develop into contempt rather than compassion and the constructive exercise of social responsibility. The Southern professor is either relatively indifferent to poverty problems of others, or his concern about them leads to frustration. With colleges cluttered up with students, how can the capable poor be "handled" also? He is troubled about the poor, but he is fully occupied with the problems of the financially secure.

The problem of ethnic differences is slowly being resolved within the South. The prospects for alleviating the problems of poverty are brighter than ever. But, integrally related with race and economic circumstance is the attending handicap of mediocre schooling through the elementary and secondary school years. Here the Southern professor faces his most trying bewilderment. He knows there are thousands of college-capable students who can never hope to succeed without some special encouragement and competent remedial instruction. Yet the status symbols of his social system in higher education place a strong taboo against working with academically substandard students. The professor loses face enough by committing himself to instructing students in standard freshman and sophomore courses. For him to stoop beneath this level of indignity and guide the learning of students who have no legitimate claim upon his services is presumptuous indeed.

Meanwhile, with the growing clamor for education beyond high school, the problem of making adequate provision for the educationally disadvantaged Southerner continues to mount. The relative supply of competent instructors is diminishing. The Southern region lags behind the rest of the nation in providing adequate faculty staffing, which makes imperative a concentrated attention to the recruitment, training, and retraining of able young people for college teaching.[16] Meanwhile, as the volume of disadvantaged pupils continues to increase, the South has a disproportionately large share of poorly schooled youth wanting to get on the magic carpet of higher education. If opportunity for higher education is to be provided in some form for all who seek it, discrepencies between conventional admissions levels and the achievement levels of entering freshmen in institutions of open or low selectivity will continue to expand. T. R. McConnell and Paul Heist pointed out the South's historic plight as early as 1959: "The mean ACT [American College Test] scores of freshmen in the Protestant and liberal arts college of the north central region varied from 94 to 123 . . . the variation in means in the northeast of the same type was from 111 to 131. In the South, excluding Negro colleges, it was

[16]See: Winfred Godwin, foreword in N. Z. Mendalia, *On Becoming a College Teacher, A Review of Three Variables*, Monograph No. 6 (Atlanta: Southern Regional Education Board, 1963), p. iii.

from 68 to 123. "[17] In succeeding years, conditions appear to have deteriorated. Only the more highly selective institutions have shown evidence of improvement.

Unless the Southern professor has had special preparation or appropriate secondary school teaching experience, he cannot deal successfully with the acute and chronic problems of the educationally disadvantaged. He can only live with them, or move away from them. The "typical" college professor simply cannot fathom the problem. In the "Upward Bound" and "Second Chance" projects, and in similarly funded efforts, some professors are conscientiously and commendably learning how to cope and aid. Often, however, a professor or college administrator reports a pending approval of a project for "Upward Bound" or "Second Chance" educational programs. Then comes the query, "Where do we find staffing?"

The normative pattern of collegiate professors has been to blame the educational ills of their students on the secondary schools. The high school teachers, prepared for their tasks in colleges, have earned a share of this guilt; but to blame others about the past is not to take corrective action in the present. The problem of developing basic study skills, of teaching reading speed and comprehension, the elementary principles of mathematics, the fundamental concepts of the social sciences, the substance and methodology of general science, and the communication skills involved in oral and written English are matters beyond the competence of most college professors. These disadvantaged students do not know enough yet for typical professors to teach them.

In past years, the professor might have been inclined to give attention to the needs of these students, because students were once in such short supply. With the classrooms now being filled by students who can pay or easily borrow their way, and who have reasonably adequate background, there is little genuine inducement for professors to make provision for the talented but educationally disadvantaged. The Southern professor recognizes the predicament, but cannot burden himself with this additional tribulation, a thankless task accorded low esteem, unless a grant is attached. In sum, then, the Southern professor's predicaments related to race, to poverty, and to educational disadvantage will not go away. He, himself, is caught in the inexorable struggle of status symbols and aspirations.[18] He is mobile, however, and can move out of their visible presence. Wherever he moves, he can perform valuable professional services to society, which will be materially rewarded and gain him the plaudits of his peers. Yet he is troubled as he sees himself in company

[17]McConnell and Heist, "Do Students Make the College?," *College and University*, 35:4 (Summer 1959), 443.

[18]In one Southern institution, the faculty protested having to use the same parking stickers as those used by the staff, although they shared a reserved parking lot. They were "better" than the staff, the faculty believed, and insisted that their parking stickers should make the point clear. The administration reluctantly conceded the point.

with those other highly regarded citizens who passed by on the other side of the Jericho road.   The white professor privately decries the way in which Negro professors have smugly alienated themselves from lower class Negroes in their upward and lateral mobility into the historically white world.   Then he looks at himself, and sees that the Negro professor is too much like his white counterpart.   Then, he looks away.

RECOMMENDATIONS

Is it necessary to point out that each professor who "professes" to instruct should work toward excellence in that endeavor; that he should value his own activities or remove himself from them? Should academic scholars be reminded that a continuing intellectual stretching for self-improvement is as characteristic of the profession in instruction as it is in any research endeavor? Should exhortation be explicit to the effect that innovations in curriculum and instruction should be studied in the educational interest when that fact is so implicit in the nature of the profession? Yet resistance continues to stymie unsubsidized efforts at progress; subsidized innovation, however capricious and transitory, tends to get a go signal. Should we need, in short, to remind ourselves that higher education is not established for professors, but only requires the services of professors in the public interest? Fortunately, for many professors these imperatives are obvious and guide their professional lives.[19] There are large numbers of individuals, a potentially dynamic, submerged minority, who see the broader vistas of higher education, who personally feel the predicaments described in the preceding pages.   But Southern professors require substantial encouragement and assistance from many who are outside the faculty ranks. With that encouragement and assured support, a creative minority of faculty members within the South can emerge in active response to these predicaments.   They must know, however, that they are a part of a sustained effort to deal with chronic problems of Southern higher education, not simply invited, on a transitory basis, to administer seasonal palliatives. If professors are "job hoppers," the migratory workers of higher education, it is because there is a lack of permanence in the commitment of supporting organizations for their services, especially in the areas of singularly Southern predicaments.   Nevertheless, professors with conviction and a sense of commitment to these problems are not helpless without funding support.

The Professor's Search for Identity

1. The professor, like the student, faces the continuing question of personal identity.   His self-concept may cause him to drift along accepting the artificial status symbols in a social system where individuals are rated by wealth, or skin-pigment, by early educational advantage, or by earned

---

[19]No institution was visited in connection with this study without discovering professors dedicated to professional service. The disheartening fact was in their isolation, or their lack of concerted effort.

graduate degrees or faculty rank or seniority, or by parking stickers. He may, on the other hand, place a value on individuals based on their evident desire to become personally and socially significant. In real life, of course, these forces continue to battle. This recommendation is that the professor continue to engage in that battle, and ally himself with professors of like spirit on his campus.

2. This second kind of self-concept leads to "unbecoming" behavior, that is, professional service beneath one's station. It mandates a commitment to teach on lower collegiate levels as well as higher ones, to instruct students who require instruction as well as those who could do almost as well without it. Academic status derives from less teaching, not more. Professional behavior must insist on achieving the avowed institutional goals, including an allegiance to first-rate teaching. Collectively, the professors are obligated to protest financial discrimination on the basis of the students taught; they must insist that salary be based on the qualifications of the instructor rather than the academic or intellectual level of the students.

3. The professor should volunteer for a fair share of student advisees, appropriate to his field. In the interest of students, however, he must adamantly refuse to accept an oppressive load that will preclude the student-professor relationships inherent in such an assignment. (Some junior-ranking professors are assigned scores of advisees.) Unless he volunteers to have some part in the nonacademic affairs of student life, he severs a bond with students that sharply curtails his potential for effectiveness.

Academic Preparation of the Faculty

4. Professors in graduate schools have shirked too long their inescapable obligation to develop teaching competence among the students who expect to perform instructional duties. The concept of a two-year graduate program, with its foci on scholarship and pedagogy, should be implemented in several public and private universities. Such a program might properly be completed on a terminal basis or in direct route to the doctorate, with the final year of the doctoral program consisting of intensive research activity. Multi-institutional programs, insuring observation and instructor internships in institutions differing in ethnic, intellectual, and social-class composition, would be especially desirable.

A category of teacher education, embracing senior high school and junior college levels, needs to be inaugurated in a number of institutions, especially in the general education areas. In addition to the needs of regularly educated youth in senior high schools and junior colleges, such instructors should become uniquely competent in working with educationally disadvantaged youth.

Professional Growth of the Faculty

5. The conventional notion of professional growth has deteriorated into routine expectations. Leaves of absence for study and research, attendance at professional meetings and the like have their points, but they are not always good ones. They sometimes provide occasions for professors to speak at each other when they neither have a great deal to say, nor an inclination to listen. The concept of leaves of absence should be extended beyond research for a semester of creative teaching—of instructing under optimal conditions with reduced load and with student assistance. Such leaves should also provide for short-term exchanges of duties for a quarter, trimester, or longer in other institutions—a "quick dunking," as it were, in another institutional culture.

Faculty Holding Power

The starts and stops of professional progress are attributable in part to increasing faculty mobility. Of comparable academic turbulence, however, is the corresponding attitude of the sheer likelihood of moving. An instructor may remain in an institution for several years without becoming rooted in institutional purposes because he feels he may be moving at almost any time. Academic tenure is coming to be less of a problem while faculty desertion of the institution, "taking up with another college," creates a problem of holding power.

6. Salary contracts for new faculty, or for those on term appointments, should provide an incentive bonus at the end of four years of service, accruing annually, but not payable until contract fulfillment. The amount of such bonus is a debatable item, but probably should be in the range of 40 percent of the average annual salary over the quadrennium. In this way, a stability and upgrading of faculty commitment to institutional planning could be encouraged.

CONCLUSION

In viewing the plight and the promise of Southern professors, the fact is apparent that they read the cues for advancement well. They understand the ritual behavior of very influential people who say one thing and mean another, the people who determine their rank, their salary, and their faculty load. Many professors, however mixed their motives, seek the inner satisfaction of rendering significant service to society in their chosen academic specialties through teaching, research, consultation, and writing. If the cues are favorable, they will move their energies into coming to grips with problems of race, poverty, and of cultural disadvantage. Many would prepare themselves for temporary or extended service were it not for the risk and financial sacrifice imposed by such commitments. Provision for financial advancement must be made within job specialties, rather than up and out of them. There must be a bringing together of genuinely concerned professors with financial resources to support their efforts in these educational tasks. It must have been for such responsibilities as these that college and university presidents were invented.

SELECTED REFERENCES

Albright, A. D., and John E. Barrows. *Preparing College Teachers. A Project Report.* Lexington: The University of Kentucky and the Southern Regional Education Board, 1960.

Baskin, Samuel (ed.). *Higher Education: Some Newer Developments.* New York: McGraw-Hill Book Company, 1965.

Brown, James W. *College Teaching, Perspective and Guidelines.* New York: McGraw-Hill Book Company, 1963.

Fischer, John. "Is there a Teacher on the Faculty?," *Harper's,* 230:1377 (February 1965).

McGrath, Earl J. *Memo to a College Faculty Member.* New York: Institute of Higher Education, Bureau of Publications, Teachers College, Columbia University, 1961.

Mendalia, N. Z. *On Becoming a College Teacher, A Review of Three Variables.* Research Monograph No. 6. Atlanta: Southern Regional Education Board, 1963.

8. THE PRESIDENT'S CHALLENGES

To praise or to indict presidents of institutions of higher learning *en masse* constitutes an obvious fallacy, but an all too common one. William and Mary College, founded in 1693, was a pioneer institution within the South. Under the forceful leadership of its president, James Madison, it enlarged and modernized its curriculum in 1779. The old rigidity of program prescription gave way to a degree of student option in electing some courses and ignoring others. Bishop Madison was wont to speak of heaven not as a kingdom, but as one great republic with no distinction of rank, where all men would be free and equal.[1] There were other strong presidents of vision in those days. Jasper Adams is reported to have raised the College of Charleston "out of the rut."[2] President Jonathan Maxey of South Carolina secured the foundation of a chair of chemistry in 1811, and procured physical apparatus for demonstration teaching. He arranged courses in French—radical that he was—for those who did not wish to take Greek or Latin, a tradition-shattering feat. President Horace Holley was largely responsible for lifting the University of Transylvania in Kentucky to the first rank of western colleges.[3] These presidents were among the creative minority of administrators whose common character was that of concern for the present and orientation for the future. They were concerned about excellence, equality, and societal relevance in higher education.

There were other presidents of strong will whose views were oriented to the status quo. Signs of change at the University of Georgia were largely due to the efforts of Professor Joseph LeConte and other faculty members, protested by their president. In 1859, they effected the decision to discontinue the freshman and sophomore classes because of the university's central projected mission of specialization in schools of medicine, law, engineering, and agriculture. President Church promptly tendered his resignation. Before this educational innovation could be implemented, as history would have it, the Civil War erupted and the entire plan was

---

[1]See: George P. Schmidt, *The Old Time College President* (New York: Columbia University Press, 1930). pp. 156, 168.

[2]*Ibid.*, p. 162.

[3]*Ibid.*, p. 163.

abandoned.[4] More than a century later, Florida Atlantic University is giving the idea another try.

But the strong presidents in the South, whether advocates of change or opponents of it, were not all in yesteryear.[5] A number of them are at work in the Southern region today, administrators of resolute will who have managed, by paternalistic or by democratic means, to effect change or to resist it against heavy pressures, rather than drift in moving waters or simply float unmoving in the still backwaters of Southern higher education. Presidents of colleges and universities are not an aggregation of weak-willed individuals who follow the lines of least resistance. The courage and vision of at least a considerable minority among them, their prudence in strategy and tactics, are often far more circumspect than meet the public eye. If presidents have a collective weakness, it is in their ineffectual attempts to work collectively, perhaps their lack of zest for it, or their preoccupation with the presses of their own isolated duties.

Nor is it accurate to assume that the strong presidents are in the great colleges and universities, and that the weak ones are in the institutions that struggle without high reputation or financial strength. Strong presidents are at work in every category of Southern institutions of higher learning, along with their weaker counterparts. The "group fallacy" classification of presidents is complicated by the fact that every president has his personal profile of courage and weakness, of wisdom and imprudence. Some, weakened by personal ambition or by insensitivity to the associates with whom they work, employ questionable means in the interest of presumably worthy ends and manage to scale their way to exalted positions in the higher education establishment. Others, like the statesmen described in J. F. Kennedy's *Profiles in Courage,* make hard decisions that run counter to consensus.

There is a way out of the morass of problems in Southern higher education, and only the presidents of institutions of higher learning can lead that exodus. In doing so, they will require a different kind of moral and financial support from their constituent bodies. They will require a more dedicated level of professional commitment from their faculty and administrative personnel. Perhaps most difficult of all, they will find multi-institutional cooperation no longer optional, but educationally mandatory. Most especially they will need to cooperate, in order to deal effectively with the problems of ethnic differences, financial problems, and the special requirements of educationally disadvantaged youth.

---

[4] *Ibid.*

[5] A "strong" president may be characterized by strength of character or by sheer stubbornness. The line separating these differences is often thin. Our use of the term strong refers to its more positive connotation of strength of integrity in the public interest.

THE SELECTION AND PREPARATION OF SOUTHERN PRESIDENTS

The qualifications of college and university presidents, and procedures for their selection, have been subjects of widespread attention. A recent study in this area, conducted by authorization of the American Council on Education, delineated the typical ways in which college presidents are currently chosen.[6] The national picture is not encouraging. In the South, many choices have not followed the logic of determining criteria with reference to the central mission of the institution, nor have procedures been followed which were always calculated to select the best qualified prospect for a position. It is important to acknowledge that within the South, both written and unwritten requirements enter into the selection of the college president. Some relate to race, religion, sex, and temperaments of adjustment rather than of promising leadership in innovation.

In ethnic terms, the South has undergone a transformation. In the predominantly white institution, the Southern white male Anglo-Saxon Protestant is typically an odds-on favorite. Yet no institution, unless it be church-connected, would specify this set of qualifications in its written criteria. Furthermore, among the candidates whose qualifications are considered without reference to these, a person holding other valid qualifications would more than likely be Southern Protestant as well. Thus, while criteria have genuinely become more liberal, the net effect is not correspondingly apparent.[7]

The history of the predominantly Negro college presents a different picture. Until the recent past, presidents of Negro colleges have customarily been white. In an effort to develop and recognize the leadership potential of Negro educators, however, the trend became pronounced toward electing Negro presidents to predominantly Negro institutions of higher learning. With so few other opportunities for leadership open, it is now almost unthinkable for a historically Negro institution to search for a president without reference to race. The college presidency is the last position in higher education likely to become desegregated.

Not only are presidents sought in terms of race, but they may also be sought for their weakness as well as for their strength. Some must be weak in the sense that they concur with the consensus about the outlook of their governing boards on controversial issues. They must be strong, however, in pursuing relentlessly the objectives they have been implicitly instructed to accept. In the case of a university system, which searches for numbers of presidents each biennium, there is an understandable quest for stability and an attempt to recruit able presidents who will work well within the higher education harness. In church-related and other nonpublic

---

[6] Frederick deW. Bolman, *How College Presidents Are Chosen* (Washington, D.C.: American Council on Education, 1965).

[7] In one private college's search for a president, the religious affiliations of prospects have been considered virtually irrelevant.

institutions, an increasing emphasis is placed upon the fund-raising potential of the presidential prospect, a potential threatened by the innovative president.

The fact is heartening, however, that when presidents come to assume that office, within the South, they tend to work with zeal in achieving success for the institution as well as for themselves. This appears to be less true in the case of fully secure presidents who have become authoritarian personal institutions themselves, who view themselves as patriarchs of their institutions. Some know they will not advance any further in the status system of educational administration, but know that they are not threatened where they are. They can relax and hold dominion over their limited higher education estate. In such instances, a variation of Gresham's theorem is manifest. Poor presidents, whatever the institution, tend to repel good professors. Yet, in the South, there is a residual faculty expectation of paternalistic leadership from their presidents. Despite some encouraging exceptions, the Southern college is "run by its president." Professors are left free to conduct their private (classroom) affairs, and major decisions of the college are made with only perfunctory recognition of professors' stake in the decisions and their judgment about them. In turn, the professor is free to rule his students in academic affairs.

The preparation of the Southern college president reflects an important difficulty in higher learning. President Emeritus Goodrich C. White, of Emory University, relates the story of a conversation concerning a professional program designed for prospective administrators. A young college president engaged in the discussion remarked, "But if that kind of thing had been required, I never would have been president." The quick reply was, "No, Bob, but you would have been prepared." [8]

The new college or university president faces difficulties in trying to raise the level of his qualifications. The pressures of time, and choices of how to use it, constitute a great deterrent to further learning. The immediate pressures upon the president, and his inability to extricate himself from such crucial urgencies as ceremonial appearances, early convince him of his indispensability. Some successful efforts, perhaps most notably at the Harvard Business School, have been made to provide advanced training for college administrators after their selection for their new post but before they assume it. As far as the South is concerned, however, there are many lessons in college administration that the Harvard Business School is not prepared to teach. One of them deals with the educational dimension of the enterprise in relation to business efficiency

[8] White, *The Education of the Administrator* (Nashville: Board of Education, The Methodist Church, 1957), p. 10.

in Southern culture. Another deals with the cultural realities of the Southern regions themselves.[9]

ROLE CONFLICTS OF THE PRESIDENCY

Presidents of institutions of higher learning vary considerably in the jobs they face and in the ways they face them. The fact that presidential salaries range, across the nation, from about $5,000 to more than $50,000 per year emphasizes the diversity in their formal qualifications and circumstances.[10] Despite these marked differences, fundamental similarities appear in the nature of problems they encounter. Administrators and professors of educational administration have been criticized for their value systems and their ways of working. Lloyd T. Williams, for example, recently criticized them for aligning themselves with the holders of status and power. He believes they are unduly inclined to conservatism except where innovation is financially attractive and nonthreatening to the community power groups. He called attention to their neglect in giving direction to social change, as in recent situations relating to desegregation.[11] He believes they have failed to set examples of "unflinching dedication to freedom, accompanied by willingness to take political action consonant with desired needs"; and further believes them to be unduly concerned with "things" rather than with giving effective release to human talents through "imaginative enlightened human relations."[12]

Criticisms of value systems come easy. They neglect, however, to take into account a number of inescapable realities, in particular, those attending the office of the presidency. President John Oswald, of the University of Kentucky, has provided a convincing picture of the various pressures on heads of such institutions.[13] While recognizing the ease with which school leaders can mistake process for purpose, he explains the numerous inescapable roles, including the ceremonial functions that cannot easily be delegated, of the symbolic head of an institution. The

---

[9]See: Raymond F. Howes (ed.), *Toward Better Preparation of College and University Administrators* (Washington, D.C.: Association for Higher Education, 1964), pp. 2-4. Longer-range programs at the University of Michigan and elsewhere are well known. Efforts to prepare junior college administrators have also been undertaken at two Southern universities, in Texas and Florida. The University of Kentucky has done a bit. Nowhere in the South, however, is any university addressing itself effectively to the crucial, expanding task of presidential development.

[10]See: William Graybeal, *Salaries Paid and Salary Practices in Universities, Colleges, and Junior Colleges, 1965-66* (Washington, D.C.: Research Division, National Education Association, March 1966).

[11]Such a position appears to be based on the premise that administrators solidly believed in desegregation. That premise, of course, is false.

[12]See: Robert E. Ohn and William G. Monahan, *Educational Administration, Philosophy in Action* (Norman: College of Education, University of Oklahoma, in cooperation with the University Council for Educational Administration, 1965), pp. 35-36.

[13]Oswald, "Pressures on Heads of Institutions," *Current Issues in Higher Education*, Proceedings of the Twentieth Annual National Conference on Higher Education (Washington, D.C.: Association for Higher Education, 1965), pp. 159-162.

president, he agrees, is more likely to accommodate himself to a range of differences than to instigate innovations that may run counter to the power groups associated with the institution. In the first place, the risky innovator is not generally sought for the presidency. In the second place, the "idea men" are not likely to feel comfortable or to remain for long in the chafing restrictions imposed by institutional compromise. This issue at least introduces us to the role conflicts of the college presidency, where everyone seeks a strong president who espouses his causes and accepts his value system.

Business v. Educational Priorities

The central role conflict of the college president is that of the educational function of the institution in relationship to its business function and its fiscal strength. In optimum circumstances, of course, each strengthens the other, but that is not always the genuine situation. The conflict takes many forms, some of which are often misunderstood outside the administrative circle, and sometimes within it. For example, the previously discussed conflict between an emphasis on instruction and one on research is often a direct consequence of the financial pressures or incentives of the institution, luring it into research activities and away from instructional functions. The president may get the brunt of the criticisms though he and his faculty are simply joint victims of financial circumstances.[14]

Within the South, the financial situation is rapidly improving in public higher education. There the growth in financial investment has been almost incredible. During the period 1963-1965, the investment in public colleges and universities in the South was raised from approximately $600 million to more than $830 million.[15] The financial condition varies widely, however, both with reference to the level of educational offerings and to the size of enrollments in public and nonpublic institutions. Within the states represented by the Southern Association of Colleges and Schools, the presidents of junior colleges expended only $683 per student, while on the senior college level, the figure was $1,030. Within institutions offering the doctor's degree, the expenditure per student was $2,200. While more than a thousand dollars per student was spent by institutions offering only the baccalaureate degree, only $930 was spent in those institutions that also offered the master's degree but not the doctorate.[16]

---

[14]This creates the unofficial dual-salary system, that of the "grant" professor as opposed to the college-funded professor, which also creates a subtle schism in faculty morale and commitment.

[15]Based on legislative reports of the Southern Regional Education Board as quoted in "Southern Colleges Do Better," *Southern Council on Teacher Education Bulletin*, 111:2 (November 1965).

[16]See: Gustave E. Metz, *Current Fund Expenditures* (Atlanta: Southern Association of Colleges and Schools, 1964), p. 11. Some institutions would have been better advised to give that year to a prefreshman level rather than a postbaccalaureate one.

Presidents of small nonpublic colleges face the greatest dilemma. The expenditure per student in institutions with an enrollment of less than 500 is approximately $760, while the comparable expenditures in institutions enrolling more than 2,500 students is reported to be $915.[17] The president of the poor college is forced to decisions that test his wisdom and try his character. With the best of motives, he may find that inferior programs of teacher education, for example, are the only forms of higher education that promise fiscal solvency. Among the stronger institutions, presidents face so many pressures for excellence that similar role conflicts appear in different dress. No president is immune from the conflict of loyalty between financial and educational interests.

The Present v. the Future

The second role conflict of the college president is related to the first. It involves the choices between the exigencies of the moment and those of the long-range needs of the institution. There is a striking parallel here between the person and the institution. Psychologists have referred to the characteristic of culturally deprived citizens as being unable to "delay their impulse for gratification," who thus settle for short-term gains. The history of these deprived individuals, however, shows that they have learned that long-range planning is unrealistic. Too many barriers are in their way on the long journey. The succession of disappointments and the disillusioning shocks have taught them that long-range planning does not result in a reward, and a series of cold realities in their experiences have taught them to be cynical about a distant Utopia. Today is all that is real.

In a similar way, the "developing institutions" have learned that it is unsafe to count on a steady flow of support from uncertain sources. Repeated disappointments in their efforts give them less reason to be sanguine about long-range planning than the more heavily endowed institutions or the state-supported colleges and universities. While presidents of some institutions can count with confidence on continuing or expanding financial support, others face grim prospects. The nonpublic institution of limited financial means has increased difficulty in getting "into orbit" in performing services for higher education. The president has to do the best he can for the time being, hoping that, as he moves into a more promising and tolerable administrative role, he can leave his institution a little better than he found it.[18]

---

[17]*Ibid.*, p. 22. If public institutions were removed from this total, the contrast would be even greater.

[18]A highly publicized and useful document on long-range planning was prepared by Sidney G. Tickton, *Letter to a College President on the Need for Long Range Planning* (New York: Fund for the Advancement of Education, 1963). But the financially harassed president is less interested in pie in the sky than in bread on the table.

Personal Ambition v. Professional Service

One of the more difficult conflicts of the college president is that within himself, between his desire to rank high in the profession and to be of maximum service to it. Status symbols of success are all too clear. The most highly regarded president holds dominion over the largest or the most selective institutions, and receives a salary commensurate with his recognition. In achieving professional distinction therefore, the president is tempted to subordinate educational considerations to his own career advancement.[19] The president can only attempt to resolve this conflict, of course, by examining each educational and financial end with reference to the specific means by which he seeks to accomplish it. For him there is no general ends-means issue. It is painfully specific.

CONFRONTING SPECIAL PROBLEMS

Within the South, the college president has for many years directly felt the impact on higher education of problems associated with race, with poverty, and with educational disadvantage. Now, national attention is being focused on these problems. The critic of the Southern presidency can find good cause to censure his leadership for failing to accept the responsibility of facing these problems constructively and with dedication. The apologist for the president, however, can give some cogent arguments in his defense. The president's hands have been too full of other problems to undertake these with the attention they merit. But the problem remains, and it is no longer about the past. It is about the present and the future.

The Ethnic Issues

The greatest single area of difficult decisions within the past two decades has pertained to desegregation. The president's first dilemma has often been the disagreement between his private opinion and his public position on the rightness or wrongness of desegregation and its concomitant effects. He has needed to temporize or reconcile his views with regard to gradualism. He has been troubled concerning his public responsibility to effect social change or to work within the forces of social change in an obedient educational role.

Fund raising functions have caught the president in a moral squeeze. He has been forced to be for segregation and against it; for gradualism and for exercising strong initiative. The white president in some instances has honestly sacrificed his personal convictions in what he regards as the larger interest of institutional stability and solidarity. For some Southern presidents, this ambivalent role has been too easy; for others, it has been exceedingly difficult. The Negro college president has faced similar

---

[19] The rapidly growing Burger Chef system has established an "exclusive new club" to honor franchise holders who have sold a million or more hamburgers. This club is symbolic of higher education, where volume of business is privately regarded as the highest good.

problems. In the interests of protecting his institution, he has found it expedient, on occasion, to "go along with" stalling tactics in the direction of desegregation. Other Negro presidents have seen their own institutional development threatened by the progress of desegregation itself. They have thus needed to support the cause of desegregation publicly while working exceedingly slowly to implement steps to accomplish it. Others have been under steady pressure to applaud segregation as being mutually preferred.

Although the public issue of desegregation has been legally resolved, the educational and extralegal dilemmas remain to confront the presidents of Southern institutions of higher learning in the emerging postdesegregation era. The succeeding chapter of this study will deal in fuller terms with this subject. At present, we can point out that the college president is weary from the travail of the struggle, but finds that at last the resolution of subsequent ethnic issues rests squarely on his shoulders and won't "shuck off."

The Issues of Poverty

Whatever the economic circumstance of his institution, the president faces a number of economic issues. He has his battle with the budget, and he has to do some short-range and long-range speculation on decisions governed by economic considerations. In the more financially secure institutions, the problem of rising expectations in all spheres of the institution's activities continue to perplex him. If his college is in dire financial circumstances, he faces a decision of stretching out poverty or of insisting on sound educational programs as long as the money or credit lasts. As one amiable president facetiously remarked, "If this college has to go the poor house, I intend that it shall go there in style."

Sidney Tickton's proposed long-range economic planning for colleges and universities was footnoted earlier, and there is a great deal of merit in his proposition.[20] But as one college president observed, long-range planning is much like a developing sales program. Regardless of the care and thoroughness exercised in promotional work, or how steadfast the efforts to implement it, no type of planning is effective unless you make the sales. Until the recent provisions of the Higher Education Act of 1965, the outlook of many nonpublic colleges was melancholy. It is still true that in many institutions a kind of bargain basement educational program is necessitated by the limited funds available.

The presidents also sense a fragile quality associated with various forms of federal and private funding. The loan provisions of the National Defense Education Act, for example, were not originally incorporated into the congressional budget of 1966-1967. In one small institution, this meant that three hundred students, then borrowing an estimated quarter of a million dollars within an academic year, would need to turn elsewhere for financial support or drop out of college. To expect an institution with

[20]Tickton, *Letter to a College President.*

limited funds to undertake long-range planning and program expansion with special reference to the academically talented student with financially limited means is patently unrealistic, however worthy. The assured financial support is not precisely where the poor students are, and college presidents continue to struggle with the long-range character of this problem.

The Untouchable Problem—Educational Disadvantage

Because of the cultural character that favors the advantaged and penalizes the disadvantaged in status terms, what self-respecting institution would deliberately seek out educationally disadvantaged students? Some institutions, with selective potential, make an effort to sprinkle in a few such students to provide cultural diversity and a token commitment to the solution of society's problem. In the main, the college president who accepts such students in large numbers is in the poorest position to make provision for their educational needs. With the recent support of the Office of Economic Opportunity, and private funding organizations, college presidents have made sporadic headway in dealing with this problem. Here again, though, the presidents sense a short-lived commitment. The problem of assisting capable, educationally disadvantaged youth is not something that can simply be treated as a collateral duty of instructors whose main commitment lies elsewhere. To accomplish this task in effective fashion, some college presidents must declare themselves as being committed to exert a major effort in behalf of this category of students. They raise the honest question, however, to "make a special effort with what resources and with what personnel?"

The Endemic Problem Cluster

These problems generally do not come to the campus as separate entities. Where any one of these three problems appears, at least one or two others will be likely to accompany it. Thus the cluster of issues combines to bewilder the president who lays serious claim to confronting and coping with any one of these special problems. In the academically selective institutions, which have not had much direct experience with financial hardship, the president is exempt from the stark responsibility of facing this problem. Yet as an educational leader who senses a shared responsibility for directing social change and for coming to grips with the basic social issues of our time, he is also wondering about the proper responsibility of his institution in its broad social context. Within the flux of social change in recent years, a few presidents, in their separate ways, have furthered the cause of higher education with special reference to one or more of these special Southern problems.

SOME ACHIEVEMENTS OF SOUTHERN COLLEGE PRESIDENTS

The South has its strong presidents now as truly as it did in the past. They do not tower over their peers as some did in yesteryear, but many have their moments of greatness or show the steady strength of leadership that spurs their institutions to respond to new challenges. Sometimes this is shown by a stance of personal courage in the face of considerable odds, and of prudence in reducing these odds. At times their strength is apparent from the fortitude to persist at discouraging, lowly honored tasks in the slow climb toward educational adequacy. Less perceptible, but sometimes more substantial, the strength of presidential leadership can be found in the action of deans, professors, and students whose creative potential is released and energized by supportive presidential action.

Faculty Development

Every college and university president, directly and through administrative subordinates, is on the continuous lookout for prospective capable professors and administrative personnel. While his success in marshalling and retaining a qualified faculty is of great consequence for his institution, if that is all he does, the net gain for higher education is negligible. If those professors are not contributing to one institution, they will be to another. Only as presidents and their deans work capably at the professional improvement of their faculty, away from the reciprocal competitive bidding and raiding practices and the hackneyed practices of encouraging advanced formal graduate work and perfunctory faculty research activities, will they be contributing to the crucial teaching function in higher education.

A number of Southern presidents have made a point of working at the stimulation and improvement of their own faculties, as revealed in a recent regional investigation. This study of faculty development procedures in small colleges points to a number of significant efforts, including some in which presidents and their deans have taken strong initiative, both without the benefits of incentive grants and with them.[21] Yet here again, the president who leads his faculty in an authentic long-range set of faculty development activities is in a small uncoordinated minority.

The Racial Sector

In the present investigation, a score or more of examples of presidential achievement and courage in connection with desegregation could be cited. We shall refer to a few. The president of one predominantly white university, himself a segregationist, interceded with his governor to gain permission to admit one or more Negro students, reasoning that the ultimate resolution of the issue was certain and that it would be far better to select students who sought an education rather than to permit the NAACP to pick their own candidates in an atmosphere of tension and potential

---

[21] See: W. Starr Miller and Kenneth M. Wilson, *Faculty Development Procedures in Small Colleges / A Southern Survey*, Southern Regional Education Board Research Monograph No. 5 (Atlanta: Southern Regional Education Board, 1963), especially chap. VII, "Reflections and Impressions," and appendixes in which the procedures of eight selected colleges are described.

violence. The governor held fast. Subsequent events proved the president to be right. The governor's "stand" at another state university was ineffectual. Despite his private convictions, the president sought to assure every right and courtesy to Negro students who were afterwards admitted. He was eminently successful in doing so.

A Negro presidential candidate was interviewed for a position in a college where the search was evidently for a "safe" Negro who would not become involved in issues of civil rights, who would stick to the "educational matters" of the college. With tact, but without equivocation, the prospect made clear that he could do no less than encourage the support of the laws of the land; while he had no personal intention of crusading, he could not ask his students to refrain from abiding by the dictates of their conscience within the law and college regulations. He was not offered the position. This may not, of course, have been the decisive factor.

The president of a predominantly white university put his own position "on the line" in a bold step to permit full desegregation in every aspect of collegiate enrollment and functions. Despite some resignations from the Board of Trustees, he held fast, and virtually no difficulties were encountered.

The president of a state university worked toward conciliating diverse power groups, and eventually left the university to assume another presidency where he knew he would encounter ethnic issues in a church-connected setting. He left behind a legacy of administrative integrity that won for his successor some decisive battles in the contest for educational opportunity.

Each of the presidents of four of the most outstanding private universities of the South (Duke, Emory, Tulane, and Vanderbilt) arranged to admit approximately ten Negro freshmen each year under Rockefeller Foundation scholarships. This added dignity to the concept of desegregation on the highest social rungs of the South's educational ladder.

There are examples of weakness, of deception, and of cowardice within the Southern presidency, as well as those of courage and vision. The above examples and others like them attest to the fact that valor and prudence among presidents of Southern colleges and universities is not relegated to the past. And throughout this epoch, no case has been discovered of a president losing his position because of a forthright public stance. Whatever known errors in judgment have been made, they have all been on the side of timidity, not temerity.

The Plight of the Poor

The president of any institution of higher learning is governed in dealing with problems of students' financial stress by the economic strength of the institution. Rice University can continue to provide its students with a strong academic program, and can assure any admitted student that he will be helped through financial difficulties by a liberal scholarship system. Some other financially secure institutions virtually assure this same condition. Living in an economically affluent institutional culture, however, places subtle financial stress on students who cannot participate regularly in fraternity, sorority, and other extracurricular activities of importance. Some presidents have worked, with good effect, to offset this economic pressure as well. Berea College, in Kentucky, and Berry College, in Georgia, are not among the more heavily endowed institutions, but they manage to provide substantial self-help for students through college-connected employment. The president of one small institution has students report directly to him if the financial aid system of the college is insufficient. He has thus far been successful, without exception, in preventing any worthy and industrious student from needing to interrupt his college career for financial reasons.

The other side of the poverty picture is the more pathetic one. In an effort to bring college education within the financial reach of the poor student, numerous short cuts and sacrifices are necessary in the calibre and diversity of the educational opportunities afforded them. Presidents have worked vigorously at faculty development, and some have achieved a good deal with the problem of getting maximum educational mileage out of the college dollar; of husbanding institutional resources in a way that does not exploit the faculty, that helps them toward greater qualitative productivity. But many have been ineffectual against these heavy odds.

Educational Disadvantaged Students

Assisting the educationally disadvantaged student who has sufficient aptitude for continued learning has not been a respectable activity in the upper social echelons of higher education. Even now, there is evidence of a kind of opportunism, a sudden burst of subsidized compassion for students in this category. But even when such efforts were inglorious, a number of presidents were working assiduously at that task against overwhelming obstacles.

The president of one predominantly white junior college has provided a systematized year of intensive college preparatory work for high school graduates prior to their admission into junior college standing. The president of a predominantly Negro university faced a new statewide selective admissions policy, based on test scores, to be uniformly applied to all public institutions. His initial effort was to oppose such action in view of its failure to make due allowance for the disadvantaged backgrounds of many otherwise college-capable students. Unsuccessful in that effort, he achieved an unofficial exemption for his institution and others facing similarly massive problems. His next major problem, of course, is to confront students with their own deficiencies and to find ways to help them overcome them rather than simply to receive an inferior baccalaureate degree.

Some presidents have been responsible for sustained efforts and measured success in this effort. In Tennessee, for example, both Knox

College and East Tennessee State University have accomplished a good deal with limited resources. The Wood Junior College, in Mathiston, Mississippi, on a personalized rather than a systematized basis, has enjoyed more than moderate success.

The president of a comprehensive public junior college provides opportunities for high school or remedial work. Academic, technical, and vocational education are available. The junior college is fully integrated, and makes educational success, with guidance, possible for virtually every high school graduate willing to stick with his learning task. The art of achieving the possible finds a model here. Without the vision and persistance of its president—and adequate public financing—the goal could never have been achieved.

In each of these three special problem dimensions, a few presidents stand out as being personally committed to improving the opportunities of the college-capable youth who are ethnically, economically, or educationally disadvantaged. With limited faculty and financial resources, their effectiveness has been limited, and there has been no great coordination of regional effort, even among the dedicated presidents themselves. The case has been, regrettably, to each his own.

PRESIDENTIAL VIEWS OF SOUTHERN PROBLEMS

Sooner or later, presidents get around to acting on what they believe in. As F.H. Allport once expressed it, a man's attitude is what he does. To gain an insight into the views of college presidents about higher education problems associated with race, poverty, and educational and cultural disadvantage, a combination of interviews and opinionnaires were used, representing a total of more than eighty presidents of Southern colleges and universities extending beyond those identified in this study. Some responses to specific questions are reported below, although not all of the responses were obtained in direct response to questions in the precise wording here indicated.

What of the Negro? Query Number One

"The higher education of the Negro Southerner is of concern both to the presidents of predominantly Negro and predominantly white institutions. If Negro Student A attends a predominantly Negro college, he wants to be sure that this decision will not jeopardize his best future interests as an economically secure citizen. If he attends a desegregated institution as a member of an ethnic minority, he seeks the assurance of acceptance, understanding, and adequate counseling. What should be done for him or her, and who should do it?"

> *President Able.* A survey of Southern colleges and universities would be helpful to determine operational attitudes about on-campus minority groups. Such a report should be distributed to every college and senior high school in the South.

President Baker. The answer is difficult, because we have not yet had any full-time Negro students. We expect to have some soon. I hope they will receive full acceptance in the community, but I cannot be certain this will happen. Our authority and influence do not extend beyond the campus.

President Charlie. If the Negro chooses to attend a predominantly white college, he must condition himself to the pressures and discomforts of the small segment of the college community which will seek to ostracize him. It is important for him to remember that not all white students receive acceptance, understanding, and individual counsel either. Yet the responsibility falls on the administration and student leadership to extend the concept of acceptance by as many students and faculty as possible.

President Domino. The image that Negro colleges are inferior ought to be challenged more than it is; and those Negro colleges which are inferior ought to do something about it. The Southern Association of Colleges and Schools should help by setting and assuring compliance with at least minimum standards in accordance with policy.

President Edgar. If a student, white or Negro, is enrolled in an institution consisting predominantly of another race, and thinks he will be fully accepted into all segments of the institution's society, he is completely unrealistic, seeking what is untrue in any segment of this nation's social order. He has to overcome—as an individual—the invisible barriers imposed by custom on all minority groups around the nation.

President Fox. I believe that if the Negro student has it in him he will make it in spite of the disadvantage of any college. . . . Our [white] students and faculty have to struggle to withstand the temptation to provide compensatory factors.

President George. At this [white] institution, I believe the student would be accorded what he sought: acceptance, understanding, and counsel as an individual.

President Harvard. The all-Negro college has been and is performing a vital function in the South. The more personally or academically anxious Negro student would feel more comfortable and secure here. The point is for a student to find a college that takes him where he is and helps him onward and upward. Some Negro students are able to "have their cake and eat it too," by doing graduate work and professional work at substantially desegregated universities.

President John. The basic need is to exert a universal effort to educate the general public to the worth of *the* individual. Every college, including our own, can and should make positive contributions to this effort.

In summary. The Negro should not get "over his head" in academic pressures or overwhelming social circumstances. On the one hand, there is the need for more Negro pioneering effort to change the long accumulated and distorted stereotypes of the Negro. Conversely, there is the need for a socially secure setting in which one's academic and personal life will strengthen a positive self-concept. The predominantly Negro college is uniquely fitted to serve this function. It would help, too, if Negro colleges could achieve at least token desegregation among both students and faculty in an increasingly desegregated, open society.

What of Financially Limited Means? Query Number Two

"Student B, white or Negro, wishes to attend college. He is clearly capable of academic success in your institution, but is of financially limited means. The plain truth is, he's 'busted.' What can or will you do for him?"

President Andrew. We will either accept him, and help him get through, or explain to him that we're sorry but we can't. It's about as simple as that. It seems to me unfair to encourage a student with offers of partial aid which are obviously inadequate.

President Bill. Such a student should receive our first consideration. We should discontinue giving lures of token aid to the students not in financial need, and athletic scholarships to the nonscholars. If the college is to be an academic community, financial assistance to the academically able should come first. The idea, however, is hard to sell.

President Charles. Financial aid in abundance is available to the needy from church groups, federal grants, and loans, and direct institutional funds. Cooperation between alert high school counselors and college admissions officers should resolve any difficulties. It is no longer a major problem.

President Daniel. I believe students should earn some money to attend college, no matter how bright and financially needy. It is one thing to be needy; another to be deserving. A student should have at least a nest egg of $50 or so before entering. This, with the combination of subsequent government loans and part-time employment, should help him along.

President Easy. I have never known a student who really wanted to go through college who wasn't somehow able to find the necessary money.

President Friday. A student with such financial limitations should be expected to assume a heavy burden of debt for his college education. This is a capital investment and his increased earning power should make repayment a proper part of a long-range career plan. In addition, it might prevent students' taking college education quite so lightly.

President Gemini. The establishment of community colleges gets at the heart of this problem. The commuter college makes higher education practically free. Its extension, coupled with other developments, should provide access to higher education for every academically capable student.

President Hiway. In our college, the National Methodist Scholarship is often the wonderful vehicle we use to help get such a student started in college, or the boost he needs at some other financially critical period during his college days.

President Jackson. If impoverished white students would keep asking; if high school counselors would keep pushing and helping them search; if colleges would utilize all available resources for providing such assistance, press for additional funds—and lend a sympathetic ear—then the economic barrier would be overcome. It requires team effort, all along the line.

In summary, there is a general recognition of the problem, an awareness that it is lessening in intensity, and a feeling of a collective responsibility. If there is a team captain, it is the financial aids official, but his teammates are not helping him. Interviews revealed that the job was growing far more rapidly than personnel were being found to perform it.

What Of Educationally Disadvantaged Youth? Query Number Three

"Student C, intelligent enough and without financial barriers, is handicapped by low academic achievement. His motivation is moderate. Without special encouragement and assistance he will most likely be an academic dropout. With a sufficient amount of help, his continuation and success in higher learning are distinctly possible. What is the prospect of Student C, and where lies the responsibility for his success in college or university?"

President Anthony. Institutions of higher learning should not be burdened with heavy remedial responsibility. The state government should shoulder this responsibility in high schools and junior colleges.

President Bolivar. Such a student should be sent to a junior college, and there be given remedial reading, personal guidance in study skills, smaller classes, and more individual attention. If successful, he could subsequently transfer to a senior college. Because of his environment no senior college would be a good place for him. Such a student could be almost hopelessly lost with such a handicap.

President Chester. High schools should give post graduate courses in basic and college preparatory subjects. The long-range solution is to encourage better college students to enter the teaching profession, eventually upgrading the elementary through high school program. The college should, however, make remedial courses available, without credit, in English, math, history, and geography.

President David. A pre-college training period, as several preparatory schools and colleges in New England have demonstrated, should be available to this student, without collegiate credit, and perhaps without cost to the student. A grant for this purpose might be obtained.

President Emmett. The college should provide a type of crash program designed to bring students up to normal levels of achievement. Students, generally anxious to avoid delays in their program, should be informed as to what is being done and the reason for such action. *We must discontinue the practice of teaching on college level and giving p a s s i n g g r a d e s to students who read on the grammar school level. We are only fooling ourselves.*

President Friday. There is no way, in my opinion, to eradicate snobbery and arrogance in American life. I know Ivy College men, for example, who feel an inherent superiority over others. This attitude, in my opinion, handicaps *them* more than it does others who have had lesser advantages. President L. B. Johnson is an excellent example of the point I make. Institutions show snobbery too, of course. Whether our college is geared to help Student C or not, we have the responsibility to inculcate the value that helping students learn is always worthy of commendation, regardless of social class or academic disadvantage.

President Gentile. This student is unlikely to make good in a reputable senior college. A small private college ordinarily does not have the financial and faculty resources for such a program. Certainly a college with a stretched budget cannot develop an appropriate remedial program. We can only screen them out or wish them well. The solution is a broadly based remedial program, and that involves curricular revision and funding. A student could help himself a bit, of course, by taking a lighter course load and extending the four-year interval normally required for earning a degree, but that is a risky course of action.

President Honor. This is a problem with which we have always been faced. A given college should understand its own purposes and be true to them. *Students should not be misguided into i n s t i t u t i o n s unprepared for them.* There should also be a concerted effort in higher education to remove the stigma so frequently attached to guiding the learning of youth who have already been discriminated against by inferior schooling or cultural undernourishment, or by accident or design.

In summary. Presidents feel that assisting the educationally disadvantaged is not a proper function of higher education, that it is especially outside the sphere of duty of a senior college. Most presidents assume that a temporary program might boost students over that hurdle of disadvantage (although many such students range from two to five years below grade level, and might require up to half that time to catch up, even with above-average scholastic aptitude). Many presidents have a limited comprehension of the magnitude of deprivation. Approximately a tenth of the institutions questioned by opinionnaire or by interview described some special effort to deal with these problems. In some cases, the efforts were subsidized and the subsidy marked the beginning of such efforts. In a half dozen cases or so, the effort was independent of supplementary support.

RECOMMENDATIONS

The president of a college or university is helpless without his deans, his professors, and a supporting governing board. As a career optimist, he calls all his predicaments "challenges." Whatever the functions of his institution, those of high quality instruction and of close faculty advisory relations are likely to go lacking. Presidents are not apathetic about the matter, but they feel restricted by financial limitations or by faculty recruitment on the one hand and professorial immunity from administrative supervision (academic freedom) on the other.

1. Every college president within the South having publicly assured civil rights compliance should seek to accomplish some degree of *de facto* desegregation in student and faculty relationships. In some instances, this should take the form of institutional desegregation or its extension. In other cases, it should involve multi-institutional projects or activities in which students can unlearn distorted stereotypes and come to feel a comfortable part of the larger academic community regardless of race or social class.

2. The problem of student poverty is only of peripheral interest in some institutions. Every president should shoulder with his administration and faculty the responsibility to minimize the financial stress of students and to de-emphasize in the institutional culture the prestige of spending money.

3. The role of higher education with reference to the educationally disadvantaged is not a proper responsibility of the large majority of public and private colleges, and certainly is outside the major function of most state and private universities. Theirs should be an attitude of genuine respect, however, for those institutions that undertake that important function, and they should be willing to accept these students once their handicap has been removed.

4. The presidents of approximately thirty institutions, public, private, and church-connected, should band together to pioneer in the provision of opportunities for students handicapped by economic, ethnic, or educational disadvantages, or some combination of these limitations. There is already a measure of success, however fragmentary, on which to build; a new level of societal commitment to the worth of the task; and potential sources of support for such efforts if undertaken in a setting of long-range planning and continuing commitment.

5. The presidents of universities and deans of graduate schools are morally impelled to support efforts to instruct educationally disadvantaged

youth by developing a new type of college teacher, one who can step out-side the mold of the professor to guide learning effectively in a new con-text of requirements, especially in the tenth-to-fourteenth grade range. He need not be encumbered with a Ph. D. degree.

CONCLUSION

With such conflicts built into the American college presidency, and with the added Southern dimensions, it is difficult for any president of a South-ern college to avoid major pressures that test his strength of character , his patience, wisdom, and sheer endurance. There is little virtue in saddling him here with additional recommendations. There are impli-cations for the president in virtually every recommendation contained in this study. His task is not to yield to the temptations of power or status, but to use them in the public interest; not to achieve prestige by its cur-rently popular symbols, but to recast the status system of higher education in such a way that a man's worth is measured not by his title but by the societal use to which he puts it. The college president requires support and he needs loyal opposition, for he cannot rise far above nor will he descend much lower than his governing board and his educational team.

SELECTED REFERENCES

Bolman, Frederick deW. *How College Presidents Are Chosen.* Washing-ton, D.C.: American Council on Education, 1965.

Dodds, Harold W. , with the collaboration of Felix C. Robb and R. Robb Taylor. *The Academic President, Educator or Caretaker?* New York: McGraw-Hill Book Company, 1962.

Howes, Raymond F. (ed.). *Toward Better Preparation of College and University Administrators.* Washington, D.C.: Association for Higher Education, National Education Association, 1964.

Jones, Thomas E. , Edward V. Stanford, and Goodrich C. White. *Letters to College Presidents.* Englewood Cliffs: Prentice-Hall, Inc. , 1964.

Metz, Gustave E. *Current Fund Expenditures.* Atlanta: Southern Asso-ciation of Colleges and Schools, 1964.

Miller, W. Starr, and Kenneth M. Wilson. *Faculty Development Pro-cedures in Small Colleges / A Southern Survey.* Research Monograph No. 5. Atlanta: Southern Regional Education Board, 1963.

Schmidt, George P. *The Old Time College President.* New York: Colum-bia University Press, 1930.

Tickton, Sidney G. *Letter to a College President on the Need for Long-Range Planning.* New York: Fund for the Advancement of Education, 1963.

PART III.

SOME SHAPING FORCES

SOME SHAPING FORCES

The shaping forces of higher education in the South are difficult to identify and describe. The mere task of cataloging these forces is a considerable one. Our purpose here is not so ambitious. The spectrum of forces connected with the promotion and resisting of desegregation may not properly be classified as a shaping force. Yet desegregation's various vectors cannot be ignored in looking at the major forces affecting higher education.

Accreditation, and the regional association charged with giving it direction and meaning, is a more logical category in the identification of forces acting on higher education. Its consideration in this study is particularly relevant as the Southern Association of Colleges and Schools comes to examine anew the scope of its leadership functions beyond accreditation as well as the further exercise of its accreditation functions.

The force of the federal government in these days needs no explanation for inclusion. Nor does the private foundation, which has assisted the South in many forms for a century, require justification in being classified as a major shaping force in higher learning.

A consideration of these heterogeneous influences in Southern higher education constitutes the present portion of this study.

9. DILEMMAS OF DESEGREGATION

The forces for and against desegregation have battered against Southern colleges and universities almost incessantly for nearly twenty years, while the consideration of many other significant social and educational issues has had to wait. But, with the exception of a few isolated "mopping up" operations, the legal and *de facto* struggle against segregation in higher education has been won.

There is the ever present possibility, however, of winning the war and losing the peace. The conflict concerning segregation of the races in America has passed its climax in nearly all major public sectors. Its most victorious battles were those of the Supreme Court decision of 1954, the Civil Rights Acts of 1957 and 1964, and the Voters Right Act of 1965. In 1966, Congress occupied itself with the civil rights issues of housing, jury duty, and federal jurisdiction over crimes against civil rights workers.

The early skirmishes in that general conflict were in higher education, a legal battleground selected by the National Association for the Advancement of Colored People on the bases of valid claims and odds for success. Virtually no provision had been made in the 1930's for the separate education of Negroes in graduate and professional fields in any of the Southern states.[1] If there was a hope for victory, this would be it. And by the beginning of 1966 only one public institution had not yet signed an Assurance of Compliance with the Department of Health, Education, and Welfare, according to the provisions of Title VI of the Civil Rights Act of 1964. This was a junior college in Mississippi with an enrollment of 280 students. But even there, sentiment was almost evenly divided with reference to the wisdom of compliance.

In the nonpublic sphere of Southern higher education, circumstances were different, but only a few of the smaller colleges had not agreed to comply with the desegregation provisions of the Civil Rights Act. By 1966, no university had declined to do so. The policy of segregation continued to be the prerogative of nonpublic institutions, unless they

---

[1]See: Jessie P. Guzman, *Twenty Years of Court Decisions Affecting Higher Education in the South* (Tuskegee: Department of Records and Research, Tuskegee Institute, June 1960), p. 1.

chose to take advantage of public funds. Among the remaining "noncompliant" segregated institutions, eighteen were Baptist or Southern Baptist, six were Methodist, four each were Presbyterian and Catholic, and nineteen were private institutions. Four among this total group were colleges for Negroes.[2]

The new Commissioner of Education in 1966 made clear the point that progress in desegregation would be sought in the form of a change of attitude as well as an insistence upon genuine compliance with provisions of the law. Commissioner Harold Howe II, who had provided leadership for ethnic progress in North Carolina and elsewhere, commented that "as the South moves into much greater integration, a new element must come in, the creation of a spirit which supports this sort of thing. This isn't easy to come by, but it can be done."[3]

In previous years, the onus of responsibility for desegregation had been upon the courts and upon Congress. Just as educators were exhausted or becoming weary of the conflicts concerning desegregation, they were handed the central responsibility for leadership beyond desegregation. Among the many lessons learned in connection with the desegregation era, one was that desegregation cannot be effectively dealt with as an isolated phenomenon.

The desegregation era has been described in some depth in a recent publication of the Southern Higher Education Study,[4] and while it is important to understand some of the main threads of this transformation, the present chapter is confined to higher education's responsibility for its own present and future. The courts, the Congress, and the executive branch of the federal government have freed higher education to provide leadership for ethnic integration through education, broadly conceived. The question now confronting Southern colleges and universities is how this responsibility can be exercised in the best public interest and with the least injury to Negro and white citizens. There is an evident danger that higher education at this crucial juncture in social history will abdicate its responsibility because of the uncomfortable complexities attending it.

A VIGNETTE OF THE RECENT PAST

No single point in time marks the beginning of the Negro's yearning for freedom and equality in America unless it be the date on which the first

---

[2]See: "Colleges and Universities Which Have Signed an Assurance of Compliance," Cumulative List C-26, November 26, 1965; with supplement C-26-D, January 7, 1966, U.S. Office of Education; *Education Directory, 1964-65, Part 3, Higher Education* (Washington, D.C.: U.S. Office of Education, 1965). An indeterminate number of other institutions were not yet in fact desegregated, however.

[3]See: G. K. Hodenfield, "Education Chief to Push Integration," *The Nashville Tennesseean* (December 23, 1965), p. 17.

[4]Sam P. Wiggins, *The Desegregation Era in Higher Education* (Berkeley: McCutchan Publishing Corporation, 1966).

slave touched American shores. The story of that striving for citizen-ship has already been told, in a scholarly and vivid manner, by Frank Tannenbaum.[5] In our time the movement toward equality in a desegregated context has changed so considerably that the past is difficult to understand in the perspective of the present. Some general descriptive passages about the racial dilemma of the South in Gunnar Myrdal's *An American Dilemma* are helpful in providing some insight into the views of the period of his study (1942).[6] But for higher education in the South, an understanding of the present day requires some factual review of desegregation's history in Southern higher education itself.

The Opening Door

Pioneering efforts to achieve desegregation in higher education go back in time for more than a century. Prior to the Civil War, Oberlin Collegiate Institute in Ohio, and Berea College in Kentucky, admitted students without reference to creed or color. Soon after the Civil War, Tougaloo Southern Christian College, a predominantly Negro institution in Jackson, Mississippi, accomplished faculty desegregation in the deep South. These and a few other such instances were nineteenth century "oddities" in the culture of Southern higher education. Then in 1933, court litigations began to come into prominence with the case of Hocutt *v.* North Carolina. Yet another fifteen years elapsed before the segregation barriers really began to crumble. The cases of McLaurin *v.* Oklahoma State Regents for Higher Education (1948) and of Sweatt *v.* Painter *et al.*, against the University of Texas (1950) proved to be the crucial court decisions in the historical chain of desegregation events. As the eminent sociologist Guy B. Johnson expressed it, "Those were the cases that cracked the state universities and led to the admission of Negroes to truly Southern institutions for the first time."[7]

In the early 1950's, nearly fifty institutions of higher learning in the deep South and the border states were already desegregated, a majority of which were nonpublic institutions. All but one of the public institutions had been required by court order to desegregate. Thus the 1954 decision of the Supreme Court in the case of Brown *v.* Board of Education of Topeka came after the courts had made it virtually clear that public higher education was not to remain segregated. This did not mean that the

---

[5] Tannenbaum, *Slave and Citizen, The Negro in the Americas* (New York: Alfred A. Knopf, Inc., 1946).

[6] Myrdal, *An American Dilemma, The Negro Problem in American Democracy*, Twentieth Anniversary Edition (New York: Harper and Row, 1962). See particularly, "Postscript Twenty Years Later," by Arnold Rose, pp. *xxvii-xlv.*

[7] Johnson, "A Survey of the Admission and Integration of Negro Students into Public Institutions of Higher Learning in the South," (1953), an unpublished working paper for the "Harry Ashmore Project," Section of Special Collections, Joint University Library, Vanderbilt University, Nashville, Tennessee. Also see Guzman, pp. 10ff.

ultimate decision, of course, would not be stalled and often circumvented.[8]

During the period 1948-1954, a number of regional organizations and agencies in the South, publicly and privately, were laying the ground work for the desegregation era. The Southern Regional Council predicated much of its research and dissemination activities on the belief that segregation itself had to yield before other social and educational problems could be grappled with fairly and effectively. Its emphasis on equal opportunity for all residents within the South caused it to align itself with any worthy efforts in the direction of desegregation in higher education. It did not equivocate; it did not compromise; it stood with dignity for a basic social change against what were then heavy odds.

The Southern Education Foundation worked in a far more moderate fashion to support the interests of Negro education, insofar as the political and social realities seemed amicably to permit. Sometimes this effort appeared to strengthen the cause of desegregation; at other times, it supported developing educational leaders in segregated circumstances. The guiding view was that the concept of desegregation and the legal steps toward its fulfillment must be brought about together to avoid the hazard of an empty victory in the area of human rights and educational opportunities.

The Southern Association of Colleges and Secondary Schools faced a distinctly different set of educational tasks and of social and political circumstances. This was the meeting ground of educators whose views were quite diverse and often contradictory, concerning both ends and means on the issues of desegregation. Within the open context of varied outlook, firm steps were taken to insure full membership of qualified historically Negro institutions in the Association.[9] Among the major developments of this early desegregation period was the financial and educational assistance to a large number of Negro institutions, which enabled many of them to measure up to the accreditation standards of the Association.

The Statistics of Desegregation

The Southern Education Reporting Service was established in 1954, under a grant from the Ford Foundation, in response to an evident need for factual and objective reporting on the extent of desegregation in public education in the South. In serving this purpose, it clearly advanced the cause of desegregation as well. The records of the Southern Education Reporting Service, coupled with a variety of other sources, make it possible to graph a statistical account of the opening door of college

[8]See: J. P. Guzman (ed.), *The Negro Year Book, 1952* (New York: Wm. H. Wise and Company, Inc.. 1952). pp. 239-252. Data based on a survey of the *New York Times* in 1950.

[9]See: William H. McEniry, "Educational Progress in the Southern States," address delivered to the (Negro) Association of Colleges and Secondary Schools, December 1961. Prior to this period, institutions for Negroes were not members of the Southern Association, but were on the "approved list," holding a quasi-accredited standing.

admissions, of desegregation in public Southern institutions of higher learning. Such an account is not fully accurate, of course, since desegregation may mean achieving an above zero condition of desegregation in one college or substantial numbers in another. The timeline through this crucial eighteen-year period provides, nevertheless, a general indication of the increase in desegregation in institutions of higher learning.

From the standpoint of Negro enrollment in predominantly white Southern institutions, it is estimated that fifteen hundred Negro students were enrolled in such institutions in 1954. Approximately two-thirds of these students were enrolled in public institutions. Ten years later that number had increased tenfold, but the ratio of public to private enrollment remained almost constant. In addition, approximately 25,000 Negro students in 1964 were attending predominantly Negro institutions in which a few white students, virtually all non-Southerners, were enrolled.[10] Fifty-thousand other Negroes were enrolled in segregated colleges. Thus in 1964, approximately 85 percent of Negro college students were enrolled in all Negro or predominantly Negro institutions with a non-Negro enrollment of less than 5 percent.

By 1966, the doors of admission to most Southern colleges and universities were open, grudgingly or with welcome mats outspread, to Negro students. The thousands of Negro students in historically white institutions gave testimony to the fact that there would be no turning back to the predesegregation era in higher education. To understand the depth of meaning in further change it is necessary to know the present legal circumstances.

The Hand of the Law

The political and legal history of recent years has been one of using the law and of circumventing it for diverse ends. The law has generally been supported, but it has been variously circumvented or flouted by both conservative and liberal groups in the interest of their contradictory goals. Little would be gained here by recounting the story of the political aspect of the desegregation era. It is only necessary for us to understand the force of current law to determine the real limits of the options of public and nonpublic institutions of higher learning. Public colleges are required to be desegregated now, whether they have signed the Assurance of Compliance or not, in every officially sponsored aspect of collegiate life. There is virtually no doubt in legal circles that any lawsuit pursued to test the principle of practices along these lines would receive an affirmative outcome.[11] With reference to the nonpublic institutions, a

[10]See: Guy B. Johnson, "Desegregation in Higher Education," *Higher Education,* XX:9 (June 1964), 6.
[11]See: Jerre S. Williams, "Implications of the Civil Rights Act of 1964," *Proceedings of the Sixty-ninth Annual Meeting of the Southern Association of Colleges and Schools,* Louisville, Kentucky, December 1964 (Atlanta: Southern Association of Colleges and Schools, 1965).

GRAPH 1

DESEGREGATION IN 170 PUBLIC, HISTORICALLY WHITE COLLEGIATE INSTITUTIONS IN THE ELEVEN CONFEDERACY STATES, 1954-1966

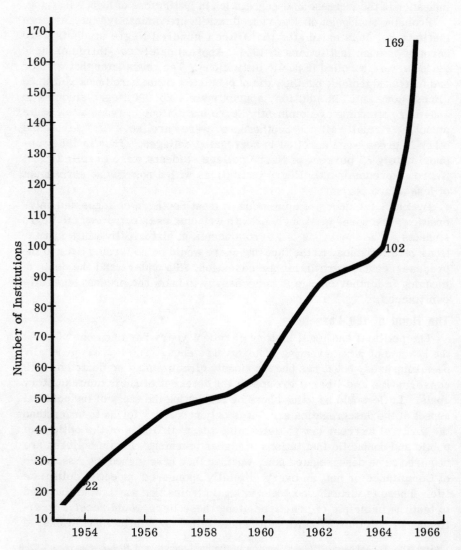

Sources: "Ten Years in Review," *Southern School News* (May 17, 1964), p. 3, and cumulative list #C-24 of "Colleges and Universities which Have Signed an Assurance of Compliance," to March 1, 1966.

GRAPH 2

Desegregation in 70 Public, Historically White Collegiate Institutions in the Border States of Delaware, the District of Columbia, Kentucky, Maryland, Missouri, Oklahoma, and West Virginia, 1954-1966

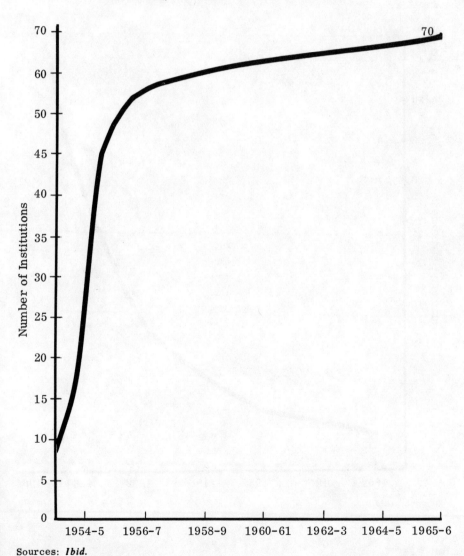

Sources: *Ibid.*

GRAPH 3

DESEGREGATION IN 45 PUBLIC, HISTORICALLY NEGRO COLLEGIATE
INSTITUTIONS IN THE ELEVEN CONFEDERACY STATES, 1954-1966

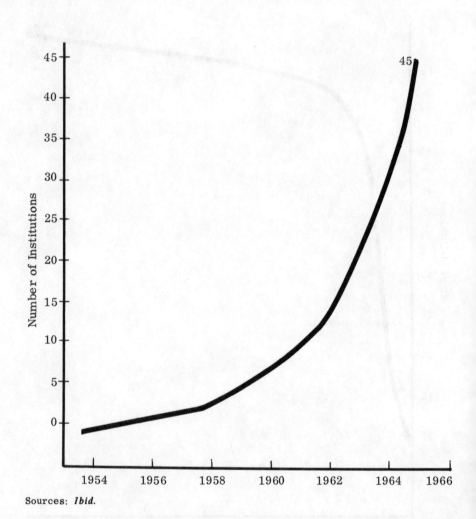

Sources: *Ibid.*

GRAPH 4

Desegregation in 10 Public, Historically Negro Collegiate Institutions in the Border States of Delaware, the District of Columbia, Kentucky, Maryland, Missouri, Oklahoma, and West Virginia,

1954-1966

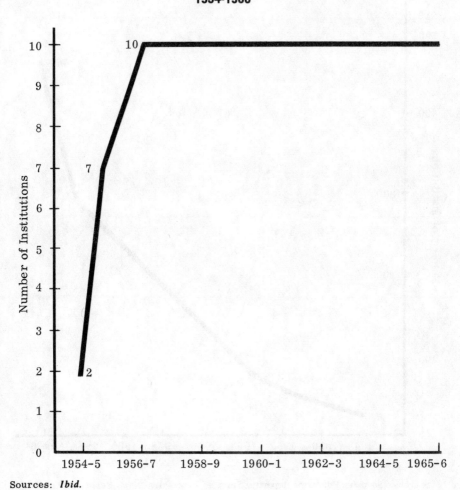

Sources: *Ibid.*

GRAPH 5

Desegregation in 513 Southern Higher Education
Public and Nonpublic Institutions, 1948-1966

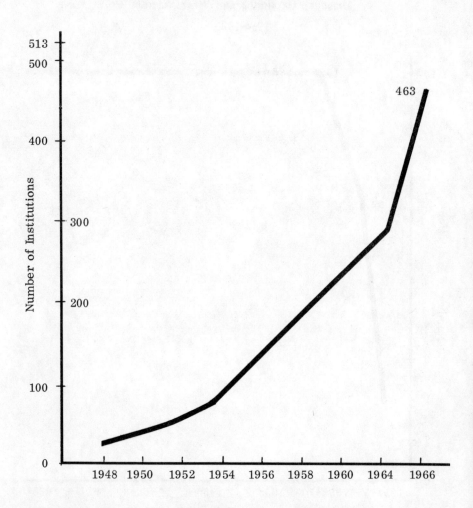

Sources: Southern Education Reporting Service, especially, News Release of October 8, 1964, and *Southern School News* (May 1964, and May 1965). Unofficial sources are from church and private groups, the United States Office of Education, and other agencies. The eleven states of the deep South area, including Arkansas and excluding Kentucky; and the 214 public institutions and 299 private institutions are included in this estimate.

great deal of freedom remains as long as the institution does not participate in any federally assisted programs or does not have employees
involved in interstate transportation, that is, out-of-state residents. That
freedom is largely an illusion, however, as is readily manifest by the
increased dependence of nonpublic institutions on federal support. Within
governing realities, the independently wealthy private institution may
choose to remain segregated, but none has made that choice. The so-called
independent institutions have concluded that such freedom is bought at
too dear a cost. Even church-connected colleges are becoming more
government connected, some receiving more funds from the federal
government than from their religious parent body.

The opening of collegiate doors in the South has been attended by much
cultural turmoil and personal travail, but it has been accompanied by
remarkably little violence or personal injury. Its damage has been more
psychic than physical. The hand of politics, in historic "race baiting"
terms, has long since been played out. The law is clear, and its enforcement is increasingly certain.[12]

THE BENEFITS AND IRONIES OF DESEGREGATION

Before we can see beyond the desegregation era, it is necessary to understand some of the benefits and ill effects that have attended it. From one
standpoint, Negroes in the smaller segregated colleges will be left behind
in the mainstream of progress unless those colleges do something significant to revitalize their programs. As partly mendicant institutions, they
stand little chance of doing so. Yet they provide a culture in which there
is less of an overwhelming threat of failure and more of a feeling of
congeniality. If theirs is not an "academic" community, at least it is a
"learning" community. But unless the predominantly Negro colleges
can be assisted to maintain or obtain adequacy, they will be increasingly
regarded as imitations of higher learning institutions rather than as the
genuine article. Such institutions are further handicapped by the loss
of some of their outstanding students to predominantly white institutions.
The Negroes who will be left behind in a changing social order are needless casualties of desegregation, but there is no simple solution to their
dilemma.

White students in predominantly white institutions are rearranging their
views of the nature of the Negro through desegregation. These contacts
have been highly educational in the main because their earlier contacts
with Negroes were limited to those of the atypical servant class, the
unschooled and obsequious domestics.

[12]The Office of Education continues to review the compliance assurance from colleges and
universities, so that signing a piece of paper is not a perfunctory matter. A strengthening
of that effort became apparent in the spring of 1966, with five colleges affected by an announced withholding of federal funds.

The white student in the segregated college is, of course, affected, too, but in ways quite similar to his segregated Negro counterpart. When he was a part of a noisy majority, he was conforming to a fashionable prejudice. Now, as a part of a quiescent and vanishing minority, he is dubious about being left behind in a segregated, isolated, minority group of whites. A number of highly regarded Southern universities have publicly announced their recruitment of and available scholarships for Negro students as well as their desegregated admission practices, and the white Southerner is puzzled, fearing that he may be losing caste by remaining in a segregated context. A decade ago he would have lost caste by taking precisely the opposite course of action. Long a devoted conformist, he is uncomfortable about being a deviant.

A few white students have elected to enroll in predominantly Negro colleges. In some of the border states, that number is substantial. Further South, the number not only dwindles rapidly, but such white students are generally non-Southerners. Some of the more prestigious, predominantly Negro universities, such as Fisk University, are making a concerted effort to recruit white students from the South and the non-South. There the odds for success are improved by a nucleus of white students and a desegregated faculty. Hampton Institute, near Norfolk, Virginia, has already made long strides toward desegregation in reverse. Even so, passing over into the predominantly Negro institution is still looked on askance among a preponderant majority of white Southerners.[13] A temporary or part-time enrollment is highly favored by many students, but a complete breaking away from the majority group on a long-range basis continues to be virtually unthinkable.

Becoming a voluntary member of a minority group, for white or Negro students, is not an altogether attractive prospect. This explains in part the reticence in achieving faculty desegregation in both directions. A number of college presidents would be pleased to accomplish this, but professors, including those of most liberal leanings, are not anxious to forsake the culture of which they have come to be so integral a part. Thus, as desegregation becomes more personal in higher education, there is more reluctance to accomplish it in terms of sustained commitment.

The central historical purpose of desegregation in higher education, of course, was to provide access for Negroes into historically white universities and colleges. Thus the major evaluative question refers to the consequences of desegregation for those students. The National Scholarship Service and Fund for Negro Students undertook the task of ascertaining the academic and social effect of such desegregation. The evidence from that investigation, while far from being conclusive, is

---

[13]For an authentic and revealing report on desegregation in historically Negro institutions of higher learning, see: Ponchitta Pierce, "Integration: Negro Colleges' Newest Challenge," *Ebony*, XXI:5 (March 1966), 36-46.

certainly persuasive, that if Negro students are appropriately selected on the basis of their achievement and scholastic ability, coupled with financial support and personal encouragement, their achievement in the academic and social life of the college community is virtually assured.[14] Qualified Negro youth, in large numbers, can do well in predominantly white institutions of high academic standards.

A comprehensive review of research evidence on the effects of desegregation has been compiled. This research considers the related factors of social threat and of academic threat, showing how each may magnify the other.[15] As the social threat eases in Southern higher education, which it has continued to do with surprising swiftness, the veil of educational disadvantage is lifted. This constitutes a new source of acute discomfort to Negroes and whites alike, both needing to pretend that disadvantage, if unnoticed, will disappear. Meanwhile, the more competent Negroes forge ahead and proudly assert that Negroes should be given no preferential consideration. For their part, they are surely right. But the question of the nature and purpose of preferential assistance goes unanswered, while athletic nonscholars, Negro and white, get tutorial attention as a matter of course, as well as financial assistance above the table and underneath it.

There is a mingled benefit and irony regarding the most academically outstanding Negro youth. It is illustrated by the recently developed National Achievement Scholarship Program, which is administered by the National Merit Scholarship Program expressly for Negro students, recognizing that their backgrounds place them at an unfair disadvantage in open competition for National Merit Scholarships.

The first round of such scholarships, in 1965, included a list of 224 recipients, 128 of whom were Southerners. Of the 224 students, only forty-two elected to remain in or enter the South. Most of the others showed a preference for the prestige institutions of the East and the Midwest. Of the forty-two who remained in the South, twenty-one chose to enter predominantly white institutions. Of the twenty-one remaining students, seven entered Fisk University in Nashville, Tennessee, and four entered Morehouse College in Atlanta, Georgia.[16] The benefit of this widespread choice, of course, is to extend the opportunities of these students in many ways. Viewing the matter from the point of view of the historically Negro college, however, shows it losing 90 percent or

[14] See: Kenneth B. Clark and Lawrence Plotkin, *The Negro Student at Integrated Colleges* (New York: National Scholarship Service and Fund for Negro Students, 1963).

[15] See: Irwin Katz, "Review of Evidence Relating to Effects of Desegregation on the Intellectual Performance of Negroes," *American Psychologist,* 19:6 (June 1964), 381-399.

[16] Based on information from the National Achievement Scholarship Program. The broader picture is more hopeful. Three thousand commended Negro candidates were listed in September 1966. From this list about 1,000 finalists were selected; and from them about 200 award winners. From this broader base of good students, predominantly Negro colleges may fare well.

so of its best students to predominantly white institutions, and running squarely into society's taboos if it attempts to recruit a corresponding number of academically talented white youth.

BEYOND DESEGREGATION

The imponderable question before Southern colleges and universities is whether they shall float along in the new social age or whether, by determined action, they propose to participate actively in shaping its character. The years of 1966 to 1970 will record higher education's response to this question. In considering it, we should be less concerned about achieving massive desegregation, and more concerned about giving it a chance to prosper in a climate conducive to growth, being mindful not to thwart that chance.

It is also important to recognize that the solution of one problem often creates additional ones. Desegregation in higher education has been of most benefit to the already privileged and talented Negroes, the top rung of their social ladder. This privileged group is, in one sense, the least deserving of compassion. It is inclined to segregate itself on the basis of social class, alienating itself from the Negro poor, just as any social group that is clearly beneath another will determine to subordinate some other group to it. As desegregation in higher education continues then, the privileged Negro student, like his white counterpart, becomes enamored of privilege and has decreasing feeling for those in his own former estate. Meanwhile, the historically Negro college, in its efforts to help the more disadvantaged Negroes, is in jeopardy—in the ironical name of human rights.

Substantive Conditions for Progress

Progress in social affairs comes about through a combination of individual and joint effort. This effort must be accompanied by sustained commitments rather than by capricious attention to the publicized crises of the moment. Until this coordination of effort and depth of individual, institutional, and government or foundation commitment can be achieved, progress will continue to be sporadic and uncertain. With such individual commitment, multiplied many times and given financial and administrative support, the benefits will magnify as the ironies of desegregation diminish.

Desegregation can no longer be properly viewed as a single phenomenon for focal attention, however, and if the postdesegregation era moves beyond its present plateau of achievement, higher education's homework must be directed toward the broader demands of society.[17]

---

[17] The following proposals are treated more fully in Wiggins, *The Desegregation Era in Higher Education*, chap. VII.

RECOMMENDATIONS AND DISCUSSION

The press for extended desegregation in public school systems continues to be largely stymied even in 1966, despite the Civil Rights Act of 1964, and the formality of compliance with an often pharasaic "freedom of choice."[18] Although "massive tokenism" continues to prevail on lower levels, higher education is providing genuine access in a demonstrable and commendable manner in an increasing number of public, private, and church-connected institutions. With this increase in *de facto* desegregation, the South needs to see a model of success, not a reflection of failure, beyond desegregation. Unless it does, little hope remains for public education on lower levels to grasp the concept of liberty, equality, and fraternity.

The Precollege Circumstance

Instruction: Many college instructors of freshman courses in English, mathematics, and science should teach in high schools, either a single regular course or occasional senior classes. Frequently, their instruction should be in high schools in which they are in the minority ethnic group. This contact and experience will benefit high school students who aspire to college, and should be beneficial to college instructors in their own freshman classes as well. Such action may, in addition, facilitate successful faculty desegregation in public schools.

Counseling: High school counselors need to obtain and compile, for Negro and white students alike, reliable information concerning the social threat of institutions in relation to ethnic groups and social class; the failure threat of academic attrition, of limited remedial or special instruction available to disadvantaged students; and the financial threat based upon information relating to scholarships, work-study programs, loans, and other benefits.

B o o s t e r projects: Such booster programs as "Project Opportunity" of the Ford Foundation and the College Entrance Examination Board, which begins with bright seventh graders, and the "Project Upward Bound," initiated by the Office of Economic Opportunity, which provides a kind of last academic precollege chance, are based on sound concepts and have a great deal of merit. Such programs need to be guarded, however, by such principles as the following:

1. The goals must be reasonable in relation to the amount of disadvantage to be coped with and the time to do it. Past efforts have tried to span too large a gap in a few months of miracles—which were never wrought.

---

[18] See: *School Desegregation: Old Problems Under a New Law* (Atlanta: Southern Regional Council, September 1965). Less than 6 percent of Negro Southerners enrolled in public schools are in desegregated schools in the eleven states of the Confederacy.

2. Continuing assistance to individual students must be assured. Temporary concern, followed by anonymity, can be both educationally detrimental and personally disastrous.

3. White and Negro students should be helped without preferential consideration for either group. Except in Appalachia, and some other areas of the rural South, however, Negroes will continue to be preponderant in such chronically disadvantaged groups.

Recruitment: Predominantly white institutions need to become increasingly active in recruiting Negro students who show good promise of success in their respective programs. The three thousand "commended candidates" of the National Achievement Scholarship Program is a good list of such prospects. To assure more continuity of desegregation practices in the more reluctant "compliance" institutions, small groups of Negro students, academically able and socially mature, should be encouraged and enabled to attend these institutions to prevent a regression to segregation. "Cluster" scholarships, or individual financial incentives in some cases, would be fully in order.

Conversely, the more prestigious and academically demanding among the predominantly Negro colleges should seek to recruit and offer "cluster scholarships" to Southern white students, at or near the level of the National Merit semifinalists, on a one- to four-year basis.

On the College Campus

The white student facing his tomorrow has a responsible challenge to give the concept of desegregation a fair chance regardless of his a priori views. The mature student's mind is one of open commitment; in the undefined present it should neither be made up for him by the weight of tradition nor by an uncritical acceptance of change, but in response to the situation of the moment with intelligence, sensitivity, and good manners.

The Negro, likewise, must be a realistic student of the facts of prejudice, whether it be pro-Negro or anti-Negro in nature, his own or that of others. He has to guard against ascribing failure to prejudice when it is due to his own inadequacy or lack of effort. Half of the white college students will not finish college; so failure is surely not a race-related phenomenon. But like others, it will be more "human" for him to look for causes of failure outside himself. His race may come in handy as a respectable explanation for difficulties in a desegregated college.

Student leaders today have an unparalled opportunity for helping their institutions to move beyond the mere achievement of physical desegregation, but their work needs to be marked by a broader view than simply a consideration of the occasional plights of Negro students or of white students confronted with race-linked problems. A Committee in the Student Interest should see to it that legitimate concerns of all individual students are heard, are properly channeled, and are given constructive attention, and that spurious gripes are checked or at least exposed. This committee should have a "safety valve" function to prevent untimely demonstrations and to organize any that seem warranted.

The efforts of student leadership must be combined with those of student aid coordinators, with directors of student personnel, with deans of students, and with coordinators of faculty advisers. Such student groups can serve effectively, informally and unofficially, as a referral body, and can avoid the despair of individuals facing financial, psychological, or academic crises alone.

The professor needs to overcome the learned bias that the greatness of an institution, and hence of its professors, is measured by its student failure rate, or its size, or its wealth, or the number of its eminent faculty. These are the measures of reputation for greatness, but they may not be reliable indicators of the true character of greatness. That character, in its humanistic sense, is a measure of the educational change accomplished within students as a result of their total college life. Thus the college, if it is highly selective, is highly successful only as it responds to its challenge of student talent, a talent that may develop or atrophy, that may be put to social use or to crassly selfish purpose. The college that is largely unselective can achieve comparable greatness through a service that raises the aspirations and achievements of other youth commensurate with their talent. This is where the disadvantaged Negro student, with college success potential, enters the scene of special opportunity for the professor.

The non-Negro professor takes justifiable pride, alongside his Negro associate, in the historically liberal position he has taken with reference to desegregation, but now his responsibility becomes a personal matter. He needs to work either toward a college admissions policy consistent with academic expectation, or an academic expectation consistent with admissions policy. In colleges with open admissions policies, this need for a consistency of expectation results in a mandate to provide, at some point, remedial or "bridge" courses for college-capable youth, not for Negro students alone, whose academic backgrounds have been meager, or who are, for other reasons, "underachievers."

The challenge of the present is for professors to demonstrate in overt, though not necessarily dramatic ways their willingness to be liberal in service as well as exhortation. Such action calls for living up to the credo of the professor—who "thinks otherwise"; who is not bound by the conventional kudos, but who takes his examined assumptions along the paths of logic to their intellectually demanding conclusions.

The president, on matters of policy and its administration, may feel lonely, but he is never alone. He is in company with his Board of Trustees in matters of policy formulation. He is in company with his administrative staff as he works with the intricacies of management, of budget, and educational leadership. He needs, first of all—and however difficult—to make clear the institution's stance, its *one voice,* on the matter of desegregation, with due sensitivity to students, faculty, patrons, and others who may or may only seem to support that institution. No other recommendation can avail much so long as ambiguity pervades in administrative practice. The private segregated college will not be subject to censure for the integrity of its principle if it lives by its conviction without intrusion upon others.

The hypocritical institution, however, is increasingly vulnerable. Once the president, his board, and central administrative team have made clear the position of their institution, the desegregated college can forget about inch-by-inch anguish of gradualism and tokenism, of making certain that the "right" things are said to the "right" private audiences in the "right" places. The president, thus unshackled, is free to be his institutions's president.

The president who can muster sufficient initial support from his constituency, can serve the cause of Southern higher education well by repudiating the conventional claims to greatness. He can lead his college toward evolving a miniature democracy in which higher education can flourish with a minimum of "social threat" because it will be an ethnically open society; of "failure threat," because students will be helped to achieve attainable standards; and of "financial threat" because students will be assured of adequate resources through scholarships, labor, and loans, and will be accepted in the college community regardless of their socio-economic class.

Beyond the Campus

Leadership on state, regional, and national levels can serve in a strategic role to effect improvement, and to preclude fragmentation of effort at the institutional level.

In the public sphere, the selection of new college presidents must be a point of increasing concern. The "program oriented" president, rather than the "hotel oriented" president, will be more apt to bring about improvements on matters of due concern. New presidents of all institutions should be favorably disposed toward selecting central administrative staff without regard to race, but with regard to educational production.[19]

In the merger of collegiate institutions, predominantly Negro institutions must not be expediently merged with those that are historically white. Despite physical proximity they may be years apart in admission standards, and in program offerings. In some cases, one institution might properly become a distinctive desegregated community college, with precollege instruction available. A terminal program of vocational,

[19]To press for a desegregated faculty at all costs can lead to educational bankruptcy. For a predominantly white college to appoint a Negro professor of marginal competence would be an awkward error. Likewise, for a predominantly Negro college to appoint an incompetent white professor would boomerang on the purposes of desegregation. It has, indeed, done so.

technical, and general education should be provided, and the other institution should keep its door open to students whose aptitude and achievement warrant further higher education, leading to graduate or professional studies.

It would be presumptuous to suggest what specific regional agencies might do to advance educational opportunities in a postdesegregation era. The Southern Association of Colleges and Schools might, however, see fit to focus upon the endemic problems related to race and poverty, either through emphasis at conventions or through study groups of its College and Secondary School Commissions. In addition, some effort toward coordinated study and action by other appropriate agencies would prove highly beneficial.

Private philanthropy is both relieved and concerned at the way its traditional role has been modified by the federal government. It has been relieved by the massive furtherance of some of its own objectives. It has been concerned about the uprooting effects of some hastily contrived efforts to solve, with panacea-like patterns, some complex problems whose roots go deep. What a foundation now does to help higher education beyond desegregation depends, of course, upon its resources and the special nature of its objectives. Among many possibilities, these opportunities appear to have merit:

1. Short-range programs, in colleges and senior high schools attempting to move "beyond desegregation," should be encouraged and supported, especially where such efforts can be well evaluated, and where they show promise of a spread of effect if taken over subsequently by governmental agencies. Federal government agencies should be invited to participate in the evaluative phases of such programs experimenting in a evolving social democracy.

2. Scholarships to white and Negro students enrolled in institutions of a predominantly different race should be provided with an established assurance to students of continued interest and support, similar to those under the aegis of the National Scholarship Service Fund, but expanded and available without racial preference.

3. "Faculty differential scholarships" to encourage temporary faculty assignments of one year or less in an ethnically different institution should be provided. (For example, if a $12,000 professor accepted a $9,500 assignment, a foundation scholarship should provide for this difference, a small salary increase, and defray expenses for travel and housing accommodations.)

CONCLUSION

The shaping legal forces of the desegregation era in higher education have ended, but desegregation has not come near its intended destination. There are no longer pressures upon local institutions from federal or private agencies, once gestures to erase segregation have been made.

The issue is now placed in a new perspective where colleges enjoy a new kind of freedom and a new dimension of responsibility. Southern higher education faces the task of viewing constructively the ethnic issues in a new social context. Whether vanquished or victorious in the eighteen-year struggle, educators feel a tired reluctance to give the matter further attention. "It will work itself out," they say; and so in time it will. But the results for the South will be pathetic indeed, if one of higher education's greatest moments of opportunity catches it too preoccupied with miscellaneous proposal writing to take concerted action. Such action must be directed toward a new cultural enrichment among the rich and the poor, the Negroes and whites, the educationally privileged and the disadvantaged, all aspiring to equality and excellence of opportunity according to their diverse talents and goals.

SELECTED REFERENCES

Clark, Kenneth B., and Lawrence Plotkin. *The Negro Student at Integrated Colleges.* New York: National Scholarship Service and Fund for Negro Students, 1963.

Cliff, Virgil A., Archibald W. Anderson, and H. Gordon Hullfish (eds.). *Negro Education in America,* Sixteenth Yearbook of the John Dewey Society. New York: Harper and Row, Publishers, 1962. See especially: Nelson H. Harris, "Desegregation in Institutions of Higher Learning," chap. IX.

Daniel, Walter G. (ed.). *Studies in the Higher Education of Negro Americans, The Journal of Negro Education Yearbook,* XXXV. Washington, D.C.: Howard University, 1966.

Harleston, Bernard W. "Higher Education for the Negro," *The Atlantic,* 216:5 (November 1965), 139-144.

Johnson, Guy B. "Desegregation in Southern Higher Education," *Higher Education,* XX:9 (June 1964), 5-7, 10.

Katz, Irwin. "Review of Evidence Relating to Effects of Desegregation on the Intellectual Performance of Negroes," *American Psychologist,* 19:6 (June 1964), 381-399.

Kvaraceous, William C., *et. al. Negro Self-Concept, Implications for School and Citizenry.* New York: McGraw-Hill Book Co., 1965.

Pierce, Ponchitta. "Integration: Negro Colleges' Newest Challenge," *Ebony,* XXI:5 (March 1966), 36-46.

Wiggins, Sam P. *The Desegregation Era in Higher Education.* Berkeley: McCutchan Publishing Corporation, 1966.

10. ACCREDITATION AND QUALITY ASSURANCE

In dealing with higher education's problems associated with poverty, with race, and with mediocre precollegiate schooling, consideration of the regional accrediting association may be open to question. The decision to deal with it seems warranted, however, by three facts. First of all, the Southern Association of Colleges and Schools has moved far in recent years in the direction of qualitative aspects of accreditation, a fact that will increase the prospect of considering the worth of an institution in a new frame of reference. Second, the Association has increasingly come to view itself in broader terms than accreditation, however significant that function may be. Third, the regional leadership functions subsequently discussed in this chapter as accrediting, supportive, and mediative in nature must be assumed by some existing organization or by a newly formed agency. New agencies should be established only when existing agencies of established reputation and high promise cannot, or do not, choose to assume responsibility for significant emerging functions.

The recently formed Regional Educational Laboratories provide an ironic case in point, across the nation, of how American regional associations of colleges and schools have defaulted in their broader responsibilities, and are being by-passed in educational developments beyond accreditation. Yet the Southern Association has given recent evidence of a substantive effort to look at the broad educational landscape, and to assume a larger share of responsibility for uplifting Southern society through better education at all levels. In changing its accrediting and other roles, the Association must introduce some fresh and actionable points of view, and working proposals will require an undergirding of strong, although not massive support. A number of such proposals emerged from the Southern Region Conference on Education, in December 1965. The president of the Association gave assurance that the Association would "study carefully recommendations that have relevance for a regional agency in an attempt to upgrade and increase the Association's contributions to Southern education."[1] The Southern Association can become a major

---

[1] *Proceedings of the Southern Region Conference on Education, Education: The Southern Hope* (Atlanta: Southern Association of Colleges 1966).

force in the fulfillment of the hope for a prosperous South at peace with itself, largely through a transformation of lower and higher education.

A crucial decision now facing all of the regional associations is whether they shall be, in fact, single purpose accrediting bodies or move into a broader sphere of educational leadership. Their historic tradition would suggest the latter course, as would the formal statement of objectives of the various regional bodies. Through the years, however, accreditation has come to be regarded as an important means to the end of improving higher education; and, in operational terms, it has sometimes come to be equated with the end itself.

The historic character of accreditation as an American institution was summed up thirty years ago by George F. Zook and M. E. Haggerty in their monograph, *Principles of Accrediting Higher Institutions.* [2] The first forty years of experience with the accreditation concept of the North Central Association of Colleges and Secondary Schools, only the latter half of which had included college accreditation, led to the public admission that some colleges that met the standards for accreditation were not effective while other excellent institutions were clearly deficient in meeting them. Thus, thirty years ago, a "new plan" for accreditation in higher education was developed, with General Education Board support, under the leadership of Zook and Haggerty, with the assistance of John Dale Russell and Floyd Reeves.

Three conceptual patterns were emphasized. Now, in the 1960's, there is a rebirth of those same emphases in accreditation, especially within the South. That renaissance is a hopeful and ambitious one. Below is the 1936 version, in brief:

1. The term "standard" was to be discarded, and hopefully the negative concept associated with it. In its place was a series of educational principles laid out on a "pattern map" on which could be traced a profile of institutional adequacy, recognizing that superiority in some characteristics might compensate for deficiencies in others.

2. Emphasis in the "new plan of 1934" was on flexibility and growth of institutions with reference to their differential purposes. The objective was to move out of the ruts of minimal conditions of acceptance, uniformity of pattern, and mediocrity of status. [While subsequent history has brought some pains of disillusionment to the concept, it is still seeking a mature resolution in higher education.]

3. Control of accreditation involved a social purpose. The accrediting agency was viewed in 1934 as representing a "revolt from the unprogressive and autocratic manner in which government frequently deals with all things in evolution . . . and an attempt to prevent the cause of educational standards from falling into confusion, low standards, and ill repute."[3]

[2]Zook and Haggerty, *The Evaluation of Higher Institutions. Vol. I. Principles of Accrediting Higher Institutions* (Chicago: University of Chicago Press, 1936).

[3]Zook and Haggerty, p. 95.

[It will be recalled that this was during the frantic struggle of this nation to arise from its societal trauma, the "panic" of 1929.]

A new generation has brought with it new struggles for control of various segments of accreditation in higher education; until 1949, with the establishment of the National Commission on Accrediting, accreditation was a national open contest without rule book or arbiter. The issues of accreditation have become more complex, and the need for accreditation has increased. A number of these new complexities were described by William K. Selden in his treatise on the general subject of accreditation.[4] Even in 1960, the question of voluntary or governmental accreditation was raised as being of major importance. In private circles, the issue continues unresolved. The accrediting associations were then, and are now, on trial for numerous reasons. A part of the problem has been that administrators of institutions of distinctively high quality have seen accreditation as peripheral to their concerns, since they rise so far above a number of accredited institutions that have met only dubious minimal standards. With the Southern Association's emerging concept of qualitative growth, however, even the eminent, unthreatened institutions report benefits from the experience of decennial accreditation visits.

The explosive accreditation issue of the early 1960's focused on the National Council for the Accreditation of Teacher Education. The 1965 report by John R. Mayor and Willis G. Schwartz to the National Commission on Accrediting, supported by the Carnegie Corporation of New York, provided a definitive analysis of accreditation in this major dimension of higher education.[5] In this report the false dichotomy of quantitative versus qualitative standards in accreditation was again examined, and an effort was made to relegate to regional associations the emphasis upon minimal qualifications of higher institutions.[6] In explicit terms, the report dealt with the power structure of accreditation in teacher education, which sooner or later comes to be, publicly and privately, the core issue in the struggle for control of accreditation of higher education and, to a lesser degree, for control of higher education itself.

The regional accrediting associations have tended to limit their approval by accreditation to the over-all purposes of institutions rather than to their separate component parts. The regional map of these associations looks more like a joke of history than a rational division of function or a natural geographical division of America. Of the six regional associations, for example, two of them serve thirty of the fifty states.

---

[4]Selden, *Accreditation: A Struggle over Standards in Higher Education* (New York: Harper & Bros., 1960).

[5]Mayor and Swartz, *Accreditation in Teacher Education: Its Influence on Higher Education* (Washington, D.C.: National Commission on Accrediting, 1965).

[6]*Ibid.,* p. 234.

North Central Association 19
Southern Association 11
Northwest Association 7
New England Association 6
Middle States Association 5
Western Association 2

The question of general geographical control arises therefore, and there is no Supreme Court to mandate a reapportionment of responsibility in the recently established Federation of Regional Accrediting Commissions. The National Commission on Accrediting does not have the power of reapportionment and there is no historic tendency, personally or organizationally, to "cooperate one's self" out of business. The emerging function of the regional associations will have to be resolved further before power negotiations, or friendly settlements, can be reached in a more operable system of regional accreditation. For the present, however, the concern here is with the American South and how its regional accrediting association can help systems of higher education to become more relevant and more coherent in dealing with regional educational problems.

THE SOUTHERN ASSOCIATION OF COLLEGES AND SCHOOLS

The accreditation picture in the South is unique both in its achievements and in its hope for the future. The Southern Association of Colleges and Schools is arbitrarily considered here to encompass the South, although there is a reluctance since Arkansas and the southern portions of Missouri, Illinois, Indiana, and West Virginia are not included with the eleven states comprising that Association.

The Southern Association was not established primarily for the purpose of accrediting institutions. Its founding purposes were (1) to facilitate cooperation and mutual assistance among schools and colleges, (2) to raise the level of scholarship, (3) to achieve a greater uniformity of college entrance requirements, and (4) to develop college preparatory schools.[7] Accreditation came to be regarded, over the years, as a means toward these and other worthy ends, and the first accredited college did not receive this recognition until twenty-five years after the establishment of the Southern Association, which then approved thirty-three of its forty-four members.[8] Then the accreditation struggle began.

The charter members of the Southern Association of Colleges and Secondary Schools were the universities of Vanderbilt, North Carolina, Duke (then Trinity College), Mississippi, Washington and Lee, and the University of the South (Sewanee).[9] The historic and current distinctions

---

[7] See: *Proceedings*, p. 2.

[8] Guy E. Snavely, *A Short History of the Southern Association of Colleges and Secondary Schools.* Reprinted from the *Southern Association Quarterly*, IX (November 1945), 93.

[9] Invitations to the organizational meeting were extended by a committee appointed by the faculty of Vanderbilt University. *Proceedings of the Seventeenth Annual Meeting of the Southern Association of Colleges and Schools*, p. 2.

of this cluster of institutions did not come by way of the "eminence" of accreditation—but of professional and academic laurels individually attained. Meanwhile, however, the federal government, various private foundations, foreign countries, and parents of college youth continue to rely on accreditation as a symbol, if not an indicator of quality.

During the early years of the Southern Association, the recognition of the importance of accreditation grew to the point that accreditation came to be regarded as the major function of the Association rather than as simply one means toward achieving its basic purposes. Until 1962, quantitative standards were uniformly employed within this pattern of accreditation.

The Association has performed its accreditation function, and other functions growing out of it, in a creditable manner despite modest financial support. Its total budget for the fiscal year ending June 30, 1966, amounted to $522,671, of which $186,383 was allotted to staff salaries and fringe benefits. Yet the Association attempts to provide a measure of leadership for 417 colleges (with accreditation visits to more than forty each year), for 2,868 secondary schools, and for 4,578 elementary schools. Thus the expenditure for staff services per member institution amounts to less than $24 per year.[10] Major contributions have been made, of course, through the untiring efforts of the Association's staff and the widespread sense of dedication of school and college officials who perform services within the Association either on a gratis basis or for nominal remuneration. It has been calculated by a staff official of the Association that 5,600 individuals (including duplications) within a recent year served on accreditation committees. To state the matter on a different basis, if accreditation visits were accomplished in the present pattern by staff members, ninety full-time employees would be required to perform that function alone. With such an effort, it is easy to see how the accreditation function has served to eclipse other means of achieving coordination of higher education activities.

The present purpose is not to relate the historical function of the Southern Association nor to present a presumptuous analysis of the accreditation movement within it. Yet some major elements in the evolving past continue to live in the present, and of these it is well to take note.

A DECADE OF PROGRESS, 1957-1966

From its beginning, the Southern Association did not seek, except in ethnic terms, to become an exclusive fraternity of the elite among higher education, but sought, instead, to assist institutions to earn the recognition reflected by its standards for accreditation. In 1957, however, many Southern educators came to regard the Southern Association as having a duality of purpose, of being an accrediting agency and providing an annual meeting for a reunion of the educational fraternity and the exchange

[10]*Proceedings,* pp. 12, 75ff.

of professional experiences and ideas. These circumscribed purposes
were worthy ones, and they laid a foundation for the past decade of unusual
achievements.

The Association's most delicate and difficult task during the first five
years of this period was to unite in common purpose the historically Negro
and historically white institutions. It has approximated that achievement,
for the most part against heavy odds. In 1957, the Association adopted
a standard of accreditation applicable alike to historically Negro and white
colleges and universities. Through financing on-campus visitations, the
General Education Board assisted the Association in its efforts to raise
the quality of Negro colleges sufficiently to meet quantitative accreditation
requirements.[11] The Danforth Foundation then proceeded to provide sufficient direct support for selected Negro colleges to merit accreditation.
When the effective date of the new policy arrived on January 1, 1962,
twenty-six of the twenty-eight colleges for Negroes that had been assisted
by the Foundation earned and were accorded full accreditation.[12] The
general picture of accreditation trends is shown in Table 11.

Following this achievement of a measure of ethnic unity and the application of single standards (1957-1962), a second major task was undertaken, this time to move from a quantitative orientation to a qualitative
base of standards. Although this development occurred a quarter of a
century after the Zook-Haggerty proposals, the South was moving force-
fully toward building the concept of quality into its accrediting policies.

In November 1962, the "New Standards" became effective, placing an
increased faith in a decennial plan for Institutional Self-Study and Periodic
Visitation.[13] In 1964, the Executive Council of the Commission on Colleges requested Dr. Sidney T. French to review the Institutional Self-
Study and Periodic Visitation (SSPV) Program. The first ten-year period
of that program began in 1957, and the new standards had been in effect
for two years. Dr. French completed his study in 1965 and reported that
the program was working well, and that it required no major modifications.[14]

The evolution from quantitative to qualitative requirements for accreditation has been exceedingly slow and difficult, but the Southern Association has advanced with good effect. The emphasis on quality gives
hope to those institutions that have a considerable distance to go, but that

---

[11]See: Donald C. Agnew, "Accreditation in the Southern Region," in Lloyd E. Blauch (ed.),
Accreditation in Higher Education (Washington, D.C.: U.S. Office of Education, 1959),
p. 67.

[12]*The Danforth Foundation Annual Report for 1963-64* (St. Louis: Danforth Foundation,
1964), p. 7. The fact of double standards in accreditation prior to 1962 was recognized
and openly admitted.

[13]The Staff of Commission on Colleges, *General Accreditation in Higher Education* (Atlanta:
Southern Association of Colleges and Schools, 1963).

[14]The principal recommendations of Dr. French pertained to revisions in the Manual
(the SSPV Program), modified procedures for the self-study timetable, and more extensive
follow-up at the midpoint of the ten-year cycle. *Proceedings*, p. 47. This study was by no
means exhaustive, but a part-time, one man, informal inquiry into "how things are going."

at least are making progress. Rather than paying homage to the more elite institutions, this emphasis recognizes and honors uniqueness of function, the total effort, and the institutional setting in which the function is fulfilled. Thus the colleges working with educationally disadvantaged high school graduates are entitled to accreditation, one may presume, if they are performing their tasks creditably, even on a subcollegiate level (interpretation is by this author).

TABLE 11

FREQUENCY OF ACCREDITATION OF HISTORICALLY WHITE AND NEGRO INSTITUTIONS OF HIGHER EDUCATION, 1954-1964

State	1954				1964			
	White		Negro		White		Negro	
	Senior Colleges	Junior Colleges	Senior Colleges	Junior Colleges	Senior Colleges	Junior Colleges	Senior Colleges	Junior Colleges
Alabama	12	3	6	0	14	14	5	1
Florida	8	4	3	0	9	12	3	2
Georgia	15	13	9	0	18	15	9	0
Kentucky	14	13	1	0	22	9	1	0
Louisiana	12	1	4	0	15	1	4	0
Mississippi	9	13	4	0	10	17	3	0
North Carolina	20	15	11	0	23	18	11	0
South Carolina	15	1	4	1	15	3	3	1
Tennessee	22	4	5	1	27	5	5	2
Texas	32	22	7	1	41	34	5	1
Virginia	22	6	4	0	25	8	4	0
Total	181	95	58	3	219	126	53	7

Source: Furnished by courtesy of the Executive Secretary, Commission on Colleges, Southern Association of Colleges and Schools, who cautions that some minor notations of explanation would add to the precision of this table, but that as a base of reference, it is substantially correct.

A third major achievement of the Association during this decade has been the development of communitywide educational programs on the elementary and secondary levels for poor and educationally disadvantaged children and youth. Supported largely by the Ford and Danforth foundations, the multimillion dollar Educational Improvement Project is a potential testimony of imaginative vision and aggressive action. Project Opportunity, in cooperation with the College Entrance Examination Board, represents another milestone of strategic achievement in which the Southern Association has had an influential part.

A fourth contribution of the Association has been the safeguarding of institutions of higher education against the threat of political interference with educational affairs. The latent power of its intervention in the Ole Miss desegregation crisis is regarded by some educators as a dominant force in saving Ole Miss and other institutions of the state's monolithic higher educational establishment from virtual disintegration and shambles. More recently, the previously mentioned North Carolina case of 1965 caused the Association to take a forthright stand in the interest of academic freedom. This case pertained to a 1963 North Carolina law regulating visiting speakers at state-supported colleges and universities. The Executive Council of the Association's Commission on Colleges concluded that "the law constitutes political interference with the necessary authority of the affected governing boards."[15] The Association was instrumental in effecting a viable compromise in the law and its application.

In doing so, it held true to its time-honored tradition of intervening in behalf of higher education when it is seriously jeopardized by political activity. Governor Eugene Talmadge of Georgia, more than twenty-five years earlier, had overplayed his political hand and was curbed by the Association's firm stand—a stand of resilience characterized by a hard core of professional integrity. That is the Southern Association's well-earned tradition.

In 1963, during this decade of progress, the Association became incorporated and reformulated its purposes. Its first stated purpose was that of accreditation, but it recognized six others as well, including two that pertain generally to the subject of this study: (1) To operate programs of action that are designed to bring about specific and concrete improvements in educational practice. (2) To discover and disseminate information bearing upon the solution of important problems.

The Southern Association of Colleges and Schools has served its region well during the past decade. The decade ahead, however, will be far more exacting of it. The Association can become a central shaping force in Southern education, or, if it chooses, it can content itself with merely observing the parade of progress until it passes out of view. That decision has, in words, been made. The ensuing years will write the record of that decision.

THE FUTURE OF THE SOUTHERN ASSOCIATION
IN HIGHER EDUCATION

Barring unforeseen major developments among regional associations and national accrediting bodies, the Southern Association will have to carve out its own educational future. It will, as it should, work in concert with the recently established Federation of Regional Accrediting Commissions to explore a mutuality of interests. Sovereign associations can, as a

---

[15] *Proceedings*, p. 59.

federation, learn much from each other. The Association must also continue to depend upon the National Commission for Accrediting for due recognition and for ground rules of operation, if it is to avoid a regression to a national chaotic state of affairs.[16] It must also seek to strengthen, rather than to sever, relationships with the National Council for the Accreditation of Teacher Education.[17]

All of this can be done, regrettably, in a relatively static and impoverished context. The Commission on Colleges of the Southern Association must have a financially healthy body before it can provide substantial strength to its institutional arms. Conversely, only as member institutions make a substantial investment to its fuller functioning can they expect it to become much more than a struggling holding operation until the federal government preempts much of its function, not by choice but out of necessity. The staff alone cannot make that decision. It is an Association policy matter.

The Commission on Colleges of the Southern Association is confronted with one of the most difficult decisions in its history—whether to be governed by its preoccupying function of accreditation or to assume a broad aggressive leadership role in areas now untouched by the accreditation function. With imagination and widespread commitment, it can pursue the latter course; with more conservative and limited goals, it can nonetheless continue to serve a useful function on matters of accreditation and professional fraternity. The Association can go either route honorably and to good purpose, but the need is urgent for it to commit itself either as the Southern Association of Accreditation or as the Southern Association of Colleges and Schools. Fortunately, a Committee on Policies and Functions has been recently formed to give mature and well-informed attention to this issue and to address itself to the task of making recommendations concerning it.

RECOMMENDATIONS AND DISCUSSION

A creditable beginning has been made by the Association in getting a vision of what it can become and what it can do for Southern higher education. But that vision does not appear to be widely shared among college administrators. None would "plough the Association under, " but some see its function as that of a perfunctory body, charged with excluding the degree mills and giving an aura of respectability to most higher education institutions. The annual convention of the Association provides limited hope for sustained planning and action, although a measure of prior committee deliberation maximizes the value of convention programs and committee deliberations. The Association is viewed by some as serving primarily

---

[16]The present director of the National Commission on Accrediting, as many readers know, moved into that position from brief but distinguished service as Executive Director of the Southern Association of Colleges and Schools.

[17]See: Mayor and Swartz, *Accreditation in Teacher Education, passim.*

to provide a rite of passage into the respectable, but not always distinguished subculture of higher education. Yet it is already more than that.
Even if accrediting remains its preoccupying goal, it remains a high mountain to climb. If the Association accepts supportive and mediating responsibilities of leadership, its climb must be even more strenuous.

Collegiate Accreditation

The general problems of this study's concern are already of interest
to the Committee on Policies and Function of the Southern Association,
which has within its purview the activities of the entire Association. The
following recommendations might therefore be considered by that committee, or some ad hoc committee that is able to concentrate on these
problems, and that can propose action for the Association. This should
be a funded, sustained effort designed to yield results that can be acted
upon.

In the application of new accreditation standards, the Association has
recognized the need to provide, for historically white and Negro marginal
institutions alike, a systematic diagnostic service to pinpoint deficiencies
and give sustained assistance to institutions in overcoming them. The
Association's responsibility for rating is coupled with its opportunity for
helping institutions, as it has demonstrated effectively in the past. It
must not stop, but must increase the tempo of that assistance. Title III
of the Higher Education Act of 1965 is an implicit invitation to the Southern
Association to provide extended leadership in this direction.

A review of quantitative standards, and an interpretation of qualitative
standards is already being undertaken to assess the relevancy of new
standards now obtaining,[18] such as those relating to library acquisition
with little regard to the care exercised in choosing library materials and
the nature and extent of their use by students. Similarly, in setting a
fixed percentage of earned doctorates on a given faculty, the Association
should in fact recognize that there are some third-rate doctorate holders,
and some first-rate instructors who for a variety of reasons have not
earned this coin of the higher education realm. The Association is at
work in dealing with these difficult issues. It can do even more.

1. The Association should seek out and encourage institutions that show
a depth of commitment to a special educational cause, coupled with initiative and reasonably adequate resources. Such a commitment to become
centers of excellence in a variety of educational programs should be encouraged and publicized. In the past, the Association has generally been
permissive of flexibility, but in the future it needs to be |m o r e| *supportive*
of those institutions that have a genuine inclination to launch pioneering

---

[18] The Southern Region Conference focused on the need "for new and realistic accrediting
standards to properly measure all of the major facets of the junior college program." See:
Education: The Southern Hope, p. 24. In like vein, collegiate accreditation requirements
merit review with reference to these developing colleges seeking to serve the disadvantaged
youth focused upon in the present study.

efforts in the areas of desegregation, of developmental education for disadvantaged students—white and Negro—to combat the problems of talented
students of financially limited means, or of working at this cluster of
commonly associated problems. The Association needs to champion the
cause of both junior and senior colleges that have unique potential for this
important service to higher education.

2. Institutions should be encouraged to develop *measures of c h a n g e*
among college students, in intellectual acumen, professional competence,
and values, that reach beyond quantitative accreditation. Institutional
research should be encouraged that would reveal both intellectual development among general and specialized lines, and attitudinal change from the
standpoint of social responsibility and its behavioral manifestations. Such
programs as the work programs at Berea College, voluntary community
service, and VISTA-type services illustrate this idea. In this same ser-
vice-oriented context, institutions might more properly be judged by their
holding power than by their academic flunk rate.

3. The Association should focus on the special problems that are widely discussed, but rarely acted upon, such as that of a new level of commitment to creative college teaching—or at least to the improvement of
teaching on freshman as well as graduate levels. A project along such
lines in any of the major areas of instruction would reinforce a qualitative
emphasis on higher education. An excellent teacher of developmental
reading or mathematics may be contributing as much to the general welfare as a professor of advanced ichthyology. Accreditation, with its new
qualitative emphasis, must seek to get at measures of relevant faculty
development for instruction and academic guidance, rather than inferring
competence on the basis of transcripts and publications.

4. Innovations in reaching for qualitative standards and steady improvement should carry some "outward symbol of an inward grace." The
capstone of these efforts to achieve general or specialized excellence
should be publicly acknowledged beyond the inclusive accreditation of
quasi-respectability. There are risks, of course. This recognition should
probably not take the form of an exclusive superaccreditation. Instead,
a few institutions should be recognized as "centers of excellence" for distinguished achievement and/or effort in some aspect of Southern higher
education. The prototype for such an arrangement has been already set
by the National Science Foundation. Why should there not also be recognized centers of excellence in dealing with the spectrum of higher education tasks, including its effective democratization? *Any* accredited institution might reasonably aspire to such achievement, including successful
efforts with desegregation against heavy odds, or of helping students to
overcome their "inherited" problems of socio-economic disadvantage.
Such awards should not be slanted toward these areas but should recognize achievements in providing for excellence and/or equality of opportunity in all of Southern higher education.

These proposals, and others of far greater merit, could strengthen the Association's hand of service to the South. None of them, however, can be given sustained attention without additional staffing and funding. At its present size, the commission's staff would be unable to perform its present duties creditably and give due attention to these matters as well. The commission would indeed face a hazardous conflict of interest. The present staff has achieved an experienced *savoir - faire* in accreditation. In moving beyond the accreditation sphere then, either a relatively separate staff within the Association, or a separate agency outside the Association should deal with the subsequent needs of higher education, in the categories of supportive and mediative functions.

The Supportive Function

Within its central full-time staff and a continuing part-time staff, the Association or some new agency of Southern higher education can perform a number of supportive services, both to collegiate institutions and to college-bound, or college-capable students. This supportive function should be an ever-changing one, characterized by an alertness to immediate and imminent problems that are not competitive with other agencies, but complement them. In many instances, the agency can properly initiate a supportive service and transfer its function in the evolving course of its development, as that function is no longer needed, or as some other agency assumes responsibility for it. The Association has already begun to provide low-cost consultative services in the area of business management without direct reference to accreditation. Such services, if provided at less direct cost, in the educational problem areas, would be a valuable extension of the supportive concept of the Association.

1. The Southern Association, or a separate agency, could perform a signal service by establishing a clearinghouse for Negro and non-Negro professors who seek to exchange professorships, or to be awarded temporary or permanent assignments in institutions unlike their own in racial composition. Such an organization as the Woodrow Wilson Foundation might enter into such a partnership effort. The purpose of such a clearinghouse would not be to foster desegregation among faculty per se, but to make available the total field of available professional talent so that institutions could move in the direction of recruiting faculty without reference to race. Some desegregation would presumably be a growing concomitant of such a plan, but not out of compulsion. Indeed, faculty desegregation is not a legal requirement in higher education—only in elementary and secondary schools—by a curious legal circumstance. Yet we need to build a body of experience along these lines to test out the relevance of faculty desegregation for strengthening the fabric of higher education.

2. Case studies of efforts to move beyond desegregation in Southern institutions of higher education should be actively supported. The era of

desegregation is now largely concluded in its physical and legal dimensions. The next few years will determine the gains and losses of that effort. A study of institutional effort in the interest of extending higher education beyond superficial academic desegregation could be properly fostered by the Southern Association. As it assumed some leadership in its earlier development, now it should promote efforts to assess the present and plan beyond it.

   3. In the South, a lower percentage of college-age students are enrolled in colleges than elsewhere in the nation. Especially is this true among the Negro youth, and, as cited in a previous chapter, the Negro male is statistically rare in higher education. We must not give our exclusive attention to the most acute sector of the problem, of course, but consider it in its entirety. Wherever and whoever disadvantaged college-capable youth are, regardless of race, or sex, they must receive appropriate counseling and assistance so that their choice about higher education becomes a well-informed decision. In that context, high school counselors are in dire need of materials that will be of assistance in working with all youth, but particularly with disadvantaged ones, with reference to higher education. The recent publication by John R. Hills and others, *Counsellor's Guide to Georgia Colleges, 1965,* for the University System of Georgia, illustrates a segment of what might be done on an interstate or regional basis. The Association, or a separate agency, could make a substantial contribution to higher education by providing suitable data for high school counselors, in assisting students to learn how to gain admission, to determine their probable level of achievement in various institutions, to discover means of self-support, and to achieve a sense of success in an appropriate college environment.

   The suggestions made above are not ordered in any priority of significance or validity. Their purpose is only to illustrate that problems in the categories of racial, educational, and economic disadvantage are proper concerns of educational leadership within the South. The Southern Association of Colleges and Schools needs to decide whether to assume such leadership or not.

The Mediative Function

   The concern of regional, voluntary accrediting associations is that their function will, sooner or later, come under government control. The anxiety persists, with a number of new developments for it to feed upon. A more constructive use of concern is that of helping collegiate institutions to clarify their special reasons for existence, and to assist them in the "achievement of the possible." The area is a delicate and controversial one, but with increased familiarity with public and nonpublic institutions, the Association could serve as a highly valuable resource link between colleges and universities on the one hand, and public and private national funding agencies on the other.

The flurry of proposal writing for government and private grants provides a classic case for illustration. Under educationally sound conditions, the grantor and grantee should achieve a "meeting of the minds" in both the goals of a project and the means of achieving it. Often, the opposite condition obtains. The "developing" institution has no finesse in proposal writing, and may have difficulty reconciling its needs with the "grant categories." The Association can be of help to institutions seeking aid from foundation and governmental agencies because of its increased knowledge of the strengths and limitations of institutions, and of the possibilities of genuine multi-institutional cooperation, etc.

It can be, at the same time, a friendly mediator in the best interests of colleges and of funding agencies, serving only at the request of institutions or of such agencies. The quick concern arises, of course, that prejudicial information may be passed along against the grants sought from a foundation or public agency. However, the Association can help institutions to decide against making applications when they might conflict with the economic and educational interests of the institution. In addition, no privileged information would be passed along to a prospective grantor without the institution's knowledge and consent.

One position is that the Southern Association should virtually double the scope of its function, continuing to expand its accrediting services, and moving ambitiously into other leadership roles as well. A strong case can be made for the opposing position, that if the Association performs its accreditation task with distinction, it should not be expected to do much more. Unless the Association makes its own decision, that decision will be made around it, by governmental and private funding agencies. The pivotal point is not so much who does the job, or even who gets credit for the performance, but that, within the South, ways be found to coordinate leadership effort with higher education problems in general, and with the distinctively regional problems of higher education, its neglected vacuum, in particular.

THE ENDEMIC PROBLEM

The problems associated with race, with poverty, and with educational disadvantage have not been singled out as isolated responsibilities of the Southern Association. They are integrally related to its broad pattern of action as a potential major shaping force. If the Association's horizons of responsibility expand, and if it can muster enough fiscal strength to undertake its proper obligations, the Southern Association, and its Commission on Colleges, may yet prove to be a good bet for giving general leadership to the South in higher education. That is what it conceived its purposes, historically, to be. At times, it has lost the way. At times, it has been pushed aside. Over the years, the internal struggles for power between the secondary and higher education interest groups have on occasion caused it to lose sight of its common purpose. Now it is largely preoccupied with the highly significant tasks pertaining to accreditation, and extracurricular projects somewhat peripheral to the Association's main body.

Time may not be running out, but certainly there is no abundance of it remaining. If the Commission on Colleges takes its stand on the most salient issues of Southern higher education, it can give sustained leadership to colleges, some of which are drifting almost without purpose, and can achieve a cosmos from the fragmentary efforts now being made in behalf of excellence and equality. If it elects not to do so, a separate agency or a new association of modern pioneering institutions will be required to meet the higher education challenges confronting this new era of opportunity within the South.

SELECTED REFERENCES

Blauch, Lloyd E. (ed.). *Accreditation in Higher Education.* Washington, D.C.: U.S. Office of Education, 1959.

Dickey, Frank G. "Accreditation and Excellence," *American Association of Colleges for Teacher Education Yearbook,* 15 (Washington, D.C.: AACTE, 1962), 128-134. (Proceedings of the 1962 Annual Meeting, Chicago, Illinois.)

Dressel, Paul L., *et al. Evaluation in Higher Education.* Cambridge: Houghton Mifflin Co., 1961.

Gardner, John W. *Excellence — Can We Be Equal and Excellent, Too?* New York: Harper and Row, 1961. (See especially chap. VIII, "College and the Alternatives.")

Mayor, John R., and Willis G. Swartz. *Accreditation in Teacher Education: Its Influence on Higher Education.* Washington, D.C.: National Commission on Accrediting, 1965.

Proceedings of the Seventieth Annual Meeting of the Southern Association of Colleges and Schools: Education: The Southern Hope, 18:4. Atlanta Southern Association of Colleges and Schools, 1966.

Sweet, Gordon. "General Accreditation in Higher Education." An unpublished work paper developed expressly for this study.

Zook, George F., and M. E. Haggerty. *The Evaluation of Higher Institutions.* Chicago: University of Chicago Press, 1936.

11. THE FEDERAL GOVERNMENT'S EMERGING ROLE

Four years before the present United States Constitution was adopted, the federal government entered the business of education—in 1785, an education act was passed under the Articles of Confederation. Since that time, Americans have continued to debate whether it should do so. That debate approached its end in 1965.

In 1862, a successful merchant and member of the United States Congress, Justin Smith Morrill, who had been a school dropout at the age of fifteen, introduced in Congress a bill giving each state 30,000 acres of federally owned land in the western states for each of its members of Congress. The Morrill Act provided for the income from the sale of these lands to be used to endow institutions at a new kind of college, one that would "promote the liberal and practical education of the industrial [i.e. working] classes in the several pursuits and professions of life."[1] A hundred years later, a centennial committee, in developing a theme statement for the commemoration of the land-grant colleges and universities in America expressed the conviction that: "Education faces always the problem that the Land-Grant movement founders discerned a century ago: the requirement for reappraisal, reorganization, and redirection to meet the needs of time and change. Persistence in old patterns, however resourceful and responsive in their day, are not sufficient."[2]

In this decade, a new impetus has been given to that concept. The federal government has had a great deal to do as a force in American higher education generally, and in Southern higher education most of all. The government has been a respondent to change, as a corporate student of social forces and educational needs, but it has been an initiator of change as well. The National Defense Education Act of 1958, one of many responses to the Sputnik shock, set the government in motion in both of these capacities, with an anxious focus on "excellence." Soon thereafter, Mr. John W. Gardner effectively exposed the imaginary dilemma that a society has to choose between educating the "elite"—however identified—exceedingly well, or of educating the "masses" in a mediocre fashion. Mr.

[1]Contained in foreword by Richard Harvill, in Herman R. Allen, *Open Door to Learning, The Land-Grant System Enters Its Second Century* (Urbana: University of Illinois Press, 1963).
[2]*Ibid.*, pp. *v-vi*.

203

Gardner, who has since become the key guiding force in implementing functional concepts of government in education, advanced this now familiar position: "It is possible to have excellence in education and at the same time to seek to educate everyone to the limit of his ability. A society such as ours has no choice but to seek the development of human potentialities at all levels. It takes more than an educated elite to run a complex, technological society. Every modern, industrialized society is learning that hard lesson." [3]

American society is now embarked on the difficult course of examining that point of view, and the government is seeking to give leadership and guidance in that effort. It is getting a great deal of advice. In 1962 the American Council on Education focused on the theme of "Higher Education and the Federal Government" at its annual meeting, where the conference heard a report from Nathan Pusey on the Carnegie Study of the Federal Government and Higher Education.[4] Not far behind came the Educational Policies Commission of the National Education Association with its official recommendations on *Educational Responsibilities of the Federal Government,*[5] and the White House Conference on Education, which also indirectly served to usher in Mr. Gardner as the new Secretary of Health, Education, and Welfare.

A BIPARTISAN RATIONALE

A review of such materials as those cited here, off-the-record interviews with leaders in higher education, including responsible officials within the federal government, and direct activities concerning institutional recipiency of federal grants combine to show both the range of the possibilities and the real hazards associated with relationships between the federal government and the institutions of higher learning. Underneath the differences of Republican John Gardner and Democratic President L. B. Johnson is a bipartisan bias toward achieving excellence and equality of opportunity in education, including and beyond the high school years. If the American commitment were limited to the vagaries of political fortune, its foundation would be shaky, indeed. But while the form and size of support will vary with political leadership, and international war and peace, that commitment is coming to be regarded as a continuing proposition of the new American way of life.[6]

[3]Gardner, *Excellence: Can We Be Equal and Excellent, Too?* (New York: Harper & Bros., 1961), p. 77.

[4]Charles G. Dobbins (ed.), *Higher Education and the Federal Government: Programs and Problems,* papers presented at the forty-fifth Annual Meeting of the American Council on Education, 1963 (Washington, D. C.: American Council on Education, 1963).

[5]Washington, D. C.: National Education Association, 1964.

[6]In March 1966, a letter from Senator Albert Gore to his constituents cautioned that Congress was blanketed by the Vietnam crisis, and could do little else of far-reaching consequence because of it.

Federal aid has acted historically to stimulate local initiative. Thus, the states took over activities initiated and encouraged by the federal government, invested their own funds in them, and then ran them in their own ways, according to their needs, aspirations, and selfish interests. Federal assistance to education has been, from its beginning, *stimulative*. Much of it has taken the form of support of research in new fields. Support has also been characteristically *strategic*. It has been designed to initiate needed developments not likely to come about through the unassisted efforts of the various states.[7] The Morrill Acts were designed to stimulate new areas of education that would revolutionize the nation's agriculture and its economy. They accomplished that by supplying, in the long run, only a tiny fraction of the necessary resources.[8] The service academies are obvious examples of federal investment in education to meet specific national needs that could not be met by the states. Other examples could include the stimulation of progress in specific fields of critical importance, such as nuclear physics and oceanography, through grants for research and aid to students.

A more recent emphasis of the federal effort is of designing many of its programs to reduce the inequality among the states in the level of educational opportunity they provide. This objective has profound implications for our present focus of concern, among which is an order of magnitude of federal investment far beyond that of the present. The rationale for the changing federal role merits examination.

We live in a society whose members are unwilling that any among them shall have to endure hardship and deprivation without limit. We are unwilling for the unfortunate, the afflicted, and even the undeserving among us to starve, to go without shelter, or even to be deprived of certain minimum levels of comfort and pleasure. In such a society, it is necessary to collect and redistribute, arbitrarily, a part of the wealth of the population. This is done at the local level through private and public agencies. The process is repeated at the state level because there are local areas incapable of maintaining acceptable minimum levels of economic welfare. The process is repeated at the federal level because there is more variation among the states in their ability to provide adequately for the minimum needs of their citizens than our society is now willing to abide.

This pattern of local, state, and federal cooperation is found over and over in our society: in the construction of roads and highways, so that

---

[7] The nature of this likelihood is swiftly changing, as witness the Education Commission of the States coming into fruition in 1966 through the efforts of North Carolina's "Education Governor," the Honorable Terry Sanford, and other educational politicians and political educators.

[8] Like the National *Defense* Education Act of 1958, the Morrill Acts were linked with the matter of national security, directly or remotely.

all areas may be reasonably accessible; in the conservation and development of natural resources; in the development of agriculture and the
stimulation of economic enterprise. All these efforts have a common
objective: to promote the welfare of the people and to help all people
to make progress toward self-sufficiency—and not so incidentally, to
increase the Gross National Product each year.

In a day when some education is a necessity for even limited individual
success, when the high school diploma is often not much of an economic
asset, and when the progress of the nation and the areas within it depends
so greatly upon the advancement of learning, it is essential that great
emphasis be placed upon the provision of universal educational opportunity.
Educational opportunity and economic development, as our society has
learned, cannot live in estrangement.

So long as our society includes large numbers of individuals who have
been denied a reasonable opportunity to develop themselves through education, it will be necessary to take from those who are more productive,
by virtue of greater opportunity for development, in order to provide for
the deprived citizenry. What is true of individuals is true of areas in
which access to educational opportunity is severely limited in amount or
quality. The people and the resources in those areas will continue to be
underdeveloped, and it will be necessary to redistribute to them a part
of the resources of other areas. To perpetuate educational deprivation
is to perpetuate the necessity for redistribution of the fruits of education.
Conversely, collective support of education, at local, state, and federal
levels, is directed toward the development of greater self-sufficiency
on the part of areas and individuals, and spreading the responsibility for
economic productivity over a broader population base.

Not only do industry and economic development follow education, but
each nourishes the other. Where educational opportunities are low, those
who somehow get a good education are tempted to move to other areas in
which business and professional opportunities are greater. The developed
areas get richer and the underdeveloped areas get poorer, both economically and in the cultural development of the population. The provision of
a reasonable level of educational opportunity everywhere is the only means
of reversing the trend. No section of the country should be penalized
for inability to pay for education, and no individual should be denied education because he cannot pay for it. To deny education either to the individual or to the geographical areas is to reduce the corresponding potential
for productivity and contribution to society's success.

But there is an aspect of the provision of educational opportunity that
goes beyond even so vital a matter as the economic and scientific progress
of the nation. It is the dignity and intrinsic worth of each individual. When
the people of the townships in Massachusetts decided to tax themselves
in order to establish common schools, they did so out of conviction that
in a democracy each child must have an opportunity for education, that

he should not be excluded from this opportunity, set apart, or denied adequate training because of the economic or social status of his family, or any other circumstance beyond his control. Thus the basic justification for the setting up of tax-supported schools in the beginning was the need for provision of an adequate educational opportunity to all. This was also the justification for state legislation permitting local districts to tax themselves to support local schools. It was, again, the justification for early state legislation that provided for state taxes to assist the local districts and counties, which were and are unevenly equipped to meet the educational needs of their children. Many states cannot now, of themselves, lift educational opportunity to a reasonable minimal level. The logic that has led the states to assist counties and districts within them, leads also to the conclusion that the federal government must assist the states.

In the past, we Americans have tended to respond to educational needs in relation to crises—Sputnik, for example—rather than out of positive and forward-looking philosophies. The same forces that caused the past generation to raise educational standards to include the secondary level now clamor for still greater intellectual maturity. We know the importance of education in relation to research and technology, to economic and social change, and to international developments. We know that in order for a society to grow by innovation, education must provide the skills needed by creative and discriminating individuals, and inspire them with a zeal for service and a sense of direction to make the future better than the past. We know all of these things, and yet we as a nation might not yet be stirring ourselves from educational lethargy were it not for the recognition that educational assistance in the South, in Appalachia, and elsewhere, would really help the whole nation head off a downhill plunge to another crisis, a crisis brought on by the dissatisfaction of inequality in a society that prides itself on equality of opportunity and continuous striving for excellence.

The fact that the South, and Appalachia, and a few other places have been singled out as examples of needs in education may not be good for regional pride. But what is lost in pride may be compensated for by the satisfaction of being the catalyst for educational improvements across the country; indeed, around the world. For there is a growing realization that the best road to real progress lies not in patronage, at home or abroad— although some patronage may be necessary—but in helping people to help themselves. Only by fulfilling our educational aims can we accomplish the other, perhaps more lofty, aims of economic and social progress.

Education—relevant and coherent education—is the major factor that determines the difference between progress and stagnation for the individual, for the local community, for the state, for the region, and for the nation. Higher education's task for self-examination and for innovative growth was placed in accurate perspective by William Friday, president

of the Consolidated University of North Carolina, in his October 15, 1964,
address to the Association of Governing Boards of Universities and Colleges:

> What we refer to as a "tidal wave" of enrollment growth in American
> schools and colleges is but a ripple of the world population explosion.
> What we refer to as increased emphasis on research and investigation
> relative to teaching is but one facet of the world-wide explosion of knowl-
> edge—vast, accumulative, and accelerating new outreaches of scientific
> and technical knowledge. What we call inflationary trends is but one
> segment of world-wide economic adjustment necessitated by new fiscal
> patterns, new political alignments, and what some authorities have aptly
> described as the "revolution of rising expectations." What we see as a
> basically altered relationship between educational institutions and the
> government, alterations affecting both public and private institutions and
> tending to minimize the difference between them, are but side effects of
> the pervasive and perplexing cold war, of the global confrontation between
> forces of liberty and forces of coercion.[9]

Our task, in the South as elsewhere, is not to judge the past as a per-
petrator of the ills of the present, but to recognize the meaning of the
present, and to raise in the classrooms the really big questions in life.
We can thereby help our youth to develop the powers of discrimination for all
kinds of learning, in school and out, so that they can meet the uncertainties
with equanimity and with commitment to a better future within their own
thinking and within their own dealings with their fellow men. The rationale
for federal assistance to education is attached to such lofty motives as
these, as well as to some less noble political ones.

The South's Recent Past and Its Present

The problems of education in the South were recognized by some far-
seeing Southerners long before civil rights legislation made the quality
of this education a national concern. In 1936, Charles William Dabney
noted the additional burden of a dual school system in the South, and
questioned the financial ability of the South "to educate and train the
children of poor tenants, black and white, as they should be, as they
must be, if the next generation is to be any better off than their parents."
He pointed out that "the South spends a larger portion of her funds on
education than do other sections," and that "if the South spends far less
money for schools than the average of other states, it is because she has
not the money to spend." [10] He employed census figures to show that, in
1930, the average expenditure per pupil for white children in the South
was less than half that of the national average, and that for Negro children
it was only about a fourth of that for Southern white children, or about an

[9]Friday, "Views of the Future," *Association of Governing Boards Reports,* 7:2 (1964), 4.
[10]Virginius Dabney, *Universal Education in the South,* Vol. II (Chapel Hill: University of
North Carolina Press, 1936), pp. 489-495.

eighth of that of the average in the nation. As a solution, he suggested a national equalization fund:

> We have shown that this great work of educating the poor whites and the Negroes of the South cannot be done by the southern people unaided. As it is impossible for a single locality to meet more than a small part of the expense of the school, making it necessary for the state to help, so it has come about that the state cannot bear all the expense of its schools, making it necessary for the Federal government to help. The training of these neglected people is not merely a state task; it is a national task— a national duty.

We share the indictment, as an entire nation, that we have waited nearly thirty years since this pronouncement before the enactment of the Elementary and Secondary Education Act of 1965. We can ill afford any additional lags of this character, scratching off another generation from opportunity.

What the South can now do in higher education is intimately related to what it has been doing in elementary and secondary education. The quality of such education and the proportion of young people who complete it have a profound effect upon the quality of higher education that can be undertaken and the proportion who attempt it. This is one of the South's major recognized handicaps. States in and bordering the South rank at the bottom of the scale in median school years completed and in the percentage of the adult population with at least four years of high school or with at least four years of college.[11] With the relatively low percentage who enter college, there are problems of staffing the schools of each generation—and the cycle of educational disadvantage grows more intense in the same way that the cycle of poverty feeds on its own hunger. This works the other way around, too. Where higher education serves a relatively large percentage of the population, there is a pool of educated individuals from which to draw educational staff and leadership for business and the professions.

And yet, the South is anything but lazy or indifferent regarding education. In 1963, per-capita personal income in the South was only about 75 percent of what it was in the nation as a whole. The ten states with the lowest per-capita personal income were all in the South or bordering it. In that same year, as shown in the following table, when public school revenue for the nation was only 1.7 percent of personal income, it was 2.7 percent in Alabama, 2.8 percent in Georgia, 3.9 percent in Louisiana, 2.8 percent in Mississippi, 3.3 percent in North Carolina, and 3.4 percent in South Carolina. But not *one* of these states approached anything near the national average per pupil expenditure for current expenses in the schools.

[11]Digest of Educational Statistics (1963), pp. 96ff. See also: *Senate Hearings of the Elementary and Secondary Education Act,* Part I (Washington, D.C.: Government Printing Office, 1963), p. 592.

TABLE 12

EDUCATION—THE TASK AND THE RESOURCES—IN STATES IN AND BORDERING THE SOUTH, COMPARED TO THE UNITED STATES AVERAGE

States	Dimensions of the Task				Resources			Efforts		Problems		Aid
	Median School Years Completed, Persons 25 and Older, 1960	Percentage of Population Illiterate, 1960 (14 Years and Older)	Percentage Draftees Failing Mental Tests, 1963	Recipients on Public Assistance, per 1000 Population, 1964	Percentage of Per-Capita Income in Relation to National, 1963	Percentage of Households With Incomes Less Than $2,500, 1963	Percentage of Nonpublic School Enrollment, 1961-1962*	State Tax as Percent of Personal Income	Percent of Personal Income Spent on Public Schools, 1963	Percentage of Instructional Salary in Relation to National Average, 1964-1965	Percentage of Expenditure per Pupil in Relation to National Average, 1964-1965	Per-Capita Federal Aid to States, Local Units, and Individuals, 1963
United States	10.6	2.4%	24.7%	40	100.0%	22.3%	14.2%	5.3%	1.7%	100.0%	100.0%	$58
Alabama	9.1	4.2	43.2	64	67.6	35.8	4.0	6.9	2.7	75.5	59.6	65
Arkansas	8.9	3.6	49.1	54	65.6	39.4	2.8	6.8	2.0	66.7	65.6	79
Delaware	11.1	1.9	23.0	35	134.7	15.3	20.0	6.4	3.5	105.4	111.0	67
Florida	10.9	2.6	33.8	34	86.2	33.0	7.2	5.9	2.3	97.2	83.4	45
Georgia	9.0	4.5	40.1	45	76.1	26.0	3.1	6.4	2.8	80.2	68.3	61
Kentucky	8.7	3.3	34.6	49	73.2	34.9	12.7	6.4	2.3	76.0	66.9	66
Louisiana	8.8	6.3	51.2	76	72.5	34.0	16.9	8.9	3.9	83.0	86.5	85
Maryland	10.4	1.9	31.7	31	113.8	14.1	19.2	5.2	1.3	109.4	104.1	48
Mississippi	8.9	4.9	52.3	77	56.8	41.0	3.1	7.4	2.8	65.4	56.5	70
Missouri	9.6	1.7	18.7	56	102.8	24.6	16.5	4.3	1.2	89.9	90.5	62
North Carolina	8.9	4.0	43.8	41	73.8	30.1	1.5	7.3	3.3	81.1	66.7	44
Oklahoma	10.4	1.9	14.2	69	79.7	33.1	3.8	6.8	1.3	82.4	75.8	92
South Carolina	8.7	5.5	50.7	29	64.8	32.8	2.7	7.1	3.4	70.3	59.8	46
Tennessee	8.8	3.5	31.3	41	72.8	34.7	4.3	6.2	2.2	76.4	62.1	68
Texas	10.4	4.1	28.1	32	84.4	28.2	6.9	5.3	2.4	87.1	82.0	53
Virginia	9.9	3.4	35.8	17	84.0	29.9	6.8	4.9	1.6	86.8	78.7	48
West Virginia	8.8	2.7	38.3	88	76.9	30.5	3.6	6.9	2.3	73.7	65.2	62

*United States average for fall 1962, calculated from *Digest of Educational Statistics*, 1963 edition, USOE-10024-63, p. 85. Data for states from "Shared-Time Programs: An Exploratory Study," Research Report 1964-RIO, Research Division, National Education Association, as quoted in Hearings, *op. cit.*, p. 453.

Source: Senate Hearings of the Elementary and Secondary Education Act, Part I, pp. 453, 588, 592-595, 597, 600, 604, 613, 622, as taken from *Rankings of the States, 1965*, Research Report 1965-RI, Research Division, National Education Association.

Furthermore, the South has few students in private and parochial schools compared to the nation as a whole. While no citizen would expect to shirk his public education responsibility, we may as well recognize that the public burden is relieved to the extent that it is carried by private and parochial schools.

Obviously, when there is little with which to work and when the task is enormous, it takes a greater amount of effort. But education is not the only burden on the South. There is also a heavier welfare and public assistance load. In January 1964, for example, the seven states with the largest proportion of public assistance recipients were either in the deep South or in the bordering states.

One does not really need precise data to realize that poverty and lack of education in one segment of the population add to the burden in other segments. That fact is evident in the way state and local taxes have to be levied upon those who have, in order to provide some measure of the necessities of life for those who have not. In 1963, per-capita federal aid to states, localities, and individuals was $58 for the nation as a whole. In Alabama, such per-capita aid was $65; in Arkansas, $79; in Kentucky, $66; in Louisiana, $85; in Mississippi, $70; in Tennessee, $68. Such figures further attest to the need for redistribution of income in an effort to offset educational disadvantages.

It is better for the nation, and for us as individuals, to invest in our future through educating our youth rather than wasting their talents, which limits our productive potential, and thereby lowers the resources out of which we shall have to pay for the welfare of the uneducated—which becomes a vicious circle. We have come—Republicans, Democrats, and Independents—to accept a new version of that duty.

The Changing Nature of Higher Education

The proportion of our population who went on to higher education a generation ago is a crucial factor in staffing our schools and colleges today, and the proportion who attend college today will be a crucial factor in the kind and quality of education we can offer tomorrow. The matter of who goes to college and who does not go is more than a problem of identifying academic competence and providing adequate finance. Student selection itself is a social force, and educational opportunity is a public responsibility. Leadership or lethargy in providing educational opportunity for our youth today will determine the kind of leadership we will have to handle the public issues of tomorrow. When, or whether, a boy or girl goes to college should not be simply a question of his academic aptitude and ability to pay for it. It reflects the hopes and aspirations of parents, of the school, and of the community. This social force is not just a matter of getting the student into and through college; it is also a matter of whether he is inclined to use his education in socially productive ways in his postcollege years. College success is not enough; it is a relative matter. In some cases, it may mean the conforming, compulsive, dependent, and unoriginal accumulation of information. In other cases, it may mean creative, purposeful learning and commitment to continuous learning and service throughout life.

Providing for higher education in the South, as elsewhere, is not simply a matter of increasing faculty and facilities, in itself a formidable task. Although better utilization of staff and facilities will help, there is still the need to adjust programs and practices to accommodate emerging needs. To prepare our youth to act with judgment, composure, and purpose in the face of rapid social and technological changes, our colleges and universities must re-examine their objectives in terms of today's society and initiate innovations to provide the kind of climate conducive to a "self-renewing society. "[12] Since economic realities increasingly demand at least some higher education for almost all lines of work, the concept of higher education must be expanded to include a wide range of community college programs for students interested in subprofessional and technical work. The fact that students are succeeding in college does not warrant the conclusion that colleges are succeeding with students.

Higher education is no longer merely the province of the academically oriented individual who finishes a degree and aspires to graduate study. It is also the province of the individual who wants the abilities necessary to shift jobs as conditions change, and aspires to the understanding and appreciation necessary for coping with the leisure time resulting from a shorter work week. More and more, higher education must serve not only to prepare young people for the world of work but also to prepare adults for changes in the world in general. In the years ahead, the demands for higher education for adults may multiply far faster than current demands are growing for our youth. These conditions in America, and these views about them, support the proposition that the federal government must participate massively in the public education task, in the interest of the general welfare.

FEDERAL AID—A SYMBOL OF NATIONAL RESPONSIBILITY

This nation has always taken pride in the state and municipal autonomy within the system of public education, and the independent initiative of private colleges and universities. New funds provided by federal legislation are a form of acknowledgment that higher education is also a public responsibility in the national interest. The urgency of that recognition is manifest by the annual increase in higher education enrollments: 1964, five million; 1965, 5.9 million; 1966, seven million (estimated).

Before 1958, financial assistance available to all of higher education through the United States Office of Education was only a little more than $5 million, largely from land-grant funds. In the fiscal year 1965, it

[12]See: John W. Gardner, "Renewal of Societies and Men" (New York: *Annual Report* of the Carnegie Corporation, 1962).

exceeded $700 million, the major part of which was for National Defense Education Act programs and higher education facilities.[13] These figures exclude programs such as Cooperative Research, which provide funds on a contractual basis. It will be helpful to review, for background purposes, some of the provisions of funds made available to higher education through action by the 88th and the 89th Congress, between January 1963 and March 1966, which pertain to problems associated with poverty, with race, and with educational disadvantage.

The 88th Congress

1. The Health Professions Educational Assistance Act of 1963 (PL 88-129) authorized a three-year program of grants to help construct new teaching facilities and improve existing facilities for the training of additional physicians, dentists, pharmacists, nurses, optometrists, podiatrists, and professional public health workers. The act's loan provisions are designed to assist students who have the capacity and a career ambition for these fields, but who would not otherwise be able to afford training. Loans are limited to $2,000 per student per academic year. The program is administered through the Bureau of State Services, Public Health Service.

2. Title III, Education Provisions, of the Mental Health Facilities and Community Mental Health Centers Construction Act of 1963 (PL 88-164), authorized grants to help public and other nonprofit colleges and universities to train a corps of teachers and other professional staff for education of the handicapped. The act also seeks to stimulate needed research and demonstration projects through grants to institutions and research organizations.

3. To extend the enrollment capacity of higher education institutions, the Higher Education Facilities Act of 1963 (PL 88-204) authorized a $1.2 billion investment by the federal government in the academic facilities needed by public and other nonprofit colleges and universities. There are special provisions to accommodate the unique role of public community colleges and technical institutes to spur the development and better geographic distribution of graduate schools.

4. Title I authorized a five-year program of grants to construct and improve academic facilities, with 22 percent earmarked for public community colleges and public technical institutes and the remainder available to public and nonprofit private institutions for the construction of teaching or research facilities in the natural or physical sciences, mathematics, modern foreign languages, or engineering, or for libraries. The five-year program of grants authorized by Title II will expand and improve academic facilities in present graduate schools and centers and assist in developing topflight new ones.

[13]See: "What the 88th Congress Did for American Schools and Colleges," *Milestones in Education* (January 1963-October 1964), OE-10031-A, p. 45.

5. Title III authorized loans for academic facilities, thus extending available aid beyond that authorized in the first two titles. Appropriations for the fiscal year 1965 were $463 million, including loans and grants.

6. Portions of the Vocational Education Act of 1963 (PL 88-210) are applicable to higher education, and the criteria call for junior colleges, technical institutions, and other institutions offering vocational training to be represented on advisory councils charged with carrying out state plans. The act makes permanent the area technical education programs which were established under Title VIII of the National Defense Education Act of 1958; provides construction and equipment funds to be used for the vocational education quarters of high schools and colleges meeting certain conditions of instruction, as well as for area vocational centers; makes special funds available for locally administered work-study programs; and provides grants for the construction, equipment, and operation of residential vocational schools (upon appropriation of funds) to state boards for vocational education, to colleges and universities, or, with state board approval, to local public education institutions. Ten percent of funds authorized by the act are to be channeled into grants for research, experimentation in the curriculum, development of instructional materials and teacher training, and other projects of a related nature.

The act, which is administered by the Division of Vocational and Technical Education of the Office of Education, is highly flexible in the level of the educational continuum to which funds can be made available, so that it is difficult to say how much of the $158 million in its fiscal 1965 appropriations went to higher education.

7. The National Defense Education Act has had an impact on virtually every college and university in the United States, as well as on elementary and secondary schools. Through its Amendments of 1963 and 1964 (PL 88-210 and PL 88-665), it has been extended through the fiscal year 1968. In the six years following its passage, more than 640,000 undergraduate and graduate students took advantage of the loan provisions of Title II. The federal government provides about 90 percent of that money. Over the first six years, loans averaged $484 each, for a total of $443 million. The amendments liberalize loan provisions in a number of important ways and increase the amount of authorization.

Amendments to Title IV provide for substantial increases in the number of graduate fellowships, liberalize the qualifications for fellowships, and provide additional funds. Title V, which initially was directed to improvement of guidance, counseling, and testing in the secondary schools, has been amended to include public junior colleges and technical schools. It also broadens and liberalizes guidance training institutes set up by colleges and universities. Title VI, as amended, continues and expands the activities of language and area centers in their efforts to provide instruction in neglected languages, and in their teacher-training institutes. In fact, the language institute program produced such interest and activity that the 88th Congress separated it into a new Title (XI) which will not only continue to support foreign language institutes but will establish institutes for school librarians, for educational media specialists, for teachers of history, geography, English, and reading, and for those teachers who work with disadvantaged youth. The 1964 legislation continued the annual authorization of $5 million for research to promote more effective educational use of television, radio, motion pictures, and similar media, and to increase the flow of information about their use to the schools.

The Vocational Education Act of 1963 made Title VIII permanent and authorized $15 million annually for technical education. Except for Title IX, which is concerned with science information and is administered by the National Science Foundation, the massive program of the National Defense Education Act is administered by various divisions of the Office of Education. The bulk of fiscal 1965 appropriations of $349 million were for higher education.

8. Titles IV and VI of the Civil Rights Act of 1964 (PL 88-352) are concerned specifically with education. Title IV authorized the Commissioner of Education to conduct a survey for the President and the Congress on the availability of equal opportunity in education because of race, color, religion, or national origin.[14] The title gives the commissioner the means to help communities deal not only with the desegregation process itself, but with the educational challenge issuing from it. Through it, scores of educational institutes have been arranged with colleges, universities, and school districts for teachers and administrators to provide assistance in planning and executing improvements in the educational program for children involved in desegregation.

In Title VI of the Civil Rights Act, Congress outlawed discrimination in federally assisted programs and imposed on each agency the responsibility to insure that such discrimination is ended—by voluntary compliance if possible, but if necessary by the prospect of the discontinuance of federal assistance. This title therefore touches every area of federal assistance in higher education. Those parts of the act concerned with educational assistance programs are administered by the Program of Equal Educational Opportunities of the Office of Education. Institutions of higher education filing assurances of voluntary compliance with the Office of Education were discussed in Chapter IX.

9. Through the Juvenile Delinquency and Youth Offenses Control Act (PL 88-368) and 1964 amendments, fourteen training centers at as many universities were established to prepare youth workers for a variety of fields. Provision is also made for curriculum development, for short-term workshops, and for traineeships in connection with the training centers and workshops. Included in the education provisions of the Economic

---

[14] This survey has been conducted under the direction of Dr. Ernest Q. Campbell, Chairman of the Department of Sociology at Vanderbilt University.

Opportunity Act of 1964 (PL 88-452) is the College Work-Study Plan, which provides funds to colleges and universities to enable them to offer needy students useful part-time work. Such work may be on campus or in the community, but it must serve some public interest, and must be work that would not otherwise be accomplished. The program is administered by the Division of Student Financial Aid of the Office of Education.

10. The Nurse Training Act of 1964 (PL 88-581) authorizes construction grants to boost the enrollment capacity of colleges, universities, junior colleges, and hospitals. The bill also authorizes support for a wide range of teaching improvement projects, for a student loan program to attract new recruits to nursing and for traineeships to provide staff competencies. Various divisions of the Public Health Service are responsible for administering the Nurse Training Act.

The above programs of the Office of Education all grew out of the legislative activities of the 88th Congress. Among the benefits from earlier legislation, as previously mentioned, are funds to land-grant colleges, which in fiscal 1965 amounted to about $14 million, and those through Cooperative Research (PL 83-531), which in fiscal 1965 amounted to nearly $16 million, and went largely to colleges and universities for educational research and related activities.

Through the years, legislation has also provided benefits to higher education through a variety of other government agencies. Most of this legislation has been directed toward the establishment of programs or the encouragement of specialized training considered important to the national welfare. Although each agency's programs have generally focused upon its particular area of concern, the support generally falls into one or more of the categories of research and development; facilities and equipment; institutional grants; fellowships and traineeships; training grants; federal schools and training of personnel; and other student support.

In addition to research and development, and other programs under general administration of various departments, there are special programs by such agencies as the National Science Foundation, the Atomic Energy Commission, the Public Health Service, the Vocational Rehabilitation Administration, the National Aeronautics and Space Administration, the Veterans Administration, and the Housing and Home Finance Agency. One example will suffice to suggest the scope and focus of these specialized programs. In 1965, the National Science Foundation provided support for facilities and equipment for specialized research and institutional science programs, for institutional grants and specialized science education grants, for fellowships and traineeships in science, and for training grants for institutes and other training programs in science. The National Arts and Humanities Foundation, with its beginning grant of $2.5 million, has not yet determined how humanistic and how humane the direction of its services will be. Already there appears some division within those ranks.

Measured by dollars, the specialized programs of these and other departments and agencies have made an enormous contribution to higher education. They have filled important needs in the nation's welfare and, in one way or another, have assisted most colleges and universities. But they are inclined to leave peaks and valleys in areas of emphasis. The growing realization of these gaps, along with other forces, led to the passage of the Elementary and Secondary Education Act (PL 89-10) of 1965, by the 89th Congress, along with the Higher Education Act of 1965.

The 89th Congress

Public Law 89-10 which authorized $1.3 billion initially, is the most far-reaching education bill ever passed by the American Congress. It is a striking assumption of national responsibility for assisting in the development of quality education programs at all levels and in all states. It is too early to say just how much of the funds will go to higher education institutions. That tends to miss the point a bit anyway. Certainly, the colleges and universities will have to provide a measure of leadership, including consultative services, training, and important research to help carry out the intent of the act, even though most of the titles provide that funds are administered through the states. Many colleges and universities will be particularly interested in Title IV, which is directed toward improvement of educational research and training. This title enlarges the Cooperative Research program and authorizes $100 million over a five-year period for the construction and development of regional educational laboratories for research and action purposes.

These laboratories aim to provide a network for research and educational action, and frequently cross state lines in an effort to establish natural regions insofar as practicable. The first nine tentative laboratories show the emerging regional pattern of areas across the nation:

Southeastern Education Corporation, Tallahassee, Florida
(Alabama, Georgia, and Florida)

Appalachia Regional Educational Laboratory, Morgantown, West Virginia
(West Virginia and parts of Pennsylvania)

Mid-Continent Regional Educational Laboratory, Kansas City, Missouri
(eastern Kansas, western Missouri, and parts of Nebraska)

Central Mid-Western Regional Educational Laboratory, St. Louis, Missouri
(eastern Missouri, western Kentucky, western Tennessee,
eastern Illinois, and northeastern Kansas)

Upper Midwest Regional Educational Laboratory, Minneapolis, Minnesota
(North Dakota, Minnesota, Iowa, and South Dakota)

Northwest Regional Educational Laboratory, Portland, Oregon
(Oregon, Washington, Montana, Idaho, and Alaska)

Far West Regional Educational Laboratory, San Francisco, California
(northern California and western Nevada)

Continental Divide Consortium, Boulder, Colorado
(parts of Wyoming, Colorado, New Mexico, Utah, Arizona,
Nevada, Montana, Idaho, South Dakota, Kansas, and Nebraska)

Research for Better Schools, Inc., Philadelphia, Pennsylvania
(southeastern Pennsylvania, southern New Jersey, and Delaware)[15]

The Higher Education Act of 1965 was the culmination of effort in the federal response to the growing needs of higher education.[16] Its Title III, "Strengthening Developing Institutions," seeks to help the institutions where the poor and educationally disadvantaged youth are, and where they continue to be penalized by further disadvantage rather than receiving equitable remediation. The "in between" colleges, whether they be junior or senior colleges, which dip down below usual college-level instruction, offer the greatest potential hope for disadvantaged college-capable youth. Here, at least, they need not apologize for their own earlier mistreatment by their society.

Title IV, with its provision for student assistance, again extends opportunities to those who are deserving. Title V, "Teacher Programs," can eventually establish a nationally significant Teachers Corps to get at the roots of some educational problems of areas of low-income families. Title VI, designed to strengthen the quality of undergraduate instruction, can do so despite some of its categorical restrictions. Title VII, with its extensions and amendments to the Higher Education Facilities Act of 1963, can also be of significant help.

In 1966, congressional attention has shifted to study of international education, but not at the substantive expense of the Higher Education Act of 1965. Neither the Vietnam War, nor President Johnson's haste to land Americans on the moon before 1970 has forced a moratorium on the achievement of the enunciated goals of American higher education. The president's message to Congress, on March 1, 1966,[17] and the "Higher Education Amendments of 1966"[18] provide sufficient reassurance on that

---

[15]Source: *Newsletter*, American Association of Colleges for Teacher Education (March 1966), p. 6. Planning for a tenth laboratory is under way at the Center for Urban Education in New York City.

[16]For details, see: *Higher Education Act of 1965, Section by Section Analysis*, OE-50045. For more current information, contact the Assistant Commissioner for Legislation, U.S. Office of Education.

[17]"Review of Achievements in the Fields of Health and Education and Further Recommendations for Attaining Goals," 89th Cong., 2nd sess., H. Doc. 395.

[18]HR-13174, 89th Congress, 2nd session.

point. In all of this legislation, the government's effort to equalize regional inequities of educational opportunity has concentrated its aid program on the South, and that concentration will continue.[19]

THE PROOF OF THE PUDDING

The federal government's intervention in the support of education for the general welfare is a sudden extension of the American dream in the new world, one of equality of opportunity and excellence of attainment. The government's action extends this concept to institutional as well as to individual opportunity, so that a college can be what it is "cut out to be" in the public interest, rather than be doomed to dubious status and questionable service.

Higher education for economic productivity, civic maturity, and responsible leadership is within the grasp of Southern institutions if they exercise imaginative initiative toward these ends. In so doing, they will not need to water down academic standards, but to redefine them, to match the standards against the aspiration and capacity of the man or woman who seeks to attain them.

Despite these favorable signs, there is an ominous uncertainty about the response of the South to its new challenges. It will find its rationale in the character of implementation, by Congress, by the Office of Education, and by the Southern institutions of higher learning themselves. The 88th and the 89th Congress seemed to be the most productive of educational opportunity in the twentieth century. Then came Vietnam. Even though diverted from educational needs to foreign misfortunes, the 89th Congress, in its second session, left ample slack for higher education to carve out its work for years to come.

The Adjustment of Ethnic Togetherness

The Civil Rights Act of 1964, with attending legislation and judicial decisions, has made clear the rights of Negroes within the South. But the Negro there is not sure how to act as a free man or woman, and his adjustment mechanisms are unpredictable. He must not be vindictive, or he will be a poor winner. He must not be beholden to his Caucasian peers, because this simply changes the form of his subservience. He must not press beyond his legal rights because this is not good manners; yet he must not stop there, because this infers an inherent prejudice among Caucasians. The predominantly Negro institution is in a peculiarly difficult position because Caucasians do not exercise their right to attend such institutions. They have, in the main, never regarded it as a right any more than officers have regarded it as a right to leave officer's country to eat at the enlisted men's mess.

---

[19] See: "Rankings of the States, 1966," Research Division, National Education Association, Washington, D.C., 1966.

Predominantly white institutions must "comply," whatever compliance ultimately turns out to mean. Most Southern college presidents welcome the Assurance of Compliance requirement, either as a moral compunction or as a shifting of their own decision-making responsibility to the shoulders of Uncle Sam. Yet, underneath, some Southern administrators feel a sense of guilt for taking a bribe to accomplish desegregation. Typically, they also feel a sense of honor, once bribed, to abide by its conditions in good faith. Federal monies are clearly accomplishing "togetherness." If the Office of Education does not press insensitively, the end goals of ethnic desegregation for a common humanity may yet be realized in our time.

The Perils of Prosperity

The sudden reversal of fortune, whether rags to riches or riches to rags, necessitates a considerable adjustment. The rags-to-riches adjustment is regarded by some sociologists as the more difficult. The problem of the *nouveau riche* may prove to be the greatest single peril in Southern higher education. It is possible to drown the South in quenching its thirst.

The Office of Education faces its own prosperity dilemma. With unprecedented funds for disbursement, more than a hundredfold in a decade, comes a new sense of power, and a compulsion to spend all appropriated funds before they "revert," or before appropriations are reduced because of one year's surplus—an openly recognized malpractice in government spending.

Institutional diffusion of purpose results from asking for everything for which colleges may be technically eligible. The sudden availability of funds for a myriad of purposes has caught the South off guard. Colleges are woefully unselective in their requests for aid and unprepared to fulfill their contracts in a creditable manner once awarded.

An institution ought to be what it is cut out to be, but it is apt to be lured from its true self by the encouragement of various governmental backers offering it more than it can assimilate. The South's past problems have been those of obtaining adequate funding for legitimate educational needs. It now faces the perplexity of finding professional staffing to develop suitable programs for readily available funding. Federal officials have been privately labeled "agents of seduction," enticing institutions to apply for grants unrelated to their purpose, facilities, and available staffing.

Proposal Poverty and Prosperity

Some institutions have learned to incorporate federal assistance in ways to strengthen and advance their central missions. Others have learned to "drain off" federal funds for other collegiate ends, such as unrelated graduate scholarships and the like. Others unwittingly have drained off their own resources, weakening their central program to attract marginal grants from governmental sources. The relationships between institutions and the federal government range from highly sophisticated grantmanship to economic naivete.

In institutional terms, the situation is much like the poor joke about the poverty program to the effect that everyone becomes more wealthy but the poor. Equalization does not mean indiscriminate giving to the "developing institutions." But there is an inequity in leaving the pattern of proposal writing and implementation to each institution. If any case could be made for compensatory preference, it would be in getting some of the less promising institutions into the mainstream of Southern higher education. The college with its staff depleted by being "picked over" by its affluent competitive sister institutions calls out for equality. The government should facilitate cooperation in higher education rather than reinforce the present unhealthy state of collegiate competition.

Questions and Answers

The most alarming symptom of the shaping forces of the federal government does not lie with the government at all. It lies with the basic questions that each institution asks itself. The question privately implicit in proposals for grants is, of course, "What's in it for us?" The more fundamental question, however, is "What are we in it for?" John F. Kennedy was talking to the Southern higher education establishment as well as to the other sectors of American life when he admonished us not to ask what our country could do for us, but to inquire instead what we could do for our country. The new opportunity ushered in by massive federal support is attended by an alarming money malady, and it is growing to epidemic proportions. Enlightened self-interest requires that we ask the educational questions as well as the economic ones, in the context of institutional self-control.

RECOMMENDATIONS

The road is steep and tortuous from the formulation of the concept of excellence and equality of opportunity in higher education to its realization. It has to be traveled by companions on that journey, not by wayfarers each suspicious of the other and unworthy of trust. There are no federal devils behind the legislation, though some of it clearly shows its political as well as its educational aspirations and modus operandi. Congress, the Office of Education, and the entity of Southern higher education have to work in mutual trust, and at the same time, keep themselves and each other honest with reference to worthy ends and the legitimate means by which they may be attained.

1. Congress must make a firm long-range commitment to the implementation of its avowed goals, so that higher education will know, in substance, what it can count on. The National Aeronautics and Space

Administration need not worry that its astronauts at an intermediate space station in the Apollo program will be instructed to return to the earth due to a lack of appropriated funds for the remainder of the journey. The goals of education must represent an equally firm commitment, in substantive form, to minimize the crash efforts growing out of desperation or opportunism. The near loss of National Defense Education Act loans in 1966 illustrates the constant threat of crisis that impedes efforts in higher education to provide for college-capable youth of limited financial means.

2. Congress must devise imaginative means for encouraging nonspending or delayed-spending in achieving goals. Timetables are often unrealistic. The pattern of frenetic spending to avoid reversion of funds to the federal government should not be reinforced. Hasty spending compounds problems, even with sound planning. The practice of spending in haste and repenting at leisure characterizes far too many well-intentioned congressional appropriations. The need to locate competent staff, or to develop them, cannot be safely by-passed, and imprudent spending in higher education can become its long-range undoing.

3. More "lead time" is essential between the appropriation for a federally financed activity and its implementation. Too often, the time intervals between the assurance of support for a program or its expansion, its guideline sequels, and its required implementation deadline is a monstrosity of expectation. Good ideas *have to have* a reasonable chance of initial success.[20] Saturation efforts result in limited success, placing pressure on those responsible for such programs to falsify about success and failure rather than to provide fair assessments. The Upward Bound Project, an excellent idea, along with others, has suffered from the strikes against it of unrealistic time pressures in 1965. With its Pilot Projects of 1965-1966, this lead-time principle is being more hopefully employed.

4. With rapid acceleration of functions and the needed reorganization of the United States Office of Education, the many mouths of its different branches have been saying many things. The need is increasingly imperative, however, for the office to speak with a single voice on the many major matters under its purview. With reference to the meaning of Assurance of Compliance in desegregation in higher education, for example, a college president is fully entitled to some assurance of uniformity of interpretation from one state to another. The limits of local discretionary judgment must, in fairness, be explicit.

5. In this connection, a need is evident for a coordination of federal programs in higher education that deal with the cluster of programs relating to race, to poverty, and to educational disadvantage. While

---

[20]The Teacher's Corps, for example, was being "talked up" throughout the South in March 1966 for a massive but yet uncertain program to begin ninety days later. With such time limitations, only research and demonstration projects have a chance for success.

each category has its own discrete qualities, they cannot be productively dealt with in a discrete, fragmentary manner.

6. Proposal writing often proceeds by a series of misunderstandings. The Office of Education should attempt to foster a partnership relation in the proposal-writing process. Two specific courses of action would be helpful:

a. Each institution should be invited to prepare, for the permanent records of the Office of Education an explicit delineation of its educational goals and emphases among them, clarifying the kinds of educational activities that are central and those that are relatively peripheral to its reasons for existence. All subsequent proposals should then be assessed against the background of this institutional context as well as the specific proposal itself.

b. Conferences and seminars in proposal development should be regularized so that institutions can make sounder educational decisions concerning what aid to apply for, and what procedures to employ in receiving it. The more needy institutions are also needy from the standpoint of grantsmanship. With more finesse in this department and a few key staff persons to actualize approved proposals, the grants would often get to where they would serve highly useful purposes. At present, there is a correlation between the ability to write first-rate proposals and the ability to divert, adroitly, funds provided to serve other institutional purposes.

7. The Office of Education continues to puzzle over optimum ways of becoming decentralized without adding to its present problem of organic disunity. With reference to the specific problems of most concern of the South, one useful step might be the appointment of a permanent official of the Office of Education in each of the capitals of the Southern states. Among other values, this would reduce the requirement for endless trips to Washington. It would promote state and federal articulation of effort in many funded programs, and would make it possible for the Office of Education to maintain a more coherent and accurate view of changing conditions and needs in the public and nonpublic institutions in the various states.

8. The Office of Education is both handicapped and helped by the categorical nature of much of federal legislation. It should have access to additional unrestricted funds to be expended at its discretion, and appropriately accounted for, in the interest of innovative efforts in higher education that "cut across the categories. " Of equal importance is the continuing communication with present and proposed action of major private foundations, which are not so restricted to externally imposed categorical grants. The foundations, as we shall consider subsequently, have a new role in relationship to the federal government, and the Office of Education should seek to exploit the full educational potential of it, taking the initiative in this partnership in presumably common purpose.

9. Southern institutions of higher learning must avoid being diverted from their true purposes by temptations to submit opportunistic proposals for grants. Such unstudied action can lead to a dissipation of institutional resources, both financial and human. The first and continuing order of collegiate business, in relation to the federal government, is to study the variety of funded categories with reference to the range of educational activities in which they may properly engage without detriment to the institution's major mission. No matter how attractive, the college must overcome the temptation to make money at the risk of weakening the educational enterprise.

10. As recognized earlier, not every institution can or should concern itself with academically disadvantaged youth. Every institution should reach a carefully determined decision concerning its commitments. In the affirmative cases, the access to funds for Upward Bound Projects and the procuring of competent staff to assure their success should be a high priority of college business. A moral commitment is implicit in such a decision, to make provision for such students on an integral continuing basis in the college curriculum in the freshman and sophomore years. Title III of the Higher Education Act facilitates these provisions.

CONCLUSION

The rationale for federal support in the democratization of higher education is fundamentally sound and is now almost universally accepted. The funds for giving impetus to this view of responsible leadership and support are generally ample, sometimes excessive. These conditions, in combination, provide an unparalleled challenge for Southern higher education. Whether these conditions will lead to dream fulfillment or to a travesty of crassly shortsighted opportunism remains open to question. A great hope resides in the coordinated effort of dedicated leadership of which there is a good supply within the South.

SELECTED REFERENCES

Conant, James B. *Shaping Educational Policy.* New York: McGraw-Hill Book Co. , 1963.

Corey, Arthur F. , Margaret Lindsey, *et al. Educational Responsibilities of the Federal Government.* Washington, D.C.: Educational Policies Commission, 1964.

Dobbins, Charles G. (ed.). *Higher Education and the Federal Government.* Washington, D.C.: American Council on Education, 1963.

Harris, Seymour E. (ed.). *Education a n d Public Policy.* Berkeley: McCutchan Publishing Corporation, 1965.

Higher Education Act of 1965.   89th Cong. , 1st sess. , H. Rept. 1178. Washington, D.C.: October 19, 1965.

"Higher Education Act of 1965: Whom to See and Where to Go for Funds. "
    Title by title interviews with U.S. Office of Education Officials,
    College and University Business, 40:3 (March 1966).
Higher Education Amendments of 1966. 89th Cong., 2nd sess., HR-13174.
    Washington, D.C.: March 1, 1966.
*Message from the President of the United States, Transmitting Review of
    Achievements in the Fields of Health and Education and Further Recom-
    mendations for Attaining Goals.* H. Doc. 395. Washington, D.C.:
    March 1, 1966.
Tiedt, Sidney W. *The Role of the Federal Government in Education.*
    New York: Oxford University Press, 1966.

12. PRIVATE PHILANTHROPY AND ROLE REDEFINITION

Presidents of Southern institutions of higher learning are cognizant of the educational gains rendered possible by American philanthropy. While a few may currently view the foundations as little more than financial disbursing agents with their own special angles to be deciphered in the interest of grantsmanship, many others view private benefactors as responsible servants of society working with dedication for its long-range betterment. All informed educators recognize that the South has been a major beneficiary of private giving, and that this region would be in an unthinkable state of cultural disrepair without the cumulative effects of private philanthropy.

For a full century, since 1867, Southern higher education has been materially aided and educationally lifted by the strategic beneficence of private contributions. Church-related philanthropies, as represented by the American Missionary Association, and a diversity of private benevolence, as reflected by the General Education Board, have made a significant imprint on Southern culture through higher education. If the pyramiding effects of such expressions of concern for the South through the years were erased, the region would be in circumstances of disadvantage, and further political and economic instability would have resulted. The social revolution of this decade, indeed, could have erupted in armed conflict long ago had it not been averted by the indelible effects of private philanthropy. However that may be, private philanthropy continues to have a strategic role in Southern higher education.

The current social upheaval in higher education, with its demands for instant aid, for action based on hasty planning, and with its rapidly accelerating enrollments, presses in upon the foundations for new answers to urgent questions. Meanwhile, the massive intervention of the federal government into the higher education establishment, coupled with some institutional poverty amidst a higher education economy of abundance, presents almost bizarre questions of the foundation's function. Problems find their capstone of puzzlement in the matrix of claims to the "right" to higher education for the Negro, and for the poor and educationally disadvantaged without regards to race. In this educational transformation, the foundations are being asked for a new clarification of their special

227

reasons for existence. They are undergoing a self-searching assessment of their changing role in honest response to that query. Their thoughts have properly turned to the endemic problems of ethnic, economic, and educational disadvantage.

This study does not presume to resolve basic questions of foundation functions, and this author would surely not pretend the competence to do so. The questions have been dealt with in scholarly and expert fashion elsewhere.[1] They have also been treated in lighter style with useful effect.[2] The intent of this chapter is rather to follow the historical thread of philanthropic attention to the special endemic problems of Southern higher education; to identify the immediate problems and prospects in this context; and to recommend for philanthropic consideration several kinds of support that appear consonant with a corporate stewardship of wealth in the interest of the changing American South.

In developing the position here, numerous collegiate presidents and foundation officials have been helpful. A special public acknowledgment is due to Dr. Curtis Dixon, who made available the benefits of his experience and empathic wisdom growing out of many years of service as Executive Director of the Southern Education Foundation.[3]

A HISTORY OF HELPING

Since the beginning of private philanthropy, it has found America's most needy and restive region to be the South. Within this region, the focus of philanthropic effort has been upon the poor, the educationally deprived, and to a major extent, the Negro. The history of helping, however, has been fraught with delicate problems. How does a foundation help the needy citizens when the power structure of a social order is bent upon their continued subjugation and abject dependency? How could the Negro be educated, for example, when the ruling class thought it not in the best interest of the Negro nor of the ruling class? The task of assisting the disadvantaged without alienating the Southerners in positions of power was a chronic continuing problem. Senator James K. Vardaman, of Mississippi, caustically asserted that what the North was sending South was not money, but dynamite, that education was ruining the Negroes, even leading them to demand equality. Others expressed more intemperate objections, which are unprintable.

George Peabody was the pioneer to initiate the service of private philanthropy in the educational field, with the establishment of the Peabody

[1]See: Merle Curti and Roderick Nash, *Philanthropy in the Shaping of American Higher Education* (New Brunswick: Rutgers University Press, 1965), and Abraham Flexner, *Funds and Foundations: Their Policies Past and Present* (New York: Harper & Bros., 1952).

[2]See: Lloyd N. Morrisett, "A Foundation's Influence on Education," *Phi Delta Kappan*, XLVI:9 (May 1965), 442-446; and Joseph M. Russin, "The American Way of Giving," *Newsweek*, LXVII:11 (March 14, 1966), 87-92.

[3]Of particular value have been the "Preliminary Statements of the Executive Director, in Annual Budget Dockets 1958-59—1964-65, Inclusive," Southern Education Foundation, Inc. (unpublished).

Education Fund in 1867. That fund began with a million dollar gift, and a subsequent gift of another million dollars two years thereafter. Placing these funds in the trust of white trustees from the North and South, George Peabody stipulated that "the benefits intended . . . shall be distributed . . . without other distinction than their needs. "[4] He knew of the plight of the white poor as well as that of the destitute Negro. The Peabody Education Fund also served with good effect to stimulate other private philanthropy for educational purposes, as benefactions for Southern higher education continued in increasing amounts.

The John F. Slater Fund was established in 1882 as the first foundation to devote its resources exclusively "for educational purposes among the lately emancipated population and their posterity. " This preferential exclusion was based upon Mr. Slater's conviction that the ex-slave could become a responsible citizen only through education. This idea of "compensatory preference" sprang from a zeal to help the Negro because he had been singled out in Southern history as its servile tool. The first foundation, then, was established for the poor without specific regard to race; the second was for the Negro, without specific reference to poverty. The funds mainly settled, though, where the need was greatest, in the interest of the Negro poor.

The General Education Board was established in 1902 by John D. Rockefeller, and came to exert a major force in shaping Negro higher education. Mr. Rockefeller declared the board's object to be the promotion of education in the United States "without distinction of sex, race, or creed. "[5] Even women, at long last, were coming to be recognized as entitled to equality of opportunity. The General Education Board followed an agonizing policy of respecting the feelings of Southern whites. In the judgment of some critics, this practice tended to entrench the Negro more firmly in his subordinate role. If this was the effect, it was certainly not the intent, and no one can know the history that might have emanated from a different *modus operandi*. The origin of private philanthropy in the South, in these and other instances, was a manifestation of concern for the poor, for the Negro, and for the conditions of widespread educational disadvantage.

Numerous other foundations have provided varying kinds of support in these areas of need. The Southern Education Foundation, for example, was established in 1937, and the Peabody Fund and the Slater and Jeanes Funds were merged with it.[6] The Danforth Foundation, the Rockefeller Foundation, the Ford Foundation, the Kellogg Foundation, the Alfred P. Sloan Foundation, among numerous others, have made their strategic

[4] See: Franklin Parker, "George Peabody's Influence on Southern Educational Philanthropy, " *Tennessee Historical Quarterly*, XX (1961), 57.
[5] See: "Annual Report of the General Education Board, 1917-1918, New York, " pp. 84-85, as quoted by Curti and Nash, pp. 173-174.
[6] The SEF traces its origin, in unbroken line, to the Peabody Fund via the Slater Fund.

contributions. The church-affiliated groups and the mutual associations, such as the United Negro College Fund, have each provided or enlisted aid in connection with one or more of the major problems of Southern higher education. Some of them have been stung throughout their history by the criticisms of Southerners because of their preferential consideration for Negroes. Late in the nineteenth century, for example, J. L. M. Curry, a Southern administrator of several educational foundations concerned with the South, remarked that Northern dollars bought the Negro an education that was "unsettling, demoralizing, pandered to a wild frenzy for schooling as a quick method of reversing social and political conditions."[7] Conversely, some foundations have also been criticized, especially since 1938, for their lack of militant assistance in the cause of civil rights.[8] The same foundations have been privately castigated for taking such an obdurate position *for* desegregation, declining in recent years to consider segregated institutions when making grants.

Despite the contradictory criticisms, and the limited success coming from some of its contributions, private philanthropy has developed a useful strategy for ameliorating conditions of education within the South. But now its function is changing, and the rapid tempo of the social revolution could easily blur its vision. As Abraham Flexner used to admonish, the foundation has to bunch its hits instead of scattering them. There are shifting targets now, and some conventional systems of bunching foundation support are wide of the mark in Southern higher education. The prospects for maximum help depend upon viewing current problems in this changing perspective.

THE FOUNDATION IN QUANDARY

Private philanthropy will continue to be a major shaping force in Southern higher education, in part because the South is accustomed to the cooperation of foundations. A million dollars will not stretch as far as in former times, but the imaginative use of even modest funds can continue to give creative direction to many worthy activities among Southern colleges and universities. Increasingly, there is a need to examine the utilization of funds in ways that run counter to the patterns, if not the rationale, of foundation giving. Foundations, like colleges, can become institutions of habit to the point that old assumptions, no longer valid, may go unexamined and unchallenged in new circumstances.

Foundations have made commendable efforts to combine their resources, on occasion, for a common purpose. The Council for Financial Aid to Education, established in 1952, represents a joint venture of the Carnegie Corporation, the Alfred P. Sloan Foundation, the Ford Foundation's Fund for the Advancement of Education, and the General Education Board. The

---

[7]Curti and Nash, p. 172.
[8]See: Philip Stern, "An Open Letter to the Ford Foundation," *Harper's*, 252:1388 (January 1966), 83-87.

Educational Improvement Project, under the aegis of the Southern Association of Colleges and Schools, represents a jointly sponsored activity of the
Danforth Foundation and the Ford Foundation. The work of the Woodrow
Wilson Foundation, the College Entrance Examination Board, and the
National Merit Scholarship represents other efforts of foundations to work
with and through nonprofit agencies. Yet, some of the major foundations,
and some of the minor ones, have their own bureaucracies, their own
party-lines, and some find a consortium of effort to be a highly imprac-
ticable arrangement.

Furthermore, individually and collectively, foundations are not fully
approachable with "unorthodox" innovations. Besides, many dedicated
individuals in Southern higher education have only a remote idea of how to
go about getting assistance from any foundation to support educational
improvements that are appropriate functions of their institutions. In an
honest sense, they wish to help philanthropists to use their money wisely,
but being novices, do not know how to make the initial approach, not to
mention the beginning of a plan of strategy and tactics. Foundations and
worthy donees cannot always find each other, despite the extensive travel
of many foundation officials.

The foundations have a welter of problems facing them, separately and
in combination, as they try to serve the nation through Southern higher
education in these unstable years. Some of their experience in grants
abroad, with increased control over the administration and surveillance of
activity, might translate successfully to small pseudoindependent institutions of higher learning in the South.

A General Design

The need has long been evident for a general design in higher education,
so that institutions may legitimately aspire to excellence in the unique areas
of education beyond high school, however exalted or humble their contribution in conventional terms. Together, colleges and universities must
comprise an articulated effort for society, providing an ever broadening
base of technical training and professional education. This general design
cannot find expression, however, until a reasonable general design is
established for the financial support of public and private sectors of
higher education.

The foundations therefore face the problem of coordination and of
support, not only among themselves, but also with support from church and
state and, most recently, with spreading support from the federal government. On the one hand, foundations may lead the way for effective massive
federal support, as the Rockefeller Foundation has done in the international
field, discovering and demonstrating good educational directions for
large-scale efforts that have proven beneficial on a more modest scale.
Yet the federal government is frequently outstripping its private forward
defense, and not always in the most promising directions. The policy

referred to as "countercylical" giving would place the foundations in the role of correcting distortions or "filling the cracks" in government programs, a "softening of the governmental categories," as it were. Such assistance has unique possibilities.

These views are not contradictory. The point is that a mechanism needs to be established for assuring sustained communications between the private and public sectors. This communications system needs to encompass representation from the affluent and from the "developing" institutions. Honest conversations are difficult to establish under present circumstances. The foundations and the institutions tend to be guarded in their communication. There is the continuing problem among the benefactors of who gets the credit and, privately, the blame. The problems of fragmentation, of working at cross purposes or of accidental duplication of effort, must be reduced through a system of open communications before a general design for higher education can enter the domain of hopeful reality.[9] Foundations are not as prestige-oriented in their philanthropy as they sometimes appear to be. Yet the impoverished institution needs to be in two-way communication with foundations along with its more distinguished institutional peers, or it cannot hope to perform its unique, laborious mission with good effect.

The Need for Models

Tokenism has found its bastion in the South in the form of educational crumbs for the poor and educationally disadvantaged students and their institutions. The current fashionable, funded efforts at performing academic miracles in a summer provide a case in point. Except for a few exemplary public community colleges, there are hardly any models of opportunity where the threats of academic failure, of financial embarrassment, and of ethnic awkwardness are removed as a high order of collegiate business. Many institutions offer a mediocre fifth year master's degree program at the top, when they would be better advised, in the public interest, to develop a prefreshman academic year to give strength to the shaky background of their incoming students.

An Opportunity College, with a drastically reordered curriculum and an assured dignity for industrious and deserving students, needs to be established in every Southern state, as frugal examples of excellence of educational opportunity. If it becomes lavishly supported, it loses its influence

---

[9] In earlier days, a number of small foundations arranged "Stingray" conferences to look together at proposals received from various sources, minimizing duplication of effort. Foundations are too large to attempt such arrangements now, some say, but computers can do a great deal of it for them if they genuinely wish to be innovative and cooperative in their efforts.

as a model. If it is supported too parsimoniously, its limited success will render it unworthy of emulation.[10]

Similarly, a consortium among colleges in the Southern metropolis could extend the upward leveling of educational opportunities. Provisions for curricular programs of a multi-institutional nature, coupled with some joint faculty appointments, could provide an effective adaptation of the Opportunity College plan. The difficulties are genuine, but the prospects are good for initiating and advancing such efforts with some foundational nudging.

The colleges of the South are, meanwhile, handling these problems as an unwelcome expedient, or at a low order of priority. The prospect for success and spread of effect, with substantive support from foundations and other sources, could assure a large measure of initial accomplishment and give the low-prestige function a new dignity in Southern higher education. Both the Opportunity College and the Consortium of Extended Educational Opportunity represent ways of fulfilling fundamental educational obligations.

The Staffing of Programs

Well-conceived grants often go astray for lack of adequate staffing, and this fact is an open secret. Yet the myth persists that once a grant is in hand, competent staff can be procured. Often they are—from other grants. Basic to the problem of suitable educational programs for the socio-culturally deprived or ethnically handicapped student, is the virtual nonexistence of staff uniquely prepared to help them. Such a faculty do not require Ph.D. degrees, nor research sophistication, nor even the facility and temperament for writing for publication. They need an academic competency, an insight into principles of guiding learning, and a functioning philosophy that embraces the student as a learning person more than as a learning machine.

Foundations are acutely aware of this need, but the universities that could bring together the resources for such faculty development have not come to the fore, whether too enamored of doctoral programs to work at this subdoctoral task of such societal significance, or for other reasons. Private philanthropy needs to identify suitable university contexts as a basis for forging ahead with a program for staffing Opportunity Colleges, by whatever name. Whether such a program leads to a teaching doctorate, *sans dissertation,* or a Master of Philosophy degree, is not the central issue. Society doesn't really care. It simply wants the job done.

---

[10]Such colleges could be junior colleges, with flexible two-to-three-year programs, or they could be senior colleges, flexible to the point of three-to-five-year baccalaureate programs. None should offer graduate programs but should be first-rate "staging areas" for disadvantaged students of graduate-school calibre as well as junior and senior colleges with appropriate terminal programs.

The Seed and the Harvest

A time-honored assumption of foundations is that they are seed-planters, and so they are. Yet unless there is a hoe to weed the garden there is little point in planting the seed. In these years, the planter and the reaper need to get their signals straight. Sometimes the foundation needs to be one; sometimes the other. The problem of follow-through is as important as that of break-through, and the foundation that is more concerned about sustained educational success than spectacular accomplishment can do a great deal.

The county agricultural agent, in earlier days of resistance to agricultural innovation in the South, made a point of staying with his farmers until they "laid their crops by," with good advice and some physical assistance. Such a function is incongruous, of course, when a grant is made for esoteric research to a distinguished university. Full faith has to be placed in the research idea, the scholars, and the university context. Such is not the case, however, in assisting developing institutions to enrich the lives of culturally impoverished but academically talented youth. Such dependent institutions must count on professional advice, financial assistance, and moral encouragement to complete their tasks with full effectiveness. But if foundations say, "we cannot invest in such marginal, risky institutions," they must be prepared to hear the echoing option of the stronger institutions that, "we cannot afford to invest our resources in such risky, potentially volatile kids, unless—of course—they are outstanding athletes." Foundations can be of assistance to developing colleges in the husbanding of their own resources, cultivating their skills in obtaining appropriate federal grants, exploring new sources of institutional revenue, and developing curricular programs of merit and relevance.

The Threat of Evaluation

Foundations, like individuals, enjoy success. In its absence, the most acceptable substitute is an unearned reputation for it. Yet, there is a proper place for occasions of failure, which should be understood and publicly recognized. If grants grow out of honest conversations and merged goals with institutions, success and failure become a shared relationship, providing a new security of effort.[11]

The foundation has an emerging potential function of assuring independent evaluation of the net effects of its own ventures and those of the federal government as well, when engaged in like undertakings of mutual interest. Evaluative research should accordingly precede as well as follow grant activities. For example, institutional research concerning the South's endemic problems associated with the assimilation of minority groups, and

[11]Because of the lack of genuine "meeting of the minds" of the foundation grantor and the institutional recipient, funds may be sought and used for one purpose, granted for a partly coinciding one, and "evaluated" in terms showing success all around. Off-the-record examples of this phenomenon are abundant.

the various threats of academic, social, and economic failure should be conducted prior to the intervention of proposed innovative variables. Rather than aspire to unerring success in their project investments, foundations should seek to achieve success in the prospect of progress through *unbiased appraisal* of effort. In that respect, every foundation's investment should be construed as successful, if it is, in best theoretical and pragmatic terms, on the basis of informed judgment, a "good bet." Whether successful or not, the design for its appraisal makes possible the learning of basic ingredients for cumulative subsequent success.

The Minority Group Phenomenon

In considering problems of race, of poverty, or of educational disadvantage, the conventional rules of investing capital risk have little relevance. Help has to be in the context of the total institution, not merely an isolated extension of it. For a hundred years without surcease, foundations have faced the delicate problems of giving needed assistance to one group without giving offense to another. The problem persists, and some useful practices have been developed in accomplishing it. The National Achievement Scholarship Program, for Negroes, is a recognition of the ethnic disadvantage unavoidably built into the measurements of the "open" National Merit Scholarship Program, which will truly become open competition only as educational backgrounds of white and Negro youth approach equality. Even here, of course, inequities militate against culturally deprived white youth.

Problems and issues hang on. In the past, aid was provided to Negroes in a setting of docility. Booker T. Washington was a more attractive recipient, for example, than the petulant W. E. B. DuBois. In 1966, here we are again. The Ford Foundation has invested millions of dollars for the Educational Improvement Project, virtually all slanted toward Negro beneficiaries. The Carnegie Corporation made a recent $300,000 grant for further study and subsequent service to Negro colleges in the South. From non-Negro quarters comes the caustic query, "What are you doing for the white poor in Southern higher education?" From the emancipated Southern Negro, the question arises, "What are you doing to further the cause of desegregation and ethnic integration in higher education, especially among the predominantly Negro colleges?" There is no sufficient answer. There is a need for a "general design" among foundations to structure their largesse in such a way as to benefit, in cluster patterns, white and Negro students, segregated and desegregated, and to promote ethnic congeniality wherever it can be accomplished.

The foundations, as in the past, while compassionate about the fears and prejudices of white and Negro Southerners, must not surrender to them. Their avenues of service to the human community must lead higher education into the future rather than hold it to its shackled past. Through their patterns of giving, they must reveal a continuing dedication to distinctive intercultural higher education, at home and abroad, and a depth of concern for the poor whites in the urban and rural South, whose enslavement, while of a different specie from that of the Negro, remains a real barrier to dignity, and to educational incentive and opportunity.

The federal government, for understood political reasons, often has to embark upon a program of hasty action with inadequate planning. Foundations, with a view to the long-range social welfare, are not forced into so untenable a trap unless it be one they have made for themselves. Yet their tedious processing of grant proposals combines with their decisions of urgency to create varieties of problems. The first is that of a hastily contrived plan that either assumes its capable execution or that forces premature spending as a measure of expedite action. A second problem is that of first obtaining sufficient leadership staff to give projects a reasonable prospect of initial success. The foundations, like the federal government, are curiously faced with delays followed by a sometimes irrational surge of hasty action.[12]

The Trouble with Precedents

But, what is the present real value of the foundation's contribution? The conventional pattern of pump-priming matching grants is valid for universities of renown or with an affluent constituency, although there are sophisticated games played here. The further position of special project support, rather than basic support, has a validity as well, to those institutions of sound body. The recent financial tragedy of the University of Pittsburgh, however, attests to how quickly the arms may atrophy when the body itself is malfunctioning.[13]

The able and deserving youth who are being helped by the foundations because of their financial or academical handicaps may be attending institutions rich in commitment to help them, but poor in skills and basic resources. The foundation's task is not to move the students to overcrowded, unconcerned institutions, but to help some of the institutions achieve a coherent educational program for them. The greatest hope for giving long-range assistance to disadvantaged youth is to help the disadvantaged institution that deeply cares for them, so that the present authoritarian facade of education can evolve into a democratic academic community—a break-through *and* a follow-through commitment.

In these and other ways, the foundations face problems of knowing what to do, of confronting the prospect of unfair criticisms, however circumspect their course of action, and of the nauseating acclaim of sycophants, however unwise their plans. In 1967 and thereafter, just as in 1867, the need continues for foundations to commit their resources and to tax their

[12]If a foundation is making decisions for the America of 1980, the week-end drafting of a multimillion-dollar proposal from thin air becomes unspeakably risky. But "the Board meets when it meets."

[13]Like other such institutions, its ultimate financial salvation promises to be from public funds.

wisdom in the interest of the nation through helping Southern youth in whom the prestigious establishment has no history of deep concern.

The "Rule Book" of philanthropy may be as valid as ever in broad terms, but it is largely inapplicable in dealing with the South's characteristic problems of disadvantage in higher education. A new rationale is called for in this dimension of support. The classic triad principle of private grants has been that they should go where there is a well-formulated idea, with proven scholars to give it substance, in a supportive and financially strong institutional context. This principle still applies to some degree. Some prestige institutions should devote efforts to help the disadvantaged, which will give the effort some fashionable status, and provide prototypes for 1980. Getting to the crux of the matter, however, the foundation must first identify the institution that cares, a college with a history of demonstrable concern. It may need assistance in formulating its "idea," in securing specialized first-rate staff, and some basic support as well. Such support must be given. The old criteria simply won't work.

The seed-planting principle is not valid in this context. The assured continuation at the task is as important as the beginning of it. The foundation and its collegiate partner must work in partnership in securing funds for the college, and the foundation must then cast itself in the countercyclical role, helping the college where government and other categories of support are artificially restrictive or insufficient.

The conventional concept of innovation has become threadbare from its commonplace, or pasted on, gimmicks. There is no more significant innovation for reshaping society than in demonstrating the potential of a weak institution in achieving distinction, at modest cost, in educating talented but disadvantaged youth, along with their more privileged equals, in a setting of individual dignity.

In the realm of desegregation, conventional practices are obsolete. Now is the time to build for 1980. It is the time to support imaginative desegregation efforts of faculty and students in the more reluctant white institutions and in the academically well-regarded institutions of predominantly Negro enrollment. It is time to show, concurrently, an abiding concern for all disadvantaged youth regardless of race.

Every basic assumption about the role of private philanthropy requires a depth of examination with special reference to ethnic issues, problems of financial hardship of individuals and of institutions, and problems of academic disadvantage of the "almost but not quite" college student. The Flexner position, of bunching hits and insistence upon high institutional standards, made a great deal of sense for the medical schools of America in 1910, and for much of higher education in 1966. The dissimilar outlook of Tom Dooley makes a more cogent argument today in the matters of our present concern. It is better to develop a few "second rate" colleges to a position of compassionate productive service, which other such institutions will view within the realm of the possible, than to give lavish support to already strong institutions. The following recommendations provide examples of actionable efforts deemed worthy of foundations' consideration in the context of this discussion.

1. The most pressing need for strategic foundation assistance is the improvement of lines of honest conversation among officials of foundations, government officials, and Southern colleges. Such communication could be initially extended in the form of an invitational conference on the role of private philanthropy, followed by visits to different institutions, unrelated to specific proposals, and by the identification of intermediate interpreters with no conflict of interest.

2. The innovation of Opportunity Colleges, and Opportunity Programs, chiefly nonpublic, should be established from existing institutions after a depth study of institutional potential, and the need for countercyclical and basic support is estimated. A decade of commitment should be involved, with a minimum gift of $1 million to each designated institution and an estimated minimum-maximum figure beyond that point.

3. Foundations, separately or collectively, should foster consortia in higher education in the urban South with special attention to the problems of ethnic, economic, and educational disadvantage. Such grants should be withheld, however, until some general compact of prior multi-institutional cooperation is in effect, unrelated to a proposal grant.

4. High-risk projects in intercultural education, twenty years ahead of today's South, should be encouraged in elite institutions. This would involve whites, Negroes, and foreign students from many nations in studies of family life, politics and international diplomacy, economic systems, religions, and ethnic differences, studied maturely in a context of world realities.

5. University programs for development of faculty members of undergraduate colleges should be encouraged, unhampered by the irrelevant requirements of doctoral programs. A new recognized symbol of attainment should accompany such a program. Such a program should be biracial in nature and should provide teaching internships in both predominantly white and predominantly Negro institutions.

6. Research should be conducted in a number of Southern institutions to assess the index and quality of acceptance and assimilation of minority group students, and of those of financially limited means and of marginal academic opportunities who require systematic remedial instruction. Such data would be highly useful, both to prospective students and to institutions of higher learning.

7. Cluster scholarships should be provided small groups of students in selected institutions to break tradition's crust where it is hardest. In a strongly entrenched college, finding difficulty in achieving desegregation, five scholarships each, for Negro and white students respectively, should be provided as an incentive in facilitating desegregation where Assurances

of Compliance have been filed and *bona fide* recruitment efforts made without success.

8. Planning grants, of a year or so, should be made to establish a college-foundation partnership, initiate staff search, and perform related institutional research prior to a substantial long-range commitment of supplemental support. Approximately three times as many such grants should be made as subsequent major grants. In this field of assistance, more time and less money will frequently yield more substantial educational dividends. This calls for expanded part-time foundation staffing, to get to know the colleges and their officials behind the proposals they write.

9. A center for social action in Southern higher education should be established to give permanent coordination to efforts in dealing with the South's chronic "low status" problems. It should be an independent center concerned alike with public, private, and church-affiliated colleges, attached to two or more institutions of higher learning, and free to conduct independent evaluations of various educational endeavors. As a clearing-house and service center for foundations, the federal government, institutions of higher learning, and various news media, the Social Action Center for Southern Higher Education could assume a permanence of commitment to what many now perceive to be a fashionable transitory commitment. In the absence of a general design for Southern higher education, such a center appears to be the most workable option; in achieving such a design, its most likely prospect.

CONCLUSION

These recommendations rest on three fundamental premises. *(a)* Foundations and colleges must learn to work together more genuinely in common purpose. *(b)* The traditional rationale for foundation support, however valid in other dimensions of higher education, has to be discarded in consideration of the problems of central concern in this study. *(c)* Unless there should be reasonable assurance of sustained commitment to the democratization of higher education in both the public and nonpublic sectors of the higher education establishment, it is ill advised to tool up for such a noble but exacting effort.

SELECTED REFERENCES

Curti, Merle, and Roderick Nash. *Philanthropy in the Shaping of American Higher Education.* New Brunswick: Rutgers University Press, 1965.

Flexner, Abraham. *Funds and Foundations: Their Policies Past and Present.* New York: Harper & Bros., 1952.

Hall, Roy M. *Private Philanthropy and Public Purposes.* Washington, D.C.: National Education Association, 1963.

Morrisett, Lloyd N. "A Foundation's Influence on Education," *Phi Delta Kappan,* XLVI:9 (May 1965), 442-446.

Russin, Joseph M. "The American Way of Giving," *Newsweek*, LXVII:11 (March 14, 1966), 87-92.

Stern, Philip M. "An Open Letter to the Ford Foundation," *Harper's*, 252:1388 (January 1966), 83-87.

PART IV.
STUDIES IN UNIQUENESS

STUDIES IN UNIQUENESS

In dealing with the multitude of problems in Southern higher education, the need for a general design is pronounced, but the task of meeting that need is exceedingly difficult to accomplish. Various types of institutions of higher learning likewise require some coherent design for goal fulfillment. The problem of unity in diversity continues unabated if not magnified.

The junior college, with its varied functions, is commonly regarded as *the* institution uniquely fitted to deal with problems of educational disadvantage and limited financial means. While this point of view is essentially accurate, not all such institutions are, or should be, concerned with these tasks, and some other institutions are properly concerned with them. Thus, while our major attention here will be upon the community junior college and its variations, other institutional types of higher learning warrant being singled out for attention as well. One of these is the church-related college, worthy of consideration with reference to the ethnic issues as well as to those of economic and academic barriers to post high school learning. Similarly, the historically Negro college requires study in relationship to these problems because of its deep identity with all of them. Types of colleges overlap, to be sure, as in the case of a predominantly Negro, church-related, junior college. Yet each special type of college may be understood more fully, in terms of the concerns prompting this study, by means of separate attention.

In such a context, what is done—or not done—in one type of institution affects, by accident or by design, the functioning of other types of institutions. A picture of uniqueness of function therefore suggests that attention should also be given to the state colleges and universities, a number of which evolved from the land-grant institutions, historically established to provide an open door to higher learning.

In the four succeeding chapters, an effort will be made to view each of these major categories of institutions in their Southern context, in relation to problems of a racial, economic, and academic character.

13. THE COMMUNITY JUNIOR COLLEGE

If there is a solid South, it is not found in relation to the existence of junior colleges. In Texas, Mississippi, and Florida, they are long-established institutions. In South Carolina there is not one public junior college, and in Louisiana, there is no public or private junior college in its usual meaning unless one counts the University Extension Center in Alexandria.[1] North Carolina and Florida have made amazing recent strides in the development of public community colleges, each with enrollments already exceeding 100,000. North Carolina's current plan, upon maturity, will have placed a community college within thirty miles of every college-age citizen in the state. Tennessee and Georgia are joining the junior college trend, and Virginia gives strong indications of a forward surge in this area of higher education. As Winfred Godwin circumspectly cautioned, however, community colleges will be little more than "expensive white elephants" if they arise largely out of political whims or social pressures instead of genuine educational needs.[2]

This analysis of junior colleges in the South refers to the fifteen states served by the Southern Regional Education Board. This South includes the eleven states of the Southern Association of Colleges and Schools with the addition of the bordering states of Arkansas, Oklahoma, West Virginia, and Maryland.[3] Within the eleven-state area of the Southern Association, 136 junior colleges were already accredited in 1966, another twelve were candidates for accreditation, and thirty-five additional ones at various

---

[1]There is, however, the parochial Mt. Carmel Junior College in New Orleans, with an enrollment of twenty-five; and the Saint Joseph Seminary, with an enrollment of fifty-three. *Education Directory, 1964-65,* U.S. Office of Education.) A public junior college is being planned in Shreveport, La.

[2]Foreword to A. J. Brumbaugh's *Guidelines for the Establishment of Community Junior Colleges* (Atlanta: Southern Regional Education Board, 1964). North Carolina has observed this principle in exemplary fashion. See: C. Horace Hamilton's, *Community Colleges for North Carolina, A Study of Need, Location, and Service Areas* (Raleigh: North Carolina Board of Higher Education and the Governor's Commission on Education Beyond High School, 1964).

[3]The author acknowledges, with appreciation, the contribution of Dr. James W. Reynolds, of the University of Texas, from whose work document much of this chapter has been developed.

245

stages of development had expressed an intention to seek accreditation.[4] In 1965, Florida alone supported twenty-four public junior colleges and three nonpublic ones. This illustrates the rapid tempo of junior college development in the South.

THE SCOPE OF THE CHALLENGE

There were 558,270 high school graduates in the spring of 1962 in the fifteen states comprising the territory included under the Southern Regional Education Board.[5] Of this number, 502,425 were graduated from public high schools, 26,403 from private high schools, and 29,442 from the subcollegiate departments of institutions of higher education. When the 2,919 who received high school equivalency certificates are added to the number of graduates, the result is a grand total of 561,189 youth. A state-by-state division of these data is presented in Table 13. In the fall of that year 268,713 freshmen entered the colleges of those states, of whom 214,073 or 80 percent were residents of the state in which the college was located. A breakdown of this number is presented in Table 14. Most of the out-of-state residents were from other Southern states.

If the total of freshmen entrants who are residents of the state in which the college is located (214,073), is subtracted from the total number of high school graduates (561,189), this leaves a total of 347,116 or 61.9 percent of the high school graduates unaccounted for. Obviously, a number of them entered colleges outside the states in which they were graduated from high school. For purposes of this study, however, the figures just quoted will suffice. *Approximately 40 to 48 percent of the high school graduates in 1962 entered college that year in the fifteen states under consideration.*[6]

As attention turns to the approximately 55 percent who did not enter college, the question of explanation arises. The demonstrable reasons are not available, though one might reasonably conjecture that the normal reasons prevailed: they got married or obtained a job, or they entered military service, etc. In the present study, three specific categories of youth have been singled out for investigation: (1) those prevented from entering as a result of a financial barrier, (2) those prevented from entering due to a lack of motivation or adequate preparation because of inferior secondary schools, and (3) those deterred from entering because of racial deterrents.

[4]See: *Proceedings* (newsletter of the Southern Association of Colleges and Schools [March 1966]).

[5]Edmund J. Gleazer, Jr., and Alice Carroll (eds.), *American Junior Colleges* (Washington, D.C.: American Council on Education, 1963). The 1967 edition was in preparation but not available for use as this publication went to press.

[6]In general terms, there were about a million high school youth of "graduation age" of whom 558,270 graduated in 1962, and an estimated 250,000 entered college. (Other estimates, as in *Rankings of the States* by the National Education Association, run lower.) In 1964, not more than 150,000, according to normative attrition rates, could be expected to have continued their higher education.

TABLE 13

NUMBER OF GRADUATES OF HIGH SCHOOLS OR THE EQUIVALENT IN
MEMBER STATES OF THE SOUTHERN REGIONAL EDUCATION
BOARD, SPRING 1962

States	Public High Schools	Private High Schools	Subcollegiate College Departments	High School Equivalency Certificates	Total
Alabama	30,455	883	2,265	363	33,966
Arkansas	19,328	464	1,522	54	21,368
Florida	42,882	2,058	4,230	146	49,316
Georgia	36,014	1,116	1,526	197	38,853
Kentucky	25,516	2,696	572	357	28,141
Louisiana	28,492	4,274	2,299	208	35,273
Maryland	26,533	3,847	1,900	25	32,305
Mississippi	22,094	707	757	120	23,678
North Carolina	48,068	552	1,287	129	50,036
Oklahoma	27,052	838	0	123	28,013
South Carolina	23,929	622	668	211	25,430
Tennessee	33,701	1,567	1,300	437	37,005
Texas	86,518	3,720	7,592	272	98,102
Virginia	33,316	2,298	1,107	137	36,858
West Virginia	19,527	761	2,417	140	22,845
Total	502,425	26,403	29,442	2,919	561,189

Source: Edmund Gleazer, Jr., and Alice Carroll (eds.), *American Junior Colleges* (Washington, D.C.: American Council on Education, 1963).

The three categories do not, of course, possess mutually exclusive delimitations. A given individual might be classified in one, two, or in all three categories. In spite of this condition, however, it is helpful to consider the three categories separately in this investigation.

In addition to the decision to single out these causes for high school graduates not entering college, we are concerned with how the junior colleges in the fifteen states assist high school graduates in overcoming these obstacles. The question's application to other types of colleges is reserved for subsequent chapters.

We will examine the characteristics of junior colleges that, on the surface, seem likely means by which the number of students prevented from entering college can be reduced. Evidence of the presence or absence of these characteristics has been taken from existing literature dealing with junior colleges.

Ten characteristics of junior colleges appear to bear directly on the three groups of students. They are: (1) institutional proximity, (2) location in population centers, (3) financial costs, (4) financial aid for students, (5) opportunity for part-time employment in the community, (6) the nature of the student clientele (some junior colleges do not seek the three types of students listed), (7) recruiting policies, (8) summer sessions, (9) segregation status, and (10) curriculum and guidance services. Brief consideration will be given to each of these characteristics.

TABLE 14

Number of Freshmen Entering Colleges* in Member States of the Southern Regional Education Board and Percentage of Resident Freshmen in those States

States	Freshmen Entrants	Number of Resident Freshmen	Percentage of Resident Freshmen
Alabama	11,459	8,773	76.6
Arkansas	9,347	7,659	81.9
Florida	24,118	19,722	81.8
Georgia	13,940	10,970	78.7
Kentucky	13,581	10,113	74.5
Louisiana	14,597	12,927	88.6
Maryland	13,229	9,986	74.9
Mississippi	13,971	12,276	87.9
North Carolina	23,315	17,318	74.3
Oklahoma	16,930	13,726	81.1
South Carolina	9,701	7,488	77.2
Tennessee	21,626	15,158	70.1
Texas	55,735	49,331	88.5
Virginia	18,067	11,888	65.8
West Virginia	8,937	6,738	75.4
Total	268,713	214,073	79.7

*Includes junior colleges, four-year colleges, and universities.
Source: *Ibid.*

Some General Observations

The proximity of a junior college has long been recognized as a factor conducive to college enrollment. If the college costs are moderate, the financial barrier faced by some students is diminished through certain available economies, such as living at home, and the possibility of maintaining part-time employment. The student with low motivation may find

himself swept into college simply because many of his high school classmates are attending. For the Negro or white student, however, proximity
is of value only if the nearby junior college will admit him and if the community will countenance or permit such action.

A large number of all three types of students live in population centers. Thus, the presence or absence of junior colleges in the respective
states' population centers is important. This factor, while significant,
is of less significance in a number of states included in the study. In six
of the states, for example, a majority of the residents of the state live in
locations with a population of less than 2,500. Those states and the percentage of the population living in places of fewer than 2,500 population
are as follows: Kentucky, 55.5 percent; Arkansas, 57.2; South Carolina,
58.8; North Carolina, 60.5; West Virginia, 61.8; Mississippi, 62.3.

Students of financially limited means are faced with the immediate
problem of deciding whether their financial resources will permit them
to attend college or not. That decision is further complicated by the fact
that college attendance will deprive students of the time that might otherwise have been spent in full-time wage earning. This complication introduces and tests the level of aspiration, of strength of motivation, and re-
inforcement of aspiration and motivation from external sources.

The relevance of the existence or nonexistence of financial aid to help
students defray costs needs no elaboration. Opportunity for part-time
employment pertains both to income-producing work at the junior college
or off-campus in the community in which the junior college is located.

The nature of the student clientele refers to all three types of students
being studied. In one sense, it represents the difference between an open-
door policy and one of selective admissions. Selection, where it exists,
is commonly on the bases of such factors as financial status, social status,
educational purpose, or others. Many junior colleges, both public and
private, conduct vigorous recruiting campaigns. The question of greatest
moment here, however, is whether or not prospective students of the
types mentioned are actively sought in recruiting activities.

Summer sessions have significance for students with financial barriers
by permitting their taking reduced course schedules during the academic
 year in order to work part-time, and to make up academic deficiencies
accruing during the year. In addition, students with academic handicaps
may take remedial courses in the summer session before their initial
full-time enrollment as freshmen in the fall. For the latter group, such
action frequently makes possible a normal rate of progress through the
junior college years without loss of time.

The increased prevalence of desegregated junior colleges adds to the
collegiate opportunities for Negro students, and this opportunity is further
enhanced by the presence of creditable junior colleges attended predominantly by Negroes. It is weakened, on the other hand, by a facsimile of
higher education which does not prove to be functionally educative.

Finally, the provision of efficient programs in guidance and counseling helps all three types of students. The full benefits, of course, are not achieved until after students have entered the junior college. For this reason these programs accomplish much less in lowering the barriers that stand in the way of prospective students actually enrolling in the junior college.

The assumption is generally made that the junior college has certain advantages not possessed by the four-year colleges and universities in serving such students, and that these advantages will result in a larger number of local students enrolling in junior colleges. That assumption is especially valid in the case of public institutions.

But one should keep in mind that despite the greater tendency for public junior colleges to serve local clientele, the factor of statewide availability of junior college education must be considered before a valid assessment can be made. In only five states does the percentage of the total public junior college enrollment—made up of students who are resident of the respective states—exceed 90. These states are: Mississippi, 96 percent; Texas, 95; Florida, 94; North Carolina, 94; Maryland, 92.

While North Carolina and Maryland are included in this list, the distribution of junior colleges throughout these states leaves some substantial population areas unserved, a problem currently receiving active attention there. The central task, of course, is that of getting an appropriate college within reach of college-capable youth, or of helping youth to get within reach of a relevant college education. There is little doubt that, in the Southern region, the number of youth needing junior college education is far in excess of the number being served. In no more than three to five of the fifteen Southern states, are public junior colleges providing adequate service for the three types of students under consideration. According to most quantitative indicators, the three leading states are Florida, Mississippi, and Texas.

Proximity

The factor of proximity was studied on the basis of the geographic distribution of the junior colleges throughout the several states, and on the basis of the population of the towns or cities in which the junior colleges are located. To reduce the geographic distribution to quantitative terms, a three-point scale was developed with the following definitions: (1) Reasonably well distributed in relation to distribution of population. (2) Some substantial population areas unserved. (3) Poor distribution in relation to distribution of population. States were then rated on a subjective, but well-informed basis. The following tabulation presents the results of these ratings: *Rating 1*, Florida, Mississippi, Texas. *Rating 2*, Georgia, Kentucky, Maryland, North Carolina, Oklahoma, Virginia. *Rating 3*, Alabama, Arkansas, Louisiana, South Carolina, Tennessee, West Virginia.[7]

[7]From a work paper prepared for this study by Dr. James Reynolds, professor and consultant in junior college education, the University of Texas.

To the extent that these ratings are valid, the proximity factor operates to the advantage of the three groups of students being studied in only three of the fifteen states considered. *In six states, or 40 percent of the total number, the distribution of junior colleges is so unsatisfactory as to deny a preponderant majority of these students t h e opportunity presented b y living within commuting range of an inexpensive junior college.*

Population Centers

A second index involves the size of the town or city in which the junior college is located. The following tabulation includes the median size of the cities in fourteen of the states.[8]

TABLE 15

MEDIAN SIZE OF CITIES IN WHICH JUNIOR COLLEGES ARE LOCATED IN FOURTEEN SOUTHERN STATES

State	Median Size of Cities	Number of Junior Colleges in State
South Carolina	42,250	6
Texas	20,300	41
Florida	19,400	23
Virginia	17,100	15
Maryland	16,800	15
Arkansas	12,500	5
Oklahoma	8,850	16
Tennessee	8,300	7
Alabama	7,650	8
West Virginia	7,000	3
Georgia	4,700	19
Kentucky	3,550	16
North Carolina	2,900	17
Mississippi	1,950	26

Source: *The Junior College Directory, 1965* (Washington, D.C.: The American Association of Junior Colleges, 1965).

The premise underlying this tabulation is that the larger the median size of the cities in which junior colleges are located, the greater the number of students served. Thus, South Carolina would rank highest on this measure of proximity; Mississippi would rank lowest. Yet, all of the junior colleges in South Carolina are nonpublic.

[8]Louisiana is omitted from the list. St. Joseph's Seminary is described as a "minor preparatory seminary for men studying for the Roman Catholic priesthood," and Mt. Carmel's Junior College has a function apart from that under consideration here.

The preceding tabulation of junior colleges was compiled without consideration being given to whether they were public or private. There can
be no doubt that this factor, directly associated with financial costs, influences the number of resident students served. The case of South Carolina is illustrative. In this state, without public junior colleges, figures
were available on tuition charges in 1962 in four of the six private junior
colleges.[9] Median charges for day students plus fixed special fees were
$396.00. Using Texas as a comparable case, the median charge for forty
public junior colleges for which data were available was $133.00, slightly
more than a third the cost in South Carolina.

The median size of the cities in which junior colleges are located in
South Carolina is large because four of the six junior colleges are located
in four of the ten largest cities. Six cities of comparable size were selected
in Texas. The total enrollment in these six Texas junior colleges was
5,034 compared with a total of 2,667 in South Carolina's junior colleges.
The total population of the six South Carolina junior college locations was
262,450 compared with 226,800 for the Texas locations. The total junior-
college enrollment in Texas is 43,403, in South Carolina 2,667.

It will be observed from a consideration of the factors of cost and number of junior colleges that the lead position accorded South Carolina in the
preceding tabulation is, in a sense, misleading due to reliance on data
of median size alone. The necessity for relying on both the tabulation
of median size *and* the number of junior colleges, when rating geographic
distribution, is clearly demonstrated in the case of Mississippi. While
that state rates in group one in geographic distribution and second in the
number of junior colleges, it ranks last in median size, since many of
the public junior colleges stem from agricultural high schools that were
originally established in rural communities.

A brief sketch of the factors of proximity and population-center location,
in combination, will illustrate the progress and attending problems of
various Southern states.

1. Florida and Texas, which are in positions of leadership in regard
to the proximity factor, also occupy this position in relation to population-
center locations. Moreover, the location of two new junior colleges, one
in each state, will further enhance their position. The expansion of existing junior colleges into multicampus status within a given urbanized area
will add even more to their attractiveness to the three classifications of
students under consideration.

2. In Mississippi, the disadvantage noted earlier, of junior colleges
located in small towns, reflects a problem of consequence. However, the
adoption of the multicampus principle enables a junior college located in
the small town of Perkinston, to serve students in one of the ten largest
urban centers, Gulfport. It may be that in the next few years this move
will serve to dry up the parent campus.

[9]*Junior College Directory, 1965.*

3. The urbanized area of Baltimore is served by three separate junior colleges. This fact should not be confused with the multicampus arrangement since each of these junior colleges exists independently of the others. The net result, however, is to provide greater service opportunities to the three types of students considered.

4. In Virginia all junior colleges have been branches of four-year colleges, a situation that usually is not conducive to serving the three classes of students considered. But a study of higher education has recently been conducted in Virginia, and followed by supportive legislation that bids well for a change of the junior college role in that state.

5. The two junior colleges in Gastonia, North Carolina, parallel the Baltimore situation, both in the nature of the arrangement and in their prospective corresponding benefits.

6. In Arkansas and West Virginia, the Fort Smith Junior College and Beckley College, respectively, provide the benefits for the three classes of students even though each of these institutions is nonpublic.

States with a large percentage of nonurban population will have to depend on a larger number of public junior colleges if satisfactory service is provided for a substantial number of the three categories of students.

Financial Costs and Aid

The degree to which financial costs serve as a barrier to college attendance is obviously related to the extent to which the colleges involved provide scholarships or loans for defraying these costs. Private colleges, as would be expected, are more liberal in granting scholarships. Yet, federal assistance to students and state loan provisions have largely equalized the access to funds in public and nonpublic junior colleges.[10]

The costs of public junior college education are within the means of nearly all Southern youth if two related conditions are met: if the college is within "live at home distance," and if gainful employment for self-support or to provide support of dependents is not required. In a number of institutions, the cost for tuition, fees, and textbooks amounts to not more than $20 to $40 per month. The previously cited reference to Texas is an approximately typical example, with tuition amounting to less than $150 per year. In general, the tuition and fees of nonpublic institutions are more than double these amounts. Some accredited nonpublic junior colleges, however, operate on a "bare bones" budget and, subsidized by funds from private or religious organizations, provide a year of college— including room, board, and tuition—for less than a thousand dollars. They also make provision for many students to earn or otherwise receive funds to cover half of their total expenses. The Wood Junior College, in Mathiston, Mississippi, is an example. It illustrates, as well, the value of the location of some junior colleges in nonurban situations.

[10]Georgia is an outstanding example of a state that has taken notable recent steps in providing financial assistance to its collegiate citizens.

The recent forms of financial aid to students from federal and state sources render some data of 1962 virtually obsolete. The problem is no longer that of achieving aid for worthy students, in scholarships, loans, and work-study earnings. The problem is to reserve the funds for the most deserving, and to develop a balanced program of financial aid for them. In general, private junior colleges in the South award a larger number of financial grants in the form of scholarships, but scholarship stipends in the public junior colleges are more likely to defray full costs of college attendance.

Part-Time Employment

Table 16 shows the employment status of students enrolled in the junior colleges in fourteen of the fifteen states of the Southern Regional Education Board (Louisiana is again excluded for the reason previously explained). Since some junior colleges use the term "work scholarships" for employment on-campus, there are undoubtedly many instances of overlap between the characteristics of employment status reported here and that of scholarships discussed in the preceding section.

Of the ninety-five private junior colleges listed, only fifty-two or approximately 55 percent supplied data on employment status; and of the 123 public junior colleges, only eighty-nine or approximately 72 percent supplied such data. (Unfortunately, we cannot assume that the forty-three private junior colleges and the thirty-four public junior colleges that did not supply such data did not have any students who were employed. We can only infer that the figures are probably representative of all the junior colleges involved.)

On the basis of percentage of all students earning half or more of their college expenses, the first three states, having both public and private junior colleges, are Maryland, Florida, and Texas. On the basis of composite scores, and considering all states, Arkansas actually is third. (In the *1964-65 Education Directory* of the United States Office of Education, no public junior college was listed in Arkansas.)

Composite scores were computed on the basis of taking the total number of students enrolled in junior colleges in each state, the total number earning half or more of their college expenses, and determining the percentage the latter figure is of the former. Table 17 shows these percentages, state by state.

In the consideration of previous characteristics, Mississippi ranked with Florida and Texas near the top. In regard to the characteristic of student employment, it ranks well down the list—tenth out of fourteen. While there is no proven explanation for this situation, it is apparent that this is a result of Mississippi junior colleges being located in small villages where employment opportunities are limited.

TABLE 16
NUMBER OF STUDENTS EARNING HALF OR MORE OF THEIR EXPENSES AT PRIVATE AND PUBLIC JUNIOR COLLEGES IN MEMBER STATES OF THE SOUTHERN REGIONAL EDUCATION BOARD

State	Total Number of Colleges		Enrollment		Number of Colleges Reporting Employment Status of Students		Number of Students Earning Half or More of Their College Expenses		Percentage of Students Earning Half or More of Their College Expenses	
	Public	Private	Public	Private	Public	Private	Public	Private	Public	Private
Alabama	0	5	0	1,553	--	3	0	364	0%	23%
Arkansas	0	2	0	720	--	2	0	315	0	44
Florida	29	2	16,848	973	20	2	7,732	597	46	61
Georgia	9	9	5,374	2,713	6	5	389	263	7	10
Kentucky	1	10	419	2,275	1	5	251	155	60	7
Maryland	12	6	4,174	1,226	9	2	2,440	800	58	65
Mississippi	16	9	8,848	1,367	14	5	1,574	193	18	14
North Carolina	5	15	1,907	7,284	2	8	539	918	28	13
Oklahoma	12	2	4,616	397	10	1	1,250	51	27	13
South Carolina	0	5	0	1,850	--	3	0	413	0	22
Tennessee	0	7	0	2,049	--	5	0	493	0	24
Texas	31	12	19,621	2,036	23	8	5,894	708	31	35
Virginia	7	9	1,441	3,335	4	2	212	80	15	2
West Virginia	1	2	641	723	--	1	0	317	0	44
Total Public	123		63,529		89		20,281		32	
Total Private		95		28,501		52		5,174		18
Total Colleges	221		92,030		141		25,455		28	

Source: Gleazer and Carroll (eds.), *American Junior Colleges*, as reported in a work paper of Dr. James Reynolds in the Peabody College Archives of the Southern Higher Education Study.

TABLE 17
PERCENTAGE OF JUNIOR COLLEGE STUDENTS
EARNING MOST OF THEIR EXPENSES

State	Composite Percentage
Maryland	60%
Florida	47
Arkansas	44
Texas	30
Oklahoma	26
Tennessee	24
Alabama	23
West Virginia	23
South Carolina	22
Mississippi	17
North Carolina	16
Kentucky	15
Georgia	8
Virginia	6

Student Clientele

Some of the junior colleges in the Southern region are not interested in the three types of students we are considering. Some of these colleges are easy to identify, such as Marion Institute in Alabama, Gulf Park in Mississippi, St. Mary's in North Carolina, Oklahoma Military Academy in Oklahoma, Allen Academy in Texas, the Southern Seminary and Junior College and Sullins College in Virginia. These institutions have been developed to serve other groups than the three considered here. They merit commendation for having given serious attention to their institutional purpose and in a manner consistent with that purpose.

These junior colleges have further arbitrarily been identified as those that charge in excess of $900 for board and room, tuition, and special fees. However, if the junior college that charged in excess of this figure provided scholarships for half the student body or more, it was included in this investigation. Thus, thirty-nine junior colleges, or approximately 18 percent of the 221 junior colleges accounted for in Table 16, are classifiable as not being substantially concerned with the three classes of students with which this study is concerned. Moreover, two states, North Carolina and Virginia, account for more than half of these thirty-nine colleges. North Carolina has thirteen such junior colleges; Virginia has eight. But North Carolina is expanding the opportunity for enrollment in junior colleges and Virginia is rapidly beginning to do the same.

Of the thirty-nine junior colleges, Oklahoma Military Academy is the only publicly controlled college. Also, during the year for which these figures were taken, 1962-1963, 57 percent of the students enrolled there were not residents of Oklahoma.

The relationship of the total expenses (amount of board, room, tuition, and special fees) and the number of resident students in the college was checked. The system used was simple. The range of tuition cost was ascertained, and placed in four range segments. The mean percentage of resident students was then computed for the segments of the range. The following tabulation shows the results.

TABLE 18
TUITION AND STATE RESIDENCY

Range	Percent of Resident Students
$ 900 - 1,269	72
1,270 - 1,638	66
1,639 - 2,008	55
2,009 - 2,378	10

One can only conclude that so far as any consideration for the three categories of students is concerned, the amount of concern exists in inverse ratio to the junior college costs and the percentage of nonresident students.

Recruitment Policies

Recruiting policies constitute another characteristic believed to have a bearing on the extent to which junior colleges in the fifteen-state area evidenced concern for the three classes of students identified. Although no quantitative evidence is available to support conclusions about this characteristic, some postulates, nevertheless, seem warranted. Before advancing such postulates, however, one junior college, Alice Lloyd College in Kentucky, is singled out for particular consideration. While the enrollment is not large, 191 students, all students receive full-cost scholarships. Only two other junior colleges—Midway in Kentucky and Warren Wilson in North Carolina—approach the situation at Alice Lloyd. The percentage of resident students at Alice Lloyd was reported as 99, whereas it dropped to an atypical 34 at Midway, and to 9 at Warren Wilson.

The first postulate advanced is that concern for the three classes of students as evidenced by recruiting policies will bear the same inverse ratio to the magnitude of junior college costs as was suggested previously. Stated differently, junior colleges with lower college costs evince in their recruiting policies greater concern for the three types of students than do junior colleges with higher college costs.

The second postulate concerns public junior colleges. In the instances of these institutions, to the extent they implement their recruiting policies with active effort, they will manifest even greater concern for the three classes of students than will private junior colleges.

Finally, it is postulated that with the exception of such junior colleges as those singled out for particular consideration, few, if any, of the junior colleges give definite consideration to any of the three classes of students in the curriculum or the pattern of instruction.

Summer Sessions

The significance of summer sessions, as indicated earlier, is two-fold. These sessions provide an opportunity for students with high school incurred academic deficiencies to reduce the magnitude of those deficiencies by summer session attendance immediately before entering the regular session of the junior college. In addition, the availability of summer sessions allows students to earn part or all of their college expenses, by taking less than a regular academic load to afford time for work, and making up the deficiency thus incurred by summer session attendance.

Data concerning summer sessions were available from 219 junior colleges in the fourteen-state area (Louisiana was not included in this part of the study). Such sessions were offered in 151 of the junior colleges or in almost 70 percent. The length of the terms ranged from five weeks to twelve weeks. Two junior colleges reported trimester organizations. The 219 junior colleges consist of 96 private and 123 public institutions. Compared on the basis of the numbers offering summer sessions, 56 of the 96 private junior colleges, or approximately 58 percent have such sessions; while 95 of the 123 public junior colleges, or approximately 72 percent have summer sessions.

In the period from 1962 to 1966, conditions have improved in most of these states. Even with the improvements, however, it is doubtful that the relative standings or the over-all regional conditions would be changed substantially. As the programs mount, the needs for them accelerate in comparable proportion.

Desegregation

Racial segregation has lost much of its significance owing to the passage of the Civil Rights Act of 1964 and to related shaping forces. As a result, it will diminish as the law is enforced. The public junior colleges feel the effect of the act with greater force than do the private junior colleges. Since the public junior colleges generally are in a better position to serve the three classes of students than are the private ones, their earlier desegregation is highly pertinent to this study.

Figures for 1964 showed that 158 of the 219 junior colleges studied admitted white students only, twenty-three admitted Negro students only, and thirty-eight were desegregated. By 1966, the situation had virtually become reversed. Only one public junior college and ten nonpublic ones

TABLE 19

Availability and Length of Summer Sessions in Junior Colleges in Member States of the Southern Regional Education Board, 1962

State	Number of Junior Colleges	No Summer Sessions	Length of Summer Sessions								
			Five Weeks	Six Weeks	Seven Weeks	Eight Weeks	Nine Weeks	Ten Weeks	Eleven Weeks	Twelve Weeks	Trimester
Alabama	5	2	0	0	0	1	1	1	0	0	0
Arkansas	2	1	0	0	0	0	0	0	1	0	0
Florida	31	7	1	15	1	5	2	0	0	0	0
Georgia	18	4	0	5	0	1	1	2	3	2	0
Kentucky	11	2	1	2	0	1	3	0	0	1	1
Maryland	18	9	0	4	0	2	1	0	1	0	1
Mississippi	25	9	0	2	0	0	2	11	0	1	0
North Carolina	21	7	0	2	0	0	1	1	2	8	0
Oklahoma	14	8	0	0	0	3	3	0	0	0	0
South Carolina	5	2	0	0	0	0	0	2	0	1	0
Tennessee	7	0	0	4	0	0	0	3	0	0	0
Texas	43	6	0	2	0	0	3	0	0	32	0
Virginia	16	10	0	4	0	1	0	1	0	0	0
West Virginia	3	1	0	0	0	0	0	0	0	2	0
Total	219	68	2	40	1	14	17	21	7	47	2

Source: Gleazer and Carroll (eds.), *American Junior Colleges*, as reported by Dr. James Reynolds.

had declined to execute the Assurance of Compliance with the desegregation provision of the Civil Rights Act of 1964.[11]

Florida decided in 1965 to eliminate its policy of maintaining separate junior colleges for white and for Negro students in many of the districts. By September 1, 1966, all public junior colleges had become desegregated.

Guidance

In the study of some of the previous characteristics of junior colleges favorable to the three types of students considered, circumstances yielded a dearth of definitive data. Regarding guidance services in junior colleges, no useful quantifiable data are available. The absence of such definitive services illustrates, in one sense, the lack of serious consideration given in most junior colleges to the complex of activities that, when taken in the coordinated aggregate, add up to a well-developed program of student personnel services. Too often it is felt that responsibility has been discharged satisfactorily if some form of guidance and counseling service is provided. Settling for a program that provides only haphazard counseling, however well-intentioned, may ignore some of the many aspects of college life, such as admissions, testing, orientation, records, research, health, residence and dining halls, loans and scholarships, discipline, student activities, and their coordination under a professionally competent student personnel leader.

Every junior college provides most of these services in a decentralized, and frequently uncoordinated, manner. The counseling needs of the three types of students receive some attention, but until more serious consideration is given by most of the junior colleges to the development of high-quality programs in student personnel services, no outstanding results may be expected. In serving these three classes of students, public junior colleges generally perform much better than do private ones. Of the states in the Southern Regional Education Board area in which public junior colleges are located currently the best service to the three classes of students is being provided in the states of Florida, Mississippi, and Texas. Some other states, however, are showing encouraging signs of improvement.

RECOMMENDATIONS

1. A network of existing and new colleges, designated as Opportunity Colleges, or colleges with distinctive Opportunity Programs, should be established as models in each quadrant, or its geographical equivalent, of each Southern state. Its distinctive character should be its absence of economic threat through patterns of financial aid, of academic threat

---

[11]Based on information from the Equal Educational Opportunities Program of the United States Office of Education. In the public schools, desegregation has proceeded upward from the first grade; in higher education, downward from the graduate schools of the university. Thus the senior high school and the junior college have been at the end of the desegregation line.

through provision of educational programs appropriate to the backgrounds and educational goals of students, and its absence of racial threat by developing a social climate of acceptance of all students. Such colleges or programs should not be limited to students with these disadvantages, but should make a point of achieving a comprehensive student body with diverse talents and goals. In substance, the Opportunity College should take the lead in developing students' self-concepts and self-direction, and in establishing attainable goals and means for their reasonable fulfillment. Some such institutions are already in existence, but they are not characteristic of any present type of junior college or other institutions of higher learning.

2. The location of these institutions should be governed both by educational and economic considerations. Otherwise, a travesty of democratizing higher education goes on in the name of its fulfillment. While no competition should be introduced against creditable or promising nonpublic institutions, public junior colleges should complete the general design so that Opportunity Colleges or programs, uniquely oriented to the solution of the endemic problems, should be within sixty to eighty miles of all college-, capable citizenry. This does not imply, of course, that all junior colleges should undertake this combination of specialized tasks; but many should.

3. The public and private sectors of higher education should combine resources in approaching the task of developing Opportunity Colleges. This can be accomplished in a variety of ways. For example, nonresident tuition should not be charged to commuting students who may reside across a state line. In the case of a geographical area that can be effectively served by a private or church-related institution, where no comparable public institution exists, partial tuition scholarships should be paid by the state. In such instances, assurances of providing specified educational services should be made explicit to that state. Accreditation alone should not suffice for this purpose.

4. Recruitment practices, for students and faculty alike, should stress the over-all objectives of the institution, emphasizing academic, vocational, and social goals. Recruitment should emphasize the college's efforts to dignify the value of the individual and of useful labor of all types, to place a high level of confidence in the ability of students to study independently, and to demonstrate the principles of responsible participation in the collegiate society. Such recruitment should encourage qualified students to enter confidently, despite their race or their backgrounds of marginal opportunities.

5. Selective recruitment should be practiced to avoid encouraging students to enter upon programs where their chance of successful completion, with available help, is unlikely. *The Opportunity College should not be an institution for the intellectually incompetent.* That is a different category of problem requiring intensive care and limited potential. It is

out of keeping with the character of higher education in the sense employed in this study.[12]

6. Summer sessions should be pointed to more imaginative instructional programs, combining individual diagnosis and remedial instruction, basic scholastic instruction, guidance and nonbookish activities for recreational pleasure and social development. Summer sessions should become, in Opportunity Programs, the high point in the college year rather than the make-up drudgery they sometimes appear to be.

7. Student recruitment should begin at the tenth-grade level with two summer educational programs provided for rising juniors and recent high school graduates. In this way college entrance becomes a gradual transition, academically demanding but psychically reassuring. Upward Bound project funds and support from private foundations should be sought in developing innovations in this endeavor.

8. No Opportunity College can rise above the level of the competence and commitment of its faculty to the institutional goal. Nor can first-rate faculty members be recruited, developed, and retained without recognition and remuneration commensurate with their qualifications. To assure long-range success, open-ended professional opportunities must exist so that distinguished professors, at salaries of $15,000 or above, could be employed and retained. The conventional practice, of course, is that professors are paid on the basis of their students' qualifications as much as their own.

9. Educational experiences of value to general and specialized education should be officially recognized, encouraged, and even arranged on an individual basis, by Opportunity Colleges. Creditable experience with VISTA, the Job Corps, military service, and other work experience should be individually evaluated for appropriate recognition and collegiate credit, with and without examinations.

SELECTED REFERENCES

Brumbaugh, A. J. *Guidelines for the Establishment of Community Junior Colleges.* Atlanta: Southern Regional Education Board, 1963.

Gleazer, Edmund J. , Jr. (ed.). *A m e r i c a n Junior Colleges.* Seventh Edition. Washington, D.C.: American Council on Education, 1967.

Hamilton, C. Horace. *Community Colleges for North Carolina, A Study of Need, Locations, and Service Areas.* Raleigh: Board of Higher Education of North Carolina and the Governor's Commission on Education Beyond the High School, 1964.

Harris, Norman C. *Technical Education in the Junior College.* Washington, D.C.: American Association of Junior Colleges, 1964.

[12]In an arbitrary manner, we limit "higher education" to refer to post high school learning of students who have reached at least an eleventh-grade academic level or its equivalent, and whose potential is of conventional collegiate level.

Henderson, Lee G. "Junior Colleges Growing in Service," *Florida School Bulletin,* XXVII:2 (December 1964), 15-17.

Johnson, B. Lamar. *State Junior Colleges: How Can They Function Effectively?* Atlanta: Southern Regional Education Board, 1965.

Merlo, Frank P. , and Bert Schwartz. "The Burgeoning Community College," *Saturday Review,* XLVIII:51 (December 1964), 50-54.

Reynolds, James W. "Special Problems of the Southern Community College," unpublished work paper prepared for this study. Nashville: Peabody College Southern Higher Education Study Archives, 1965.

Technical-Vocational Education and the Community College. Proceedings of the Thirteenth Legislative Work Conference, Williamsburg, Virginia, August 27-29, 1964. Atlanta: Southern Regional Education Board, 1964.

Thornton, James W. , Jr. *The Community Junior College.* New York: John Wiley and Sons, 1960.

14. THE CHURCH-RELATED COLLEGE

The Gospel, often referred to by theologians and ministers as the "Good News," has a special relevance for the church's stake in providing educational opportunities without the culture-bound ties of prestige and ethnocentrism. Beyond this religious motivated mission, these problems and church-related colleges have a strange, historical mutual attraction. This treatment of the Southern church-related college attempts to describe some important present circumstances and to suggest some guidelines for action in the sacred institution's fulfillment of educational purpose.

We regretfully omit a consideration of the private secular college, which also has an important role to play.[1] On the other hand, we preempt some of the problems and issues that could almost as appropriately be treated in the succeeding chapter on the predominantly Negro college. Yet, a greater homogeneity of purpose, and of characteristic problems, may soon be realized among church-related colleges as a "type" than among predominantly Negro colleges as another type. However that may be, both will have their continuing respective challenges and perplexing problems in meeting the three points of our concern here.[2]

A NOTE ON HISTORY

"Education in colonial America was the child of religion," observed Thomas J. Wertenbaker in his *Princeton: 1746-1896*.[3] The colonials established nine college "children" before 1780; and all but one of them were church foundations, based largely upon colleges within the British university plan. Practically speaking, the early church colleges were church-state projects, for the colonies found many ways to help the institutions financially. Today, we are moving again toward church-state alliances.

[1] The forthcoming study of the American liberal arts colleges, under the direction of Dean Morris Keeton of Antioch College, should provide illuminating perceptions germane to these interests.

[2] The author is indebted to Dr. Myron Wicke, General Secretary of the Methodist Board of Higher Education, for preparing a work paper upon which this chapter leans heavily. He is also grateful to Dr. Manning Patillo, of the Danforth Foundation, for his valuable judgments and for making available the unpublished materials related to the several regional conferences of church-related colleges sponsored by the Danforth Commission on Colleges and Universities in 1965.

[3] Princeton: Princeton University Press, 1946.

HIGHER EDUCATION IN THE SOUTH

TABLE 20

NUMERICAL DISTRIBUTION OF CHURCH-RELATED, PRIVATE, AND
PUBLIC COLLEGES IN THIRTEEN SOUTHERN STATES
(EXCLUDING UNIVERSITIES)

State	Public Colleges	Private Colleges		
		Church-Related	General Private	Total Private
Alabama	9	15	2	17
Arkansas	7	8	3	11
Florida	30	10	7	17
Georgia	18	17	9	26
Kentucky	6	24	5	29
Louisiana	9	9	1	10
Mississippi	22	17	3	20
North Carolina	13	36	6	42
South Carolina	3	16	7	23
Tennessee	6	27	12	39
Texas	50	34	5	39
Virginia	8	23	12	35
West Virginia	10	6	4	10
Total	191	242	76	318

Source: *Education Directory, 1964-65. Part 3: Higher Education,* OE-50000-65 (Washington, D.C.: U.S. Government Printing Office, 1965).

A landmark in the history of higher education was the famous Dartmouth College decision of 1819, protecting the freedom of privately chartered institutions. When it appeared that the legislature of New Hampshire might void the terms of the charter of Dartmouth College, the United States Supreme Court ruled that the private charter could not be abrogated by state legislatures. The decision was to a degree a green light for the spreading of private and church-related colleges from coast to coast, unrestricted in many ways in relation to the public institutions, which found themselves hampered by state legislatures.

Unhappily the movement was often nearly unbridled, and freedom did not consistently find responsible expression. Denominational pride frequently occasioned a vicious kind of sectarian strife that knew few bounds. As a result, far too many church-related colleges were established, and many atrophied. In more recent years, however, only a few Protestant church-related colleges have been established. Roman Catholic colleges in America continue to be established more rapidly.

In 1860 there were only fourteen "permanent," i. e. still existing, Roman Catholic colleges and universities in the United States. By 1930, there were 126 and in 1960 there were more than 200. The history of church-related colleges works its way into the present circumstance to explain some of the major problems confronting church-related colleges today, both in the South and in the non-South.

WHAT IS A CHURCH-RELATED COLLEGE?

The defining of a church-related college is not a simple matter. Perhaps one useful approach would be to consider as church-related those institutions that list themselves as such in official and major directories, or that accept nomination or election of trustees by church bodies. This approach will be employed in the observations that follow, recognizing the lack of complete accuracy in such a classification.[4]

Church-related universities, of which there are a number, are excluded from our consideration since they are considered in a subsequent chapter and represent special circumstances. By university is meant an institution that gives considerable stress to graduate instruction, confers advanced degrees including the doctorate, and that has at least two professional schools not exclusively technological.[5]

Whereas Protestant colleges are normally related to local or regional church bodies, most Roman Catholic colleges are related to religious orders, which are often international in scope, and nearly if not entirely independent of local church bodies. Even so, Roman Catholic, like Protestant, colleges are heavily influenced by local and regional pressures.[6] Most students come from within a somewhat limited radius, and church-related colleges are heavily dependent upon tuition income.

Are church-related colleges significant in quantity of their student enrollments? A recent study[7] estimates that of a total of 2,100 colleges and universities in the United States, more than eight hundred are church-related. These institutions enroll nearly 900,000 students, or 18.7 percent of the total United States enrollment in higher education. If one were to include also the small private colleges in the country, with many of the characteristics shown by church colleges (for example, emphasis upon training for the teaching profession), the enrollment of the entire group would be well over 20 percent of the American total. The percentage for

[4]Such colleges are increasingly federal government "connected" in important economic terms. Privately controlled Bible colleges exist in some states, while some church-connected colleges now shun the requirements of Bible study.

[5]See: United States Office of Education, *U. S. Statistics of Higher Education, 1957-58* (Washington, D. C.: U.S. Government Printing Office, 1961), p. 119.

[6]"To be a southerner means to be religious with a southern accent," according to Joseph Fichter and George L. Maddox, "Religion in the South, Old and New," in John C. McKinney and Edgar T. Thompson (eds.), *The South in Continuity and Change* (Durham: Duke University Press, 1965), p. 383.

[7]Manning M. Pattillo, Jr., and Donald M. Mackenzie, *Eight Hundred Colleges Face the Future* (St. Louis: Danforth Foundation, 1965).

the South is higher than this—perhaps exceeding 25 percent—because of the concentration of church-related colleges in this region.

PREDOMINANTLY WHITE CHURCH-RELATED COLLEGES

In general, church-related colleges, like other types of colleges and universities in the nation, operate under lay boards of control. This fact is paramount in any consideration of racial policies in these institutions. Trustees of most Protestant colleges are, in whole or in part, elected or nominated by the sponsoring church body. There are instances, however, in which none of the trustees is so named. But the more religiously conservative the church, the more likely will be the practice that all or nearly all of the trustees are named by the ecclesiastical body. Currently, more trustees are being elected by the board itself, and most boards have a number of trustees elected by the alumni of the institution.

For many years the large majority of trustees was made up of ministers, which is still the case among the more conservative bodies. There is a tendency toward fewer clergymen, and the most vigorous colleges are now more likely to include in their board a sizable majority of business and professional men. A recommendation for limiting representation of a single profession to a third or less of the board was adopted in 1935 by the North Central Association of Colleges and Secondary Schools and probably had considerable influence upon this shift outside that geographical region as well as within it.

Little imagination is required to understand why Protestant boards of trustees in the South have been painfully slow to vote for desegregation of their institutions, even on a token basis. While national church bodies may vote overwhelmingly for integration, colleges are controlled mainly by local or regional trustees. The movement toward desegregation in the South has therefore been very slow indeed, with more than thirty such institutions still unwilling to sign the Assurance of Compliance of the Civil Rights Act of 1964. In 1966, of sixty-four institutions which had not signed the Assurance of Compliance, one-third (twenty) were private, while the remainder represented a variety of Protestant denominations and Catholic orders.[8]

In 1966, with only rare exceptions, predominantly white church-connected colleges have not admitted many Negro students, and have not developed a recruitment program on an equality basis. White church-related colleges, in spite of their religious stance, have been of little direct help in offering educational opportunity to Negroes. The fact must be recognized, however, that this inertia grows, in large part, out of honest convictions that need to be understood as a cultural inheritance.

---

[8]Cumulative List of Colleges Having Signed Assurance of Compliance, March 1966, from Equal Educational Opportunities Program, U.S. Office of Education.

Accreditation, Size, and Quality

The problem of quality among church-related colleges in general, not alone in the South, merits our attention in leading to a consideration of the ethnic, economic, and academic issues confronting them. In a recent national study, conducted by Myron F. Wicke, of 528 church-related senior colleges that met the requirements of church relationship listed earlier, about a tenth were found not to be regionally accredited. [9] Only 5 percent of those unaccredited, however, represented institutions enrolling six hundred or more students. Thus size is a major factor in achieving the minimum requirements of accreditation. In that group, no institution enrolling eight hundred or more students was unaccredited.

The two-year college situation is more severe, again mainly related to the fact that so many junior colleges are small. Actually 39 percent of 137 two-year colleges in the Wicke study were regionally unaccredited, but not one institution enrolling three hundred or more students was unaccredited. While none would contend that regional accreditation is in itself an assurance of outstanding quality, yet such accreditation is a preliminary indication of institutional quality, and the lack of such recognition constitutes a strong danger signal. Here is the basic irony. As church-related colleges become small enough to assure a sense of community, they suffer the lack of resources to establish a creditable academic condition. Meanwhile, the public multiversity achieves academic eminence while sacrificing its spirit of community. [10]

Financial Strength

The quality of educational programs is also closely related to a college's financial strength. Church-related colleges vary greatly on this criterion and in their sources of income. A nationwide study (1960-1961) of sixty-nine senior colleges related to the Methodist church indicated that 58.8 percent of educational and general income came from tuition and fees; 10 percent from endowment income; 23.7 percent from gifts and grants; and the remainder from a variety of other sources. [11]

There are, however, wide extremes in these as in other matters. The institutions with the highest dependence upon student fees received 89.5 percent from this source compared with the lowest dependence upon tuition and fees, 23.7 percent. Institutions in large urban areas, North and South, tend toward greater dependence upon student fees than those in smaller towns and rural areas, and the averages do not differ greatly for two-year institutions.

[9] Wicke, *T h e   Church - Related   College* (Washington, D. C.: Center for Applied Research in Education, 1964).

[10] While such communities in church-related colleges are more paternalistic than democratic in modern parlance they do, nevertheless, exemplify a kind of extended family institutional culture.

[11] Myron Wicke, unpublished work paper prepared for this study. Nashville: Peabody College Southern Higher Education Study Archives, 1965.

The ramifications of these facts are of utmost importance. Boards of trustees have been loath to jeopardize enrollments (hence, tuition income) by consenting to a policy of desegregation. Moreover, a point to be more closely examined later, as fee structures have of necessity been advanced, it has become less likely that the average Negro can afford to enroll in a private or church-related college.

Intervention by the federal government, in behalf of "developing" colleges (Title III, Higher Education Act of 1965) and in numerous other ways has established a supportive relationship of substantial magnitude with nonpublic as well as public institutions. Thus, church-related colleges are coming to be more federally "connected." Recently, they have come to face a new peril as federal aid to church colleges is rendered unconstitutional by a state court of appeals.[12] Facing contradictory expectations, and direly in need of financial aid from both sources, the college is hard put to strike a middle course, but sees no viable option.[13]

In general, tuition and fees are lower in the Southeast than in the United States as a whole. For private liberal arts colleges across the country, the median charge for tuition and fees was (in 1962-1963) $751, while in the Southeast the median charge was only $559. Thus it is markedly less expensive to attend a private college in the Southeast than in any other section; yet charges even in the Southeast are high for people of stringently limited means, and the institutions are pressed into a restrictive economical operation, sometimes approaching educational bankruptcy.

The most crucial among the financial factors are obviously those dealing with faculty salaries. A comprehensive study of this problem by the United States Office of Education for the year 1961-1962 is illustrated in Table 21.

More recent data (1965-1966) show that the median salary of teachers in public junior colleges has improved from $7,207 to $8,361, while that in private junior colleges has risen from $5,175 to $6,407.[14] Within the nonpublic sector, the church-related colleges presumably remain below the over-all median. On the senior college level, the median salary for state institutions increased in 1965 to $8,750. Nonpublic colleges with enrollments of more than 1,000 students paid average salaries of $8,214; those with enrollments of 500 to 999, the most numerous group, paid a

---

[12]*The Washington Post*, June 4, 1966, B-5. The Maryland Court of Appeals overruled four to three the usual defense that public grants could be made to church-related institutions, in a ruling affecting three colleges in that state. A state supreme court review is being sought. This decision has no direct effect on the Higher Education Act of 1965, but could ultimately do so.

[13]For a fuller insight into this quandary, see: Thelma Stevens and A. Dudley Ward, *The Methodist Church and Race* (Nashville: Methodist Publishing House, 1962). Also: Ernest T. Thompson, *The Spirituality of the Church* [Presbyterian] (Richmond: John Knox Press, 1961).

[14]William S. Graybeal, *Salaries in Higher Education, 1965-66*. Higher Education Series Research Report 1966-R2 (Washington, D. C.: National Education Association, 1966), pp. 53, 56.

median salary of $7,480; and colleges with lesser enrollments managed to pay an average faculty salary of $6,485. Again, we recall the church-related sector is on the lower side of these figures. Such was the picture in January, 1966. Furthermore, there is abundant evidence that salaries of church-related colleges in the Southeast are lower than those in other sections of the country.[15] Nationally, church-related colleges as a group tend to offer average salaries of from $1,200 to $1,700 *below those in other private institutions,* and $2,000 or so below those in public institutions. There are, however, many notable exceptions to these averages, in the South and elsewhere.

TABLE 21

AVERAGE SALARIES OF FACULTY PERSONNEL IN JUNIOR AND SENIOR COLLEGES, PUBLIC, PRIVATE, AND CHURCH-RELATED, UNITED STATES, 1961-1962

Type of Institution	Senior Colleges			Junior Colleges		
	Number of Institutions	Number of Faculty	Average Salary	Number of Institutions	Number of Faculty	Average Salary
Total public and private	794	79,873	$7,665	305	10,469	$6,836
Total public	274	49,424	7,918	208	8,558	7,207
Total private	520	30,449	7,526	97	1,911	5,175
Independent	161	15,005	8,104	35	895	5,628
Baptist	27	1,457	6,329	18	325	4,601
Lutheran	23	1,502	6,552	6	65	5,064
Methodist	60	3,265	6,382	14	252	4,751
Presbyterian	44	1,784	6,398	7	105	4,736
Catholic	142	4,821	6,473	9	50	4,301
All other	63	2,615	6,433	8	219	5,103

Source: W. Robert Bokelman, Louis A. D'Amiko, and Ann Jane Holbrook, "Salaries and Basic Student Charges at Private Controlled Institutions of Higher Education," *Educational Record*, 44:3 (July 1963), 255.

The problems thus far discussed, those of control, accreditation and quality, and financial strength, suggest only a part of the complex of problems confronting predominantly white church-related colleges in the South. In the main, the plight of the historically Negro church-related institution is considerably worse and its immediate prospect is surely no better.

[15]National salaries of teachers in private junior colleges in 1965-1966 averaged $6,407; in the Southeast, only $5,929. Graybeal, p. 55.

PREDOMINANTLY NEGRO CHURCH-RELATED COLLEGES

The story of the efforts of Christian churches to develop programs of higher education for Negroes is characterized by valiant effort in the face of great and persistent adversity. Understandably but unhappily, the churches have done too little, even in recent days, to merge their forces for white and Negro equality. Among some of the earliest efforts to produce something akin to higher education was the founding of Ashmun Institute in Pennsylvania by the Presbyterians in 1854, and Wilberforce University by the Methodists in 1855 in Ohio. These, like other later Negro institutions, began as elementary and secondary schools. Since that day many institutions have been established for Negroes, almost exclusively in the South, and in the case of church-related colleges, primarily by Northern churchmen.

The experience of the Methodist church may be taken as an illustration of Protestant approaches to the freed Negro. A group of Cincinnati Methodists raised money for founding Wilberforce University near Xenia, Ohio. It became the first college in America to be operated entirely by Negroes. The fact soon became apparent, however, that a college in the North was no solution to the problem of educating Negroes in the South. On August 7, 1866, the Freedmen's Aid Society was organized in Ohio to develop educational institutions for Negroes in the South. Now, a hundred years later, the Methodist church is supporting, in some instances in co-operation with other churches, ten senior colleges and one junior college for Negroes in the South. One of the senior institutions, Paine College in Augusta, Georgia, was developed by what was then the Southern branch of the Methodist church. A similar sequence could be written for other Protestant bodies and for the Roman Catholic church.

These colleges were created because Negroes were not permitted to enroll in white Southern institutions. In most instances, Negro students were incapable academically of competing successfully with white students who had enjoyed far superior educational opportunities. That basic condition, alas, remains substantially unimproved today. Negro students either went North to attend a college or university, or they attended predominantly Negro institutions. Only a few of the colleges were outside the eleven-state area of the Southern Association of Colleges and Schools, with the exception of Arkansas. In the Southern Association, as described in the earlier chapter on accreditation, there were for many years two lists of accredited institutions—one for white and one for Negro colleges, with admittedly double standards of approval.

A widely recognized student of higher education, Earl J. McGrath, identified 123 colleges and universities in the United States enrolling a predominance of Negro students in 1963-1964.[16] Of this number, seventy-five institutions reported not a single non-Negro student. Of the remainder,

[16]McGrath, *The Predominantly Negro Colleges and Universities in Transition* (New York: Teachers College, Columbia University, 1965), p. 14.

only three had more than 30 percent non-Negroes. Of these 123 institutions, 119 are in the seventeen Southern states and the District of Columbia.
Fifty-six, or approximately half of the 119 Southern Negro colleges
(there are no universities in the group in the sense here defined), according to McGrath, are church-related.

Control

The control of this group of church-related colleges parallels rather
closely the pattern found in predominantly white church-related colleges.
The institutions operate under lay boards of trustees. However, since
many of the colleges were, and are, dependent upon funds from outside
the region, there are substantial numbers of trustees who live a long
distance from the college.

Over a long period of time, many Negro colleges were literally "owned"
by the national boards of education of the parent Protestant churches.
Gradually, however, the properties have been turned over to the boards
of trustees. The Negro institutions were chartered almost without exception under the most liberal terms and are legally—though not functionally—
unsegregated. Most of these institutions do have non-Negroes on their
faculties. Few of those are native to the South or were educated in it.

Accreditation and Quality

The McGrath report concludes that many of the private Negro colleges
are among the very best in "terms of their educational programs, their
faculty preparation, their student selection, and the quality of their leadership."[17] Some are, but the word many may be misleading. The majority
of church-related predominantly Negro colleges, in any case, are strictly
marginal or even poorer. In the South, for example, while all but one of
the ten senior colleges and one two-year college related to the Methodist
church were accredited in 1965, at least two others were having a struggle
to maintain even this minimum level of achievement. The difficulties in
achieving and maintaining such standards are, as always, closely related
to financial stability.

Financial Strength

There is evidence to indicate that Negro colleges are trying to educate
their students for about two-thirds of the amount being spent for this purpose
nationally, and the situation is not improving. Over a ten-year period,
educational and general expenditures increased by 108 percent in the
nation at large, but in Negro colleges they increased by only 76 percent.
The educational erosion involved in such a differential is self-evident,
and it is tragic.

The single overwhelming factor in the financial struggle is, of course,
the limited financial ability of the Negro student to pay his own way. That

[17]Page 20.

condition again is self-evident. According to a study by Vivian W. Henderson, the median income of white families in the South in 1960 was $5,009; of the Negro family, $2,322.[18] The consequences of these figures are clear to presidents of Negro church-related colleges in the South. First of all, there are limits to possible increases in student fees. Second, the same factor would make it impossible for large proportions of Negroes to enter the white church-related colleges without heavy scholarship aid, even if the colleges were fully integrated. Earl McGrath made the point convincingly in this manner: "It is clear that the income of these Negro families [half of those comprising his study] falls below the level at which they can be expected to contribute much, if anything, to the higher education of their children."[19]

THE PROBLEMS IN BRIEF

Desegregation beyond token visibility has proceeded slowly in both the historically Negro and the historically white institutions. We have considered some of the explanations for this virtual impasse. Two factors stand out in bold relief against a background of retarded progress. Courage and prudence in some institutions, among the faculty, administrators, and student leadership, have resulted in progress believed by many to be unattainable. The unpublished sagas of valiance at Mercer University (Baptist; Macon, Georgia), Millsaps College (Methodist; Jackson, Mississippi), and Furman University, the oldest Baptist college in the South (Greenville, South Carolina) are examples. The second fact is that there is no case on record of an institution's leadership moving it ahead precipitously to the point of loss of administrative or faculty position or to institutional chaos. The errors have consistently been, whether few or many, not in the direction of prematurity but of postponement.

The second ethnic problem is likewise one of considerable magnitude. Even within Negro or white segregated circumstances, it is possible to cultivate a sense of personal dignity, to establish a democratic community, whatever its particular ethnic composition. The Judeo-Christian faith is characterized by its elevated estimate of the individual. Yet the Southern church-related college has been more given to an obsolescent *in loco parentis* culture, one of prolonged dependence, than to one in which adolescents are guided into responsible, independent adulthood.

The compounding problem of institutional poverty heaped upon the economic distress of students has been amply shown. As basic costs rise, the purchasing power of financial resources lessens. Unavoidable fixed costs leave faculty salaries as a negotiable item. But while students are increasingly aided through federal funds, only meager resources are

---

[18] Henderson, *The Economic Status of the Negroes* (Atlanta: Southern Regional Council, 1963), p. 14.
[19] McGrath, p. 39.

added to improve the educational product which the student of limited means is able to "purchase."

The problem of educational disadvantage, accumulated twelve years in school and sometimes eighteen years in home and neighborhood, places the academically deprived student in a "last chance" situation. Good intentions, prayers, and moral piety do not supplant the need for adequate facilities, competent remedial instruction, and supportive student personnel services. The church-related college, peculiarly fitted for distinctive leadership in these areas, is trapped by the culture-bound restraints placed upon it by its controlling church bodies, and it languishes in a struggle for economic survival as it wrests with a nonprestigious and highly complex cluster of problems in Southern higher education. With united effort, that task will be exceedingly difficult; without it, impossible.

RECOMMENDATIONS

There is no general agreement as to the future of the church-related colleges in the South, but their viable options require a new level of cooperative relationships and substantial resources both for endowment and for current fund income and expenditures. Their economic health, without significant educational service, however, will be of little avail in American society.

1. Church-related colleges must quickly prepare to live up to their Christian professions of equality and admit and recruit on an equal basis *all* students seeking the type of education they offer. This will call for more courage than many boards of control have evidenced in recent years. It will call as well for extraordinary financial aid for competent nonwhite and white students.

2. Church bodies that support higher education must re-examine their commitments and courageously face the need to increase their financial support, but to limit that support to those institutions that give promise of excellence in college development, regardless of their existing levels of operation.

3. Denominations must work together to eliminate ruinous competition and overlapping of effort. Church bodies must learn to cooperate with one another if they are not to lose all they have managed to build over the years.

4. The colleges predominantly for Negroes represent a special problem and one that must be approached with greatest care. That problem will be examined in detail in the following chapter. Two general cautions, however, should be stated here:

(a) Whole church bodies, North and South, must redouble their efforts to provide reasonable financial support to Negro as well as to white colleges. Only such advances will guarantee continuing service for the years ahead for all worthy institutions. In time, Negro colleges will increasingly attract white along with Negro students, just as the reverse process must now take place. The best of the Negro colleges can then assuredly become "permanent" institutions, but not alone for Negroes.

(b) There are many Negro youth who because of economic, educational, and social deprivation are not now adequate to meet the standards of most predominantly white colleges. If the white colleges approach their new responsibilities only by skimming off the best of the Negro students, then the Negro colleges will suffer an increasing lack of challenge in their own student bodies. Equally serious would be an effort by Northern (or Southern) institutions to employ the best of Negro faculty members. In a day of extreme competition for teachers, the results of such a plan could be irreparable, particularly in the already disadvantaged Southern church-related institutions.

Thus while increasing cross-enrollment is both possible and desirable, what will be more needed in the years *immediately* ahead are mutual plans to strengthen neighboring institutions. This can be done by such methods as the interchange of professors in crucial areas, by joint faculty appointments, by joint faculty and student-body meetings, and by the widest possible exchange of artistic and cultural talents. Many other opportunities will emerge where the will to cooperate is alive and vigorous. The regional college movements now springing up in many places ought increasingly to include colleges primarily for Negroes. Title III of the Higher Education Act of 1965 can now substantially bolster such efforts.

5. The concept of the Opportunity College or Opportunity Program, described in the preceding chapter, is equally timely here. If, among the numerous church-related colleges in the South, one such institution in each state were designated, by ecumenical action, as a model Opportunity College, a breakthrough in both higher education and in ecumenicity could be realized. The disadvantaged college student can be educated with Catholic, Jewish, and Protestant dollars. As we know, they do not bear the inscription of denominational faiths.

CONCLUSION

The future of the church-related college is not secure. The ferment in higher education is everywhere to be seen, and where it will lead, no one can say. However, there are many signs that Americans do not want, and will not in the long run tolerate, a monolithic structure for public university education. The extraordinary pressures now evident on the campus of nearly every multiversity will become increasingly powerful. Our society will continue to insist upon public and nonpublic education, and make provision for small colleges as well as large universities, if they perform socially significant missions.

Thus the future of the church-related college, only one segment of the entire higher education spectrum, depends on a clear view of its mission; on its ability to find the church support needed to supplement other sources of income; and on its success in interpreting its goals to students, faculty, patrons, and the general public. The church-related college in the South shares these problems. It must at once face the difficulties created by years of segregated education and of the neglect of talented students of limited financial means and academic background. It needs to learn the lessons of educational as well as economic survival. It requires as well, in order to prosper in the fulfillment of its laudable goals, the substantial support of the laity of the most affluent religious establishments the South has ever known.

SELECTED REFERENCES

Frazier, E. Franklin. *The Negro Church in America.* New York: Schocken Books, 1963.

McGrath, Earl J. (ed.). *Cooperative Long-Range Planning in Liberal Arts Colleges.* New York: Bureau of Publications, Teachers College, Columbia University, 1964.

Messersmith, James C. *Church-Related Boards Responsible for Higher Education.* Washington, D.C.: U.S. Office of Education, 1964.

Pattillo, Manning M., Jr., and Donald M. Mackenzie. *Eight Hundred Colleges Face the Future.* St. Louis: Danforth Foundation, 1965.

Thompson, Ernest Trice. *The Spirituality of the Church, A Distinctive Doctrine of the Presbyterian Church in the United States.* Richmond: John Knox Press, 1961.

Walter, Erich A. (ed.). *Religion and the State University.* Ann Arbor: University of Michigan Press, 1958.

Wicke, Myron F. *The Church Related College.* Washington, D.C.: Center for Applied Research in Education, Inc., 1964.

———. "Church Related Colleges in the South," unpublished work paper for this study. Nashville: Peabody College Southern Higher Education Study Archives, 1965.

15. THE PREDOMINANTLY NEGRO COLLEGE [1]

The Southern Negro's climb from slavery toward functional freedom has been upon a ladder with various rungs of education and vocational training. That ladder has been an insecure one, and the climb has been unsteady and slow. What has passed for higher education in colleges for Negroes has often been more of a treadmill than a ladder, due in part to the fact that the rungs of lower education immunized against higher education instead of building a readiness for it.

Negro education antedates the Emancipation Proclamation. Early in the life of our nation, forces arising from Christian missionary education in foreign countries spread to the Negro American slave. [2] This movement may properly receive the credit for the beginning of the Negro's education in America. Professor W. A. Low lists seven steps in the Americanization process of the Negro, several of which are applicable to his formal education. These steps were: (1) the decision to provide Christian and nonreligious instruction for slaves, (2) the impeding restraints upon education resulting from such insurrections as that led by Nat Turner, (3) the right to be educated as free men following the political collapse of the proslavery class in the South, (4) the religious and humanitarian Northern beneficence during the Reconstruction Period, (5) Booker T. Washington's program of industrial education popularized in the Atlanta Compromise, (6) the flourishing of Negro education under the separate but equal doctrine, and finally (7) the legal protests of the new Negro resulting in the May 17, 1954, decision of the Supreme Court against segregation. [3]

Much can be said about the conflict and struggle of the Negro over the years in trying to become educated. There were those who felt that education of the Negro, as has since proved to be true, would create an

[1] The author wishes to acknowledge, with deep appreciation, the contribution of Dr. Harold N. Stinson in preparing the initial draft of this chapter, and for his perceptive judgments in connection with its revisions. A number of other individuals, of strategic assistance, cannot be publicly identified without compromising the source of confidential data forming portions of this report.

[2] By a fortuitous coincidence, Mercer University found the rationale for its desegregation in that foreign missionary context: an African convert to Christianity who wished to go to Mercer to further his education.

[3] W. A. Low, "The Education of Negroes Viewed Historically," in Virgil A. Clift, Archibald W. Anderson, and H. Gordon Hullfish, *Negro Education in America: Its Adequacy, Problems, and Needs* (New York: Harper and Row, 1962), pp. 57-58.

awakening for his ultimate civil rights. Although there were vivid evidences of the Negro's continuing desire for civil rights even before education was freely available, there is little doubt that the education he received, however inferior, gave impetus to his struggle.

The predominantly Negro college has served an important social purpose in the lives of its people. In spite of its lack of adequate support, it has made a significant contribution to a large part of the population in the South, because the predominantly Negro institution is also predominantly Southern. Only four such institutions, in the states of Pennsylvania and Ohio, are located outside the South. The remaining 119 are within the deep South or its bordering states. The Negro American has received his higher education in the South, in the area that was in the vanguard in denying him his civil liberties. Under conditions of poor support and almost complete ostracism from the remainder of the Southern academic community, the token support that came from various parts of the country and from a number of religious denominations, although grossly inadequate, has been parlayed into whatever educational benefits the Southern Negro has received. However inferior or inadequate these institutions are now reputed to be, an undeniable fact is that most of the present Negro leadership attended them.

In one of its bulletins, a predominantly Negro university includes the following statement as a part of its definition of a university: "It is both the means and the end of a free society. It is many things—of the spirit, of the mind, of the body—in one."[4] It seems essential to add to the definition all that has characterized the institution's existence up to the present. The Negro college, as is any college, is a product of its tradition and its aspirations, its faculty, its students, its alumni, its financial support, its plant, its contribution and the surrounding impact upon it. It is a reflection of the forces that have acted upon it, and is a victim of its deficiencies as much as it is responsible for them.

The Negro college represents many of the inadequacies that have been and now are basic in our culture: the biases, the discrimination, the inequalities, and the inhumanities and failures. Some of these institutions stand as a monument to the disgrace of segregation and discrimination. Others, while reflecting some of this disgrace, also reflect the Christian conscience and the democratic ideal. A few predominantly Negro institutions are today fully worthy of the name college or university. These institutions have struggled, survived, and in a genuine measure, educationally prospered.

In the pattern of segregated higher education several decades ago, the Negro educator made significant contributions. William H. Martin, former

[4]"What Is a University?," Bulletin, 38:3 (Fisk University, September 1963). The social function of the Negro college was similarly described in 1938 from the standpoint of the bearing of higher education upon the caste system in ethnic terms. See: Buell G. Gallagher, *American Caste and the Negro College* (New York: Columbia University Press, 1938), p. 233.

Dean of the Faculty, Hampton Institute, calls these contributions unique, indicating specific contributions made by schools and colleges operated primarily by and for the Negro.[5] Uniqueness also applies to the situations within which Negro education has developed. These situations Dean Martin describes as the "low economic status of the race, differential per capita expenditures in public schools, correspondingly inferior and often inadequate facilities, and indifference among some white administrators." He acknowledges the contributions of philanthropists and the growing spirit of liberalism in the South, noting that the accomplishments of Negro education were not made, nor could they have been, *in vacuo*. A few of the institutions that can be pointed to with pride are Hampton and Tuskegee institutes, Fisk, Howard, and Atlanta universities, and Talladega and Morehouse colleges. There are others, public as well as private.

Three generalizations were expressed by Earl McGrath, in his previously cited study, as basic in the description of predominantly Negro institutions. Most of these institutions (1) arose to serve a disadvantaged group in American society, as a result of which (2) they have had to devote much of their effort to remedial work, and (3) in the past they have had to place the emphasis in their curricula on a limited number of utilitarian and vocational ends.[6] These valid generalizations also hold true for many predominantly white Southern higher education institutions, as noted in the preceding chapter. The Negro institutions labored with disadvantaged youth in spite of the hostility and opposition to education for Negroes they encountered. In effect, their work was not remedial, but was developmental since the segregated high school had never given proper instruction in the areas that supposedly needed remedial attention. These students were not being given a second chance. They had been denied the first one.

A CURRENT ON-CAMPUS VIEW

Our description of the current scene begins on a campus where most of the ethnic issues have ostensibly been solved in an academically respected college community. To illustrate the marked contrast among historically Negro colleges, we shall then glimpse an institution in which ethnic problems cannot be solved in any fundamental sense, but can only find some unstable resolution. Within that range, then, our reporting effort will be to depict briefly some of the prevalent issues and concerns expressed within the predominantly Negro college, or viewed outside it by its empathic observers.

[5] Martin, "Unique Contributions of Negro Educators," in *Negro Education in America*, pp. 60-61.
[6] McGrath, *The Predominantly Negro Colleges and Universities in Transition* (New York: Bureau of Publications, Teachers College, Columbia University, 1965), p. 11. The term "predominantly" commonly means exclusively when applied to Negro institutions. McGrath's survey revealed that in 1963-1964, seventy-five such institutions had no non-Negro enrollees, and thirty-four had fewer than 5 percent.

West Virginia State College, long recognized for its academic adequacy and its exacting standards, was the first historically Negro institution to become predominantly white. Its faculty, white and Negro, has distinguished itself in instruction, research, and writing for publication in professional journals. It is academically and economically sound, and its achievements in cultivating a respect for the individual are commendable. Its success has been described in glowing terms in the daily press.[7] Some of its persistent problems have been unearthed and publicized as well,[8] showing that any search for an impeccable model of success is bound to lead to disillusioning discoveries. For example, one factor accounting for its effective desegregation was the closing of a nonaccredited college for white students in close proximity to it.

The institution is predominantly white in its total enrollment; its residential student body is almost exclusively Negro, and its commuting student body is largely white. The Negro and white residents eat lunch in the college dining hall, while most commuters eat lunch in their cars or in off-campus inns, as well as in the dining hall or college union. With new construction, these conditions will likely change. The author's conversation with students, faculty members, and administrators; his review of pertinent data, combined with campus observations to reveal the institution to merit the wide acclaim it has received in academic as well as in ethnic terms.

Alcorn A and M College, in Mississippi, reflects conditions of striking contrast. In a cultural milieu that does not yet countenance advanced "book learning" among Negroes, much less desegregation, the college is like an eagle in a small uncovered pen, which can see the sky but cannot fly. Students demonstrated there, in April 1966, to demand the resignation of the institution's president, alleged to have discharged a number of employees for participation in civil rights activities. The Negro leader in this demonstration movement was the state's secretary of the National Association for the Advancement of Colored People, whose brother, holding that office before him, had been fatally ambushed some years earlier. The NAACP leader, an alumnus of the institution, was quoted as remarking that although a graduate of Alcorn A and M, he did not get more than a sixth grade education there. However far from the truth, the remark is less of an indictment against the institution than an expression of the social forces that limit it in economic, academic, and ethnic terms. Like a ravished maiden, such a college is ashamed of the conditions of which it has become a victim.

For our present purpose, the circumstances surrounding the Alcorn crisis are of greater significance than the personal crisis of the president and of the Negro civil rights leader who sought to oust him. The problem

[7]See: "Homecoming," *St. Petersburg Times* (January 3, 1965), magazine section.
[8]See: Ponchitta Pierce, "Integration: Negro Colleges' Newest Challenge," *Ebony*, XXI:5 (March 1966), 36-46.

goes deep. A factor in the consideration and selection of the presidents of
Negro colleges, both public and private, has been their acquiescent ability
to work well with the white power structure, to whose boards of control
they continue to be responsibly beholden. The terms of "getting along"
vary a great deal, but there is a sameness about them in Mississippi, in
northern Louisiana, in north Florida, and in many other sections of the
South. While some presidents' accommodation to the white man's rule
would be called quisling behavior by such militants as W. E. B. DuBois
and his current disciples, other Negro leaders would read the social realities with a different meaning. Booker T. Washington, for example, saw the
futility in his time of pressing for instant equality, and worked instead for
the white man on behalf of the Negro. Now the administration of the Negro
college is caught between that historic reality and a contradictory reality
of the future in an awkward present, a writhing period between the gasps
of tradition and the birth of a new freedom. Along with this all-consuming
issue, the college for Negroes is burdened with poverty and academic
malnutrition as well.

There are obviously many variations between the liberal institutions of
academic adequacy, an estimated 15 percent of the predominantly Negro
Southern institutions, and the much larger number of those yet isolated
by segregation and other major restrictions to higher learning. Some colleges are chiefly concerned about the lack of motivation among their
students, who have no sustained level of aspiration to achieve what they
are capable of achieving. While white students in the South were learning
to believe that segregation was natural and "right," Negro youth were
being culturally taught a dependence upon authority, and they learned not
to try to cultivate their intellectual powers. It is a lesson difficult to unlearn, one that requires a restructuring of a self-concept of insignificance
and futility.

Other colleges have problems with students who, despite their academic
handicaps, resist "noncredit" instruction to help them overcome their deficiencies. They seek, as do many of their white counterparts in other
institutions, to get the degree in the briefest time possible, however
spurious this symbol of academic attainment may prove to be.

In some colleges, students in anxious tones confide about their demonstrations for civil rights off the campus, and their fearful reluctance to
protest against a patriarchal rule within the institution. On other campuses,
the frequent interchange of differing viewpoints among faculty and students
show an inspiring evolving democracy.

THE ENDEMIC PROBLEMS

We have noted the fact that many predominantly Negro colleges are church
related. Fifty-six or more of the 119 Southern colleges are of this type.
Thirteen predominantly Negro Southern institutions are independent,
and the remaining fifty are public. Of the total, thirty-seven are junior

colleges, seventy-one are senior colleges, some offering master's degrees, and four are universities that offer programs leading to the doctorate. Our ensuing discussion does not refer to this latter category, nor to the few distinguished institutions among the other categories. It does apply with fair consistency, however, to the remaining hundred or so predominantly Negro colleges that constitute not only the modal picture of such institutions, but the modal description of higher education for Negroes who in the preponderant majority attend these institutions. At present it is through these institutions that Negro students can be helped in substantive fashion, however marginal such institutions may now be.

The delicate and difficult question arises here concerning the consequences of revealing some unpleasant realities. Is it better to be honest or to be polite? In this sensitive area, can one do both? Logic would hold that none would be offended about the facts unless he were more concerned about his institution's reputation than its character. But that is a callous logic. An institution's reputation and character, while not identical, affect each other. Yet if a wound is not discovered, it cannot be properly healed. The issue of disclosure of delicate data lends itself to yet another hazard. In unprofessional hands, the data can be given pernicious interpretation. At the risk of offending a little, and with the hope of helping in larger measure, some data are disclosed that reveal the fictional nature of much that we call higher education. An undetermined amount of corresponding data could likely be gleaned from some predominantly white institutions, but the relative proportion would be substantially less.

Academic Disadvantage

All of us know of the accrued academic disadvantage to which Negro Southerners have been subject, but we have neither openly admitted nor come to grips with the severity of that chronic problem. It is time to do so. Within one Southern state, which from all of our indications could safely be assumed to be typical, the average achievement level of the Negro freshman is not above the ninth or tenth grade. He thus enters college ready to do creditable high school work. It is rarely his own fault, and certainly it is not the fault of the college he enters, but the reluctance to work within these limits holds both the student and his institution culpable.

In that state, the Scholastic Aptitude Tests were given to all incoming freshmen at tax-supported institutions. Within the predominantly Negro institutions, the average total scores ranged, from one institution to another, from 530 to 650 (verbal and mathematic skills combined), within the lowest decile in national norms. The first 400 points constitute a base score earned, in effect, by being able to sign one's name. In another state where these tests were administered, corresponding results were obtained, with Negro test scores clustering in the lowest over-all quartile. While such tests do not directly purport to measure achievement level, they mean, according to psychologists' private interpretations, that such students are ready to proceed successfully with standard eighth or ninth grade work.

We take another test report from a third state. Near the completion of college comes the National Teachers Examination. With a national norm between 560 and 600, more than half of these prospective teachers scored below 450. At one large institution, not one senior scored high enough to qualify for certification on the basis of a minimum standard, which was well below the national norm.

In one of the higher-ranking predominantly Negro colleges, more than two hundred students took the Graduate Record Examination. Fewer than thirty of them scored as high as the national average, and the profile of scores showed them to range from 150 to 250 points below the national median.

The final illustration is drawn from scores on the Iowa Silent Reading test, administered to more than 450 freshmen in an institution fully accredited (by the new standards) by the Southern Association of Colleges and Schools. Among that group, only thirty students scored at or above the high school senior level, while 160 scored below the seventh-grade level. The following graph shows these circumstances in detail.

Although these figures present a grim prognosis, the problem would be manageable if the students, with their institutions, faced the facts squarely and proceeded to deal with them productively. In a number of demonstration efforts, capable students have made tremendous leaps forward despite backgrounds of marginal instruction and lack of intellectual stimulation. The problem continues, however, when it is ignored or dealt with ineptly. The faculty members of these colleges have themselves been handicapped by these same problems of mediocre schooling. Thus the cycle turns on itself. One higher education official, intimately familiar with the details of the problems of education in predominantly Negro colleges, described this cycle with emphatic accuracy: "The poorest students, from the poorest cultural backgrounds go to our poorest public schools to be taught by the poorest teachers. They go on to our poorest colleges to be taught by our poorest faculties, make the poorest records (except in teacher awarded grades) and go back to our poorest public schools to train more of their own kind. What a hell of a mess!"

Economic Disadvantage

The general economic plight of the predominantly Negro institution requires no elaborate documentation. As in the case of the cycle of educational deprivation, the cycle of poverty continues in ever-widening circles. The economic privations of Negro families were described in some detail in Part I of this report.

The institution has to cut its price to attract a sufficient number of educational customers to stay in business—whether it remains in education

GRAPH 6

GRADE-LEVEL EQUIVALENCY OF 454 NEGRO COLLEGE FRESHMEN, IOWA SILENT READING TEST

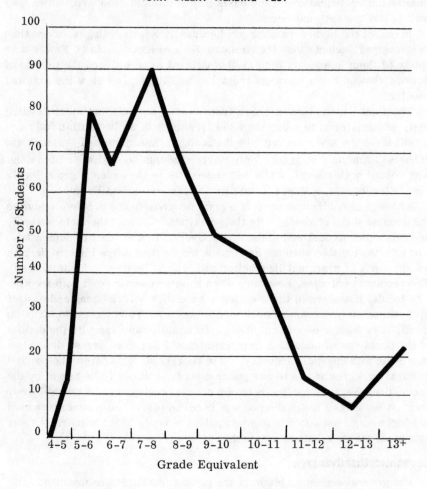

or not. One Negro president described, for example, the calculated maxi-mum tuition he could safely charge for a professional program, $500. A nearby white institution, with a tuition of $1,200, offered a similar program. The Negro president had to find the other $700 per student from other sources to provide a program of creditable calibre, or offer flimsy edu-cational merchandise at cut rates. A more widespread example is that of the required 10 percent matching provision of the National Defense Educa-tion Act loans for students. In some states no line item was budgeted for colleges for matching purposes, and some predominantly Negro institutions were unable to raise their small share locally. Thus, federal loans could not be used where they were most needed. In one state, the problem re-ceived action at the state level only when predominantly white institutions began to feel that same budgetary pinch.

There are some fixed expenditures, and some negotiable ones. When a boiler bursts, it has to be fixed, whatever the cost. The expense for neces-sary maintenance, for heating and for library books, within some elastic limits, are items not within the purchase price control of the director of finance. Teachers' salaries are negotiable, however, both for the fully dedicated and for the largely incompetent. Teaching has been a protected profession in Negro schools and colleges, and not of great concern outside that ethnic group. A fact or two will state that case. Earl McGrath's survey revealed that professors in Negro institutions (public and private) receive salaries averaging $1,200 less than professors in Southeastern institutions as a whole. Professors in private predominantly Negro colleges receive $3,045 less than do professors at private institutions in the nation as a whole. The relative contrast is greatest, however, in the private junior colleges for Negroes, where the average salaries in 1963-1964 were $3,664 compared with $5,240 in other Southeastern junior colleges. While a smaller cash difference, the percentage of contrast is greatest there. McGrath commented that ". . . the predominantly Negro colleges are hedged in by public school systems at the bottom which often offer higher compensation, by institutions of similar size and purposes in the region, some of which have better financial support, and at the top by northern universities which pay better than nearly all Negro colleges and some of which are now conducting vigorous recruiting campaigns among qualified Negro teachers."[9] In view of this raid on Negro colleges, prompt-ed in part by a desire to make visible their own racial liberality, McGrath recommends that the institutions assume the moral responsibility of assisting the Negro colleges to secure adequate replacements. The advice is wisely given, but most difficult to follow.

The presidents of predominantly Negro colleges recognize that faculty salaries are near the top in their priority list of problems, but they are stymied in their efforts at every turn. The problem deepens as it spills into curriculum determination. The problem is reduced to a curriculum

[9]McGrath, *The Predominantly Negro Colleges,* pp. 112-116.

reliance upon liberal arts and teacher education, regardless of the educational needs and aspirations of youth and the socio-economic needs of society. There are other ways to stretch the instructional half dollar. In some instances, women teachers can be employed at lower rates. Then there are ways of adding collateral services to teaching loads that do not appear on accreditation data and the like. Poverty of the person and of the institution hangs heavy on the predominantly Negro institution, and especially on the exclusively Negro institution, which is not generally in such a category by its own choosing.

The Caste and the Class System

In an effort to provide some semblance of an open, democratic society, predominantly Negro colleges have sought to recruit both faculty and students from other ethnic groups. Their success has been moderate in some instances regarding faculty employment. It has been quite limited with reference to student recruitment. The more prestigious institutions in Negro higher education have been more successful in arranging faculty and student exchange programs with Northern institutions.

There has developed an almost fashionable movement among Eastern and Midwestern universities to "adopt" a Negro college in the South. Some of the results of these efforts have reportedly proven beneficial. Yet no college wishes to be patronized by another, no matter how distinguished it may be. Probably the most important benefits of such programs come to the "supporting" institutions, and particularly to faculty members and students who have never before left their sheltered academic havens. If they survive the culture shocks and reentry crises attending such an experience in the world of reality they knew only intellectually, and therefore superficially, they will have benefited themselves and their future students appreciably.

Four-fifths of predominantly Negro institutions continue to be all-Negro in their enrollment, and virtually so in their faculty membership as well. Does this then mean that discrimination is ended because there are no whites around to discriminate against the Negroes? Unhappily, no.

Mahatma Gandhi did not become functionally aware of the injustices inherent in the Hindu caste system until he was personally discriminated against on account of race (i. e. skin color). It was then that his flash of insight occurred. Discrimination, as we know, can be based on many different status factors. Any social system that deliberately establishes vertical social distance, arbitrarily restricting a two-way free flow of information and viewpoints, sets up its own power system of discrimination. For one reason or another, the predominantly Negro college community is missing excellent opportunities to inculcate democratic principles, afforded it at no cost, by not employing principles of democratic organization and administration.[10] Years ago, Buell Gallagher described the

[10]Not for a minute should we assume that predominantly white institutions are paragons of excellence in this respect either. Benevolent patriarchs are extant in the small Southern institutions, white and Negro.

progress of the Negro college from "authoritarian autocracy" to paternal-
ism, but deplored its failure to achieve democracy. While leading the
student to believe he is a free agent, Gallagher stated, "the administrators
and faculties find themselves pulling the puppet strings, hopefully repeating
democratic phrases, often deceiving themselves into thinking that the
democratic process is being actualized through the paternalistic process."[11]
The self-deception phenomenon is a baffling one. The only evident ways
of assuring progress are through employment of added criteria in the selection of college administrators, and of making available in-service opportunities for developing further competence in democratic leadership. A
well-intentioned shift to laissez-faire administration could be ruinous.

There are valid explanations for these conditions, but there are no longer
sufficient reasons for the predominantly Negro institution to defer steps
toward democratization until it can become desegregated, only one of
several symbols of an open society. McGrath's sympathetic view is that
the president has often been the only person in the academic body who was
"capable of giving the leadership and making the decisions on which the
survival of the institution depended."[12]

This author, both through observation and as a matter of faith in the
principle of democratic administration, can understand but cannot accept
that view. He has found an inspiring nucleus of student, faculty, and
administrative personnel in every such institution he has visited during
the past eighteen years. He has been forcibly dismayed in institutions
characterized by an omnipotent administrator at the atrophy of imaginative
ideas for progress. Finally, this view is precisely the tenet that has
caused the white segregationist to deny the Negro his suffrage rights or
even justice in the courts—that he was not mature enough to participate
responsibly in matters vitally affecting him, and that it was too risky for
society to stand the consequences of his foolish judgment.

The Negro college is not to be blamed for its patriarchal posture.
Its leadership has learned this behavior through cultural conditioning and
imitation of prestigious white masters, by whatever name, much as white
Southerners have "learned" segregation to be natural and proper. But now,
as the white educator must learn to regard his Negro associates with the
deference properly accorded peers, so must the Negro in positions of
power learn to employ that position judiciously, and in humble dignity,
with responsibility for furthering the tenets of democratic ideology. There
is a place for a faculty voice, and even for responsible student participation
in college affairs in the all-Negro college. Ethnic desegregation is neither
the beginning nor the end of democratic living. It can be extended within
a police state, or diminished in a political and social democracy. At

[11]Gallagher, *American Caste and the Negro College* (New York: Columbia University Press,
1938), pp. 268-269.
[12]McGrath, p. 115.

present, the caste problem is chronic within a number of predominantly Negro institutions of higher learning.

RECOMMENDATIONS

1. The first recommendation of this chapter, happily, is already being implemented before it gets into print. That is the current study-and-service sequel anticipated for the historically Negro colleges, which has been made possible by a grant from the Carnegie Corporation of New York to the Southern Regional Education Board. Based upon data already at hand, a good deal of constructive action can soon be taken. Many salient questions remain unanswered, however, which upon discovery can help the South to proceed further. The significant current support of several other foundations in this general area will also promote that cause.

2. There is a pressing need to establish a new type of predominantly Negro college, one that caters to academically deprived youth with evident college potential. It is a variation of the Opportunity College concept, which holds some elements peculiar to its special circumstance. Six such colleges (three senior colleges and three junior colleges) should initiate intensive programs along these lines, both offering fifteen months of precollegiate and/or co-collegiate educational programs.

The junior college should recruit high school students at the end of their junior year to spend two summers and an intervening academic year of developmental learning in academic and personal-social skills, including those involving social action. Its vocational and guidance program should be so integrated with the curriculum that each student will be able to match his aspiration with his potential in planning his own post high school program. Students who are one-to-five years academically retarded should be eligible for participation in such a program, and no high school graduates who are more than two years retarded should be exempt from it.

Senior colleges participating in this experiment should conduct a similarly intensive precollegiate program. Their graduate work, if any, should be discontinued, and each institution should confine itself to a single area of concentration in its collegiate upper-division program, such as preparation of elementary or secondary school teachers, or preprofessional work in the arts or the sciences, or limited fields of technological training and semiprofessional fields.

3. A faculty development program should be instituted with a concentration of attention upon the "freshman faculty," who would be responsible for the precollegiate curriculum as well. The nucleus of this faculty should include eight or more eminently qualified staff, chosen along such lines as these: Communication skills, two; Mathematics and Science, two; Social Science and Humanities, two; Student Personnel (Guidance and Financial Aid), two.

With a cadre of adequate, enthusiastic staff, a good deal could be accomplished for students directly as well as indirectly, through stimulating and assisting other faculty members to become more effective.

The numerous ways of gaining access to sources of potential financial support cannot be explored here. They include a need for outside support for strategic staff through provisions of the Higher Education Act for developing institutions, and they include private funding for temporary appointments of outstanding instructors along with increased consultative assistance and in-service education. The central point is that, while some outside faculty recruitment will be necessary and desirable, there is a great deal of latent, undeveloped talent now unutilized. Without imaginative faculty development, there is little long-range hope. In this faculty development, far more attention must be given to function rather than to form; more attention to appropriate needs of the faculty than to the status needs of degrees that may bear only a casual relevance for the perceived and unperceived needs of these college faculties.

4. A financial aid system is required to provide minimal security for the institution and for the individual student. Churches that have supported Negro colleges are now providing smaller shares of the costs of maintaining the institutions they sponsor. They would do well to "bunch their giving" to fewer institutions, enabling them to undertake creditable, secure programs, and to relinquish their shared control over other institutions; they should provide special help along lines of special student religious centers, special educational programs for academically disadvantaged youth (endowing a chair for instruction in communication skills, for example), and direct aid to financially deserving students. A church-related college, meagerly supported, can serve better the interests of church and state by becoming a publicly supported college, with auxiliary religious services provided by church groups.

Financial support for students of limited means must be coupled with a prior assurance of that support. Their needs for psychic security cause many of them to have misgivings about vague commitments of subsequent aid. Many have been, or feel they have been, exploited by their profiteering "friends," and they suspect unworthy "angles." Financial aid must be joined by personal contacts with a college representative whom they can trust. Student recruitment therefore must not be in the form of a sales pitch, but an appeal to the hearts and minds of youth whose set of self-expectations can be modified without losing the realistic mocrings of their limitations.

Government and private aid should be provided for basic and special needs of deserving colleges, public and private, regardless of race, whose special educational and general expenditures are less than $800 on the junior college level and less than $1,000 on the bachelor's level.[13] In this way poor institutions can be kept alive for a time, and poor students will be able to attend with at least a ray of educational hope.

[13]Based upon this author's analysis of current fund expenditures of Southern colleges and universities. See: Metz, *Current Fund Expenditures* (Atlanta: Southern Association of Colleges and Schools, 1964), pp. 13-18.

5. The predominantly Negro college needs to work, within whatever limitations are imposed on it, to democratize its own educational program. Some such institutions are already active in encouraging, rather than simply permitting, student councils with important responsibilities to perform.

Similarly, the faculty needs to be strengthened in their development through sharing in decision-making on appropriate academic matters, rather than gaining administrative sanction in a patronizing manner. There are heartening signs in some institutions of this as well. Calculated risks are present, to be sure, in the delegation of authority and responsibility; excesses and irresponsible action may follow such delegation. It is incumbent upon the central administration, of course, first to develop lines of two-way communication, of listening and of talking, through faculty advisory committees, and through student councils and the like, as a prelude to achieving the condition of a democratic academic community on the predominantly Negro campus.

6. Each college should study seriously the proper scope of its program, and should not hesitate to limit its curricular offerings to the areas that best meet the needs of its constituency, with due regard to financial strength, size, goals, and realistic opportunities.

7. In his estimable analysis of the predominantly Negro institution in transition, Earl McGrath recommended the establishment of a center in at least one university, "to provide counseling and field service, on a voluntary basis so that these institutions as well as others needing assistance can get informed advice from experienced persons. Such a center should also arrange cooperative activities among institutions seeking help and make available an up-to-date information based on continuing research."[14]

The need for such leadership service is evident from our investigation as well as from the McGrath survey and other informed sources. Southern society has long since moved beyond the need, however, for any higher education center that gives exclusive attention to any single ethnic group. As suggested earlier in this report, such a center should be multi-institutional in character, and should extend its services in terms of the triad cluster of endemic problems of Southern higher education of which race is, however important, only one, and is not in isolation from those of economic and educational poverty, which the Negro poor shares with the white poor.

CONCLUSION

The fitting conclusion to this chapter was written some thirty years ago, long before this study was vaguely conceived. It was expressed by Buell Gallagher as he dealt with the "prophetic function" of the Negro college in the context of the prevailing American caste system of the predesegregation era:

[14] McGrath, *The Predominantly Negro Colleges*, p. 161.

. . . unless the Negro colleges are ready to abandon much that is the mummery of the standardized college in order to become socially effective, they will actually work to miseducate, thwart, and misdirect Negro youth. The nonfunctional college is not merely irrelevant, it is miseducative and parasitical. In fact, the nonfunctional college for Negroes is traitorous. It acquiesces in the day-by-day defeat of the desires and aspirations of the Negro, and thereby miseducatively consents to the social stultification by which America is denied a contribution which might be made by one-tenth of its people.

We dare to hope that some colleges will wish to fulfill their social function, that they will wish to become prophetic rather than monastic and servile. Higher education will become effectively prophetic when not only its formal instruction, but equally its structure and procedures are re-directed by the best available group thinking, with the aim of employing all the strength of critical intelligence, all the stamina of the human spirit, all the resources of ethical religion in the prophetic venture. Both by precept and by practice the college then foreshadows the society it fore-sees.[15]

If this is to be a self-fulfilling prophecy, there can be no scapegoating of responsibility but only a widespread assumption of it. If a creative minority of now nonelite institutions can be identified, and assisted from public and private sources to become exemplary models, and if all others can be kept economically and educationally alive long enough to view the demonstration of the possible among these new pioneers of predominantly Negro colleges, then a groundswell of effort based upon these models can be achieved within a decade. The spirit of 1976, like that of 1776, can fittingly commemorate the abiding American spirit:

> Keep ancient lands, your storied pomp . . .
> Give me your tired, your poor,
> Your huddled masses yearning to breathe free,
> The wretched refuse of your teeming shore,
> Send these, the homeless, tempest-tossed, to me:
> I lift my lamp beside the golden door.[16]

SELECTED REFERENCES

Caliver, Ambrose. *National Survey of the Higher Education of Negroes: A Summary.* Washington, D.C.: United States Office of Education, 1942.

Clark, K. B. *Dark Ghetto.* New York: Harper and Row, 1965.

Clift, Virgil A., A. W. Anderson, and H. G. Hullfish (eds.). *Negro Education in America.* New York: Harper and Row, 1962.

[15]Gallagher, *American Caste and the Negro College*, p. 380.
[16]Emma Lazarus, "The New Colossus," as inscribed on the Statue of Liberty in 1903.

Daniels, Walter G. (ed.). *The Higher Education of the Negro.* Washington, D. C.: Howard University, 1966.

Francois, Bill. "A Living Laboratory of Human Relations," *Saturday Review,* XLIX:21 (May 21, 1966), 64-65.

Gallagher, Buell G. *American Caste and the Negro College.* New York: Columbia University Press, 1938.

McGrath, Earl J. *The Predominantly Negro Colleges and Universities in Transition.* New York: Institute of Higher Education, Bureau of Publications, Teachers College, Columbia University, 1965.

Pierce, Ponchitta. "Integration: Negro Colleges' Newest Challenge," *Ebony,* XXI:5 (March 1966), 36-46.

Plant, Richard L. "Increasing the Quantity and Quality of Negro Enrollment in College," *Harvard Educational Review,* 30:3 (1960), 270-279.

Symposium, "The Negro Private and Church Related College," *Journal of Negro Education,* 29:3 (Summer 1960).

Symposium, "The Negro Public College," *Journal of Negro Education,* 31:3 (Summer 1962).

16. THE STATE COLLEGE
AND THE UNIVERSITY

The state colleges represent the central nervous system of Southern higher education. The increasing enrollments, the building expansion, the almost frenetic faculty search, and the upward budget press together to find their focus there. In addition, the state college is in a self-imposed condition of frustration. It is viewed as almost, but not quite, a university. It sees itself, sooner or later, as becoming one, and a step in that direction is to become called one. The power struggle goes on between the university, with its specialized graduate schools offering doctoral programs and emphasizing research in various disciplines, and the state college, which inappropriately models itself after the university. The contest for control goes on in the guise of cooperative efforts in the public interest, but the motives are not so constantly pure. They are sometimes an expression of the status seekers in higher education. The university, meanwhile, has enjoyed its pre-eminence too long to feel inclined to share it, preferring to remain on the inside track of political favor. Thus, like a two-party system, sometimes one is the whipping boy; at times, the other.

While the South is in dire need of a multi-purpose system of higher education, the state colleges, including the land-grant institutions, are having increasing difficulties in delineating their respective missions and fencing in their legitimate aspirations. The various efforts to coordinate state colleges and universities more often are a parody of specialized higher education functions than examples of it. Yet, as one learned observer of these chaotic conditions privately observed, "until there is a clear resolution of the issues of central authority and responsibility, college presidents must show a good deal of political *savoir-faire* or they will find themselves at the mercy of their educational and political friends." Meanwhile, the more elite private universities with their carefully selected clientele travel above these mundane controversies, relatively unfettered by the need to establish functional lines of inter-institutional cooperation. In one sense it is just as well, because the South is in abject need of an increased number of distinguished universities regardless of the specialized nature of their distinction. No university field in the South is overcrowded with graduate or professional schools

295

of eminence. But in the South, however large the state college grows or however subject it may be to political machination, it continues to enjoy a level of student comradery, and an absence of the academic pressures that, in universities with more exacting standards, constitute a threat to mental health.

The current situation of state colleges, and of public and private universities, with reference to the problems of our concern here, can be recounted in brief order. Much of that circumstance is now a matter of common knowledge.

THE STATE COLLEGE

Some state colleges are beginning to move toward a specialized focus of service, such as liberal arts, teacher education, forestry, or engineering. Others are so busily engaged in accommodating the population expansion in higher education that insufficient time or energy remains for considering the potential values of academic uniqueness of each of the several state colleges. In Florida, partly in order to prevent a recurrence of the earlier California trend of community colleges' upward aspirations, the state colleges fit into a relatively fixed pattern. The public junior colleges are legally precluded from becoming senior colleges. Nowhere, however, do senior state colleges single out any of the three endemic problems considered in this study as matters of high priority and sustained effort.

Educationally Disadvantaged Freshmen

No great academic pressure in state colleges is felt by the average student whose academic background is moderately good. If he is within a year or two of grade level, he can manage to "pass muster" with moderate effort. In those state colleges whose enrollment in general is below college level, no great difficulty is experienced. There appears to be an invisible hand of attrition that works on a percentage basis, though the causes of attrition may vary considerably. Only in rare instances are systematic programs developed to assist youth with marked educational disadvantages who are otherwise of good college potential.

This description of conditions is not a criticism of state colleges. With the swelling of enrollments, their task of providing adequate instruction for students without such handicaps is overwhelming. They can do little more. In the case of colleges that mainly admit educationally disadvantaged students, however, the educational programs require overdue modification. Such curriculum conversion should not assume that these college students are thinking on a high school level. Frequently, their intellectual perceptions may be of graduate calibre with reference to the analysis of social problems and the like. Yet, if their tools of communication and systematic problem solving are not in condition for full-fledged collegiate studies, neither the student nor the institution gains by making believe that such is the case. Much rote learning is like reading aloud in a foreign language, with ability to pronounce words but not to translate them.

Financial Limitations

The cost of state college attendance is negligible, in relative terms, for residents of the state in which a college is located who commute to college. Tuition for out-of-state residents, on the other hand, varies considerably. A paradox is created as recruiters go out of the state to attract able students, while out-of-state tuition serves to deter their enrollment. There is little interstate reciprocity developed to facilitate a free across-the-border movement of students. Recruitment of poor students with educational disadvantages runs counter to the aspirations of institutions, whether intra- or interstate. Such students are admitted, but they are not warmly recruited. Such nonresident students are denied admission. As state colleges are in short supply of students from foreign countries, so are they in short supply of students from "foreign" (non-contiguous) states, both the privileged and the disadvantaged.

Ethnic Barriers

Every senior state college in the South is a signatory to the Assurance of Compliance of Title VI of the Civil Rights Act of 1964. No college has been shown to breach or default in this assurance. In technical terms, then, the open-door policy prevails throughout the South. In the deep South, however, the state colleges may be divided into four fairly distinct categories. In the states of the old Confederacy, the predominantly white institution, caught between the still hostile camps of segregation and desegregation, is trying most of all to do "the peaceable thing." That position is not generally hypocritical. Educational leaders want to do what they have to do in good spirit, but they are not inclined to recruit students except to meet minimal requirements, or to attract promising athletes, or students of outstanding academic promise or personal qualities. They have not yet begun to recruit Negro professors, although they are discreetly looking for them in some sectors. The extrovert character of the Southern state college soon reduces the social distance between Negro and white students. Congeniality wins out in one way or another. Worthy members of a minority group, if not generally accorded a full welcome, do soon find responsive friendships among the students and faculty alike.

The predominantly Negro college in the deep South provides virtually no opportunity for a desegregated campus community. In urban settings, occasional examples of this development could be cited, but the rural state college appears to be many years away from any measure of desegregation worthy of the name. Historically Negro institutions in the border states are moving toward desegregation among students and faculty, some almost with celerity.[1] The predominantly white state colleges in the

[1] In the morning mail, for example, a letter of inquiry about a staff placement in a border state wished to identify both Negro and white prospects as a basis for selection. A telephone call from a non-Southern state inquired about the race of a prospective faculty member, expressing a personally liberal view, but stating that the community was not yet ready for a Negro college supervisor of student teaching.

Southern bordering states are in the most favorable circumstances for progress and are indeed achieving it very well.

The basic barrier for the Negro is that of achieving academic success in a predominantly white state college; for the white student, the barrier is that of getting an adequate educational experience in the predominantly Negro state college. These are the two facts that are difficult to "get around." The deep Southern taboo persists, of course, as well.

THE UNIVERSITY

The Southern university is made up of three quite disparate historical elements. From Europe has come the classic prototype of the German university system. From the British has come the concept of the residential college. Indigenous to America, of course, has been the development of the land-grant institutions, both colleges and universities, historically dignifying the worth of man and his useful pursuits, however humble, and expressing a spirit of extending educational opportunities.[2] Thus, as Grayson Kirk expressed it, "access to higher education now is regarded as the right of all young people who have any claim to intellectual promise—and is demanded by many who do not."[3]

Educationally Disadvantaged Freshmen

With this varied heritage, the Southern state university is ambivalent in its behavior. With the exception of Florida and Texas, and with one or two states soon to follow their practice in modified forms of the "California plan," state universities follow a practice of open admissions and massive initial attrition. Students with intellectual promise, but academic disadvantage, are not identified and aided. The university "weeds out" the students who do not meet its unyielding requirements.

This inefficient, wasteful practice, as reported from numerous sources, rests on two premises, both worthy enough if viewed within their separate limited contexts. The state legislator believes that every high school graduate in his district should "have a crack at" the university, however poor his chances for success. Besides, the burden of responsibility to his constituents is thus eased from his shoulders. The argument is buttressed by the fact that, in individual cases, one can never be absolutely certain in predicting success or failure. The university, in the process, gets expanded budgets which can be diverted in part to their "real" function of graduate education and research.

---

[2]The fourfold spirit of the land-grant institutions was aptly summarized by W. J. Kerr in these words: "(1) The spirit of initiative—pioneering; (2) the spirit of growth—progress; (3) the spirit of equal opportunity for all—democracy; (4) the spirit of helpfulness—service." Quoted by Herman R. Allen, *Open Door to Learning* (Urbana: University of Illinois Press, 1963).

[3]Kirk, "The University in Contemporary Society," *School and Society* (February 5, 1966), p. 63.

The second position is that of the university professors, who look at the lower division for "scouting purposes" primarily, in search of promising graduate students to recruit into their respective and respectable schools or departments. Thus, the road of open admissions policies of state universities is paved with good intentions. And the state university is at odds with itself. The facts throughout the South are that remedial or developmental education for academically deprived youth is not fully compatible with the major direct functions of the university, and it should not be called on to perform such a function. Its major function in this regard, which it has not yet assumed, lies in the graduate preparation of teachers for high schools and colleges, who will then provide suitable instruction for youth in other academic settings. The nonpublic Southern university does not face the dilemma of the state university. It is in a position to select students, in the beginning, who show reasonable promise of success. A few of these universities also could materially increase their service to Southern society by preparing teachers uniquely competent in instructing college freshmen—who range in grade-level achievement from the eighth to the sixteenth, as a conservative estimate.

Financial Limitations

For youth who do not require special instruction, but only money, the states are making possible—with substantial federal assistance—the undergraduate and graduate education of academically talented and financially deserving students. Due to the liberal provisions of federal and state funds, in the form of loans, scholarships, and work-study income provisions, the private universities are able to provide financial security for a considerable number of students as well. A number of these institutions make a pointed effort to recruit some financially needy students out of a sense of social responsibility and as a means of extending intercultural diversity among students.

The Ethnic Barrier

The university has had leadership responsibility thrust upon it. Providing the entering door of desegregation in higher education, it has accommodated itself to a new ethnic mixture in the "house of intellect." Yet it has been, and continues to be, more of a respondent to change than an interpreter of social forces or an initiator of social change. A long forward look at the ethnic barriers and pseudobarriers has not been taken in a collective sense by the Southern university. It moves with dispatch along the trail of external financial support, and with good effect, but no concerted effort has been made among Southern university presidents to look toward American ethnic goals of 1980 and plan ways of achieving them. (A preliminary effort was under way by the chancellor of one Southern state university in 1965, but upon his subsequent acceptance of a position outside the South, the matter was dropped.)

The point is crucial for the university, not only in its law schools but throughout the fabric of its educational policy and program. For better or worse, the value system of universities will be emulated by those afforded less prestige. This can be seen in those state colleges that doom themselves to mediocrity through imitation rather than attempting to achieve excellence in matters of their proper concern and within the means of their resources. The schools and colleges a decade or so hence will bear a striking resemblance in practice and values to what they now observe in Southern university life. At the present time, there is very little to see that bespeaks a joining of effort among ethnically contrasting Southern universities to achieve presumably common—certainly compatible—purposes.

RECOMMENDATIONS

The state college can achieve an education for excellence if it will identify and assume those functions, general and specific, for which it is well suited and commonly established. In many cases, it should not attempt to deal with the educationally disadvantaged student when it can serve as a referral agent to other institutions better equipped to perform such a function. It does have the special responsibility, however, of helping financially needy students to "earn as they learn," or to borrow against future earnings. In a similar fashion, the state college should work in this postdesegregation era to achieve a new ethnic outlook, which will involve a good deal of unlearning, as well as new learning, to achieve a spirit of comradery between the races.

The university has even less of a direct responsibility for the education of culturally disadvantaged youth. By the same token, however, it has central responsibility for preparing competent teachers, with the ability to raise the aspirations as well as the understanding of youth who have learned that "it doesn't pay to learn."

The university, public and private, is assuming increased responsibility in finding needed financial support for its academically talented students. It is also intellectually concerned, at least, about its leadership role in the ethnic, social evolution of which it is so strategic a part. In this setting, the following points deserve emphasis:

1. A college, as a matter of professional honesty, should select students in keeping with its academic expectations, or should modify its expectations on the basis of the academic potential of its students. Thus, the state college will do well to "keep up with itself" in accommodating the students without acute academic handicaps who seek entrance to it. Its admission policies should generally exclude the scholastically lowest third of high school graduating classes, except those students scoring above the twenty-fifth percentile on the Scholastic Aptitude Test, or the American College Test, or who demonstrate an achievement level not lower than the eleventh grade.

Those colleges in which the normative distribution of entering students is currently below the eleventh-grade level, by any agreed upon criteria within a state, should be acknowledged as "in-between colleges"—collegiate and precollegiate. While continuing to offer baccalaureate programs, its "fifth year" should be its "first year" on the precollegiate level. Its concern should be increasingly on academic foundations rather than the illusion of a prestigious superstructure.

The land-grant concept of open-door admissions needs to flourish in a new relevant form of current expression. The concept, however, need not be restricted to those institutions that were chartered as land-grant institutions. That concept provides a missing rung in the ladder from marginal high schools to first-rate colleges.

2. The state college should combine its financial resources in such a way that college-capable youth can be assured of financial assistance to make possible their continuance in college to creditable completion. Tuition costs should not exceed $200 per academic year, and the out-of-state additional tuition should not exceed $200. Interstate exchange of students among neighboring states should be encouraged. A regional accounting of in and out of state student mobility could form a basis for interstate tuition adjustments.[4]

3. State colleges should seek recruitment of a few students from one or more foreign countries as well as from "foreign" states. Honest efforts should be made, as well, to secure both Negro and non-Negro faculty members, white and nonwhite students. The point should not be to get any fixed kind of quota representation of minority groups. The purpose should be to secure a sufficient number of professionally competent faculty and academically competent students from minority and majority ethnic groups to provide the social context for intercultural education.

4. The state college, in performing its functions, must clearly delimit them. It should not seek to grow upward as a challenge to the graduate and research oriented university. There is no place in Southern higher education for a junior university, but there is an increased need for state colleges to provide a broad educational base on the lower-division level, and to feature a specialty or two, such as teacher education or technological training, beyond that level. In the current evolution of higher education, the state college must clarify its generic function as a nonuniversity as well as its specialized liberal and professional functions, in keeping with the pattern of educational needs within its state. Only then can it become distinctively productive.

5. The state university needs to come to terms with its political establishment so that it can do what it is uniquely intended to do—provide first-rate upper-division and graduate-level instruction, conduct basic and

---

[4]A student-exchange plan, involving a reciprocal "forgiveness" of nonresident tuition would be a stopgap measure. It would be unwieldy in some respects, however, especially in multi-state exchanges.

applied research, and perform public service for which its areas of specialization render it competent. Neither the public nor the private university should undertake the remedial assistance of academically retarded youth who cannot meet the rigors of exacting collegiate scholarship. Nor should students be admitted to the university who are not likely to be able to succeed in it.

Universities offering doctoral programs, whose total enrollments exceed 8,000 should, in most cases, discontinue the lower division of their collegiate offerings. The junior college program no longer has a place in a large university. In other universities and technological institutions, the freshman and sophomore years may appropriately be retained, but only for the socially mature, academically superior students who appear capable of doing creditable graduate work upon completion of their undergraduate program, or of by-passing the baccalaureate degree in direct route to the first graduate degree. The university is no place for the socially dependent or the academically handicapped student who requires compensatory education. It is unfair to him and tests the frustration tolerance of his conscientious professors to admit him into a situation where he is virtually doomed to early failure.

6. A few public and nonpublic universities can perform a signal service for educationally disadvantaged youth by preparing, in their graduate schools, some eminently qualified instructors for junior and senior colleges, especially on the subdoctoral level. The programs should involve internship experiences in considerable variety. A unique opportunity would be a graduate program in which a predominantly Negro university joins forces with a predominantly white university to this end.

7. In the desegregation era in higher education, the university has, however slowly, led the way. Now the challenge before it is to become a model of ethnic integration in the postdesegregation era. Colleges and the schools, late or soon, will follow its leadership. If this leadership potential lies dormant, the desegregation pattern may become a stagnant condition because the challenge is no longer with the legislative domain nor with the judiciary. The Southern university is called upon to move forth, by precept and example, to take the lead in demonstrating what can be accomplished in a region that seeks to develop its most talented citizenry and to dignify every person, whatever his talent.

SELECTED REFERENCES

Allen, Herman R. *Open Door to Learning*. Urbana: University of Illinois Press, 1963.

Arrowsmith, William. "The Shame of the Graduate Schools," *Harpers*, 232:1390 (March 1966), 51-59.

Kerr, Clark. *The Uses of the University*. Cambridge, Mass.: Harvard University Press, 1964.

Kirk, Grayson. "The University in Contemporary Society," *School and Society* (February 5, 1966), pp. 63-65.
Perkins, James A. *The University in Transition*. Princeton: Princeton University Press, 1966.
Singletary, Otis A. "Obligations and Services of Higher Education to the Disadvantaged and Underprivileged," paper presented to Discussion Group 14 at the National Conference on Higher Education, Chicago, March 14, 1966, contained in *Proceedings*, Association for Higher Education, 1966.
Woodring, Paul, and Bernard Baum. "Can State Colleges Educate for Excellence?," *Saturday Review*, XLVII:16 (April 18, 1964), 55-59.

PART V.
THE HISTORY OF TOMORROW

THE HISTORY OF TOMORROW

This report has described some of the principal ways in which problems of poverty and educational disadvantage, and those of ethnic disharmony, permeate the fabric of Southern higher education. Relating to the broken strands of those problems, there is a central dilemma that seeks a hopeful step toward resolution in higher education. As the American South moves out of its past and into its future, it is presented with an opportunity for achieving equality of opportunity and mutuality of respect as a way of life, a democracy that will be significant in world affairs as well as in the affairs of this nation. Southern higher education provides a handle for seizing this opportunity of democratizing the South. The crucial present dilemma in the South's search for its nobler self, and the opportunity presented by it, comprise the subject matter of the concluding portions of this study.

17. A SOUTHERN DILEMMA

The South continues to be at variance with itself. Trying to hold to the old and grasp the new, the South finds that it cannot stretch that far. It has to give up some of one for some of the other. Collegiate learning, in church and state, mirrors this ambitendency. Higher education, to boot, is run amuck by petty political problems. A university is established where none is needed, in payment of a political debt. The location of some community colleges is determined largely as a matter of political opportunism. Able young men in state departments of education are eased out of office by superintendents who are the "peoples choice." Retirement ages of college presidents are lowered temporarily by legislative action to effect a single ouster, and subsequently raised to effect an individual benefit. Despite all of this, and far more, political patronage in public higher education is far less pronounced than it used to be, when the election of a new governor in one state, for example, jeopardized the entire executive leadership of public institutions of higher learning.

The church-connected and private institutions, of course, have their political systems as well, now and again governed by pride, prejudice, and organizational or personal ambition. The nonpublic sector is not immune to, nor independent of these forces. The raising of funds, for example, forces difficult choices regarding integrity of educational function and the price at which virtue is for sale. But these are atypical situations, happily, rather than commonly prevalent ones.

Yet, to the extent that such conditions do obtain, the drive for power and position, competition supplanting cooperation, callous indifference or unstudied smugness concerning the legitimate goals of higher education, the South will be the victim of higher education rather than its beneficiary.

THE MILIEU OF SOUTHERN PROBLEMS

Religion

A religious upheaval has attended the alleged death of God in the Bible Belt. With all the semantic double talk, a new uneasiness, a defensive insecurity has shown itself. But Southern religion had contracted an illness long before. It was the illness of social irresponsibility cloaked in the respectable "doctrine of spirituality" in the churches. The laity has long been comforted by the lack of threat to salvation made possible by a culture-bound religion. Becoming more liberal in its moral code, now condoning the earlier "sins" of card playing, dancing, smoking, and social drinking, its moral responsibility has not extended itself proportionately. It is best at its priestly function of comforting, of healing personal hurt, and of providing opportunities for formal worship. It is least effective in its prophetic function of crusading against flagrant social injustice. Its former kingly function, of exercising social control over its membership, has long since lost its old-time power.

Race

The ethnic revolt has jarred the foundations of Southern tradition. Desegregation has become an established fact in most of the South, and in higher education it has been a much-publicized *fait accompli* in all but a few small nonpublic colleges. Such desegregation has been necessitated, in part, by the faculty shortage and the reluctance of liberal professors to serve in colleges where there are reports of continued student segregation or of racial discrimination. Meanwhile, however, the academically weaker Negro students create a new concern for professors who do not wish to practice preferential grading for Negro students, but who do not wish to be regarded as prejudiced against them either.

The larger racial picture, off the collegiate campus, has reached a crucial juncture. The extension of economic opportunity for Negroes, both in developing skills and professional competency and in gaining employment commensurate with ability, is pronounced. In upper levels of ability, the supply of Negro professionals is short. The demand, often growing out of efforts to make liberal employment policies visible, creates a temporarily inflated sense of values and a corresponding inequity in fair employment practices. Puzzlement grows among employed Negroes who were earlier denied opportunity because of race and now are afforded preferential consideration because of it.

In the social sphere, the legal steps of voting rights, the use of public facilities, justice in the courts, and even a remediation of housing restrictions applicable to race are increasingly assured. Living and working in close proximity, however, especially in an urban society, does not assure neighborliness, mutual respect, or a consciousness of kind. The residue of traditional sanctions and taboos lingers on. Whether the white South, as it yields to the Negro his legal rights, will continue its prevalent tradition of caring for him as a person, or will carry a hostile resentment growing out of that new equality, remains to be determined. The result depends on how gracefully the Negro uses his rights, whether with understandable haughtiness or with educated dignity. It depends on the white man, too, as he comes to terms with the fact that he is in perplexing truth freer than he has ever been before. The lot falls upon higher education to provide leadership for a new Southern hospitality, affording ethnic direction where new prestige symbols give cues for cultural change.

Poverty

The economic conditions of conspicuous poverty—of poverty amidst abundance—are nowhere more dramatically apparent than in the Southern institutions of higher learning where some colleges are figuratively going into one form of "receivership" or another, while others have difficulty in knowing how to use their abundance of resources wisely. Thousands of college-capable youth, depressed by poverty, do not get the knowledge, encouragement, and assistance to gain a foothold in higher education, except in those states with a community college boom. With a Gross National Product in 1966 of more than $730 billion, the impoverished student, along with the "developing" institutions, faces problems of educational survival.

The South is gaining appreciably in producing and receiving a fair share of the national product. It is also being assisted in a familiar variety of ways by federal action. Whether such assistance proves to stir local and regional initiative in the direction of self-help, as opposed to a welfare state in which the South would become increasingly dependent instead of less so, is an unresolved issue. Higher education, in its turn, is being put to the test of whether it will make long-range efforts to use funds wisely or will tend toward opportunism for today's urgencies.

The Family

Southern families, Negro and white, continue to be shredded as urbanization and industrialization, though trailing the nation, continues to mount. The impact of this social disorganization makes itself felt in higher education as many college-capable youth avoid the additional threats of college failure. They already have problems enough of their own. Others who do enter college bring their familial distress with them, or feel embarrassed by their humble origins or their limited means, or by the form of their parents' gainful employment. Colleges presumably will help them to gain more "respectable" employment than plumbing, or carpentry, or cosmetology, or hack driving or other low-status activities that our "educated" society, as we know it, looks upon with condescension but could not get along a week without.

The artificial symbols of respectability, of affluence and social position, even of legitimacy of birth, may be further reinforced in higher learning, or they may come to be re-evaluated with reference to other claims for personal dignity and respect. The college is the mating community of upper- and middle-class adolescents, where the new normative pattern of family life is being formed. The future of the family as the primary social institution is being strengthened or neglected in the intellectual and social dimensions of the college's educational program.

Politics

The South is undergoing a revolution in its political strategies and tactics. The Negro voter increasingly represents a potential balance of

power in local, state, and national elections. The new political circumstances spread across the South. The threat of bloc votes of illiterates,
rather than the independent votes of well-informed individuals, is by no
means limited to Alabama and Mississippi, although its dramatic focus
is there, among the Negroes and the countervailing effects of an illiterate
white citizenry. That same threat, in varying measure, exists in every
Southern state.

The principle of reapportionment was clearly established with the defeat
of the proposed Dirksen Amendment in 1966. The vagaries of political
fortunes thus reflect a new dimension of instability within the South, not
only in Tennessee where the hornet's nest of the one-man one-vote was
first stirred up. Whatever his color, and wherever he lives, the vote of
the Southerner will henceforth be counted as one vote, an incredible circumstance in Southern politics.

Vietnam

With it all, the Vietnam stalemate has braked ambitious efforts to move
toward a Great Society, in the South and throughout America. The military
draft requirements place in the front lines those men for whom America
should have the deepest compassion. Like Uriah in the heat of battle, they
are expendables in preserving a way of life for the youth whose educational
privileges permit their collegiate attendance and sufficient academic
success to avoid the draft. In the name of patriotism, the disadvantaged
serve the advantaged.[1] Norman Cousins has referred to these inequities
as Russian Roulette, commenting that "the government has proclaimed
in effect that its draftees are intellectually inferior and therefore fit for
the fighting front rather than for the classroom."[2] Senator William
Fulbright, with a band of supporters, continues to be critical of American
foreign policy. Thus the war itself, and the nature of determining who
must risk their lives in it, combine to claim the spotlight of controversy.
The question of the true role of democracy, at home and abroad, claims
to be the point at issue.

THE SOUTH'S DILEMMA

A quarter of a century ago, Gunnar Myrdal reported a disharmony, in the
North and the South, between the tradition of enlightenment and the American Revolution on the one hand and the subjugation of the Negro on the

---

[1]See: Donald Graham, "Taking a McNamara Fellowship"; Jeffrey Goodman, "How To Be
Patriotic and Live with Yourself"; Keith R. Johnson, "Who Should Serve," *The Atlantic*,
217:2 (February 1966), 59-68.

[2]Cousins, "Russian Roulette in the Classroom" (editorial), *Saturday Review*, XLIX:17
(April 23, 1966), 22. Alvin O'Konski, of Wisconsin, charged that of the hundred or so
draftees from his congressional district in a period of six months, not one came from a
family with an income exceeding $5,000. The South has a high share of youth in that cate-
gory. *Newsweek*, LXVIII:7 (July 4, 1966), 19.

other. He observed that while the Negro in the North was generally accorded his public rights, he was consistently deprived of his private rights
as a person. (Subsequent findings have revealed this to be a misleading,
partial truth.) He observed that in the South, the Negro was denied both
his public and private rights, but that the white Southerner tended to be
more indulgent in terms of the Negro's personal, private needs so long
as he remained in the place defined for him in the racial caste system of
the South.[3]

"America is free to choose," Myrdal commented, "whether the Negro
shall remain her liability or become her opportunity."[4] That issue has
since been joined, and the Negro is gaining access to economic opportunity,
to the voting booth, to public facilities, and to private residences in formerly restricted areas. The "Myrdal dilemma" has taken a new turn in
the South, as the *de jure* aspect of the dilemma has been erased.

John W. Gardner observed a different kind of dilemma, without reference to race, in the context of the aims of a free people.[5] "Can we be
equal and excellent, too?," he asked. Giving an American redefinition
of both terms, he developed a strong affirmative response to that question.
With the racial caste system being overturned, the layer of a caste system
based on economic and cultural disadvantage lies beneath it. To alleviate
the conditions of a designated minority ethnic group while remaining un-
aware of the insidious enemy of democracy in the form of poverty and
needless cultural deprivation hardly moves the South toward a social
democracy. The Southern dilemma, broadly viewed, is a fusion of the
Myrdal dilemma and the illusion of a necessary, arbitrary choice between
exclusive education and inclusive education, the Gardner dilemma. That
dilemma is whether the South shall move toward democratizing its segment of American society, in political, economic, and cultural terms, or
whether it shall only yield to the external pressures of legal sanctions,
of financial incentives, and the baubles of shallow prestige symbols to
establish a new facade of democracy.

The South's answer will take its shape and substance in the various
social institutions of church and state—and the meeting ground of these
institutions is on the campus of institutions of higher learning. That is
where the problem will most likely find its ultimate resolution. For
better or for worse, institutions of higher learning will set an example
that the status-seeking society will emulate. Higher education has within
its power the redesignation of some of these symbols of prestige, and with

[3] See: Gunnar Myrdal, with the assistance of Richard Sterner and Arnold Rose, *An American
Dilemma, The Negro Problem and American Democracy,* Twentieth Anniversary Edition
(New York: Harper and Row, 1962).

[4] Page 1,022.

[5] Gardner, *Excellence: Can We Be Equal and Excellent, Too?* (New York: Harper and Row,
1961).

it, the fashioning of a higher social order, resembling the best of the old
and the discovery of the new.

THE DILEMMA OF SOUTHERN HIGHER EDUCATION

With college enrollments accelerating far beyond earlier prediction rates,
the colleges hardly have the facilities to accommodate additional "marginal"
students, much less the staff and educational programs appropriate to
their needs. Meanwhile, each college, the excellent and the mediocre,
rushes along its separate way, remaining in a competitive position rather
than entering into a cooperative relationship. In most Southern states,
state colleges vie with each other and with universities, not to carve out
a contributive niche within their system in which to excel, but to emulate
the universities with all their diffuse functions. The conflict over reverting
universities to collegiate states is not limited to the state of Texas, although that state has been headlined in such efforts.[6] To bring cosmos
out of this chaos is difficult enough when educators and politicians keep
their eyes fixed on the legitimate purposes of higher learning. Unless
they do, the margin of hope becomes slim indeed.

The dilemma facing Southern colleges and universities is whether to
attempt the exceedingly difficult task of democratizing higher education,
or simply to give lip service to the popular trends of the moment while
catering to upper classes enjoying the privilege of culturally fortunate
birth, of social position, of affluence, and of educational advantage.

The latter course is easy to follow in these times, and can be rationalized in respectable terms so long as casual visible efforts and liberal
public pronouncements are made. There is the risk of educating for
smugness, for intolerance, and even for arrogance, but that is nothing
new. A determined commitment to democratize higher education, however,
ushers in a host of vexing and threatening problems to the higher learning
establishment and its public and private component parts.

Democratic higher education begins when students are admitted—invited
and made to feel welcome—in the college community. This is only the
beginning of democracy. Yet students must be helped to find and enter
those doors of opportunity to higher learning that are congruent with their
aspirations and abilities.

Leadership in higher education must perforce create a genuine system
of higher education, which, taken as a coherent whole, will provide for the
multitude of society's needs and accommodate itself to the tremendous
range of capacities and backgrounds, in both breadth and depth, of the
youth who will become a part of it. In such a setting, a new criterion
of success must be recognized—the criterion of institutional effectiveness
with reference to a given group of students and their achievement of
relevant, realistic goals. The dichotomy of dependence v. independence

---

[6] See any Texas daily, such as the *Houston Chronicle,* during April 14-18, 1966, or the
Denton Record Chronicle, April 18, 1966.

must yield to a concept of interdependence with recognition and support going to every useful aspect of higher learning.

Colleges, in examining the meaning of American democracy in the last third of the twentieth century, will be forced to reassess the relevance of both general and specialized education, lest they prove to be miseducative in their neglect to look forward as well as backward. The faculty must become oriented to a new function in terms of behavioral change beyond the specialized academic proficiency conventionally regarded as higher learning. This does not argue for purely utilitarian goals, but stresses that the liberal arts must be assessed with reference to their liberalizing, educative effect.

However threadbare the phrase, we learn a lot of what we live, whether it be called acculturation or progressive education. If students are in bondage to a faculty who in turn must defer to paternalistic administrators, the essence of democracy can only be intellectualized, not internalized as a way of life. Shared authority and the maturing experience of accepting consequences for decision-making are an integral part of the painful process of democratizing higher learning. There is no short cut that effectively by-passes direct confrontation with society's problems, or glosses over the present in haste to return to the comfortable reservation of an inert past. The democratic college studies and improves the social conditions on its campus and in its contiguous community.

The Southern college must become, increasingly, an open door in which both foreign and domestic subcultures interact with mutually enriching effect. Whatever the word, whether democracy or equalitarianism, the college must afford opportunities for direct, as well as vicarious, learning that forces an assessment of the raw materials out of which international tensions and conflicts are spawned. For the Southerner to be educated as a world citizen, he must get out of the web of his own subculture. South Carolinians and South Africans can learn a good deal from each other, if given the opportunity under reasonably favorable conditions. Northern and southern Louisianians and Floridians, white and Negro, can do the same.

Most difficult of all, the task of democratizing higher education requires a functional repudiation of the prestigious symbols of power through biological or social inheritance, of personal worth on the basis of the outward symbols of exclusive fraternity and sorority groupings, and of conspicuous consumption as a means of establishing a position of pomp. Higher education becomes democratized not only as it rewards achievement, but as it honors diligence of effort and dishonors the brilliant sloth; not only as it values eminence, but also the trait of mind that shows less concern about receiving credit than of serving worthy causes, in low stations as well as high ones; not only as it values the power of money, but as it values and evaluates power apart from money. Democratic higher education has the task of dignifying those traits of mind and character that declare the worth of each man's neighbor as well as of his own children. That is why the task of democratizing Southern higher education is so difficult—some will say impossible. It involves a modified value system within higher education itself, where the lowly virtues of the human condition are now regarded as substitute goals for those who cannot "get ahead" in the dehumanized society of open competition. While not minimizing the importance of competition in academic and technical achievement, it maximizes a shared responsibility for such achievement, and respects the fact that equality of opportunity invariably results in inequality of achievement, due to innate differences of individual learning capacity. Thus, realistic aspirations become a part of democratic higher learning, and a man is proud of what he may confidently hope to become.

RESOLVING THE DILEMMA

The South can never achieve a full measure of democracy, despite all conceivable legislation, without the active support of higher education. Democracy requires a political machinery, but the machinery without its spirit of motivating power makes a sorry travesty of the concept. In America and around the world, that fact has become painfully clear. From the "guided democracy" of Korea to the "peoples" democracy of China, the mockery echoes.

Higher education can take the easy route. It can enjoy the tempting rewards that accrue now as our society places so great a faith in its potential value. It can "take a dive" and make a good show of it, giving up the fight altogether. It can, in reasonably good conscience, pursue its conventional goals of education for affluence and respectability, and the values of such stabilizing education should not be too harshly discounted by public opinion. It is a strong temptation.

Throughout the Southern regions, however, is an inarticulate minority of dedicated educators whose deep convictions espouse idealistic values of higher education and who see pragmatic needs for full development of capable human resources. The future of higher education, and of the South through it, resides in the exercise of leadership by this gallant band of educators, funding agencies, and influential citizens who share the view that higher education does have, indeed, a responsibility for shaping destiny, for writing the outlines for the history of tomorrow. The dual dilemma of democratizing the South poses the central task in the shaping of that future.

RECOMMENDED REFERENCES

Gardner, John W.   *Excellence: Can We Be Equal and Excellent, Too?*   New York: Harper and Row, 1961.

McKinney, John C. , and Edgar T. Thompson (eds.).   *The South in Continuity and Change.* Durham: Duke University Press, 1965.

Myrdal, Gunnar. *An American Dilemma: The Negro Problem and American Democracy.* Twentieth Anniversary Edition. New York: Harper and Row, 1962.

Seuss, Dr. *The Sneetches and Other Stories.* New York: Random House, 1961.

18. THE TELIC FUNCTION

Forecasts of the nature and extent of change in American society are fraught with many problems, and the willingness to be cast in the role of a seer requires foolhardiness, or deep humility, or perhaps a bit of both. In large measure, of course, the American society will have the future it chooses for itself. In many respects, it remains highly indecisive. In others, its future appears highly predictable. Higher education, where clarity of vision is a societal imperative, tends to dream of a distant future but to plan for yesterday.

Social prophecy can be useful in a number of ways. It can help our armed forces in preparation for assuring our national defense a generation hence, not unmindful of the vicissitudes of Vietnam. It can help higher education to view those societal developments that are beyond its proper purview and those clearly germane to its central functions. These functions include preparing an informed, socially responsible leadership—a leadership that will be felt in politics, religion, international diplomacy, economic development, in the extension of human rights, and of opportunities through America's various social institutions. The functions also concern an active identity with the present. Just as our military forces must be in a state of perpetual readiness for both the present and the distant future, so must the higher education forces develop a state of readiness to cope with problems of the present, while shaping a society of the future to fit American ideals.

Mindful of the limitations of cultural predictions, a comprehensive effort of scholars was recently culminated under the aegis of the Syracuse University Research Corporation. The study was charged with the task of providing the best possible assessment of the United States of America and of the world in 1985. That assessment does not present a variation of Plato's *Republic* or Sir Thomas More's *Utopia* or of Edward Bellamy's *Looking Backward,* all of which are held together by an indulgence in the art of wishful thinking. It is characterized by a painstaking examination of relevant data and their extrapolation through time by physical and social scientists who collaborated in developing that social prophecy. It is a projection of present trends and a studied analysis of those factors combining for and against change in our society.

Developed expressly for the use, in long-range planning, by the United States Marine Corps, the Syracuse report viewed the evolving role of that corps to be that of a "peacemaker," preserving peace through extinguishing large and small "brush fires" of conflict, thereby preventing a world conflagration. That projection into the 1985 era, however useful it may be for the Marine Corps, contains a great deal of significant data for American higher education as well, which for less cause has put tomorrow on a low priority shelf. In an important sense, the Syracuse report is of greater moment to higher education, which shares the power to shape the era of 1985, than to our armed forces, which are charged primarily with preventing threats to our nation, whatever shape it is then in.

The Syracuse study is predicated on two basic assumptions. The first, a hopeful one, is that no general war will occur prior to 1985. The second belief is that man is, and will continue to be, slow in revising his attitudes and loyalties. That working assumption is expressed in these words: "Man's actions are motivated and directed by an amalgam of short-run self-interests—tempered and rationalized by prudence, by ethical and religious propositions, by constraints imposed by society, and by both conservative and revolutionary myths propagated by political leaders."[1] The document is a conservative one, far less dramatic, for example, than some of the spectacular predictions of David Sarnoff, chairman of the Radio Corporation of America.[2] Within the context of these assumptions, and emerging from a careful examination of trends, the comprehensive picture of American society in the 1980's takes a form which we can readily visualize. The introduction of new major variables could intervene, to be sure, and give new direction to the currently evident course of events.

AMERICA IN THE 1985 ERA

The production of goods and services in 1985 will exceed a trillion dollars, nearly double the Gross National Product of 1964. This growth, however, is expected to result in "substantial human dislocations and institutional readjustments." In two short years after this prediction, it appears to be unduly conservative. In 1966, the GNP is estimated at $730 billion, a full year ahead of "schedule."

America's population will have increased from its present 200 million to nearly 275 million. It will be a young population with a median age of less than thirty. Meanwhile, the world population will have climbed from its present three billion to more than 4.5 billion—the greatest increase being among the poor nations, with the consequence of further separating abundance and destitution. In America, nearly 90 percent of the population will be clustered in or near 240 metropolitan centers, most of which

---

[1] Syracuse University Research Corporation, *The United States and the World in the 1985 Era* (prepared under Navy Office of Naval Research Contract NOnr 4345 (00) [Washington, D. C.: U.S. Department of Commerce, 1964]) pp. 5-6.

[2] See, for example: "Switchboards in Space," interview with David Sarnoff, *U.S. News and World Report*, LIX:1 (July 4, 1965), 50-54.

already exist. Young men and women enrolled in higher education, from technical schools to universities, will then exceed 50 percent of the age group from seventeen to twenty-five. Negroes will be more fully integrated into the national economy, but unskilled Negroes will continue to constitute a majority of the urban poor.

The United States will be in a position to ward off massive world starvation through its further leadership in developing oceanic food supplies, through the use of animal protein, and major crop production, coupled with new methods of freezing, dehydration, and irradiation. America's own food problems will be largely solved, from the standpoint of minimum dietary supply, for virtually all of its citizens. Water problems will be solved through improved management of resources and the process of de-salting water. Water will cost more, but Americans will be in a better position to pay for it, and de-salted water will likely be substituted for most fresh-water resources in Southern California and other presently arid areas.

Our current modes of transportation on land, sea, and in the air, will continue to be dominant. However, in the 1985 era, our commerical airlines will include supersonic aircraft fleets, capable of speeds up to mach 3, which literate citizens will then readily translate into about 2,200 miles-per-hour. Metropolitan noise and air pollution will be sharply reduced with the development and common acceptance of electric cars for commuting purposes. There will be plenty of electricity. The installed electric capacity will then triple the present output, amounting by 1985 to about 8,700 million kilowatts.

Liquid hydrocarbons (fossil fuels) will be in sufficient supply for industrial, heating, and automotive purposes. Space technology advances will continue unabated, with more than 1 percent of the GNP (up to $10 billion yearly) being expended for space exploration and control. The Apollo lunar landing will be consummated soon after 1970 (now rescheduled for 1969), followed between 1975-1979 by a landing of eight men on Mars. The Martian landing will cost an estimated $18.5 billion, payable in ten fairly equal yearly installments. We can also buy probes to Jupiter in 1975 and to Saturn in 1985 if we wish.[3]

There will be other wonders in the field of technology. Video telephone circuits will be available, and international communication facilities will accelerate the use of English as an international language. There will be expanded use of computers for many activities, which in turn will lead to communications systems interconnecting widely separated data-processing facilities. The use of satellites in broadcasting will have become commonplace by that time. The automation of industries and offices will continue,

---

[3] See: Syracuse University Research Corporation, *Science and Technology in the 1985 Era* (1964), pp. 23-25. NASA Administrator James Webb revised the cost estimate of the Apollo Program from $20 to $22.7 billion, *Newsweek*, LXVII:22 (May 30, 1966), 65.

thus eliminating many intermediate-level supervisory and management personnel billets. There will be less need for "middle managers."

But with the miracles of science and technology, Americans will not yet have come to grips with their basic social problems of peace, of government by law, of equality of opportunity, and of a social conscience. Formal education will represent the largest single investment of public monies, and will be accompanied by increased use of teaching machines, and of programmed instruction. Meanwhile, crime and delinquency will continue to flourish as a major American concern, and family disintegration will increase with urbanization, as conservative rural traditions disappear. The Negro American will have firmly established his constitutional rights, but subtle discrimination, particularly in housing and social activity, will persist.

The government will become the "surrogate of conscience," largely taking the place of traditional charity and of private conscience. The "culture of poverty" will have its redress to the government and to its sensitive professionals, but it will be further isolated from the affluent society which, through the government, will "buy off" the poor, to keep those natives from becoming too restless. A major governmental task will be to help individuals to find meaningful social roles and a significant identity for themselves.

In politics, the South's national power will curiously decline. With fewer one-party states, the South will have fewer congressmen holding unbroken re-election records—and thus lose the value of traditional seniority appointments. Thus the two-party, one-man one-vote South will lessen the region's influence in national politics and, in direct terms, in world affairs.

Material goods will be valued as highly in 1985 as they are today. The world, and America with it, will be more "secular and more materialistic, and more oriented to the comforts of the body than the peace of the soul."[4] Ecumenical action will not bring about any "spiritual rebirth" but may affect some visible, internal church organization. The churches will show increased concern for the material well-being of humanity—they will be more a house of social concern than of conventional worship.

This view of the United States in the 1985 era has been a fragmentary sketch of America's future based on an assumption of business as usual—of uneasy peace as usual—and of formal education as usual—an assumption that our system of higher education will proceed in its presently disconnected manner, preoccupied with its cultural concerns largely of economic interests for the highly schooled. No assumption is made that higher education will modify, instead of only reinforcing, the value systems of

---

[4] Syracuse, *The U.S. and World*, p. 94. "While Americans will continue to struggle fitfully for meaning in life," the study predicts, "the majority will also have a cafeteria of transient escapes from the inevitable paradoxes of existence," p. 61.

material status symbols and of disdain for the dignity of menial labor—no matter how useful and necessary it may be.

Another view of America's future, developed as a background for higher education rather than for military defense, has been developed by Donald N. Michael, resident fellow of the Institute for Policy Studies in Washington, D.C. With his preview focusing on technological change, he makes careful predictions about cybernation—the use of automation and computers as spelling the end of full-time employment—"the end of work as a focus of life" for our population in increasing numbers. Society, through systems planning and in other sophisticated ways, will increase its efficiency in terms of economic productivity. Intellectual activity will be regulated along assembly-line patterns, much as physical activity has so largely become. Social engineering will increase the ability, through the use of the computer by behavioral scientists, to predict and control human behavior. Biological "engineering" will extend the ability to manipulate the organism, both to destroy and to modify life and the biological environment.[5]

In the nonmaterial aspects of culture, Michael foresees a deepening of dilemmas between individual responsibility to conscience and a loyalty to organizational or national purpose. The family life will provide less, not more adequate guidance for youth than it does now. Firm moral positions will be increasingly rare, and in that sense, Vietnam serves as a "prototype of things to come." Michael, in his studied fling at prophecy, observes that "the most important lesson pivotal institutions will have to learn is how to change rapidly and frequently." Without it, he cautions, we will have a society that has lost its deeper meaning to the individual.

THE DILEMMA OF OUR ASSUMPTIONS

Such views are based on good historical foundations. In 1932, George Counts published a provocative, small treatise under the title *Dare the School Build a New Social Order?* [6] In it he condemned the "slave psychology" of the pedagogue and asserted that "education as a force for social regeneration must march hand in hand with the living and creative forces of the social order." That challenge was discussed and debated for a time during the depression years. Soon, schools and colleges settled back to business as usual, including Counts' book among the relics of required reading in education courses, as good a way as any to kill off further chances for challenging thought and action. In some instances, *Dare the School* was used as a textbook for rote learning, and timid students dutifully "learned" it for examination day.

Another effort in the 1930's, this one in satirical vein, was the flight into fantastic reality (or realistic fantasy) by Harold Benjamin under the

---

[5] Michael, "The Next Twenty Years: Background Notes for Assessing the Direction and Purpose of Higher Education," in W. C. Jones (ed.), *Higher Education for All?* (Corvallis: Oregon State University Press, 1965), pp. 1-7.

[6] New York: The John Day Company, 1932.

pseudonym of J. Abner Peddiwell, Ph. D. , *Saber Tooth Curriculum*. [7]
Higher paleolithic education there became necessary for esoteric knowledge, for cultural and magical values that it became heresy to question.
Higher education as a social institution had largely outlived its usefulness.
It served only to perpetuate artificially diverse forces in society, but its
vestigial remains were highly regarded symbols of the upper class.
Peddiwell was a good lampoonist, and his satire accounted for thousands of
knowing chuckles and a good many belly laughs. Higher education, however, maintained its course and speed.

These challenges, and others of like nature, were puffs in the wind of
change, and the Syracuse professors logically assume that the higher
education establishment is not now apt to undertake a significant telic
function in society. It is not likely, in the manner of NASA, to chart a
course to achieve long-range social goals, and to discipline itself each
year with relentless team effort and unswerving purpose toward the goals
it so eloquently espouses. With reference to the vast majority of educators,
such assumptions have full face validity.

If American higher education is to make a difference in the 1985 era,
however, aside from producing a half-million technologists needed for the
space program, and the other needed millions of well-fed and precision-
tooled human cogs in an industrial society, it cannot afford to consist of
2,300 anarchic collegiate institutions. In the American South particularly,
a late hour has arrived. Bold concerted action is urgently needed by a
creative minority of leadership. That leadership now exists in the form of
potential, not kinetic energy. This concluding chapter is based upon the
assumption that higher education can and will have a creative constructive
function in the realization of man's merging social and material goals. It
can change the course of our social history.

We cannot complete this task by 1985, but we must move in the direction
that society dreams of moving—providing a sense of purpose and direction
each year of the journey toward a truly new South, one undreamed of by
those who coined the phrase. The human condition has its noble as well as
its ignoble aspects. If a nucleus of educators can be quick to revise their
loyalties, becoming motivated by long-run interests of "enlightened self-
ishness," the course of history can yet be turned to the full benefit of
mankind. If we make the proper assumptions, the 1985 era will be quite
different from that extrapolated from the data of the learned Syracuse
prophets. Our dilemma is in choosing those assumptions that will guide
our action, or those that will tranquilize us into inaction or further diffuse
our efforts.

Let us assume, first of all, that leadership will increasingly respond
to ethical impulses, and less to selfish ones; will be more inclined to
cooperation in the public interest than to competition in the private interest;
more concerned about institutional integrity of character and less about

7 New York: McGraw-Hill Book Company, 1935.

the facade of the public image. Let us assume, further, that leadership in our society, within and outside the higher education establishment, will accept a continuing responsibility for higher education's telic function, its directional force in society. Timidity will give way to a prudent boldness, a reasoning, action-oriented commitment; the focus of education will then be on our heritage—past and present—as a key to social action, not as a womb to return to in times of distress. These are the two intervening variables that can cause the 1985 era not to be the era forecast by the Syracuse analysts, but one that we in higher education have helped to shape, through suasion, through relevant education, and through personal commitment as scholarly citizens in the here and now of social realities.

As the ancient Jewish scriptures express it, it is not our duty to complete the task; but neither are we free to desist from it. This can be a time when creature comforts within the "establishment" can reach a new peak of luxury, and where we can disregard with impunity the special endemic problems of disadvantaged talented youth. Higher education can thus disconnect our nation into a Disunited States of America, divided not by state lines but by schisms of race and socio-economic class. Or this can be a time of shaping a future through coping with the vexing problems of the present, and of increasing the societal relevance of higher education within the South. The following hopeful predictions can become self-fulfilling prophecies, if enough Americans will them to become so.

HIGHER EDUCATION IN THE SOUTH: A 1975 VIEW

Southern colleges and universities in 1965 were characteristically more concerned about keeping peace with the establishment than with moving into crucial, controversial areas of social action. The phenomenon was not caused by a willful decision to dawdle with the inherent social power of higher education. Southern educators were not uniquely status driven or power thirsty. They did not entertain delusions of grandeur more than their non-Southern colleagues. They were simply not organized for collective effort, and felt that major improvement had to start somewhere else. Their hands were full of trivial urgencies.

There were the status seekers, to be sure. Some presidents were reminiscent of the fifteenth-century comment in Sir Thomas More's *Utopia,* that "[princes] are much more concerned about how to get new kingdoms for themselves than to administer well what they already have." College administrators in a growing dominion fought against this fifteenth-century "disease." There were others, however, of loftier purposes who were gripped by a sense of futility. They were harassed by building programs, by discrepancies in stated goals and the available means of achieving them, by faculty recruitment raids, by civil rights issues, and by the conflicting expectation of their many supporting and nonsupporting publics. They frequently felt forced to muddle along the best they could, hoping that much good somehow would come of their efforts—in athletics and academics, in affluence and poverty-vows. The institutions with the greatest distance to travel had the lowest supply of fuel, and both private and public funds were discriminating in favor of institutions that had less need for basic support.

Yet with the growth of higher education in material prosperity grew a restive spirit, a sense of emptiness, a feeling among an increasing number of thoughtful educators in agreement with Ecclesiastes, the preacher, that "all is vanity." In the mid-1960's, the desegregation era had come to a ceremonial end in higher education, but no sustained effort had been made to achieve, for Negroes and non-Negroes, an ethnic integration on personal and social levels. The federal government was pumping money, on a "color blind" basis, into higher education for the poor, but the poor were disadvantaged in more ways than poverty. The Ford Foundation had earmarked $15 million for Negro educational institutions, but the Negro was subtly handicapped by being singled out for assistance. Thousands of students were helped to start college—where they would soon be humiliated by the inevitable threat of failure despite their native potential and earnest efforts. There were a few brilliant poor, but even they had egregious gaps in their learning. With the gains of desegregation and the financial support for the financially limited student, the inseparable problem of educational disadvantage was an unadmitted gap, a kind of no man's land between the high school diploma and the minimum level of achieving collegiate success, especially in the historically white institution. Many colleges did not know how, or seem really to care how, to stoop below their standards to help the academically handicapped. To be an "in-between" college was to lose caste in the higher education status system, an ignominy too great to bear even in the best interest of higher education itself.

Late in the 1960's, higher education took a long step toward maturity. The yeast of change began to ferment when educators assumed increased personal responsibility for change, stopped saying "they," and some began saying to each other that "I and you must work for social and educational progress"; when they accepted the need for improvement as a first- and second-person mandate instead of a third-person escape from responsibility. Change began on a broken front at first, but soon there was a closing of ranks of educators with like commitments. There was the inevitable resistance from many expected quarters, and from some unexpected ones, but by 1970 there was a rallying to a new order in Southern higher education. This new order came to be strengthened from many sources within the South and from many supporters outside it.

These visionary, stubborn educators convinced themselves that significant progress can be initiated anywhere, and can multiply with evidence of a will to cooperate, if no one is too anxious about getting the credit, and if many are willing to share responsibility for some inevitable failure. Without a view to seeking personal or institutional credit, higher education assumed a new relevance here and there throughout the South, and the importance of that view developed as educators and businessmen showed that they meant business about higher education being an active partner in social and economic progress.

Higher education in the South in 1965 was characterized by blurred institutional objectives, by institutions promising students far more than they could deliver, by uncoordinated efforts within both the public and the church-connected (but federally assisted) institutions, by transitory commitments of fiscal expedience, largely rationalized by an illusionary sense of collegiate progress that grows out of the construction of new facilities and a plentiful supply of student customers. Like Sir Thomas More's princes, the college kingdoms were expanding, but there was a moratorium on educational progress.

Rule One: The first impasse was recognized as a lack of coordinated effort. The establishment of *Rule One* was not a new idea, the newness was that it was taken seriously. The principle read: *The academic community must work together as a matter of enlightened self-interest and as an expression of acceptance of societal responsibility. Suspicion must be supplanted by good faith, competition and conflict by cooperation on the action level.* This resulted in the creation of two systems of higher education in each Southern state to provide suitable education after high school for all aspiring high school graduates, varying widely in levels of achievement (from grade levels nine to sixteen), in ability, in technical and professional aspirations, and in potentialities.

The public system recruited students actively, on a selective basis, indicating where students of privileged opportunities and those with educational disadvantages might best be advised to go. The options of individual students were not single but multiple. The public education system contained designated colleges with special remedial and developmental booster programs containing provisions for delayed placement of high school graduates into full collegiate standing. In curricular balance, and academic guidance, the educational programs became congruent with society's needs.[8]

The nonpublic system was a parallel union, or confederation, of church-connected and private colleges and universities. This was a major "ecumenical" effort with a focus on major support of at least one nonpublic institution in each state dedicated to helping academically talented students regardless of ethnic or educational background or of financially limited conditions.

Those two systems of higher education were coordinated by a joint advisory board, and worked toward a regional system of higher education in conjunction with the Southern Association of Colleges and Schools, the

---

[8]No longer, for example, were twice as many teachers prepared as were needed, nor were there dire shortages in science, technology, and operation analysis. Students made their choices on the basis of calculated consequences, going into crowded fields only when their personal penchants overruled supply-demand considerations.

Southern Regional Education Board, and Regional Educational Laboratories, all uniquely fitted to provide guidance and to attract financial support in furtherance of this coordination effort. This coordinated system facilitated recruitment of students, faculty employment, and personalized contacts with students requiring it; it demonstrated that sportsmanlike competition can flourish in higher education. The Social Action Center for Southern Higher Education, with no dependence on tax funds or traditional function, completed the regional leadership team.

Rule Two: In that rapidly changing period, Southern higher education dealt with the nationwide problem of instability of educational effort, illustrated by the highly mobile faculties being auctioned off to colleges by the graduate schools, by the increasing rate of student transfers from one institution to another, and by sometimes staggering enrollment growths. Rule Two was the *Rule of Stability: Stability of educational effort must be assured by the increased constancy of faculty, the colleges' holding power of the student, a fixed ceiling on the rate of assimilation, and a continuing student-faculty dialogue with a focus on the student's own expanding world.*

New faculty contracts were written to provide a fourth year "incentive bonus," to reduce the tendency among young professors to move from job to job. After a year of successful employment on a college faculty, this incentive perquisite was attached to a three-year contract, which amounted to approximately 40 percent of the average annual salary for the quadrennium, payable only upon completion of three additional years of service with the institution. Some called it a bribe, but it came to symbolize an honor system of institutional loyalty, reinforced by the still standard coin of the realm, money.

In the interest of student retention, each college instituted a "retention recruitment" facility, which maintained a continuing diagnosis of those personal and institutional factors contributing to college dropouts and transfers. This facility was frequently managed by student leaders, and by the academic dean and the dean of students, and led to recurring revisions in recruitment practices, in educational programs, and in those socio-economic conditions affecting holding power and collegiate success, reducing failure threat, social threat, economic threat, and avoiding recruitment misguidance.

Recognizing that stability is achieved as a college develops its own worthy traditions such as honor systems, student participation in government, and even traditions of congenial student relationships, colleges found various ways to give traditions a chance to grow. One of the more effective means devised was to place a ceiling upon rates of increase of over-all enrollments, particularly of freshman class enrollments. They learned that although a college can "handle" as many enrollees as it can house, feed, and put into libraries and classrooms, its ability to provide higher education is restricted by far more significant and more subtle limitations. A quite different situation developed in new colleges, however, as the first four classes in as many years caught the spirit of setting precedents quickly, achieving in a genuine way, a kind of "instant tradition" social scientists explain as the "Jacobs effect."

Technology ushered in vast new opportunities for productive learning, including instructional television and programmed instruction. Such developments stressed the need for a continuing, academically intimate relationship in groups not exceeding twelve to fifteen members and including at least one faculty member. This pattern formed credit seminars in some situations, noncredit "conversations" in others. It frequently consisted of a professor and his own advisees who placed a continuing focus on "taking stock" of learning, where academic and nonbookish learning on the campus was viewed in the social milieu of local and world affairs.

Rule Three: The third and final rule was the *Rule of Relevancy: An authentic college must not simply teach what it is fond of. Its duty is to help students connect salient realities of society with their learning activities and personal commitments. Professors must be reeducated for changing realities. This is not simply a pedagogic function but a community-wide enterprise of scholars and nonscholars in which all students are teachers, and all instructors are learners.*

The *Rule of Relevancy* was the most difficult to enforce. It threatened the professoriat, and the entire collegiate curriculum, both in general and special education. It allegedly violated academic freedom. As headway was made toward it, however, and important students, faculty, and administrators supported it, the growth of that idea, too, became rapid. Students countered, "Academic freedom for whom?!" There was no place to hide from the salient issues of the new South in a world that was looking at it. The Hawthorne effect of being "singled out" as a special region gave further impetus to the effort.

The movement grew naturally out of the issues of freedom and responsibility of students on campus. Students were increasingly discontent with a curriculum that ignored the operational meaning of freedom and responsibility, or considered the meaning only in academic or detached, intellectual terms. The campus became a laboratory for learning the meaning of responsible freedom in student affairs, in matters of academic learning, and of social roles within the local community. It was still difficult to give students enough growing room without abdicating their guidance and disciplinary responsibilities. As students came to face the consequences of their power, they learned to make more judicious use of it.

As students stretched the concept of relevance beyond the campus, they became acquainted, in various personal contacts, with what Michael Harrington called the "other America."[9] Their work in Community Action Programs and in sequels to them, their election of courses in

[9] Harrington, *The Other America: Poverty in the United States* (New York: Houghton Mifflin Company, 1963). There are not only two Americas, of course, but many.

neighboring colleges of a different ethnic majority, their varied participation in political, religious, and other community movements, all helped them to become directly acquainted with the underlying problems of freedom and responsibility in a new society, an acquaintance their professors had formerly known only in vicarious terms. They were finally moving off the campus "reservation" as adolescents and returning to it as mature young, pensive adults.

Beyond the three telic rules, a number of supportive actions followed. With the ground rules of higher education changed, the value system of higher education's subculture began to change, slowly at first, as if in disbelief that any lasting difference could be made. Many clung to traditional assumptions about higher education being a thing apart from society, a Doctrine of Detachment that bore a striking resemblance to the church's "Doctrine of Spirituality," for which it had been so thoroughly castigated by "liberal" colleges in earlier times.

The Collegiate Scene

Access to higher education came to involve questions of institutional purposes and programs, of recruitment and holding power. Where the status of institutions had been earlier judged by its high standards, a high selective admission or a high "flunk" rate, status came to be based upon holding power, whatever the bases for recruitment and admissions. Failure and success came to be viewed as a relationship between student and college, and a combined attrition and out-transfer rate beyond 20 percent marked a weak institution, constituting a threat even to accreditation, and especially a warning to the distinguished centers of excellence in higher education anxious to retain that hard-earned distinction along those precise lines.

For a time public universities were in a mean squeeze. Required by law to observe an open admissions policy, they were not interested in the community college function. They were primarily and properly interested in graduate education and research. Some universities developed remedial programs that provided palliative student relief; others instituted delayed placement plans and decelerated baccalaureate programs of five years (four with summers). One state university sent notices to its high-risk applicants saying in substance, "public law requires our admitting you, but our experience teaches us that you do not have a fifty-fifty chance of success. That chance is yours to take."

All of this missed the point, because of the university's primary loyalties. By 1970, admission of freshmen to universities was limited to the top quartile of high school graduates wishing to pursue a master's-level program. By 1974, all in-transfers who were admitted in the junior year met requirements for pursuing master's degree programs.

Throughout its perplexity with the admissions problems that had been swept under the rug, or sent home, for years, colleges assumed a shared responsibility for student success, implicit in admitting students into the community of higher learners. Once beyond the failure threat, the social threat was largely removed. Selective admission, to in-state and out-of-state students alike, conveyed a sense of welcome as well as academic access. Baccalaureate programs were commonly discontinued in both public and large nonpublic universities in the early 1970's, and lower divisions were discontinued in most of the major universities, including the larger private ones.

A different kind of pressure, felt by community colleges and by unselective senior colleges, was openly recognized as being acute. Many students received a high school diploma with measured achievement at only the eighth, ninth, or tenth grade levels. The historically Negro college was chronically affected, for this condition had long been privately acknowledged. Due to the circular, cumulative disadvantage of Negro students who were both academically and culturally handicapped, the moment of truth became an unavoidably traumatic one. Some white students were in this same predicament. Post high school programs were hesitantly, but successfully, instituted on designated college campuses to bring capable students within two years of college achievement level, within reach of achieving genuine college success in a decelerated program. Some achieved by dint of unusually high aptitude; others more by determined effort.

Conditions of academic learning improved when the realigned power structure of the higher education establishment made the fact clear that faculty promotion of rank and salary would include estimates of instructional quality as much or more than the conventional yardsticks of research and published articles. Both faculty and student groups set about the task of differentiating the adequate "garden variety" of instruction from that which was superior on the one hand and that which was inexcusably poor on the other. That was all the administration needed for building the academic learning factor into the rewards system of the academic market place. No high precision qualitative measuring instrument was required. A high correlation, not surprisingly, was found between good instruction and performance of faculty advisory duties. The few exceptions were those of a few distinguished lecturers who had mass appeal as public speakers, but little else.

A helpful innovation in institutions offering precollege remedial work was the designation of a "freshman faculty" drawn largely from senior high schools and junior colleges, who were especially qualified to help students master the tools of learning, in reading and English composition, mathematics, and elementary science, and the social studies. This faculty's work was largely tutorial in small groups of college freshmen and subfreshmen, as they unfortunately came to be called.

The rising power of the students, predicted after the "Berkeley incident," did not materialize, except in sporadic responsive fashion. The

"Year of the Student" was not the wave of the future in the South. Indeed, aside from the civil rights demonstrations, Southern higher education was only on the periphery of the student movement. That was not the way of Southern ladies and gentlemen. They held a deeper respect for duly constituted authority. Besides, student groups were stimulated to accept a shared responsibility for educational progress. This development had proved to be exceedingly difficult until responsible involvement on "things that count" was assured. Until then, elected student leaders found a flood of apathy among the student body, their own electorate.

Contacts with other segments of American life, such as work experience in different subcultures in the urban South, helped to develop a fuller awareness of the several Souths. Upper classmen came to be "stockholders" in the educational enterprise, like grown sons and daughters in a new partnership of effort. *In loco parentis* lost its child-adult connotation, but gained a new bond of mutual familial concern which became strong and deep. With help from student personnel professionals, a tradition of respect for all individuals began to grow, and traditions of inclusiveness emerged so that fraternity and sorority life assumed a new meaning of commitments. Student life and academic learning were slowly merging into a coherent pattern. The campus was no longer an adolescent reservation, but a miniature model of democracy that stretched beyond its confines to study and help the larger democracy to cope with its urgent problems and to seize its unprecedented opportunities.

Student life pervaded the range of thought and action in higher education. In point of prominence, for example, students served jointly with the faculty on a number of standing and *ad hoc* committees. In some colleges, the president of the student body served as a voting member, *ex officio*, of the Board of Trustees. Frequently, student groups met in faculty homes for coffee, for fellowship, and for intellectual grappling with profound issues—past and present. The administration encouraged these arrangements by providing a modest budgetary item for faculty entertainment of students, a variation of a practice quietly encouraged by a private foundation for years.

Community work and volunteer service programs, long established at some institutions, were adapted for urban settings and became a rallying center of student activity. Professorial sabbaticals were increasingly granted to permit instructors to work in new domestic settings to keep abreast of the changing South and to examine educational implications of these changes. The undergraduate college responded to the graduate school's "research semester" by granting a periodic "instruction semester," where a professor was given a small teaching load and excused from committee duties, thus permitting him to teach under optimal conditions, tied neither to experimentation nor precluded from whatever innovations of an experimental nature he chose to explore.

Desegregation appeared to have reached a stalemate in the mid-1960's. No one was pressing for it anymore. It had been achieved, in token fashion, almost everywhere. The United States Office of Education was busy assuring compliance of Title VI of the Civil Rights Act of 1964 in elementary and secondary schools. College officials, Negro and white, were weary of the two decades of litigations and disillusioned about the unrealistic expectations of what desegregation alone could accomplish. In the mid-1960's, colleges were "catching their breath" on the matter. In early 1966, only five colleges were singled out for noncompliance, all having racial restrictions in their charters. Later in the 1960's, however, three significant trends moved higher education well along toward an ethnic congeniality beyond nonsegregation.

The first action grew out of a "self-convened" conference of university presidents and chancellors to look beyond desegregation in Southern higher education. A pointed effort was made in faculty recruitment to identify and consider the broad field of qualified candidates without regard to race or sex, the two traditional bases of discrimination. A regional clearing-house for location and preliminary screening of faculty candidates was established, and professors were employed on both short-term and continuing contracts, as "minority professors," Caucasian and Negro. This development ushered in a period of natural faculty desegregation as a general pattern of recruitment, establishing lines of communication and greater "visibility" of competent (and incompetent) professors, Negro and white.

In metropolitan areas, where many institutions of higher education were located, luncheon seminars of presidents were inaugurated. These seminars, for which Kiwanis and Rotary Club "credit" was allowed, were prompted by an interest in extending various forms of interinstitutional cooperation. (The idea was in fact initiated with an eye to foundation grants, as the foundational mood for cooperation was at that time clearly deepening.) After the initial phase of administrative jockeying for position, the presidents found nonthreatening ways to cooperate. Among them was a student-exchange system, for a quarter or semester, which gave participating students a college experience as minority group members. The plan moved slowly because it interrupted the "sanctity of sequence," a serious roadblock in some major academic fields. In increasing numbers, however, curricular adaptations were made to extend this option to students who sought it. They did, in increasing numbers.

The federal government's influence on Southern higher education was substantial after 1965. The sudden flush of prosperity occasioned by the Higher Education Act of 1965 subsided with the need for increased funds for the Vietnam military-political operation. But the federal government's Office of Education, becoming a department in 1969, began to make long-term plans and commitments. This aided the South, in its turn, in getting its own long-range higher educational bearings. It learned what it could and could not count on from the federal government.

Following the governmental preemptions of some former roles, and with some misgivings, major private foundations took a large calculated risk. They made known their interest in the furthering of efforts that showed an institution's:

(a) special reasons for existence;

(b) demonstrated ability to cooperate with neighboring institutions;

(c) commitment to improving the quality of instruction, broadly conceived.

(d) sustained dedication to helping college-capable youth surmount their economic, ethnic, and educational hurdles;

(e) active reshaping of educational programs consonant with changing social realities and anticipated manpower needs.

This assurance of commitment strengthened the purpose of institutions already inclined along these directions. An Institute for Higher Education of the Talented Disadvantaged (IHETD) was established as a part of the Social Action Center to serve as an advisory nucleus for sustained philanthropic support of institutions and of specified programs among deserving institutions seeking to show model efforts toward program development, with a special emphasis on students not otherwise adequately cared for by federal, state, or church-connected funding. The IHETD evolved a close relationship with efforts at coordination of regional effort in higher education, focusing upon those missions beyond the scope of the accrediting associations and the regional educational laboratories. While foundation support was extended to include basic support for selected institutions, more "money mileage" was gained from special ventures in educational pioneering through obtaining public funds not previously available.

CONCLUSION: 1975

Now, in 1975, Southern higher education has come to grips with its basic dilemma of whether to continue its function as a vehicle of transportation into affluent America with an attending gout of pedantry, or whether to encounter as a main order of business, the social and economic problems of the South with resolute effort. The South has been slow to learn that its own material progress and peace of mind would be increasingly hampered by not helping all citizens to develop their ability to become socially and economically productive. (Lewis Blair made a cogent argument for that position in the nineteenth century.[10]) But higher education learned that lesson and is teaching it to all the South. What the South learns, as its history has always attested, it will not soon forget.

The task is far from completed. Higher education has served in a brief decade, however, to achieve a new unity in diversity rather than to divide further the rich against the poor, the white against the Negro, and class

[10]Blair, *A Southern Prophecy* (Boston: Little, Brown, and Company (1889), 1964).

against class. The South does not like the word Utopia, because it implies fixed dead-end goals, while Southern society is in a continuing state of thoughtful change. Within the flux of a society in which higher education is at last fulfilling an impelling and compassionate telic function, through knowledge, suasion, and through the inspiration of dedicated leadership, some fundamental constants shine through. One of them was expressed in 1888 by Dr. Leete, in Edward Bellamy's *Looking Backward:* "It is precisely because we are all social equals whose equality nothing can compromise, and because service is honorable in a society whose fundamental principle is that all in turn shall serve the rest, that we could easily provide a corps of domestic servants such as you never dreamed of, if we needed them . . . but we do not need them."[11]

Southern higher education is not only improving the South, but has inspired the American non-South, the rest of America. Other developing areas of the world are coming to study this new South that has "come to itself," has cradled a new democracy amidst social travail and anguish. It is no accident, then, that the sages from Syracuse are in 1975 preparing a new report—*The United States and the World in the 1985 Era (Revised).* That revision has been rendered necessary because many responsible citizens made unorthodox assumptions about the role of higher education in the South, and with the stubbornness of Southern tradition, acted on them.

SELECTED REFERENCES

Bellamy, Edward. *Looking Backward.* New York: Houghton Mifflin Co. , 1888.

Blair, Lewis H. *A Southern Prophecy.* Boston: Little, Brown, and Co. (1889), 1964.

Brumbaugh, A. J. *Statewide Planning and Coordination of Higher Education.* Atlanta: Southern Regional Education Board, 1963.

Conant, James B. *Shaping Educational Policy.* New York: McGraw-Hill Book Company, 1964.

Hero, Alfred O. , Jr. *The Southerner and World Affairs.* Baton Rouge: Louisiana State University Press, 1965.

Institute of International Education. *Open Doors, 1966.* A Report on International Exchange. Washington, D.C.: Institute of International Education, June 1966.

Jones, William C. (ed.). *Higher Education for All?* Proceedings of the Twenty-seventh Annual Pacific Northwest Conference on Higher Education, April 1-3, 1965. Corvallis, Oregon: Oregon State University Press, 1965.

[11]Bellamy, *Looking Backward* (New York: Houghton Mifflin Company, 1888, republished by World Publishing Company, 1946), p. 119.

McConnell, T. R. *A General Pattern for American Public Higher Education.* New York: McGraw-Hill Book Company, 1962.

Syracuse University Research Corporation. *The United States and the World in the 1985 Era.* Prepared under Naval Research Contract NOnr 4345 (00). Washington, D.C.: U.S. Department of Commerce, 1964.

Appendix A

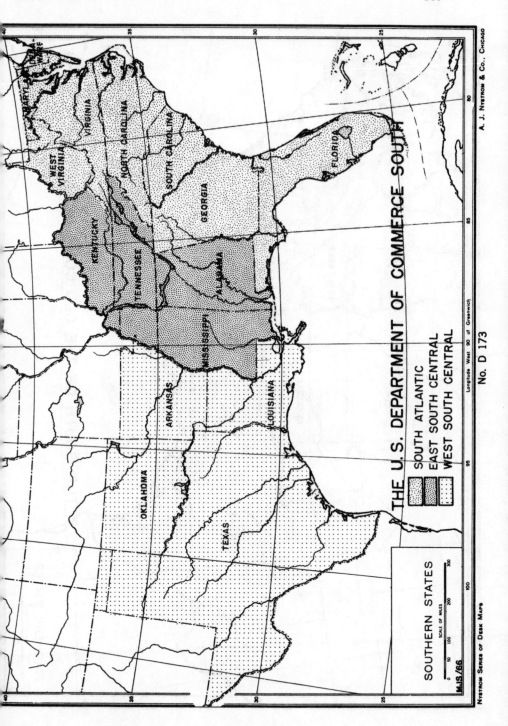

THE U.S. DEPARTMENT OF COMMERCE SOUTH

SOUTH ATLANTIC
EAST SOUTH CENTRAL
WEST SOUTH CENTRAL

No. D 173

A. J. NYSTROM & CO., CHICAGO

SOUTHERN STATES

SCALE OF MILES

0 50 100 200 300

MJS/66

NYSTROM SERIES OF DESK MAPS

Longitude West 90 of Greenwich

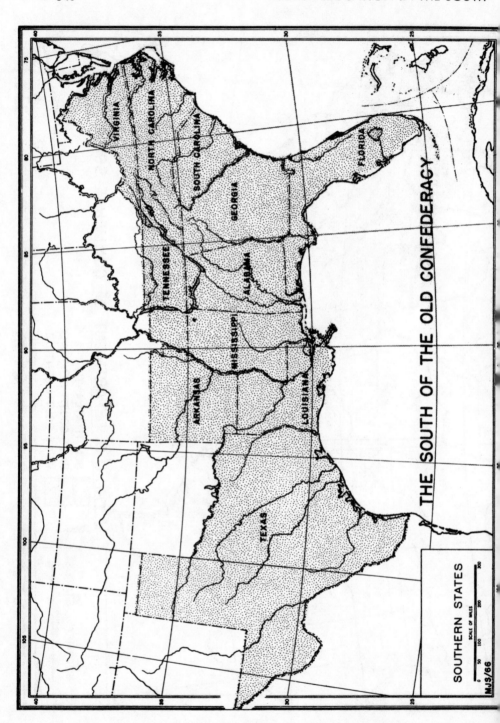

THE SOUTH OF THE OLD CONFEDERACY

SOUTHERN STATES

SCALE OF MILES

0   50   100   200   300

MJS/66

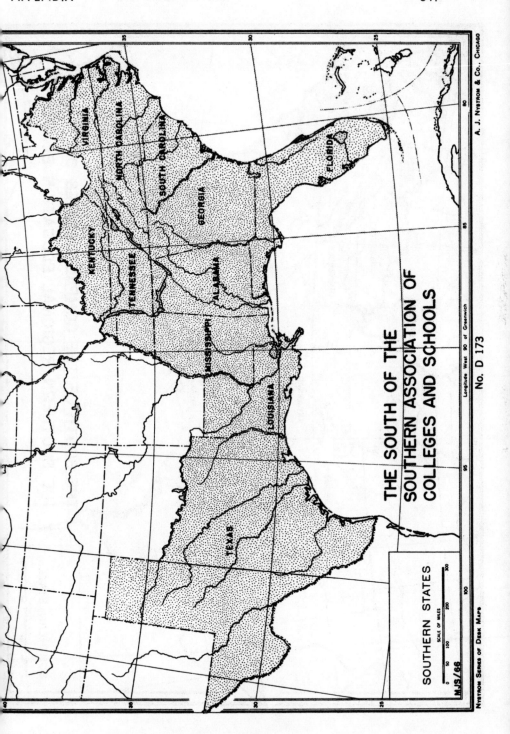

THE SOUTH OF THE
SOUTHERN ASSOCIATION OF
COLLEGES AND SCHOOLS

No. D 173

SOUTHERN STATES

SCALE OF MILES

0   50   100   200   300

M/S/66

NYSTROM SERIES OF DESK MAPS

A. J. NYSTROM & CO., CHICAGO

Longitude West 90 of Greenwich

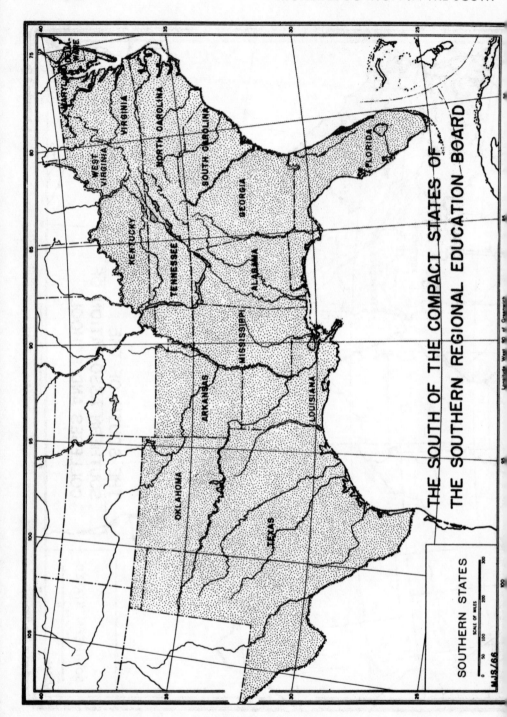

THE SOUTH OF THE COMPACT STATES OF
THE SOUTHERN REGIONAL EDUCATION BOARD

SOUTHERN STATES

SCALE OF MILES

0   50   100   200   300

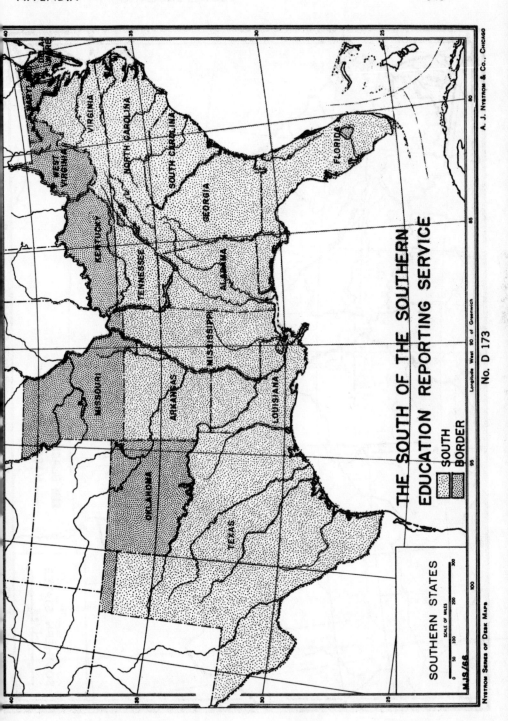

THE SOUTH OF THE SOUTHERN
EDUCATION REPORTING SERVICE

SOUTH
BORDER

SOUTHERN STATES

SCALE OF MILES
0   50   100   150   200   250   300

M.15/66   No. D 173

NYSTROM SERIES OF DESK MAPS

Longitude West 90 of Greenwich

A. J. NYSTROM & CO., CHICAGO

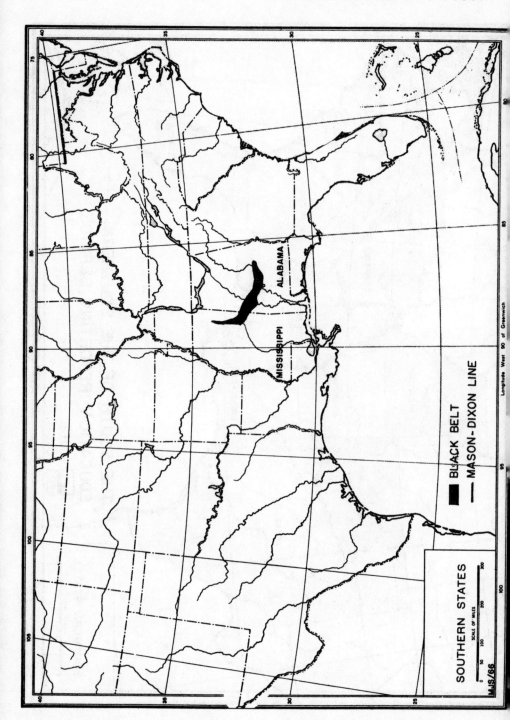

Appendix B

The Advisory Board *
Southern Study in Higher Education

Mr. William C. Archie, Executive Director
Mary Reynolds Babcock Foundation
Winston-Salem, North Carolina

Mr. Howard R. Boozer, Director
State Board of Higher Education
Raleigh, North Carolina

Mr. A. H. Calloway, Director
Information Service
West Virginia State College
Institute, West Virginia

Mr. Rufus Clement, President
Atlanta University
Atlanta, Georgia

Mr. Milton Cummings, President
Brown Engineering Company
Huntsville, Alabama

Mr. R. P. Daniel, President
Virginia State College
Petersburg, Virginia

Mr. Frank Dickey, Executive Director
National Commission on Accrediting
Washington, D. C.

Mr. Curtis Dixon
National Representative
Woodrow Wilson National Fellowship
   Foundation
Atlanta, Georgia

Mr. Luther Foster, President
Tuskegee Institute
Tuskegee, Alabama

Mr. Rufus Harris, President
Mercer University
Macon, Georgia

Mr. Herman Long, President
Talladega College
Talladega, Alabama

Mr. Hugh McEniry, Dean
Stetson University
DeLand, Florida

Mr. John Popham, Managing Editor
The Chattanooga Times
Chattanooga, Tennessee

Mr. Reed Sarratt, Director,
   Journalism Project
Southern Regional Education Board
Atlanta, Georgia

Mr. A. B. Templeton, President
Sam Houston State College
Huntsville, Texas

Mr. Bernard Werthan, Sr., President
Werthan Bag Corporation
Nashville, Tennessee

Mr. Stephen Wright, Director
United Negro College Fund
New York City, New York

Miss Flora Rhind (Unofficial)
Special Assistant to the President
The Rockefeller Foundation
New York City, New York

---

*Two names are omitted at the request of early contributors who felt they had not influenced the study sufficiently to be formally identified with it.

345

Appendix C

Southern Colleges and Universities Visited in Connection with the Southern Higher Education Study, 1964-1966

Alabama A and M College
Huntsville, Alabama

Arkansas A, M, and N College
Pine Bluff, Arkansas

Armstrong College
Savannah, Georgia

Atlanta University
Atlanta, Georgia

Auburn University
Auburn, Alabama

Augusta College
Augusta, Georgia

Berea College
Berea, Kentucky

Birmingham Southern College
Birmingham, Alabama

Clemson University
Clemson, South Carolina

Fairmont State College
Fairmont, West Virginia

Fisk University
Nashville, Tennessee

Florida A and M University
Tallahassee, Florida

Florida State University
Tallahassee, Florida

Mercer University
Macon, Georgia

Miles College
Birmingham, Alabama

Millsaps College
Jackson, Mississippi

Northeast Louisiana State College
Monroe, Louisiana

Oakwood College
Huntsville, Alabama

Paine College
Augusta, Georgia

Philander Smith College
Little Rock, Arkansas

Rice University
Houston, Texas

Savannah State College
Savannah, Georgia

Scarritt College
Nashville, Tennessee

Southern University
Baton Rouge, Louisiana

Southwest Texas State College
San Marcos, Texas

Texas Southern University
Houston, Texas

Fort Valley State College
Fort Valley, Georgia

Georgia Southern College
Statesboro, Georgia

George Washington University
Washington, D. C.

Grambling College
Ruston, Louisiana

Jackson State College
Jackson, Mississippi

Kentucky State College
Frankfort, Kentucky

Little Rock University
Little Rock, Arkansas

Louisiana Polytechnic Institute
Ruston, Louisiana

Louisiana State University at
New Orleans
New Orleans, Louisiana

Memphis State University
Memphis, Tennessee

Tougaloo College
Tougaloo, Mississippi

Trinity University
San Antonio, Texas

Union College
Barbourville, Kentucky

University of Arkansas Medical
School
Little Rock, Arkansas

University of Mississippi
Oxford, Mississippi

University of Tennessee
Knoxville, Tennessee

University of Texas
Austin, Texas

Vanderbilt University
Nashville, Tennessee

West Virginia State College
Institute, West Virginia

Wood Junior College
Mathiston, Mississippi

Appendix D

A Partial List of Respondents to Opinionnaire
Exclusive of Numerous Additional Interviews
In Reference to Chapter VIII*

John R. Bertrand, President
Berry College
Mount Berry, Georgia

Donald C. Dearborn, President
Catawba College
Salisbury, North Carolina

D. Grier Martin, President
Davidson College
Davidson, North Carolina

J. M. Eqing, President
Delta State College
Cleveland, Mississippi

John R. Mumaw, President
Eastern Mennonite College
Harrisonburg, Virginia

Rudolph Jones, President
Fayetteville State College
Fayetteville, North Carolina

R. A. Thomas, President
Georgia Military College
Milledgeville, Georgia

Taylor Reveley, President
Hampden-Sydney College
Hampden-Sydney, Virginia

James H. Landes, President
Hardin-Simmons University
Abilene, Texas

T. Felton Harrison, President
Pensacola Junior College
Pensacola, Florida

B. J. Jarman, President
Pikeville College
Pikeville, Kentucky

Joseph M. Gettys, Academic Dean
Presbyterian College
Clinton, South Carolina

William Quillian, Jr., President
Randolph Macon Woman's College
Lynchburg, Virginia

Brother Raymond Fleck, President
St. Edward's University
Austin, Texas

Dale H. Gramley, President
Salem College
Winston-Salem, North Carolina

A. B. Templeton, President
Sam Houston State College
Huntsville, Texas

Law Sone, President
Texas Wesleyan College
Fort Worth, Texas

Luther Foster, President
Tuskegee Institute
Tuskegee Institute, Alabama

*These names correspond, only in small part, with the quoted and paraphrased comments contained in this study. They do constitute, however, a major portion of paraphrased statements in Chapter VIII, "The President's Challenges."

LeRoy A. Martin, President
University of Chattanooga
Chattanooga, Tennessee

Alexander Heard, Chancellor
Vanderbilt University
Nashville, Tennessee

Henry W. Jensen, Dean
Warren Wilson College
Swannanoa, North Carolina

J. R. Noonkester, President
William Carey College
Hattiesburg, Mississippi

Charles S. Davis, President
Winthrop College
Rock Hill, South Carolina

Appendix E

The Several Souths

In our references to numerous geographical regions, for a variety of purposes, we have identified a number of Souths. Each has its rational historical antecedents. Arkansas, for example, is not within the Southern Association of Colleges and Schools, in part because of that association's arbitrary position on accreditation in contrast to that of the North Central Association a generation ago. The Southern Regional Education Board embraces Maryland, in part (and formerly Delaware) because of the favorable attitude of political leadership on issues in its formative period—gerrymandering if you will. Several maps are provided here as convenient reference for the reader as we jump from South to South. These are the principal Souths to which references are made from time to time in this study.

1. The South of the Southern Association of Colleges and Schools:

Alabama	North Carolina
Florida	South Carolina
Georgia	Tennessee
Kentucky	Texas
Louisiana	Virginia
Mississippi	

2. The South of the Old Confederacy (commonly, the Deep South):

Alabama	Mississippi
Arkansas	North Carolina
Florida	South Carolina
Georgia	Tennessee
Louisiana	Texas
	Virginia

3. The South of the Compact States of the Southern Regional Education Board:

Alabama	Mississippi
Arkansas	North Carolina
Delaware	Oklahoma
Florida	South Carolina
Georgia	Tennessee
Kentucky	Texas
Louisiana	Virginia
Maryland	West Virginia

4. The South of the Southern Education Reporting Service:

South	Border States
Alabama	Delaware
Arkansas	Kentucky
Florida	Maryland
Georgia	Missouri
Louisiana	Oklahoma
Mississippi	West Virginia
North Carolina	
South Carolina	
Tennessee	
Texas	
Virginia	

5. The United States Department of Commerce's South:

a. South Atlantic   b. East South Central
   Delaware   Kentucky
   Maryland   Tennessee
   District of Columbia   Alabama
   Virginia   Mississippi
   West Virginia
   North Carolina
   South Carolina
   Georgia
   Florida

                          c. West South Central
                             Arkansas
                             Louisiana
                             Oklahoma
                             Texas

6. The Black Belt and the Mason Dixon Line.
   The black (soil) belt is depicted on this map. A different "Black
   Belt," consisting of areas of substantial (40,000 or more) Negro
   population is alluded to in V. O. Keys' Southern Politics (New York:
   Alfred A. Knopf, 1949), stretching also in crescent shape, from
   Virginia through North Carolina and Georgia westward and north-
   ward to Arkansas. Source of this Black Belt map is C. L. White
   and others, Regional Geography of Anglo-America (Englewood
   Cliffs: Prentice-Hall, Inc., 1964). The Nystrom Series of Desk
   Maps were used for these map drawings by courtesy of the A. J.
   Nystrom and Co. (Chicago).

Index of Names

353

356